CLIVE OF INDIA

Other books by Nirad C. Chaudhuri

The Continent of Circe
The Autobiography of an Unknown Indian
A Passage to England
Scholar Extraordinary: The Life of Max Müller

NIRAD C. CHAUDHURI

CLIVE OF INDIA

A Political and Psychological Essay

'State business is a cruel Trade; good-nature is a Bungler in it.' *Halifax*

BARRIE & JENKINS
COMMUNICA - EUROPA

First published in 1975 by
Barrie & Jenkins Limited
24 Highbury Crescent, London N5 1RX

Copyright © Nirad C. Chaudhuri, 1975

ISBN 0 214 20021 3

All rights reserved. No part of
this publication may be reproduced
in any form or by any means without the
prior permission of Barrie & Jenkins Limited.

Printed in Great Britain by Flarepath Printers Ltd, St. Albans, Herts.

Contents

Table of Contents v
Preface vi
Introduction 1

Part I Rise of Clive 1725–1755
1 The Political Stage 14
2 Clive comes to India 38
3 Young Military Leader 68
4 Gestation of the Empire 106

Part II Conquest of Bengal 1756–1759
5 Loss and Recovery of Calcutta 141
6 War with Siraj-ud-daula 174
7 Plassey 200
8 Settlement in Bengal 240

Part III Clive against England 1760–1774
9 Victor of Plassey in England 269
10 Tussle for Power in the Company 296
11 Saving the Conquest 326
12 The Lone Wolf 370

Appendices
1 The Expedition to Tanjore 412
2 Genesis of the Arcot Expedition 417
3 Sources used for Chapter Seven 421
4 Some Disputed Points 423
5 Mir Jafar and Siraj 426
6 Grant of the Jaghir to Clive by Mir Jafar (1758) 430
7 End of Mir Qasim 431
8 Death of Clive 433
Chronological Table of Clive's Life 435
Glossary 438
Select Bibliography 440
Index 443

Preface

Christopher MacLehose is the begetter of this book. One evening in 1970 we were dining at Worcester College, Oxford, as guests of Harry Pitt, and he asked my wife, by whose side he was sitting, whether I would write a biography of Clive for Barrie & Jenkins. She told him to put the question to me, which he did, and without taking any time to think, I replied that I might. Within a few days the matter was formally settled.

I did not know then that 1974 would be the year of the 200th anniversary of Clive's death, and 1975 that of the 250th anniversary of his birth. But I had for many years been thinking of the British Empire in India *sub specie aeternitatis* (into which after ceasing to exist it had passed) and wondering whether an adequate history of that phenomenon would ever be written. In this state of mind I myself had often toyed with the idea of writing a sort of essay on it, with the qualification of a relative kind which I certainly had, and here was an invitation. The train of thought which influenced me will be found set forth in the introduction.

Therefore, whatever sense of satisfaction I might obtain from the fulfilment of a desire, I owe to Christopher MacLehose. Next, I have to thank Ursula Owen for undertaking the laborious and (due to the character of authors) the thankless task of finally editing the book for press. She has done this thoroughly and conscientiously, and I am deeply obliged to her. I would also thank Dr R. J. Bingle of the India Office Library for helping me to examine the Strachey papers and in procuring copies of documents. Furthermore, anyone who works at Oxford on any Indian subject is bound, ipso facto, to be under an obligation to the library of the Indian Institute. I am also.

Lastly, I would set down my gratitude to an institution to which, it seems to me, authors do not acknowledge their debt adequately. It is the London Library. If in England there is a national health service for writing books, it is provided by the library, and it does this without claiming or getting a share of the bureaucratic loot. Of course, authors pay a subscription, but as they pay much more to the same bureaucratic leviathan without getting anything in return, they should not think that their subscription entitles them to regard the Library as anything but a charitable institution. Through its invaluable service I have been able to borrow from it books published in the eighteenth century and read them at home. For a man of my age this was providing the equivalent of an invalid chair in addition. Besides all this, the courtesy of Douglas Matthews and his staff has been an ineffable extra comfort.

To conclude the preface, an explanation has to be given about the spelling of Indian names. It was wholly chaotic and arbitrary in the eighteenth century. No uniformity was observed even by one writer. With all his obsession with his *jaghir,* Clive spelt the word in at least four different ways. I have kept the old spellings in the citations, without regard for consistency, but transliterated according to the modern system in my text. The popular spelling for certain Indian words, e.g. jaghir (for jagir) has been retained. However, I have not used diacritical marks, nor departed from popular usage in respect of some well known names. For instance, I have written Alivardi Khan, and not Ali Wardhi Khan. Most of the Indian terms have been given their English meaning when they first occur in the text. Nonetheless, a short glossary is provided at the end of the book.

OXFORD 1975   Nirad C. Chaudhuri

Introduction

This book is not a work of fresh research. That is to say, it is not the product of a re-examination of the manuscript sources already drawn upon by previous biographers or of a study of new material not available before. It offers only a re-interpretation of the personality and achievements of Clive on the basis of the printed documents and secondary works.

This would seem to deprive the book of a *raison d'être*, for there are already a number of standard biographies of Clive, and they are assumed to have embodied more or less completely all the information to be found in the sources known till now. This is specially true of Sir George Forrest's biography in two volumes published in 1918. He drew upon the family papers extensively, and before him Malcolm had used them partially.

Nonetheless, it is not to be assumed that a re-reading of the manuscripts may not furnish new details. Their volume is large. The India Office Library always had the Orme manuscripts. Recently the Earl of Powis has deposited the family papers in it. Another large collection of manuscripts about Clive is in the National Library of Wales. It is not possible that all the information contained in them has been extracted. But re-reading them could take years, and the result might not be proportionate to the effort. Forrest was the first biographer of Clive to examine the family papers thoroughly; yet he did not present an image of Clive which differed materially from what was given by Malcolm, Macaulay, Gleig or Malleson, though he had his point of view. By and large, the image created by Macaulay remains the standard portrait, except for some retouching, which at times has been garish or inadmissible.

As to new material, both unpublished and unused, the India Office Library has very recently acquired the papers of Henry Strachey, who was Clive's private secretary during his third period in India. But they have not as yet been fully catalogued or described, and without going through them *in extenso* it is not possible to say what new information they contain or how many of the documents are only duplicates of the papers in the main Clive collection. I have only cursorily looked into some of them, and taken one or two items of information. I have, however, heard that others have examined them more fully. I have not seen their work.

It seems to me that the broad facts of Clive's life are not likely to be affected by any new information, for his enemies left nothing that could be set against him unearthed – or uninvented – during his lifetime and the decades that followed his death. On the other hand, his achievements and also his acquisitions were matters of public knowledge. Nothing new is ever likely to be discovered about them. Nor can we expect any light to be shed on his mind by fresh material, should any be discovered, because he was not given to introspection, and the working of his mind and his motives have to be deduced from his actions and the letters and speeches in which he explained them.

Nonetheless, a new biography of Clive may be justified on grounds other than new information. To my thinking, the inadequacy of the existing biographies of Clive is to be found not in the incomplete utilization of the sources, but in the unsatisfactory interpretation of well-known facts. This, however, is not the fault of any particular biographer, but has been virtually forced on them by a preconditioned approach.

In this respect the biographies of Clive have suffered equally with the histories of the British Empire in India. In other words, by true standards of historicity Clive has not had a better deal at the hands of his biographers than the Empire has had from its historians. The fact is that, so long as it lasted, it never moved into the light of history, but remained subject to polemics, for or against. The polemical approach has not been given up, though the Empire has disappeared. Thus a genuinely historical history of that great political phenomenon was never written, and as it seems to me will not be, unless there is a radical departure from all the extant modes of thinking about it.

The polemical approach was created by the very manner in which the Empire came into existence. The British people were not prepared for it either intellectually or morally. So when they saw it emerging they not only failed to understand what was happening, but took up a hostile attitude. Chronologically, British anti-imperialism was in being before the appearance of the Empire. The great French historian and political thinker

Alexis de Tocqueville, who once thought of writing about the foundation of the British Empire in India, pointed this out in his notes. Writing between 1841 and 1843, he said that an empire two-thirds the size of that of Alexander the Great was founded against the formal orders of the authorities at home. According to him, more singular was the failure of the deliberate attempts made by the East India Company, the British government of the day, and even British public opinion to arrest the growth of the Empire. Altogether, he said, the birth and growth of the Empire of India appeared to the world as an unexplained puzzle, almost as a miracle. This bewilderment lingered even as late as the middle of the nineteenth century. So Tocqueville thought it necessary to say that the time had come to dispel the clouds which hid the foundation of the Empire.

But they have not been dispelled. Different kinds of clouds follow one another. There was first the cloud of incomprehension; then that of hostility and moralizing; the clouds of false glorification came after that, only to be chased away by the clouds of false contrition or, less dominantly, false romanticizing.

Owing to the absence of any kind of psychological preparation to face the Empire as a political responsibility or even as a *fait accompli*, the establishment of British rule in India was seen intellectually and judged morally in the light of the traditional political doctrines of the British people, just as today the expansion of American power in the world is being seen in the light of the political principles created by the War of Independence, which are obsolete. So, the most notable and significant pronouncement on the Indian Empire in the first fifty years of its existence was the indictment of Warren Hastings by Burke. This was as natural as Burke's denunciation of the French Revolution.

The first history of British rule, and the only one that remains impressive by virtue of its conception and execution, appeared in 1817 when the Empire could no longer be opposed as fact. This was James Mill's *History of British India*. Even then Mill could not break with the old controversy. It may actually be said that he gave the first historical version of the condemnation of the Empire. His history was severely critical of the actions and methods of the founders. But he was critical in the light of English principles, not out of any regard for the character and civilization of the Indian people, for neither of which had he any respect. His history set the trend for the histories that followed, for when they did not fall in with Mill's thesis they could only put forward a counter-thesis, thus maintaining the affiliation.

Until the last quarter of the nineteenth century the theoretical and doctrinaire controversy about the Empire in India ran its course quite independently of the practical task of governing India, which so far as it was influenced by any political theory at all was affected only by utilitarianism, and in the moral aspect by evangelism. But in the last decades of that century a conscious pride in the Empire made its appearance. This epoch was ushered in by the proclamation of the Queen of England as the Empress of India. No less significant was the fact that the new title was assumed at the instance of Disraeli. All that was symbolic, for it preceded the rise of an imperial sentiment or at least an appearance of it. However, it is one of the ironies of history that the most effective and beneficent application of British imperialism in India was seen when there was no imperialistic bragging. When the glorification began it produced a conceptual imperialism which was quite unworthy of the greatest empire seen in history.

Quite naturally, this imperialism influenced historical writing. But it did not make it more historical than the old moral condemnation. The new style only created an aggressive defence, often with the help of very specious arguments. The special pleading became worse and worse as the challenge of Indian nationalism grew stronger and stronger. For some time the imperialistic sentiment cornered the old radical condemnation. But after the First World War it was the turn of imperialism to be cornered, and the symbol of this transition was a novel – E. M. Forster's *A Passage to India*. The two camps remained facing each other till the end of British rule in India in 1947. The histories written from both the positions were equally biased, superficial and insipid. True history went by default.

With the exception of a small number of works, all the histories of British India stand in deplorable contrast to the few pages written by Tocqueville on the rise of the Empire. They were not included in the collected edition of his writings edited by Beaumont because they were very fragmentary and were left in a confused state. But they have now been published in the new collected works issued under the direction of J.-P. Mayer and sponsored by a National Commission appointed by the French Government. The pieces on India are to be found in volume III of the series.*

Though based on incomplete reading, these pages show a quality of historical thinking and understanding which would have made de Tocqueville's work on British India, had it been completed, a companion volume to his *Democracy in America* and the *Ancient Regime*. But a mind like Tocqueville's was never fully brought to bear on the Empire in India. And yet as a political phenomenon it was not less significant than the United States created by the American Revolution and the Europe created by the French Revolution.

It cannot be said in extenuation that the raw material for a great history of the Indian empire was not available. The British administrators were continuously discussing the problem of ruling India empirically, and embodying their ideas and opinions not only in public papers but also in books. A large synthesis could be constructed from these. But the histiography of the Empire and the practical thinking and writing on it ran along different channels.

The Empire has now disappeared, but the prospects for its history have not improved. If anything they are worse today. There is no longer any practical motive for any effectual application of the intellect to it. The emotional urge, too, is not only weak, but of a kind which is likely to make those who still want to write about it unjust to it. The fact is that some people in Britain need consolation for the loss of the Empire, and the natural impulse is to find it by representing it as something less than what it was. This is behind the current talk of cutting everybody down to size, which means nothing more than cutting the great men of the past to the size of an inferior generation.

There are others who have adopted a definitely hostile attitude to the Empire. This is part of a general rancour against every form of British greatness. The greatness was almost exclusively the creation of a class, and the hatreds that are so marked in Britain today are bound to extend to the achievements of the upper classes.

*Alexis de Tocqueville, *Oeuvres Complètes:* definitive edition published under the direction of J.-P. Mayer. Volume III: 'Ecrits et Discours politiques'. Text edited and annotated by André Jardin. Introduction by J.-J. Chavalier and André Jardin (Gallimard, Paris 1962), pp. 441–553.

Both British administrators and historians had a bad conscience about the acquisitions in India. This was given expression in a far-fetched pun attributed to Napier about his conquest of Sind. He is said to have sent the message: *'Peccavi'* (= 'I have sinned'). This tendency has become strengthened, and it is trying to pass as historical justice.

Owing to all these emotional pressures a sort of revisionism has already appeared even among the established historians of British India. Some of them seem to consider the Empire only as the seed-bed of the Indian nationalist movement, and not as a political phenomenon in its own right. Therefore, many writers are pulled by a gravitation which makes them toe the line with Indian historians and their views, not only in respect of the Empire, but even about ancient Indian civilization. And it must be said that Indian historians even at their most scholarly are, with very rare exceptions, propagandists in disguise.

The only corrective to the dubious revisionism which can be seen is the immense amount of academic research on Indian subjects. This research is providing a good deal of new information, but it is often directed towards relatively unimportant aspects of the government of India. What is more serious is the unreality of some of the work. Most of the researchers are young men, who are not affiliated to any tradition formed by the Empire as a reality, and without some such relationship, however collateral, historical reconstruction and interpretation are bound to go astray.

These conditions that affect the writing of a new history of the Empire in India are bound to influence the biographies of the founders as well. In fact, in the historiography of British India, the current ran in the opposite direction. That is to say, the lives of the founders as lived, and afterwards as written, influenced the writing of the general histories. It was the controversies raised by the activities of the two founders, Clive and Warren Hastings, and the parliamentary inquiries into their conduct, which set the pattern of writing of the histories of British India. The men as microcosms determined the treatment of the macrocosm – the Empire. The moral issues raised by these two men in the sphere of practical politics were carried into the biographies, and from the biographies into the histories, so that it may be said that Clive and Warren Hastings cast their shadows on the entire historiography of British

India. Moral criticism and appraisement became the main purpose of both history and biography.

This is best illustrated by the two essays on Clive and Hastings written by Macaulay after his return from India, where he held the appointment of a member of the Governor-General's Council. These essays, published in 1840 and 1841, were not apologetic about the Empire as such, for Macaulay had taken part in the government of India. On the contrary, they revealed him to be as much of an imperialist as it was possible for him to be. He gave expression to his pride in the Empire in his well-known introduction to the essay on Clive. In it he chided Englishmen for knowing less about their own empire in India than about the Spanish Empire in America:

> Every schoolboy knows who imprisoned Montezuma, and who strangled Atahualpa. But we doubt whether one in ten, even among English gentlemen of highly cultivated minds, can tell who won the battle of Buxar, who perpetrated the massacre of Patna, whether Shuja Dowla ruled in Oude or in Travancore, or whether Holkar was a Hindoo or a Mussalman.

Nevertheless, he was also a good Whig and heir to the most liberal traditions in English politics and ethics. So he could not ignore the moral issues raised by the doings of Clive and Hastings, and delivered his moral judgements without reserve. In passing them he was led to set down contradictory opinions about the same moral question: he condemned Clive for forging the signature of Admiral Watson or being a party to it; on the other hand, he condemned Hastings for getting Nuncomar (Nanda Kumar) hanged for forgery. In doing so Macaulay applied the English standard to Clive and the Bengali standard to Hastings. Forgery, he considered, was a crime in an Englishman in all circumstances, whereas it was natural in a Bengali, whose character he summed up in a very famous passage:

> What the horns are to the buffalo, what the paw is to the tiger, what the sting is to the bee, what beauty, according to the old Greek song, is to woman, deceit is to the Bengalee: large promises, smooth excuses, elaborate tissues of circumstantial falsehood, chicanery, perjury, forgery, are the weapons, offensive and defensive, of the people of the Lower Ganges.

But the moralist in Macaulay could never suppress the historian in him, so as to make him incapable of giving a dramatic and colourful reconstruction of the past. As the two essays on

Clive and Warren Hastings influenced all subsequent writing on them and even the writing of general histories of British rule in India, it is as well to take note of the special quality of Macaulay as historian. This can be best done by quoting de Tocqueville's opinion of him.

After reading the concluding volumes of *History of England* he wrote to his friend Beaumont: 'C'est presque aussi superficiel, mais plus amusant qu'un roman.' But he explained what he meant by adding: 'Et même quand je dis *superficiel* je parle de la profondeur d'esprit qui fait apercevoir au-dessus des passions particulières de temps et de pays le caractère général d'une époque et la marche de l'esprit humain.'

Apart from this, de Tocqueville wrote: 'L'ouvrage n'est pas superficiel quant aux faits particuliers dont parle l'auteur et qui sont bien étudiés par lui.'

As to the impression left by Macaulay's history, as a whole de Tocqueville made this penetrating remark: 'Il faut lire cela pour voir comment le fond d'honnêteté, de bon sens, de modération et de vertu qui se trouve dans une nation et les bonnes institutions que ces qualités ont établis ou laissé subsister, peut lutter contre les vices de ceux qui les dirigent. Je ne crois pas qu'il y ait eu dans aucun pays des hommes d'Etat plus malhonnêtes que ceux dont parle Macaulay dans cette partie de son histoire comme il n'y a point de société plus grande que celle qui a fini par sortir de leurs mains.'

And Tocqueville drew a final historical moral: 'Il y a chez les peuples comme chez les individus de certains tempéraments qui luttent non seulement contre les maladies, mais contre les médecins.'*

---

*Translations: 'It is almost as superficial as, but more interesting than, a novel. . . . And even when I say superficial, I speak of the depth of mind which brings out, transcending the particular passions of the times and countries, the general character of an epoch and the march of the human spirit.' . . . 'The work is not superficial as to the particular facts of which the author speaks, which are well examined by him.' . . . 'It should be read to see how the underlying honesty, good sense, moderation, and virtue which are to be found in a people, and the sound institutions which these qualities have created or allowed to remain, can fight against the vices of those who lead them. I do not think there were in any country statesmen who were more dishonest than those of whom Macaulay speaks in this part of his history, just as there never was a society which was greater than that which finally emerged out of their hands.' . . . 'There are among nations as among individuals certain dispositions which fight not only against the maladies but also against the physicians.'

Tocqueville called all these remarks 'cat immense bavardage'. But his chitchat is more profound than the pretentious holding forth of many historians, and his remarks apply equally to the small-scale essays of Macaulay as they do to the large history. His essays showed that a basically great historical phenomenon could arise out of very corrupt conditions and high-handed or dubious actions. If there was to be any moralizing on the life of Clive it should have been at this level, accompanied by a forceful and vivid presentation of the realities of politics and history.

But the moralizing that became a general feature of the lives of Clive and Hastings remained throughout on a lower level, as if the historians were dealing with dishonest officials or tradesmen. The moralizing was not unnatural as long as the Empire lasted, for during that time everything that Clive and Hastings did remained a live moral and political issue. The challenge from Indian nationalism made their actions even more compelling ones, and the actions in respect of which doubts were raised had either to be extenuated or condemned. So the historian was driven to be a prosecuting or a defending counsel.

How difficult it was to avoid moral judgements can be illustrated by the biography of Clive by Gleig, published in 1848. He declared in its preface that his object was to treat the individual of whom he wrote as a strictly historical character as if he were dealing with the career of a statesman or a hero who had flourished in some remote age or a foreign land. Yet his book was full of such judgements, and he grasped some of the nettles by condemning Clive outright.

The confrontation between the new imperialistic historians and Indian nationalists gave another twist to the moralizing. It became very difficult for these historians to admit that anything done either by Clive or by Warren Hastings could be wrong, and on all heads of the condemnation they spun out specious justifications. This apology has ceased, but the moralizing tradition has not been given up, though the disappearance of the Empire has made it wholly out of date.

It is this tradition of writing about Clive that gives scope for a new presentation of his life. A truly historical biography of Clive today should exclude criticism or apology altogether, and present him as he was, and his age, too, as it was. The story must be told as if the writer was watching the events as realities present before his eyes, but with a detachment which the passing away of the Empire should make possible. This is all that I have attempted in this biography. Some discussion of the moral issues will be found in it, but it has been introduced only in the interest of historical truth.

I have also had to face the problem of establishing the facts of Clive's life. Strangely enough, in spite of all the work done on him there still remain a number of uncertainties about what he did. Certain things attributed to him are wholly apocryphal. Certain others, though accepted, are not established fully by any kind of evidence. In regard to his death, for example, the biographers have accepted what has appealed to them without discussing the value of the testimonies. In this book I have been very scrupulous in distinguishing between what is fact and what is only inference or merely supposition. Moreover, wherever I have felt it necessary to give a particular version of the facts differing from what is current, I have discussed the evidence in an appendix. When no reservation is made the reader may assume that I have followed the most reliable sources, even when my account of certain incidents differs from others.

In regard to the topics included in the biography it will be found that there is a good deal that is not about Clive, and would seem at first sight to belong to history rather than to biography. But these had to be brought in because in this period Clive and British India coincided. The historical situations furnished the setting in which Clive worked and rose to power. His was a dormant nature which was roused and brought to life by India. Without describing all that was happening there, it is impossible to explain him.

In short, I will say that I have only tried to show Clive as he was and his age as it was without feeling called upon to pronounce any judgement for or against. But I am not insensible to the fact that the reader might think that I have projected a view of Clive that comes very close to the imperialistic, though with neither boastfulness nor apology. I would not excuse myself for that, for if the view seems to be imperialistic it has been forced on me by the nature of the subject. It is not possible to write about the foundation of an empire without seeming to be imperialistic. For myself, I only claim freedom from preconceptions about Clive and the British Empire, not because I did not have them, but because I have outgrown them.

I feel I ought to explain this. I was born early enough – in 1897, the year of the Diamond Jubilee of Queen Victoria – to become familiar with the view that educated and thoughtful Indians held about British rule in India before nationalist agitation began as an active and widespread movement in 1905. These men were not reconciled to subjection, and emotionally they were anti-British, but intellectually not one of them denied that British rule had rescued India from anarchy and brought peace and prosperity to the Indian people.

This attitude wholly disappeared with the nationalist movement. Henceforth the same men thought of the rule as one of oppression and exploitation, and the climax of this attitude was seen when Mahatma Gandhi called British rule in India satanic. Naturally, in my young days I shared this antipathy and even hatred.

Moreover, to Indian nationalists, both Clive and Warren Hastings became symbols of British usurpation and oppression, and they, together with the battle of Plassey, passed into the literature of nationalism. Something about this will be said in the body of the book. Here I would give a personal detail. I myself as a boy of ten took the part of one of the Jagat Seths in the scene of conspiracy against Siraj-ud-daula from a Bengali epic poem which we acted out on the home stage; my elder brother lay flat on it and declaimed the dying speech put into the mouth of Mohanlal, who did not die in the battle of Plassey.

But in my university days I was a student of history, and as I gave considerable attention to methodology I became a staunch believer in the ideal of objectivity in history. I did not give up my nationalism, but I learned to keep my historical views independent of it. At the same time, I found the apologias of the British historians of the day to be both superficial and influenced by considerations of national self-interest. Thus it happened that by the time British rule was ending I had arrived at a neutral position.

Even so, I do not claim that I have written this biography without involvement in the present and future of my country. The ideal of objectivity does not require that. If the historian or biographer does not impose the present on his interpretation of the past, it is perfectly legitimate for him to go to the past so that as citizen he might understand the present. I shall give an instance to explain what I mean. In a speech in the House of Commons delivered on March 30 1772, Clive observed:

Indostan was always an absolute despotic Government. The inhabitants, especially of Bengal, in inferior stations, are servile, mean, submissive and humble. In superior stations, they are luxurious, effeminate, tyrannical, treacherous, venal, cruel.

Anyone who reads this and does not see its relevance to the conditions in both Bengals today, or does not realize how the old Roman motto for imperialism – *parcere subjectis et debellare superbos* – took on new meaning for the British conquerors, might go to history for any other purpose, but not for that which is the most urgent. That is to orient oneself in time. For the historian or the biographer this is far more important, because he will constantly be led to pronounce judgements on the past under the influence of unexamined opinions absorbed from the present unless he is able to see the similarities and the dissimilarities between the past and the present with equal clearness. I would say for myself that I have been particularly careful in defining my position in writing this biography.

Nonetheless, I realize that this may not affect its reception. It is not simply that hagiography may chime in with the mood of one age, and debunking with another; even historical truth set down with the most rigorous honesty may be acceptable and unacceptable according to the moral and intellectual fashions of an epoch. It is not readily admitted even by those who write history that there can be neither a Marxist interpretation of history nor a Christian, neither an imperialistic interpretation nor another that is anti-imperialistic – the only legitimate interpretation is the historical one. In respect of both Clive and rise of the British Empire in India I have tried to give that. With that I shall leave the account given in the book to take care of itself.

Part I

Rise of Clive

1725–1755

Chapter One
The Political Stage

How the Empire came into Existence
It has become a convention in writing biographies of Clive to prefix to them an account of what is called the fall of the Mogul Empire. This is not irrelevant, for without this historical phenomenon there would never have been a British Empire in India, nor Clive its founder.

The Indian Empire was born like the child of an inexperienced unmarried girl, that is to say, without any design to found it, or even awareness that it could come into existence, or any admission of its legitimacy. The East India Company wanted only facilities to carry on trade profitably; but its agents in India saw that, in the political conditions that had developed by the middle of the eighteenth century, it was impossible to have these facilities without a prince friendly to them in the regions where the Company had settlements. Moreover, when a friendly prince was secured he had to be given military protection to remain on his throne; and finally, he could not be given this protection without some amount of control over him. It was in this manner that the British trading concern was caught in the chain-drive of Indian power politics.

However, this trading interest was local and for Britain it had only a relative importance, not to be compared at all with the interests of various kinds she had in North America. By itself the Indian interest would not have induced the authorities at home, whether the British Government or the Company, to employ military power for political purposes. But the local agents committed both the Company and the Government at home to this course because they also had an interest in doing so and it was not less compelling than the interest of their employer. Thus, one after another, they created situations from which the home authorities could not retreat and financial and other interests which they could not abandon. At the beginning even the Government at home was influenced by a crude monetary motive, and if the embryonic empire had not begun to provide the parent state with money from the outset it would not have grown.

Even for this, very large forces would not have been furnished from Home. It was during the War of the Austrian Succession and the Seven Years' War, two European wars which had nothing to do with India, that the employment of Britain's naval power in a general pattern of strategy created a background situation favourable to the Company's political adventures in India. It is certainly one of the ironies of history that the British possessions in North America, which were regarded as valuable (and to retain which a national effort was made), were lost, but the unsought Indian acquisition became what was afterwards grandiloquently called the Brightest Jewel in the British Crown.

Thus the British involvement in India was brought about by a series of small *faits accomplis*, often the outcome of chance and unpredictable circumstances, whose significance was not fully understood at the time. Furthermore, it was helped by the distance from home and the delays in communication. The home authorities were always anything from a year to two years behind the events. Their instructions arrived too late to be applicable to specific situations and even as general indications of policy these were, not infrequently, out of date. This isolation from home was an essential element in the growth of the British Empire in India. The men on the spot took their chance. If they failed they paid the penalty, and when they succeeded the home authorities were not unwilling to appropriate the gain, though they would not encourage further adventurism.

This gradual infiltration into Indian politics was not only made possible by circumstances, but also by the presence on the spot of certain persons at the decisive junctures. When the man was not matched to the hour, that is to say, when the type of individual who was ready to exploit a tempting situation or act defiantly to meet a dangerous one was absent from the scene, the process did not make headway.

Among these personalities, Clive was the most important. Even when he was officially in a subordinate position it was still he who was the most decisive personal factor. He was the nearest approach in British history to a historical figure of the type to which Napoleon belonged. The latest historian of

Napoleon has described him as a temperament; and Clive, above all, was the embodiment of a temperament. The strongest trait of his personality was an irrepressible urge for self-assertion. And by reason of his character he became the main instrument of the political commitment of Britain in India. If he did not loom as large in the public imagination as Napoleon and has not occupied the same place in historical writing, that is because he played his part on a stage apart from the European and even the central British one; because his deeds did not affect the life of great nations with very developed literary traditions; and because his genius in its intellectual aspect was neither so powerful nor so many sided as Napoleon's. But the results of the process which was set in motion by his wild personality were more permanent.

For all that, neither the Company nor the men who conducted its affairs would have found any openings for imposing British rule on India if the façade of Muslim power in India had not presented breaches everywhere. It is this disintegration that has been given the name of the decline and fall of the Mogul Empire. However, it is necessary to be clear about this historical phenomenon. The decline and fall of the Roman Empire has created a concept of imperial decline which has been extended to the Mogul Empire. This, like many other concepts about Indian history, is quite unhistorical. The Roman Empire and the Mogul Empire were quite unlike each other in their rise, existence and disappearance. No historical phenomenon like that which was seen in the West after the age of the Antonines was ever seen in India, and the decline of the Mogul Empire, such as it was, had a wholly different character. It is this that has to be described.

The Dynasty
The very first thing that has to be noted is that the Mogul Empire was not an organized empire; it was not even like the contemporaneous Ottoman and Persian Empires, not to speak of the Roman Empire. These two had inherited stable administrative organizations, the first from the Byzantine Empire and the second from the old Persian, and had become national states. It was owing to this that Turkey, even as the Sick Man of Europe, withstood the designs and efforts of two great powers like Austria and Russia to put an end to its existence; and Persia, too, in spite of the incompetence of the Qajar dynasty

and attempts to partition it like Poland, has survived to be called the Immortal Kingdom and regarded as the successor to the Achaemenid monarchy. The Mogul Empire never became anything of this kind. It was an assemblage of territories which a dynasty of conquistadors held by naked military power and by virtue of the energy of the rulers. And so far as it took root in India, it was an ensemble of scattered military colonies founded by Turkish, Persian, Afghan or Pathan soldiers of fortune. Its dazzling pomp and splendour was that of a military camp.

Even at the height of its power, i.e. during the combined reigns of Akbar, Jahangir, Shah Jahan and Aurangzib (1556–1707), it had only a relative stability. Extension of territories, suppression of rebellions and wars of succession made up its history, and all the rest was incidental. In an empire that depended for its effectiveness on the personal ability of the ruler, succession was the crucial question, and it was never given any legal basis. Normally, it was secured by the member of the family who was the most capable and most ruthless, and who had the most able among the commanders of the soldiers of fortune on his side. Even Akbar, the real founder of the Empire and an irresistible personality, could not determine the succession between his son Salim (afterwards Jahangir) and grandson Khusru.

Worried by the growing rivalry and ill-feeling between the two, Akbar thought he would seek an omen in the outcome of a fight between two champion elephants, one belonging to his son and the other to his grandson. This was arranged, but to prevent any killing Akbar ordered his own champion elephant, Rantamhan, to stand by and come to the rescue of whichever elephant had the worst of it. As it happened, his son's elephant Giranbar cornered his grandson's, Apurva, and his own elephant charged. But both were wounded and put to flight by Salim's elephant, to exultant shouts from his followers. The grandson rushed to Akbar and complained, but the son when summoned and reproached protested complete innocence. From the mortification the Emperor fell ill of fever, which was worsened by diarrhoea, and he died some days later, on October 17 1605. After his death there was a conflict between the son and the grandson, and the grandson was killed, while his mother took poison.

This precedent was followed; and Aurangzib, the last great Mogul emperor, ascended the throne by killing three brothers and imprisoning his father, the reigning emperor, who remained in captivity for eight years. After Aurangzib's death in 1707, there began a process of decline of military power of the dynasty and of the ability of the individual rulers, which made the wars of succession not only more frequent but more ferocious.

Aurangzib totally forgot the episode of his own succession and divided the empire among his three sons. They fought, two were killed, and the eldest, Shah Alam I, succeeded. When he died, again the eldest, Jahandar, succeeded him by killing three brothers. But a nephew disputed the succession and was able, with the help of powerful supporters among the nobles or commanders, to defeat his uncle in battle. The deposed Emperor was at first put in prison with his beloved mistress, but soon the new emperor's soldiers entered his cell, tore him away from the arms of his mistress and tried to strangle him with a strap; when he did not die, a heavy-heeled soldier kicked him in a vulnerable spot and put an end to his life. Then the executioner was sent for to cut off his head. After his death he was given the name of Khuld Aramgah – 'In peace in Paradise' – the only kind of real peace the later Mogul emperors could hope for.

The nephew who succeeded him was Farrukh-siyar. This was the emperor who, out of gratitude to an English doctor who cured him of a painful disease, granted to the East India Company the right to trade in India. But he quarrelled with the two powerful Sayyid brothers, who are known as the king-makers, and was deposed by them. One of the Sayyids had him blinded with the pin with which collyrium is put on the eyes, and kept him imprisoned in a very unclean cell, where he could not seek consolation by reciting the Quran. Afterwards, he was strangled, and the beggars of Delhi (a wealthy guild), who loved him for his charity, fed the poor of the city to honour his memory.

Two insignificant and short reigns followed, and in 1719 Muhammad Shah was made emperor by the Sayyids. He had seen about a dozen of his relatives killed in battle and was determined to live. He managed to do so, had the Sayyid brothers killed, and then sank into debauchery. He reigned till 1748 and in 1739 Nadir Shah of Persia invaded India, sacked Delhi, and put an end to all effective power of the Mogul emperor.

The first events in the establishment of British rule took

place after his death. His successor was the son of a dancing girl, a young man of twenty-two, already enfeebled by debauchery, and in 1754 he was deposed and blinded together with his mother. The next emperor was stabbed to death in 1759, i.e. two years after the battle of Plassey. The emperor who followed him, Shah Alam, was a vagrant prince for many years, and even a refugee emperor for some years after his accession.

What the power and prestige of the four emperors from Akbar to Aurangzib were able to do was to make the powerless dynasty the repository of legitimate status for all subordinate rulers in India. All of them could be independent *de facto*, but none legitimate *de jure*, without sanction from the Emperor. So, in 1765, Clive had to legalize the Company's right to manage the finances of Bengal by taking a grant from Shah Alam. But in 1788, i.e. twenty-three years after this exercise of legal right, Shah Alam was seized in his own palace by a Ruhela (Afghan) soldier of fortune and freebooter, who blew tobacco smoke into his mouth, and afterwards blinded him. He asked: 'Emperor, can you see anything now?' The blind man replied: 'Yes, the Quran between you and me!' The plunderer insulted and tortured the princesses, some of whom died of hunger and thirst. He also sent for the court painter to paint a picture of himself – sitting on the chest of the emperor and gouging out his eyes. Afterwards the freebooter was put to flight and captured, and his eyes were brought to the blind emperor, who fondled them with his fingers.

The Emperor of Delhi was at last freed from personal danger in 1803, by being taken under the protection of the British rulers whose legal suzerain he was. The Mogul Empire in India was the rule of a dynasty, and this was the status of the dynasty when the British began to gain political power in India.

Weakness of the Empire
As the Mogul Empire, like all Islamic kingdoms, was an autocratic monarchy, its fall was the result of the decline of the energy, power and position of a dynasty. In fact, its powerless monarchs far outnumbered those with power. Of the seventeen titular emperors of the dynasty, two were precursors whose work did not survive, the third really created the empire; after him three more exercised power, but the next eleven progressively lost it, and of them the last three remained on the throne under British protection.

Strangely enough, the power of the Mogul Empire lasted only as long as the period of effectiveness assigned to a dynasty by the Muslim historian Ibn Khaldun, the first propounder of a secular philosophy of history. Writing in the fourteenth century, he set down the general law that no dynasty could enjoy power for more than three generations, or 120 years. He had arrived at this conclusion by studying the history of all Muslim dynasties from the age of the Caliphate down to his times.

He divided the life of a dynasty into five stages: the first, of growth in which the conquistador was identified with his people, adherents, and helpers; the second, of success and consolidation when he gained complete control over his people and claimed all power and authority for himself; the third, of leisure and tranquillity, in which the fruits of authority were enjoyed; the fourth of contentment and peace; and the fifth and last of waste and squandering.

This process, according to Ibn Khaldun, was also, from the psychological point of view, a transition from the 'desert qualities' of 'desert toughness and cruelty', to the spirit of 'sedentary culture'. The luxury which the latter engendered at first strengthened a dynasty, but in two or three generations enfeebled both the rulers and the people. When this senility once set in nothing could counteract it. With amazing insight Ibn Khaldun observed that the monuments, i.e. the large edifices built by a dynasty, were proportionate to the original power that brought it into existence, and the impression that a dynasty left behind was also proportionate to that power.

The reason for the decline, according to him, was to be found in the very nature of the dynastic kingdom. Its authority rested on two foundations: in the first place, on the might of the ruler and the 'group spirit' of his people, both of which found expression in the military sphere; after that it was money which secured the soldiers and sustained the authority. Disintegration attacked a dynasty at these two sources of power. Basically, the dynasty was destroyed by the passing away of the energy of the rulers and the collective aggressive spirit of his people.

If Ibn Khaldun had lived in the eighteenth century to see the decline of the Mogul Empire with his own eyes, he could not have summed up the process more fully and correctly. What he had read and seen of Islamic history for seven hundred years led him to propound this deterministic view. It was not falsified either in India or in the rest of the Islamic world in the three centuries after him, in spite of the greatness of the Ottoman, Safavi, and Mogul dynasties in western Asia and north Africa, Persia and India.

By the beginning of the eighteenth century the energy of the Islamic peoples was ebbing everywhere, and most of all in India, where the empire was the least organized and the environment most unfavourable. The Mogul Empire was a military state and nothing else, and it was overwhelmingly dependent on the military ability of the Turks and to a lesser degree of the Persians, all of whom came from outside India. Towards the end of the reign of Aurangzib the recruitment of new soldiers from outside fell off, and both the army and the administration began to pass into the hands of the Indian Muslims and the Hindus. This resulted in a rapid decline of both military and administrative efficiency.

Henceforth the Mogul army was composed of mercenaries from all over northern India with adventurers from Afghanistan and the Pathan country. They acknowledged loyalty to nobody, and would serve any pretender or governor aspiring to independence provided they were paid well and regularly – if they were not, they either mutinied or went over to another employer. During the reign of Ahmad Shah (1748–54) the government was in the hands of his mother, the one-time dancing girl, and her chief adviser, a eunuch called Javid Khan, who was also a lover of hers; and they could not pay the soldiers. These discontented men one day tied up a black bitch and a donkey at the gate of the palace, and forced everybody who went in to salaam the 'Begum Sahiba' and the 'Nawab Sahib', as they described the animals, and the salaries were paid for the occasion. As late as the time of the establishment of British power these mercenaries were the scourge of the rulers as well as of the people.

Even before this reign the Delhi treasury had begun to feel the pinch. One of the reasons was the cost of the wars of succession, and of the rebellions and their suppression. Rebellious governors expected to be compensated if they were to be brought back to their allegiance. During the reign of Muhamad Shah one rebellious Hindu governor agreed to call off his rebellion only when the Emperor agreed to pay him a large sum of money as costs of the rebellion and compensate him with another governorship. Drums were beaten at the imperial camp upon this victory.

Collection of revenue became more and more difficult with

the growth of anarchy. The governors had the first claim on the collections, and they were often unwilling and at times unable to send the emperor's quota to Delhi. The poverty of the emperors became chronic. Some of them sold their household effects, and all the rulers had to borrow money from the Hindu bankers, who acquired ever greater power both in the imperial and provincial governments and played an evil role.

From the beginning of the eighteenth century the provincial governors began to assert their *de facto*, though not *de jure*, independence. Bengal was the first to do so, and in about ten years the whole of the Mogul territories in the Deccan, which had formed a viceroyalty over six provinces, became independent. Similar independent governors appeared elsewhere. Military adventurers, both Muslim and Hindu, established new principalities wherever they could. These had neither geographical nor ethnic logic, and kept shifting their borders all the time. They were kingdoms of what might be called predatory rulers and predatory dynasties. Not one of these was secure without the support of mercenaries.

The greatest of the new predatory regional powers in India was the confederacy of the Marathas. Originally created by the rebellion of Sivaji against Mogul rule and established as a Hindu national state, it extended its power and split at the same time. Even the dynasty was split, and ruled only in name. The real power lay in the hands of the chief minister who was called the Peshwa, and he was the first among a group of military and political adventurers. Their armies, consisting mostly of Marathas but partly of freebooters of varied origins who would join them for plunder, carried out raids for money everywhere in India. The Maratha leaders claimed sovereignty nowhere, but a quarter of the revenue everywhere. They were the greatest threat to the regional Muslim dynasties both as enemies and as friends. To the people they became an object of terror.

Conditions in the Carnatic
The general pattern of dynastic politics at the centre of Mogul power in Delhi was repeated in all the provinces where the Muslim governors became independent or semi-independent. They also established dynasties, but the power of these dynasties often came to an end after the death of the first ruler, and in most cases they disappeared after two or three generations.

As the power of the Mogul emperors declined these minor

dynastic principalities appeared all over India. Of these, two have to be described because it was there that the first intervention of the British in Indian politics took place. Clive also found his field of action in these two. These were the nawabships of the Carnatic and Bengal. Though the second was very much more important than the first, it was in the Carnatic that the political adventure began.

This nawabship was in South India, in territories adjacent to the English settlement at Madras and the French at Pondichery. It was a vassal kingdom of a greater vassal kingdom. the Nawab of the Carnatic, with his capital at Arcot, owed his immediate allegiance to the Nizam, who was legally the Emperor's representative in the whole of the Deccan, but was in fact a powerful independent ruler. No Muslim ruler in South India had any affiliation with the native people of the south – they were all adventurers from the north or officials from the court of Delhi, and their authority rested mainly on Muslim soldiers from north India and even from outside India. Even more than in the north, Muslim rule in the south was military colonialism. So for the natives, the later establishment of British rule was the replacement of one kind of foreign rule by another.

The principality and dynasty of the Carnatic were founded in the early years of the eighteenth century by an official and soldier named Saadat-ullah. But tensions began to appear within his family from the first, though he himself ruled efficiently and became popular. After the death of Saadat the rivalries grew, and developed into cruel and bloody feuds. It was these that brought in the French and the English, first as friends of the rival claimants, and afterwards as their active helpers. Robert Orme, the first historian of these events, describes the struggle for power and possession in detail, and he incidentally makes some general remarks about the character of Muslim rule in India which illustrate concretely what has been said in general terms about the Empire. The microcosm exactly reproduced the macrocosm. These remarks are extremely valuable for understanding the circumstances out of which the British Empire in India arose.

The first feature that Orme pointed out was the purely personal character of political power in India. He wrote:

> There is no country in which the titles of descent are less instrumental to the fortunes of men than they are in Indostan, none but those of royal blood are considered as hereditary nobility; to all

others the exclusion is so absolute, that a new act from the sovereign is necessary to ennoble even the son of the Grand Vizir of the Empire. The field of fortune is open to every man who has courage enough to make use of his sword, or to whom nature has given superior talents of mind.

In this world of politics open and naked military force was the decisive factor, but when it was absent, use of treacherous violence was the alternative. Orme wrote about this:

> The constitution and defects of their government have rendered poisons and assassinations, in the practice of the great, the common method of removing those who stand in opposition to the ambition of others; insomuch that a history of one century of Indostan would furnish more examples of this nature than can be found in the history of one half of the kingdoms of Europe since the time of Charlemagne. From the frequency of these enormous practices, even the deaths which happen in the common course of nature are attributed to the iniquity of those who receive immediate advantage from them.

The rivalries and suspicions were naturally strongest between close relatives and especially between fathers and sons. On this Orme's statement of facts reads like a satire:

> The great men in Indostan bear great affection to their children during infancy; but as soon as these arrive at the age of emancipation, the perpetual intrigues of an Indian court render them, from being a consolation to their parents, the objects of their mistrust: for there are never wanting those, who endeavour to engage them in parties, and even in plots: from hence it often happens, that a prince, in his latter days, lives without affection to his own sons, and gives every kind of paternal preference to his grandchildren; and this recurs so frequently to observation, that one of the oriental poets has said, 'that the parents have during the life of their sons, such overweening affection for their grandchildren, because they see in them the enemies of their enemies.'

Though military force was the only sanction behind every ruler, and had to be used continuously, the soldiers were unreliable. On this, too, Orme is clear and emphatic:

> The armies of the Mahomedan princes of Indostan are composed of a number of distinct bodies of troops enlisted by different leaders; who with their bands, enter into, and quit the service of different princes, according to the advantages which they expect to receive. Hence the degree of reliance which a prince can have on his army is proportioned to the treasures of which he is possessed, joined to his

inclination to disburse them, and it is common in the wars of Indostan to see large bodies of troops going over to the enemy on the very field of battle.

Among the mercenaries employed by these princes the Afghans and Pathans were the worst in respect of treachery and unreliability, as they were also the best or at all events the most ferocious among the soldiers. Orme is very graphic and realistic on them:

> The Pitans, whose country is in the most northern part of the Empire, are the bravest of the Mahomedan soldiery levied in Indostan. From a consciousness of this superiority together with a reliance on the national connection which exists amongst them however dispersed into the services of different princes, they have acquired an insolence and audacity of manners, which distinguishes them, as much as the hardness of their physiognomy, from every other race of men in the Empire: they treat even the lords they serve with very little of that respect which characterises all the other dependants of a sovereign in Indostan. From the known ferocity of theirs, it is thought dangerous to inflict punishment on them, even when they deserve it, as a strong spirit of revenge has familiarised them with assassination, which they seldom fail to employ whenever the smallness of their numbers disenables them from taking vengeance by more open attacks.

Last of all, Orme's description of the Maratha method of making war has to be quoted, because these predators were an important factor in all the political and military happenings of the age:

> They avoid general engagements, and seem to have no other idea of making war, but that of doing as much mischief as possible to the enemy's country. This they effect by driving off the cattle, destroying the harvests, burning villages, and by exercising such cruelties as makes the people of the open country take flight on the first rumour of their approach. The rapidity of their motions leaves the prince with whom they war little chance of striking a decisive blow against them; or even of attacking with effect any of their detachments.

Therefore, when threatened by them, the Muslim princes tried to buy them off, paying the blackmail they demanded (as Orme added). Peoples of both south and north India were finally saved from the depredations of the Marathas by British military power. But that also needed three wars, as a result of which the central Maratha state was destroyed, leaving a few vassal states and dynasties as survivors.

Orme was in India from 1742, lived through the events about which he wrote, and set down the views that he developed through his experience. These are fully corroborated by all contemporary accounts, whether by Europeans or Muslims, and these were so well founded that descriptions of the actual events in the Carnatic that brought about the British intervention appear as if they were only illustrations of Orme's general remarks.

It was a question of dynastic legitimacy in the nawabship of the Carnatic and a rivalry over the succession in the dynasty of the Nizam of Hyderabad which led to the British involvement in the politics of south India. The British entered the field only because the French decided to take sides in both these quarrels. Both the dynasties demonstrated the truth of the biblical saying that 'a man's enemies *are* the men of his own house,' and there were so many deaths in quick succession on both sides from battles and murders that the whole story has been made almost unintelligible by a string of names; their roles in the struggles cannot be understood without keeping a genealogical table by one's side. Yet the general character of the disputes is clear. As the dynastic rivalry in the Carnatic was the primary cause of the European involvement, it will be explained at this point.

There a local governor named Saadat-ullah became a quasi-independent ruler, made himself popular and left his principality to one of his sons, Dost Ali, and the subordinate governorship of Vellore to the other son, Bakar Ali. Dost Ali had many daughters. One of them was married to Bakar Ali's son, Murtaza Ali, and another to a distant relation, Chanda Sahib, a very able man, who became the *diwan*, or controller of revenues and finances. Dost Ali's son Safdar Ali and Chanda Sahib seized the Hindu principality of Trichinopoly, and Chanda Sahib was left behind to govern it.

But the Nizam was not pleased with the spirit of independence shown by the dynasty founded by Saadat-ullah, nor with their acquisitions, and it was believed that he incited the Marathas to invade the Carnatic. In any case, a great Maratha army did so in 1740 on the pretext of collecting the tribute that was due to them. In the battle that followed Dost Ali was killed. The Marathas plundered the province, but Dost Ali's son, Safdar Ali, induced them to leave the province by agreeing to pay them a tribute of ten million rupees at stated periods. As soon as they left, he proclaimed himself Nawab of the Carnatic.

As a result, there grew up a rivalry between Safdar Ali and his brother-in-law Chanda Sahib, and Safdar incited the Marathas to invade the principality again. They laid siege to Trichinopoly, took it in March 1741, and took away Chanda Sahib as prisoner to their capital, Satara.

Safdar Ali thought that he would now reign in peace, but a rival appeared in the other brother-in-law, Murtaza Ali, who was the governor of Vellore and very wealthy. This man was both treacherous and cowardly, and he intrigued against the nawab. Murtaza inveigled him to his house and gave him poison with his food. But the nawab recovered. Then Murtaza got a band of assassins, led by a man whose wife the nawab had seduced, to murder him, and he proclaimed himself Nawab. But the soldiers mutinied against him for arrears of pay, and he fled to his fort Vellore in a palanquin, in the clothes of a woman. After that the boy son of Safdar Ali, Sayyid Muhammad, was proclaimed nawab.

At this point Nizam-ul-Mulk, the Viceroy of Deccan, decided to intervene and settle the affairs of the Carnatic. He went there, took charge of the persons of the young Nawab, and appointed one of his generals to administer the principality. This man was, however, found dead on the day he was going to leave for the Carnatic, and another able soldier in the service of Nizam-ul-Mulk, Anwar-ud-din Khan, was at once appointed to succeed him. People suspected that he poisoned the other man, whom he knew he would succeed.

Nizam-ul-Mulk found a chaotic state of affairs in the Carnatic. Every subordinate governor and commander of a fort had assumed the title of nawab, and one day at a durbar he saw not less than eighteen nawabs in the Carnatic when he thought that there was only one. He ordered his guards to whip any one of these who would still call himself a nawab.

He entrusted the affairs of the province to his nominee Anwar-ud-din Khan, but as its people were very much attached to the old dynasty, he recognized the boy Sayyid Muhammad as the titular nawab. After that he left the province.

It was then that Murtaza Ali, the young ruler's uncle, made use of the discontented Pathan soldiers to get him assassinated. When the boy Nawab was attending a wedding as head of the family, the Pathans appeared before him and demanded their arrears of pay in very insulting language. They were expelled. Strangely enough, they came again and apologized.

In the evening thirteen of them came to attend the durbar, held to receive Anwar-ud-din Khan, who had also come to attend the wedding. Their captain indicated that he wanted to show his repentance by falling at the feet of the young nawab, and, approaching him, stabbed him to death. The guards immediately killed the Pathans, and there was commotion in the city. The whole intrigue was hatched by Murtaza Ali with the Pathans. As the people suspected this and showed their anger against him, Murtaza fled to Vellore. Anwar-ud-din Khan pacified the people, but he was also suspected of complicity. In any case, Murtaza accused him, but he was able to prove his innocence to his superior Nizam-ul-Mulk, and was allowed to become the nawab.

For a time he had no trouble, as the only capable representative of the old dynasty left was Chanda Sahib, who was a prisoner of the Marathas. But popular dissatisfaction with the outsider remained, and when Chanda Sahib was released by the Marathas a new struggle for succession began, and it was this that brought in both the French and the English.

Bengal: 1740–56
British power in India was really founded in Bengal and not in the Carnatic, and there, too, all the features of Muslim politics described above, viz., substitution of one dynasty for another, rivalries within the ruling family, incursion of the Marathas, and mutiny of Afghan and Pathan mercenaries, were seen in a more aggravated form, though the ruler himself was a man of very strong character and exceptional political and military ability. He was Alivardi Khan, whose death in 1756 was followed by the succession of his grandson, Siraj-ud-daula, and within a year by the battle of Plassey and the imposition of British military and political control of Bengal.

Alivardi Khan's ability was recognized even by the Muslim historians hostile to him; his bad faith and treachery to his master, the previous nawab, was admitted even by the most friendly of them. The plot by which he became the ruler of Bengal by killing the young nawab of the reigning dynasty may be regarded as an exact prototype of that which led to the defeat, dethronement and death of his grandson, with this difference – that the Europeans were not a party to the older coup.

He and his eldest brother Haji Ahmad had come as destitute adventurers from Turkestan, and had entered the service of the second nawab of the previous dynasty in very humble capacities; Alivardi became the commander of a small body of troops, and his brother, it was said, began as a pipe-bearer. By that time Bengal had become virtually independent of Delhi under a very able governor, Murshid Quli Khan.

Murshid had no son, and was succeeded by his son-in-law, who ruled from 1727 to 1739. He was an easy-going man, given over wholly to sensual enjoyment, and left the government to his officials. The people of Bengal liked him very much, for in India King Log is always preferred to King Stork. His son, Sarafraz Khan, who succeeded him, was young, violent and suspicious, and also extremely licentious. In all this he resembled Siraj-ud-daula, whose doings made the British masters of Bengal. But he was personally brave, whereas Siraj-ud-daula was a coward.

Sarafraz was distrustful of the two brothers, Haji Ahmad and Alivardi, of whom the first had risen to high office and remained at court, and the younger had become very powerful and was almost independent as the governor of Bihar. But he was also afraid of Alivardi. He quarrelled with his own ministers, and dismissed the trusted Hindu adviser of his father. He alienated others, and more especially the influential banking family of Jagat Seths. So the disgraced Hindu minister, Haji Ahmad, and the Jagat Seths entered into a conspiracy to replace Sarafraz by Alivardi; the latter accepted the proposal and marched against the Nawab on a flimsy pretext in 1740. In the battle that followed Sarafraz was killed, fighting bravely till he was cut down. Alivardi entered the capital and was proclaimed Nawab of Bengal, Bihar and Orissa.

He was at first disliked as a traitor and usurper, but his ability soon reconciled the people. He treated the family of the dead nawab kindly. He was also respected for his austere private life and abstention from sexual indulgence. He had only one wife, and when after the death of Sarafraz fifteen hundred pretty young women were found in his harem he would not look at them, and allowed his brother and his nephews to take them over.

But two years after his installation his troubles began. The Marathas began to raid Bengal in large force from their base in central India, demanding the usual tribute of a quarter of the revenues. Alivardi rejected their insolent demands, and prepared to fight. He was, however, heavily outnumbered, and on account of the Marathar strategy of avoiding pitched battles, he could not always engage them. By outflanking his forces and overwhelming them in skirmishes they even came near Murshidabad. Alivardi won some battles. But the Marathas retreated when beaten and came again, plundering, burning, and killing everywhere, whether they were advancing or retreating. They were helped by one of the Muslim commanders of Alivardi, who turned traitor and furnished them with information.

At last, in 1744, when the Marathas had come for the third time, Alivardi employed a strategem. He deceived their commander, Bhaskar Pandit, by making proposals for peace, and when he came to a conference with all his leading commanders, had them slaughtered by his soldiers, who were hiding behind curtains. Orme commented on this incident in these words: 'The annals of Indostan scarcely afford an example of such treacherous atrocity, and none in which persons of such distinction were the actors.'

The panic-stricken Marathas fled, but rallied soon to continue their attacks, and later large reinforcements were sent by their chief, Raghuji Bhonsla. The fighting went on for seven years without any decisive result. Tired out at last, Alivardi made peace with the Marathas in 1751 by agreeing to cede Orissa to them and pay an annual tribute of twelve lakhs of rupees.

But the Marathas were not the only enemies Alivardi had to fight. While engaged in resisting them he had to face two serious rebellions by the commanders of the Afghan mercenaries whom he was employing to fight them. He was compelled to recruit these foreigners because the local soldiers were wholly undependable. The most important Afghan commander, who had a body of seven thousand faithful countrymen of his with him, was Mustafa Khan. He was responsible for the success in resisting the Marathas in the first invasion, and also played an important part in the assassination of Bhaskar Pandit. Though Alivardi had promised him the governorship of Bihar, he hesitated for fear that the man would become too powerful and perhaps wholly independent. Provoked by this, in 1745 Mustafa marched on Patna and laid siege to the city, which was held by Alivardi's son-in-law, Zain-ud-din. So dangerous was the situation that Alivardi advised him to retreat to the capital. But Zain-ud-din at first resisted and then took the offensive. In the battle that followed Mustafa was killed, and when his head was shown to the Afghans they fled.

The other commanders combined and revolted in 1747, and this time they were able to seize Patna. This was done through ruse and treachery. Zain-ud-din tried to make some of them defect by enlisting them in his army. The terms were agreed upon at a meeting with a section of the Afghans, but suddenly one of them stabbed Zain-ud-din, and when he did not immediately die, another Patnan fell on him and cut him to pieces. Then the Afghans sought out his father, Haji Ahmad, scourged him publicly, painted his face black and white, and mounting him on an ass with his arms tied behind him paraded him through the streets. They found six million rupees in his house, and tortured him to disclose where he had hidden more. His sufferings would have been prolonged if his daughter-in-law had not sent him poison, which he took. The Muslim historian, Ghulam Hussain Khan Tabatabai, though a partisan of Alivardi, attributed these misfortunes of Haji to God's wrath for his treachery to Sarafraz Khan and for dishonouring the women of Sarafraz's harem.

For three months the Afghans held Patna, looted and terrorized the city and the surrounding country. Alivardi, though overwhelmed by grief at the death of his son-in-law and heir-designate, marched to Patna and defeated the Afghans, after which they did not give him any more trouble. During these years he had to fight both the Marathas and the Afghans.

For the last five years of his life Alivardi had some respite from invasions and rebellions. But his peace of mind was disturbed by dissensions in his family. Already, while he was still engaged with the Marathas, his favourite grandson, Mirza Muhammad (later Siraj-ud-daula), whom he intended as his successor, became impatient, and at the instigation of some adventurers turned to revolt. He tried to occupy Patna, but when his supporters were killed he surrendered, and his infatuated grandfather forgave him. In 1753 he was formally nominated as successor by Alivardi. This created ill-feeling in the family.

Alivardi had no son, but only three daughters, whom he married to three of his nephews. Siraj-ud-daula was the son of the youngest daughter and the preferred son-in-law and nephew Zain-ud-din, who was killed by the Marathas. The pampered young man grew suspicious of his uncles and aunts, especially the eldest aunt, Ghasita Begum, and her husband, Nawazish

Khan. They had a very able commander, Hussain Ali Khan, whom Siraj asked his grandfather to remove. Alivardi, however, would not order this unless his son-in-law consented. Siraj tried to influence his uncle through his aunt. This lady, though hostile to Siraj, had a temporary grievance against the commander. The Muslim historian Ghulam Hussain Khan Tabatabai attributed this grievance to a trivial cause, but gossip of the times did not regard it as so trivial. It was said that the commander, a dark and powerful man, was taken as lover by Ghasita Begum, whose husband was supposed to be impotent. In reality, however, the husband preferred to play the woman, and so, it was said, he had made the commander his active lover. There were heated arguments between husband and wife about Hussain Ali. But this would perhaps have been overlooked if the commander had not transferred his heterosexual love affair to the youngest sister, Amina Begum, Siraj-ud-daula's mother. The eldest sister in a pique, after getting her husband's consent, had Hussain Ali openly murdered in Murshidabad by Siraj's men. All this was gossip, but was accepted in Murshidabad long after Siraj-ud-daula's deposition and death. Alivardi's last days were certainly made unhappy by these rivalries and intrigues.

Both the surviving sons-in-law of Alivardi died in close succession, and Siraj's younger brother was also dead. On April 10 1756, Alivardi himself died in his eightieth year. Siraj succeeded him.

Condition of the People
Very little information is available about the condition of the natives of the country while all these things were happening in the political sphere. The rulers, the soldiers and the officials of high rank were mostly foreigners, and they were concerned only with their own interests. They did not pay any attention to the people or to their welfare unless it affected their revenues. Besides, in India, from very ancient times, the general life of the people and the lives of the rulers had run along parallel lines, so that the state and society had few connections with each other. As a result, there could be stable social conditions even when there were changes among the rulers; and unless, owing to their weakness, there was widespread anarchy, mere political changes did not affect the people adversely. This separation was widened during Muslim rule, because the rulers and their manner of living were foreign. In the eighteenth century this was

especially the case because most of the provincial rulers were upstarts. On the other hand, the life of the Hindus had become so simple, and even primitive in some respects, that they could ignore the fluctuations of politics.

There is a very interesting comment on this subject by Luke Scrafton, an Englishman who lived in India in the middle decades of the eighteenth century and described the historical events from 1735 to 1758, with his reflections on them. He published the book in London in 1763, and in it he wrote:

> An Englishman cannot but wonder to see how little the subjects in general are affected by any revolution in the government. It is not felt beyond the small circle of the court. To the rest it is a matter of the utmost indifference, whether the tyrant is a Persian or a Tartar; for they feel all the curses of power without any of the benefit, but that of being exempt from anarchy, which is alone the only state worse than what they endure.

The only relationship between a ruler and his subjects which was permanent and unbreakable was monetary, arising out of the former's right to take a share of the earnings of the people in the form of taxes and land revenue. As India was overwhelmingly agricultural the main source of money for the rulers was land revenue, and from ancient times the theory had been accepted that, whoever might till the land or have a right to it on the strength of different kinds of title, it ultimately belonged to the king. Thus in the most vital relationship between the state and the subject, the ruler with his collectors of revenue, who were organized in an immense hierarchy, stood on one side, and the people on the other, and there was always a tug of war between the two. A wise and farsighted ruler naturally discouraged and often punished exactions that would kill the golden goose, but such wise rulers were not common. Normally, the ruler and his revenue-farmers tried by every means to get as much as they could out of the tillers of land or any subordinate member of the collecting hierarchy. In Bengal at the time of Murshid Quli Khan the exacting of money at the top had become very ruthless, and, naturally the lesser revenue-farmers had also become more extortionate, partly from their fear of the nawab, and partly to retain an adequate share for themselves after meeting their master's demands. This had hardened the traditional distrust between the people and their rulers.

This was also commented on by Scrafton. He wrote:

> The Rajas never let their subjects rise above mediocrity; and the Mahometan governors look on the growing riches of a subject as a

boy does on a bird's nest; he eyes the progress with impatience, then comes with a spoiler's hand, and ravishes the fruit of their labour. To counteract this the Gentoos [Hindus] bury their money underground, often with such secrecy as not to trust their own children with the knowledge of it; and it is amazing what they will suffer rather than betray it: when their tyrants have tried all manner of corporal punishment on them, they threaten to defile them; but even that often fails; for, resentment prevailing over the love of life, they frequently rip their bowels, or poison themselves, and carry the secret to the grave; and the sums lost in this manner in some measure account why the silver in India does not appear to increase, though such quantities are continually coming into it, and going out of it.*

As to defilement, Bengali tradition had it that Murshid Quli, both out of love of money and his hatred for the Hindus (as a Muslim convert from Hinduism), had a pit full of human excreta, in which he put high-caste Hindu landowners when they did not pay the land revenue he demanded. There was nothing more unclean to a caste Hindu than human excreta, though he used cow dung for cleaning his floors and ovens materially, and ate it to purify himself spiritually. Even now orthodox Hindus take a bath and change clothes after using the toilet.

Nor did the artisan get much more from his labour. Orme illustrates this with reference to the weavers of Bengal of his time, of whom he had first-hand knowledge. He writes:

> The weaver . . . living and working with his wife and several children in a hut, which scarcely affords him shelter from the sun and rain; his natural indolence however is satisfied in procuring, by his daily labour, his daily bread; and the dread of extortion or violence from the officers of the district to which he belongs, makes it prudence in him to appear to be poor; so that the chapman who sets him to work, finds him destitute of everything but his loom, and is therefore obliged to furnish him with money, generally half the value of the cloth he is to make, in order to purchase materials, and to subsist him until his work is finished.

Apart from this quest for money from its subjects, for which it

---

*My grandmother found a pot full of gold coins when digging in the garden of our house (called the New House because it was built in the early part of the eighteenth century), and I saw some of them with my father. They were very fine and heavy, with inscriptions in Persian, and must have been buried underground before my great-great-grandfather bought the site from some wealthy iron workers. Despite living in British days my grandmother also kept the money in great secrecy, hiding it even from my mother.

was always groping with the tentacles of an octopus, the Muslim state performed its other functions very perfunctorily. There was indeed some sort of Great Mogul's peace, but it was enforced very superficially. In case of serious breaches of peace the *faujdar,* or the commander of the local forces, with whom lay the executive power of maintaining law and order, often intervened. But for the most part, and especially in the countryside, it was the local landowners or chiefs, and even village headmen, who kept the peace on their own initiative, and this prescriptive local jurisdiction was not questioned by the provincial government.

This was no effective guarantee, however, of the security of life and property, and the people tried to provide it for themselves as best as they could by living together in closely built villages, and also by living unostentatiously and even miserably so that they might not attract the notice of the *dacoits* or robbers. Robbery was a regular profession, and many high landowning families practised it through their retainers. Owing to the growth of anarchy in the eighteenth century, hereditary clans of robbers like the *thugs* had grown up. Travelling was extremely dangerous, especially at night. Over and above this, there was great insecurity arising from family feuds and vendettas.

In addition to this pervasive and chronic state of insecurity, there was danger from the wars of the eighteenth century. The soldiers killed, plundered and raped, and in this respect the Marathas established what might be called an all-time record for India. Under their popular name, Bargi, they remained in the memory of the Bengali people as an embodiment of abominable cruelty. The trials of the population of westernmost Bengal during their invasions from 1742 to 1751 were worse than those of their ruler Alivardi Khan. Contemporary Bengali poets referred to their ferocity, lust and cruelty, and there is in the Bengali language a whole poem called the *Maharashtra Purana,* which describes their atrocities.

The poet says that when the Marathas approached villages the people ran away – the Brahmin with his books, the tradesman with his balances and the peasant with his plough. Men of the highest castes as well as artisans, men as well as women, fled. Gentlewomen who had never walked on any road were seen trudging with trunks on their heads. The raiders demanded money and if it was not given cut off noses and ears, or even killed with one stroke of the sword. Their outrages on women were vile. They seized beautiful women, dragged them along, and raped them one after another in whole gangs, while the women, reeling under their weight cried, 'Save us, save us!' After perpetrating these abominations they let the women go where they could.

Such was the state of the country on the eve of the rise of British power in India, and it was in this political and social milieu that Clive's life and career were cast. There are no books in which he or the other actors and observers set down what they *felt* at the time the events occurred. They seem to have taken the conditions for granted, strange as they must have been to them. When they did write, they wrote about the events objectively, not even introducing as much feeling as Thucydides expressed in describing the horrors of the civil strife in Corcyra. The earliest historian of the war in the Coromandel, R. O. Cambridge, even consciously formulated a method of dealing with his subject, setting down the alternatives, and choosing the most colourless deliberately. He was aware of what could be expected from him by the reading public in England.

> It will not appear strange that the generality of the world, through the habit of reading novels, and works of imagination, should expect from an history of the East (which has generally been made the scene of most of their ideal stories) a tale of adventures full of wonder and novelty, and nearly bordering upon romance. Neither are we to be surprised if others of a serious cast, having also, at the same time, an elegant turn of mind and a taste for ornament, should have expressed an expectation, and, perhaps, hinted their advice, that, in order to engage the attention of the reader, the work ought to be embellished with the strange manners of a remote people, the works of art and the wonders of nature in so very distant and different a climate from our own.

But, Cambridge explained, the design of the work was 'to lay before the more informed, an exact, clear, and impartial state of facts, drawn entirely from authentic papers'. This being the real design of the work, he added, '. . . every kind of decoration that was not necessary to illustrate facts would have diverted the attention of the reader from a close view of the conduct of the two nations i.e., the English and the French, by which he is to form his judgement'.

Cambridge even said that greater literary ability than his would have been out of place in the work. As he put it, 'Had these materials fallen into the hands of any person capable of rendering them more pleasing, by his superior taste in composition, and a happy elegance of style, surely he would have employed those talents injudiciously.'

This method of narration in a neutral style was adopted not only by Lawrence and Clive in their accounts of the events, but even by Orme, who only slightly heightened the effect, not by comment, but by some telling narration. The result was that a series of events, compared with which Mrs Radcliffe's horrors would have appeared tame, were described in a way that destroyed all their particularity.

Chapter Two
Clive Comes to India

The presence of Europeans and of Clive in this political world has now to be considered. The conditions just described did indeed lead to the rise of the British Empire in India, but the first impetus that pushed Europeans into Indian politics did not come from these, nor from commercial competition, but from a phenomenon of European history, namely the Anglo-French rivalry, which had been breaking out in the form of intermittent wars since 1688, and the global results of those wars.

The two European commercial companies in India became involved in this struggle with the outbreak of the war of the Austrian succession in 1740, but no actual clash between the two took place until news of the declaration of war by France on Britain, on March 15 1744, reached Madras on September 15 of the same year. There was also an interesting coincidence. Clive had arrived at Madras a few months earlier, in June 1744. In order to understand, or rather not to misunderstand, what followed, it is necessary to take note of the position of the companies just before the beginning of the first Anglo-French conflict in India.

The English Company
To take the English company first, at the time when the war of the Austrian succession broke out in 1740, without as yet involving England directly, the English East India Company had become a very prosperous trading concern. It also profited from the peace established by the Treaty of Utrecht in 1713. Its trade in exports and imports doubled between 1708 and 1750.

It had three separate centres of operation in India, called presidencies: Bombay on the western coast, Madras on the eastern coast of peninsular India, and Calcutta in Bengal. Of these, Bombay was a possession of the Company in its own right, and the other two were occupied on the strength of grants obtained from the local Muslim rulers, endorsed by the Great

Mogul. However, these stations were for all practical purposes British territory, somewhat like later concessions in China. The Company exercised full police and judicial authority over them, as also over the villages and lands that were attached to the cities proper. There were smaller stations subject to these three centres, both on the coasts and inland.

The three so-called presidencies were wholly independent of one another, and in direct relationship with the Company in London. Each was under a governor assisted by a council. The governor was the president of the council – hence the name presidency. All decisions had to be taken by the council as a whole, but naturally the president at this period had more practical authority than the members of the council, and when he was a man of forceful character he dominated his colleagues.

The English servants of the Company in India were divided into four classes: writers, factors, junior merchants and senior merchants. First appointed as writers at a very young age, and working in this capacity doing the routine work of the establishments for five years, the servants were promoted to factors, i.e. heads of the smaller stations. They became junior merchants after three more years, and senior merchants after another period of three years. Their formal pay was small, and even the governor did not get more than £300 a year. Merchants and factors received £30 and £20 a year. Even after the assumption of political authority in Bengal in 1757, the salaries were, for a councillor, £250 a year, for a factor, £140 a year and for a writer, £130 a year. These rates created a duality in every servant of the Company, with one side looking after the interest of the Company and the other to personal interest – the latter tending to dominate.

The servants had been granted the right of private trade, which they carried on with great energy and some rapacity. As a rule, after a relatively short stay in India they could return to England as rich parvenus and objects of envy to their neighbours. Though not as prominent in English society as they became in the second half of the century, they were already attracting notice. But there was no means of attracting men to do the Company's work in India other than by offering monetary incentives outside their formal work. Life in India was risky, drab and irritating. There was no attractive society, and though the native women might assuage the *rage de la culotte*, as Dupleix himself described the elemental necessity, they were at best palliatives, at worst dangerous. Dour pursuit of money by any means was the only counterbalancing attraction.

This private trade by its servants did not diminish the possible gains for the Company. What in these days would go to an extortionate bureaucratic state would in those days have gone either to the nawab and his harpies or have been swallowed up in the expenses of the trade had it been carried on by the Company. It was on too large a scale, too scattered and too complicated to be carried on by one concern. On the other hand, by leaving the private trade in the hands of its servants the Company saved on salaries and wages. It was not very willing to spend money on these. For instance, it always chartered vessels just below 500 tons, because government regulations required that every ship of 500 tons and over must have a chaplain. So in order to save the salary of the ecclesiastic, it hired ships up to 499 tons.

No one who has not had experience of the traditional methods of transacting business in India can have an idea of the number of middlemen who interpose themselves between the real buyers and the producers. Even for the Company's trade in cotton fabrics, its English servant was at five removes from the weaver. He had, first, to have his native secretary, called the *banian*, who in his turn hired brokers called *gomashtas*, and there were several others after them. Ignorance of the language and manners of the people of the country compelled the English servants of the Company to employ these intermediaries.

Many of the natives employed by the English in the early epoch of their trade later became the moneyed aristocracy of Calcutta. These men with their vested interests became powerful agents for the establishment of British power in India.

At this time the Company had no desire whatever to become involved in the quarrels of the Indian princes. Nevertheless, its spirit and policy were never purely mercantile. When the Company came to the eastern seas in the seventeenth century, its agents had something of the buccaneering spirit of the Elizabethan seamen. They not only preyed upon the trade and shipping of other European nations, but were also ready to put pressure on the Mogul Emperor by harrying his ships in order to get trading concessions. This they did even in the reign of the powerful Aurangzib.

They showed themselves equally assertive on land in order to protect their settlements and further trade. As a very aggressive servant of the East India Company, Sir Josia Child, wrote even in 1685, the Company's aim was 'to establish such a politie of civil and military power, and create and secure such a large revenue to maintain both ... as may be the foundation of a large, well-grounded, sure English dominion in India for all time to come'. This was anticipating Dupleix by nearly seventy years.

In Bengal Job Charnock put pressure on the Mogul government in a different manner. When attacked by the local governor at Hughli, he abandoned the settlement and, by resisting him, at last made the governor agree to his return to Sutanooti, which later became Calcutta. In 1688, under instructions from home authorities, an English naval force carried out an attack on the port of Chittagong. Though it was not successful, peace was concluded in 1690, and the English settled themselves firmly in Calcutta, which they fortified in 1696.

In dealing with the central and local Muslim authorities the English showed a determination to trade on privileged terms, and they generally secured the concessions they wanted. But in the early part of the eighteenth century their policy was to secure concessions from the Emperor of Delhi and to overcome the opposition of the local nawabs by pleading this superior concession. They employed this method against Murshid Quli Khan, Nawab of Bengal, who was very hostile to them, and they partly succeeded.

They had similar trouble with the lower Muslim functionaries, who often refused to obey the orders from Delhi or the local nawab in order to make money by extortion from the prosperous Company. Against this kind of harassment the Company's governors appealed to whatever effective higher authority there might be in the region in question.

For instance, in 1744 they appealed to the Viceroy of the Deccan, Nizam-ul-Mulk, when he came down to the Carnatic to settle its affairs. Though legally entitled by an imperial grant to trade in that region without paying the customary dues to the Muslim government, the local functionaries often forced them to do so. To put a stop to such levies, Nicholas Morse, Governor of Madras, wrote a very flattering letter to the Nizam-ul-Mulk. He began by saying that 'Your Excellency's appearance in these parts the English looked upon as the most favourable circumstance that could possibly happen to them.' Then he went on to say:

> By the blessing of God the affairs of this province are now settled and Your Excellency as I am informed on your departure from us, before which I beg leave to hope Your Excellency will grant us some mark of your favour as shall be agreeable to your great wisdom and generosity. This will shew the world your kind acceptation of our services to the Circar, and is what I have waited for with the most earnest desire, and which I should not have doubted to have been honoured with before now had the English been so fortunate as to have an advocate to put Your Excellency in mind of us when matters of great consequence would have admitted it.
>
> Since I have failed in that point, I humbly presume to ask it myself of Your Excellency, whose goodness I shall now rely on without any intercessor. This will be an addition to my happiness as it will give me an opportunity of making this particular address to so great a Personage as Your Excellency, of whom I beg a favourable ear to what I am about to represent.*

After this preamble, Governor Morse laid his request before the Viceroy of the Deccan. It was to issue an order so that the Company might not have to suffer from unreasonable demands from the local authorities, like the *faujdars* and *zamindars*, for duties from which it was exempted by a grant from the Emperor of Delhi.

In short, in regard to commerce the Company was firm in continuing its activities by diplomacy as far as possible, and by force if that became necessary and could be employed with effect.

As to the general political situation, the only concern of the Company was to see whether any political event affected its interest. If it did not, neither the directors at home nor the agents in India were worried about it, though for the country itself it might have far-reaching consequences. This was seen in the attitude towards the invasion of Nadir Shah in 1739, which put an end to all effective power of the Emperor of Delhi. On receiving news of it in London the directors wrote to Madras on February 6 1740:

> The account laid before us of the great revolutions in the Mogul Empire by the Persian march and return requiring no answer, as our affairs have not been prejudiced thereby, we depend upon your watchful care on all such emergencies, of our estate and property.

On the other hand, if any political disturbance was likely to injure the trade or settlements of the Company its agents were

* The letter is in Persian, and the citation is from the official and contemporary English translation.

expected to defend both with energy. Thus, on learning the news of the invasion of the Carnatic by the Marathas in 1740, the directors wrote on January 20 1741:

> The Morattas invading, overrunning and plundering the Choromandell coast gives us a most sensible and deep concern, more especially as they came within our bounds and sent you a most insulting message, tuck'd to an enormous and unheard of demand, which you did well to answer from the mouths of our cannon, and thereupon to put yourselves in the defensible posture. We hope that long before now the coast is well rid of them, and that the country Powers have been roused to defend their subjects' property against all such formidable enemies in future. However, that may be, you must by no means become tributary, or suffer contribution to be levied upon us, either by the Moors or the Morattas.

Simply, the English company, even though it did not have any political standing in India, was determined not to tolerate any move by any Indian political adventurer of the kind that would now be called nationalization. The directors were, however, ready to keep on good terms with the trouble-makers and to incur any expense that was called for. So, on hearing that the Governor of Madras had sent the Maratha commanders presents when they left Madras unmolested at the time of their invasion of the Carnatic, they wrote:

> We entirely approve of your making the Generals handsome presents at the camp to keep them in good humour; the sending them by a vackeel, we perceive, rendered them very agreeable. Upon all such urgent occasions we cheerfully acquiesce in the needful expense to prevent greater evils.

This was typical of the management of the Company's affairs at all the three centres, and in order to keep themselves fully informed about what was happening in the Indian courts the governors employed native intelligence agents, who sent them regular reports. They also kept up correspondence with the rulers and notables for the sake of courtesy. This gave great satisfaction to the latter, who felt disappointed if they were not noticed.

In the last resort, however, the Company depended on its own strength, money, men, armaments and fortifications. By 1740 all three settlements had fortifications. On the Coromandel coast there were two fortified stations, Fort St George (Madras), and further south Fort St David (Cuddalore). But at this time the fortifications were not such as to be able to stand a regular siege.

The home authorities were always urging economy on the governors. The military forces were also small, and so far as the Indian soldiers were concerned were not yet trained in the European manner. The European soldiers were partly recruits sent out from Britain and partly deserters from the service of the other European settlements in India. There were in addition some half-castes called *topasses*, who were Indo-Portuguese. A large number of natives were also employed. They were sometimes given muskets, but were generally armed only with swords and shields and other traditional weapons. They also wore Indian dress. The military forces of the Company, though adequate for protecting the settlements from casual attacks, were not strong enough for serious military operations.

The French Company
At this period Dupleix was the governor of Pondichery, with authority over all the French settlements in India. In addition to this establishment, there were those at Chandernagore, Karikal, Mahé, Masulipatam and Yañaon, and Surat. Of these the first two were the really important ones.

Dupleix had taken up the post of governor on January 13 1742. His predecessor, Dumas, who had held the post from September 1735 to October 1741, had considerably raised the prestige of the Company by an expedition to Mocha, occupation of Karikal, by his firm handling of the situation during the Maratha invasion of the Carnatic in 1740, and by fortifying Pondichery. But financially it was in a weak position, and its commercial enterprises were much less extensive and profitable than those of the English company. The very activities that had contributed to the respect for the French company's power had also involved heavy expenses and had left a large deficit. These expenses, wrote Dumas to Dupleix in September 1743, would certainly ruin the Company if they continued at the rate to which they had risen. Actually, they exceeded the profits by more than three millions. This financial difficulty continued throughout the governorship of Dupleix (1742–53), and was an important pressure behind his political adventures.

As in the English East India Company, so in the French, trade was divided into two parts: the public and the private. The latter was called '*commerce d'Inde en Inde*', and included not only the coastal trade, but also trade with all countries east of the Cape of Good Hope, with the exception of China and Mocha. At first the Company also had its share in this trade, but afterwards it had to be left to its servants, because their salaries were so low that they had no inducement to work for the Company without opportunities for extra earnings. These servants bought and commissioned vessels for their private trade, and made very large profits. Dumas, for instance, when he died in 1746, left properties worth two million livres.

The Company's trade, which was with Europe and those parts of Asia reserved to itself, was dependent on the ships it owned, supported by the ships of the French navy. Between 1740 and 1744 it suffered from the uncertainties arising out of the covert hostilities by the English navy, and from insufficient shipping. After 1744 ships became available, but the trade was swept off the seas.

Like the English company, the French one was also determined to protect its interests and establishments by force. So Pondichery was fortified by Dumas for fear of attacks from the Marathas as well as from the Nawab of the Carnatic. On the land side these fortifications were so considerable that they roused great admiration in India. Indeed, as Orme remarks, these 'were at this time in such reputation, amongst a people who had never before seen anything equal to them, that the late nabob, as well as Subdar-ally and Chunda-sahib, had sent their wives, children, and treasures, to remain there during the war'. On the seaward side, however, there were no fortifications until later.

As to the military forces, all the French establishments taken together were to have 1,000 European soldiers, but their actual number was lower. At the end of 1740 there were only 350 at Pondichery and about 100 each at Karikal and Chandernagore. In addition, there were native soldiers. It was the French who first gave European military training to the Indians whom they enlisted. But there were never a sufficient number of European officers to lead them. They were commanded by native officers, who were given money for 500 sepoys at Rs6 a month for each sepoy but who recruited only 350 or so and paid them at Rs4 or Rs3, taking the rest of the money themselves.

The military works and the soldiers were entirely for the defence of the various establishments if attacked, and there was never any idea of involvement in the rivalries and wars of the Indian princes. The French East India Company had by its charter sovereign power to conquer territory and rule, subject to allegiance to the king of France. But such powers were never exercised in India. Mahé was indeed taken by force from a local raja in 1725, and Karikal in 1738; but these were not meant to be anything but commercial establishments, and their seizure was looked upon as defence of trading rights. The local princes, both in the Carnatic and Bengal, totally forbade any warlike activity between the European companies, and they were strong enough to ensure obedience.

Dupleix himself, even after he had become the governor of Pondichery in 1742, never intended to go beyond these limits. He had arrived in India in 1722 and, after being employed in a number of subordinate capacities, became governor of Chandernagore in Bengal in 1731. He did not like Bengal and found its climate abominable, though he wrote to his brother that it was a good place for making money quickly. He complained of his salary, which was 4,000 livres a year and much lower than the salary of the governor of Pondichery. More than once he thought of resigning his post, but remained because it was only in India that he could make money – at this time his only ambition. With his natural ability and enterprise he improved the Company's trade in Bengal. But once his duties had been conscientiously attended to, he devoted himself with even greater energy to his private trade. Only one-tenth of his correspondence in this period relates to the affairs of the Company, and the rest is devoted for the most part to his extremely complex private business. So many people were connected with it that his private organization could be regarded as a small company within the great.

He had begun this trading even when he was a subordinate official at Pondichery. He acquired a fine house there, with a garden ornamented with statues, and in 1729 he sent diamonds worth 2,000 pagodas to his brother in France. The trade was continued at Chandernagore, and became more important because the chief of an establishment had opportunities denied subordinates. He borrowed money and bought ships: by 1733 he had ten, all engaged in his private trade. He bought two houses at and near Chandernagore.

As it was his intention to retire to France and to live there in style after earning a sufficient amount of money, he naturally sent his gains there. This resulted in great loss to him, for one of the ships carrying Rs500,000 was wrecked in 1735 and only

Rs24,000 could be saved. Upon this he wrote to a Jesuit priest who was his friend: 'My losses have not made me murmur against Providence; on the contrary, I have submitted to Him more than ever before, and He has given me the strength and the means to continue these voyages which I put under His high protection, requesting you to join your prayers to mine to obtain better results than in the past year.'

Dupleix continued his trading, and even sent smuggled goods into France with the connivance of the *fermier-général*. But owing to his losses at various times, and also to his expensive style of living he was able only to send about 200,000 fr. to France. This was what made him accept the governorship of Pondichery – though keen on retiring to his country, he wanted to restore his fortune.

After taking up his post at Pondichery he continued his activities along the same lines. He also married the widow of an old friend, who had already had eleven children, of whom five were living. This lady was partly of Indian descent and later came to be known in India as Jan Begum. In the political sphere Dupleix continued the policies of his predecessor Dumas. The possibility of a war between France and England made him consider military problems seriously. Nevertheless, at the time when the news of the declaration of war against England reached India, in September 1744, Dupleix was neither a political dreamer nor a political adventurer.

War of the Austrian Succession
The war of the Austrian succession led to the first military clash between the English and the French in India. When Dupleix received the news of the declaration of war by France on England he had no intention of attacking the British. The two companies did indeed regard each other as serious commercial rivals, and after the start of the European war in 1740 they also expected hostilities to break out at sea. But nothing happened in Indian waters and on Indian territory. Dupleix was anxious to maintain this local neutrality. For one thing, he knew that a British naval squadron had arrived in Indian waters, and the French squadron which was there in 1741 was now away in the French islands. So any conflict would mean the ruin of French trade. Besides, he had received a warning both from the Nawab of the Carnatic and the Viceroy of the Deccan that the companies were in India for the sake of trade, and that no war would

be tolerated. At this time he also believed that the English would not be anxious to open hostilities because the fortifications and defences of Madras were very weak. So he rejected a proposal from La Bourdonnais that between them they should attack the British in India. 'It is necessary', he wrote, 'that the English should be the aggressor, which I doubt.'

At the same time, he wrote to the English Governors of Madras, Bombay, Telichery, and Calcutta, proposing neutrality. The Governor of Madras replied that he for his part could promise neutrality, but he could not be responsible for the acts of the commander of the King's ships. The Governor of Bombay wrote that his powers were not wide enough to conclude a treaty of neutrality, but the Council of Telichery accepted the proposal, while Bengal sent a reply on the lines of Madras. In any event, hostilities were opened by the commander of the British squadron. Dupleix was bitter about it, and in concert with La Bourdonnais prepared to attack Madras.

In the conflict that followed, the French were brilliantly successful both in offence and defence. The English lost Madras in September 1746, and failed to take Pondichery when they besieged it with superior forces in 1748. The war was confined entirely to the Carnatic, for in Bengal Alivardi Khan was strong enough to compel both sides to observe peace, and on the western coast the English position was too strong to be attacked. The French military achievement remained incomplete because they failed to take the English fort of St David, and was somewhat marred by misunderstandings between Dupleix and La Bourdonnais.

But all the French successes in India were obliterated by the treaty of Aix-la-Chapelle. Its terms called for mutual restitution of all conquests. Madras had to be restored to the English, and was handed over on September 1 1749. The war was an episode in a world-wide war between England and France, and had no direct connection with the establishment of British political and military power in India. Nevertheless, it was a sort of prologue, because it left behind certain states of mind which inspired later activities, and also the resources that could make them worthwhile and practicable. It is these that have to be noted.

The most important psychological legacy of the local conflict arising out of the war of the Austrian succession was Dupleix's discovery of himself. He was very able and naturally ambitious, and the war opened up to him the possibility of applying his powers to secure higher ends. As a result, the merchant developed into the political adventurer.

His self-confidence was both extended and confirmed by his success in dealing with a very dangerous situation for the French company almost single-handed. In his later claims on the Company he declared that, but for what he was and what he did on his own, French interests in India would have been ruined. The tone of his apologia was boastful, but the facts he stated were not untrue. Some of his statements might be quoted. 'The capture of Madras', he said, 'was again the happy consequence of my preparations and the bravery of the commander and his troops.' After the departure of La Bourdonnais, he pointed out, the entire burden of keeping and defending Madras and Pondichery fell on him, and it was his resources, his credit and his purse that furnished everything needed. His wife's jewellery was mortgaged, and his silver was melted for money. 'Pondichery', he added, 'would have been lost if I had waited for support from Europe, and if my foresight and expenditure had not placed this place in a state to stand a long siege.' After the peace, he declared, the French nation had the satisfaction of learning that none of the possessions of the Company in India had been seized by the enemy and that he had foiled all their designs.

Secondly, he acquired a violent dislike and even hatred for the English, and a deep-rooted suspicion of their motives and intentions. He became convinced that they would always be the implacable enemies of France in India. To this feeling, fully developed in him in 1748, he gave free expression after his recall and in his criticism of the agreements concluded with the English by his successor. He then wrote:

> It is the English who lay down the law. . . . But some may say, they are bound by treaties like us. This is a mistake; nothing binds the English except force *vis-à-vis* their interest. . . . Nothing is respected by them except *force majeure*. . . . The history of Europe since Queen Elizabeth to our days alone teaches us that the greater part of their power, their commerce, their colonies, their wealth has no other foundation but bad faith and repeated infringements of the best cemented treaties and of the Law of Nature and of Nations.

The theory of *Perfide Albion* was full-blown in him.

Next he acquired a first-hand knowledge of the character and competence of the native princes and complete confidence in his capacity to deal with them. At the beginning of the war Dupleix had not been aggressive to the Muslim princes. When warned against hostilities in Mogul's territories he had sent a conciliatory reply. But when the English squadron continued their attacks on French shipping he wrote to the Nawab of the Carnatic:

> The scant regard that this nation [The English] pays to your orders compels me to say that I cannot refrain from acting like them as soon as ships of war which I am awaiting arrive. It is wholly necessary that we should teach them how one ought to act in a country which does not belong to them. Inasmuch as the Padishah receives many nations in his empire he and his governors should forbid them to create trouble in it. [August 3 1745]

A little later he wrote to the local military commander that he did not want the protection of the nawab, and was quite capable of taking action by himself against the English. At that time he was planning the expedition that was to capture Madras the next year.

In September 1745, Anwar-ud-din Khan, Nawab of the Carnatic, paid a visit to Pondichery; and, though a good deal of outward courtesy was displayed by both sides on this occasion, Dupleix became convinced that the nawab was not really friendly to the French but only wanted to find out from which side he could extract the larger sum of money. He himself was predisposed towards the older dynasty of Dost Ali and its surviving representative, Chanda Sahib.

After the capture of Madras his attitude became more assertive. He had given the assurance that he was attempting to take Madras only to give it to the nawab, without having any intention of doing such a thing. By so doing he prevented the Nawab from taking action at a time when his intervention would have harmed the French. When, after its capture, the Nawab demanded that the city should be handed over to him, Dupleix replied that since it belonged in absolute sovereignty to the English he had the right to keep it. After that the nawab sent an expedition to recover Madras from the French. But by November 1746, his forces were twice routed by small French forces, and the city remained in their hands.

The importance of these two actions has been exaggerated, but since these were the first clashes on land between the forces of a Muslim prince and a European company – and were also successful – they undoubtedly fostered confidence in the capacity of the Europeans to deal with the armies of the Muslim princes.

The repulse of the forces of Anwar-ud-din Khan immensely raised the prestige of Dupleix among the powers of the Deccan. Even the suzerain of the nawab, Nizam-ul-Mulk, sent his congratulations to Dupleix through his minister Imam Sahib.

> I understood what you have pointed out on the subject of the unjust war which Mafuz Khan [Anwar-ud-din's son] has waged against you. I am truly charmed that you have made him repent of it. I never doubted that it could be otherwise; and I send my compliments on it. . . . I reckon that shortly Nawab Anwar-ud-din Khan will receive drastic orders and will be reprimanded for the war.

The famous Maratha chief, Raghuji Bhonsla, was more effusive and wrote:

> I cannot in truth express the joy which I felt when I learned about the reduction of the city of Madras and of the fact that you have become masters of it. . . . The reports of your victory have spread in such a manner in these parts and elsewhere that your enemies, of whatever nation they might be, are in consternation, and of this you may remain assured. All Hindustan resounds with this news.

The prestige so acquired was to rise higher after the successful defence of Pondichery. Dupleix was recognized as one of the most important persons in India. The cancellation of all the French gains by the treaty of Aix-la-Chapelle made no difference to Dupleix's personal standing in south India. It has to be pointed out however that, as a result of the fighting in the Carnatic, neither Dupleix nor the French company gained any territory or political authority. He had no plans for any intervention in the political affairs of the country, and certainly no intention of making conquests.

But a certain emotional ferment had taken place in Dupleix's personality. He had become conscious of his own powers and of the weakness of the native princes. For the moment he was also suffering from an acute sense of frustration because all his achievements, which had cost him so much, were nullified by a peace that was not influenced by the events in India. There was nothing more likely to set an ambitious and able man on a course of political adventurism for its own sake, without conscious formulation of any goal, than the state of mind Dupleix was in at this stage. Moreover, he had one clearly felt aim, which was to thwart and harm the English in every way.

To tempt him further he had the freedom to act on his own initiative, paying little or no attention to the views and instructions of the Company or to the King's government in France. The distance of thousands of miles from the authorities above him gave him the opportunity to act as he wanted. He knew that, if he succeeded, he would be acclaimed at home even if he had disobeyed orders and instructions, and, being naturally optimistic, and at that time justified in his optimism, he did not envisage failure.

Finally, he had adequate military forces at his disposal. There were at Pondichery about 2,000 white soldiers, 1,400 sepoys and 300 Negro slaves trained to fight. In addition, a contingent of 300 sepoys had been sent from Mahé. Taken together, these forces were the largest ever assembled at Pondichery, and Dupleix knew that they outnumbered the English forces. On account of their recent successes, the morale of these troops was also high.

The English Company, for its part, was in a pacific rather than a bellicose mood. In spite of its military failures, it was to recover all its possessions, and had no interest in seeking adventures. (As will be related later, it did in fact set out on one. But for this there were special reasons.) Generally speaking, it was ready, as the directors from home advised, to make use of the tranquil condition of the country to extend its commerce.

But the Madras authorities were suspicious of Dupleix and his intentions. They were very dissatisfied with the fact that he had partly destroyed the city, and deprived it of its armaments, especially cannon. There were also bickerings over the execution of the terms of the treaty, and each party accused the other of bad faith in disregarding the provisions of the treaty of Aix-la-Chapelle.

So far as the English were concerned, therefore, both the authorities in England and in India were determined to strengthen the fortifications and defences of all the English possessions. On December 8 1749, the directors wrote to St David, not being informed as yet that the governor had gone back to Madras:

> Being determined to have our possessions and estate put in as perfect security for the future as we are able by making additions to, and alterations in the fortifications and works of our several settlements in the East Indies, and the Island of St Helena, as may render them defensible against attacks of any European or Indian

enemies, we have in order thereto, appointed Benjamin Robins, Esq., in whose integrity and capacity we have entire confidence, our Engineer General, as likewise Commandant of Artillery.

The local councils were directed to regard the instructions given to Robins as binding on themselves, and he was specially advised to give his attention to artillery, on which the safety of the British settlements mainly depended.

This emphasis on fortifications and artillery would show that the mind of the Company was running on defence. But there was also a large force at the disposal of the Madras council, though not as large as that of Dupleix. A return of the troops on the Coromandel coast, sent to the Court in London on October 30 1749, shows that in the forts of St George and St David and that at Devikottai there was a total of 1,418 officers and men, of which over 1,200 were European, and the rest *topasses*. This force was made up of nine companies of infantry, one troop of horse and some artillery. Major Lawrence was in command of the whole force with 11 captains, 2 captain-lieutenants, 18 lieutenants, 10 ensigns and 2 adjutants, altogether 44 officers including the commander. There is no mention of sepoys in this return. But some must have been employed. Or it is possible that the sepoy force which was employed for the Tanjore expedition early in that year had been disbanded, and as yet no new enlistments had been made.

Since almost immediately the two companies began to involve themselves in the quarrels for power and succession of the princes of the region, it is relevant to point out that the directors of the English company were not in favour of incurring large expenses in gaining the support or favour of the princes. On learning that Madras had made large presents to Nasir Jang, the son of Nizam-ul-Mulk and his successor for the time being, the directors wrote on December 8 1749:

> You have been too lavish of our money in making such extravagant presents to Nazir Jung and the great men about him, amounting to no less than 20,518 pagodas, 4 fanams and 70 cash, more than adequate to any services we have received or may expect from them, as experience has taught us very little confidence can be placed in any Indian Powers. You must act with more frugality and caution in this respect for the future.

But a new struggle for power between the two companies was already afoot.

Enter Clive

For the subject of a biography to enter it after it is well under way is unusual. But it is not unjustifiable in this case; on the contrary, it is quite logical. In respect of Clive the biographer might imitate the second and the fourth gospel, which omit the nativity and boyhood of Jesus to begin the story with his baptism. His early life has no relevance to his career and greatness. There was nothing in it to foreshadow his later activities or even his fully developed personality. Of course, he must have had latent aptitudes and potentialities. But these were all inside a hard shell like the bird in the egg. The Hindus call their upper castes, as well as birds, twice-born. Clive was twice-born – physically in England, and again, in the only significant sense, in India.

It must be kept in mind that a career like his, or Napoleon's (and, at a lower level, Napoleon's marshals), was not possible in a stable society. A whole order had to be in a state of political disintegration to produce such men. Only crumbling established regimes could create such roles and such personalities. Clive could become the founder of the British Empire in India only because that country was at this point disintegrating politically. So he became Clive of *India*, not of England.

There is another feature of his career which makes him remarkable compared with the adventurers and *nouveaux venus* of the revolutionary era of France. Napoleon was an accomplished student of war, a fully trained officer and a mature personality, when the revolutionary wars gave him his opportunity. To mention two other young heroes of the epoch, Hoche and Marceau were trained soldiers. Clive's early life gave him no training of this kind. He had no mental training, even. He went out to India as an unskilled and callow youth, and learned his job by doing it – and went on discovering himself.

However, biographical orthodoxy has been observed in Clive's case by seeing, in the scanty and commonplace details of his childhood and youth, presages of the founder of an empire. Some incidents related about his first years in Madras, too, appear like forgotten facts transformed into legends, if not actually invented. They are to be found in all the early biographies and also in Macaulay's essay. Three of the stories in the first official biography by Sir John Malcolm, himself one of the most distinguished soldiers and officials of the East India Company, might be mentioned. That which is accepted as most authentic says that one day the young Clive went up to the top of the tower or steeple of the church at Market Drayton in Shropshire and sat on the spout with the form of a dragon's head. Old inhabitants of the town also said that Clive was in the habit of collecting money and trifling articles from the shopkeepers for himself and his band of followers for refraining from breaking their window-panes and playing other mischievous tricks. The third story is that once Clive and his followers wanted to punish a shopkeeper and so they blocked a gutter to flood his shop. But when the dam broke, Clive threw himself in the gap and remained there until the breach was repaired.

There is always an element of the miraculous, of the sub-rational or supra-rational, in the sudden rise to spectacular greatness of men who have no hereditary claims to it; and in their case, as in the case of prophets, signs are always looked for.

The eighteenth century looked for the signs even more insistently because it was given to romanticizing the drab and undistinguished life as the virtuous life – as keeping the noiseless tenor of living, along the cool sequestered vale of life. So when Clive rose to greatness, signs were looked for and found in his early life. If, however, the incidents recalled could have any real significance for what he afterwards became, there must have been, at the end of the eighteenth century, in every English churchyard many Clives guiltless of forging the signature of Admiral Watson.

Stories of the same type were related about his obscure life as a writer and a volunteer soldier at Madras. For this period too there are three stories. The first is that he behaved insolently towards a superior and was made to apologize, and when the superior, in order to let bygones be bygones, invited him to dinner he replied: 'No, Sir, the Governor did not command me to *dine* with you.'

The second story is about a duel with a fellow-officer to whom he had lost some money and whom he suspected of cheating at cards. Clive went up to him and accused him, upon which there was a duel. Clive missed, and his antagonist, holding the pistol against his head, desired him to ask for his life. This Clive did, but when he was also asked to withdraw his accusation and was told that he would be shot if he did not, he replied defiantly: 'Fire, and be damned!' The man was so astonished that he threw away the pistol, saying that Clive was mad. Afterwards Clive said that as the man had spared his life he would never do him any injury.

The third story is about his brawls with a fellow-officer who had spread reports that he had shown cowardice during the siege of Pondichery. Clive challenged him, and in the altercation that followed was struck by the officer. A fight was prevented, but a court of inquiry was held and a public apology was extorted from the man. But as the court had taken no notice of the blow, Clive demanded satisfaction, and when that was refused he waved his cane over the officer and told him that he was too contemptible a coward to be beaten.

As a result of all these stories an idea was formed that in his early life Clive was a quarrelsome and intractable young man, if not a bully, and Mill in his history, published in 1817, wrote that at Madras 'his turbulence, though he was not ill-natured, engaged him in quarrels with his equals'.

All these stories come from an early essay on Clive published in the second edition of the *Biographia Britannica* (1783) on the authority of a man named Burman. There is, however, no mention of the incidents at Madras in the records of the Governor and his council, and it was impossible that if these had taken place they would have been ignored. The last incident has been found to be a garbled version of a quarrel between Clive and a chaplain in which the chaplain was condemned and dismissed and Clive exonerated. The facts of this authentic quarrel were discovered by Sir George Forrest in the Madras records. They will be described later.

There was an even more romantic story that, either in a fit of despair or from low spirits, he once tried to kill himself. A companion coming into his room was asked to take up a pistol from the table and fire it out of the window. When this was done, Clive sprang up and cried out: 'Well, I am reserved for something! That pistol, I have twice snapped at my own head.'

In actual fact, apart from these apocryphal stories, Clive's early life was very humdrum and uneventful. Here it is only necessary to set down the bare facts, which are wholly colourless. However, this makes his later career more and not less remarkable. What sets off the process by which a man suddenly finds himself acknowledged by his fellow men as great is better left as a mystery, both objective and subjective, for certain types of historical figures.

Robert Clive was born on September 29 1725 in the hamlet of

Moreton Say near Market Drayton in Shropshire, and was baptized on October 2 in the parish church. His family was of ancient lineage, but his father, Richard Clive, had only about £500 a year and, finding it inadequate, had taken up the profession of law. Clive's mother was from Manchester, and he always said that he owed more to his mother than to any school.

As a child he was delicate, and before he was three years old was sent away to live with his aunt and uncle (mother's sister and her husband) at Manchester. There he fell seriously ill of fever and caused great anxiety to his relatives. He remained with them for some years, and when he was seven years old, his uncle wrote about his fierce temper and readiness to fight:

> I hope I have made a little further conquest over Bob, and that he regards me in some degree as well as his aunt Bay. He has just had a fine new suit of clothes, and promises by this reformation to deserve them. I am satisfied that his fighting (to which he is out of measure addicted) gives his temper a fierceness and imperiousness that he flies out upon every trifling occasion. For this reason I do what I can to suppress the heroic that I may help forward the more valuable qualities of meekness, benevolence and patience. I assure you, Sir, it is a matter of concern to us, as it is of importance to himself that he may be a good and virtuous man to which no care of ours shall be wanting.

This is the only authenticated description of his character in childhood, and the natural traits asserted themselves in his manhood. But for the intervening years there is no other information about how he behaved or was formed. There is only a report that the owner of a private school to which he was sent in childhood said about him that if 'that lad should live to be a man and an opportunity be given for the exertion of his talents, few names will be greater than his'. This prediction also comes from the article in the *Biographia Britannica,* the source of all the legendary tales of his young days.

From this private school, he was transferred to a grammar school at Market Drayton. From this school he was sent at the age of twelve to Merchant Taylors' in London. After two years he was again transferred to a private school, at Hemel Hempstead in Hertfordshire. There is no record of what he learned or showed at these schools.

When he was seventeen the decision was taken to send him to India as a writer in the service of the East India Company. At that time many members of the trading class and also of the poor middle class were coming back, having made large amounts of money after only a few years' stay in India, and this must have influenced Clive's father. He was accepted by the Court of Directors at a meeting held on December 15 1742, and a few days later a security of £500 for him was approved of.

He sailed for India on March 10 1743. The ship met with bad weather, and had to sail across the Atlantic to Brazil. There it remained for nine months to carry out repairs. It sailed again on February 11 1744 and, passing the Cape of Good Hope, anchored in Madras Roads on June 1 1744.

This is all that is known about Clive's life till he was nineteen. There is no information about what he had learned or how he had developed. But his personality can best be seen from a long letter written to his father soon after his arrival at Madras, and also from three other letters – one to his father, one to his uncle and the third to a cousin. The letters to his father show him as a typical product of the impoverished English middle class, with all their obsessions about money and economy. This pettiness is redeemed only by the recognition of filial duty and loyalty to family and clan. It would seem that the upbringing he had as a boy had quite effectually driven out the fighting spirit in him and fostered as much meekness and virtue as his uncle wished to find in him. His elaborate and abject apologies are distressing to read, but they show what India made of the typical English boy of his class.

In his first letter to his father, written on September 10 1744, he wrote:

> I shall now make it my Duty to inform you in what Manner I have acted with respect to my Expenses, which indeed are very considerable, tho I used all the Prudence and Frugality I was then master off.

(In these extracts, Clive's own orthography and syntax are being reproduced.) He admitted that after first setting out from England he was a little careless and lost several things. But, he explained, he was not the only person to do so in the fright and confusion of being driven ashore on the coast of Brazil. He was particularly sorry to have lost the silver buckles of his shoes, which were a present from a family friend, and he sensed that his father would conjecture that he was very negligent. But this was due to an accident. He had fallen overboard in heavy seas from the poop, and could save himself only because the captain threw him a bucket with a rope to which he clung. But he lost his shoes with their buckles, his hat and his ring. And he appealed to his father to 'be so candid as to excuse me and impute my losses to want of Experience rather than any careless Extravagant habit in my Nature'. Then followed a more solemn assurance: 'Since I can assure you,' he wrote, 'I have so much instructed myself in the Way of the World, as easily to foresee the bad Consequences that must attend such misdemeanours, and am willing to undergo Your Displeasure if ever I am guilty of the like folly.'

He then informed his father that during his forced stay in Brazil he had been compelled to buy articles to the value of £10, and borrow 40 shillings in money from the captain; and on arriving at Madras and finding that the man from whom he was to have received some money had gone back to England, he also took that sum of money from the captain.

His clothes had become so worn that he would have gone naked if some of the gentlemen on board had not given him shirts and stockings. So at Madras he bought some clothes, but he was afraid that his father would be surprised by the quantity of linen mentioned in the bill. This expenditure, he explained, was due to a number of causes: firstly '. . . in this place there are none but what put clean Linnen as every Day, and indeed the greatest Part shift twice, upon Account of the intollerable Heat, which sweats them to that Degree, that they are just as if they had been dipt in a River, with all their Cloaths on, and upon that Account they generally wear such things as can be wash'd again;' secondly 'besides the Washmen live three or four Miles in the Country, and bring the Linnen but once a Month'; thirdly 'they make no use of Soap here, but beat the Shirts till they are clean against a stone, so that in eight or ten times washing they are all in rags'.

After this elaborate apology about his linen, he apologized as well for the wine, and wrote: 'I hope you'll be so kind as not to take Exception at the Wine, as there are no other Sort of Drinkables here but that, and Punch, as I always shall drink it with Water, intend to make it serve me a whole year.'

He was ready, he assured his father, to buy things on disadvantageous terms,

> . . . rather than any Way detriment myself, by running in Dept [debt], which wou'd not only be a means of incurring the Company's Displeasure, but very likely of being turn'd Out of their service, there being many Instances of the like Nature which have happen'd to several Gentlemen in this Place by such imprudent Practizes.

He added, however, that most of the Company's servants 'seem to be a set of very prudent and Industrious people'.

He asked his father for some money which he could invest.

> If you shou'd think it Advisable to advance me some Money, I cou'd not only make considerable Advantages by it, by saving wherewithall out of Interest to defray Expences in Cloathing and other Necessarys, but cou'd also increase the Principal very considerably, I can Assure you we have equaly the same Priviledges when Writers, as Factors, and I dont doubt you'll take it into your Consideration, Money is let out here at Respondentia from 16 to 32 p Cent, besides many other Advantages by Private Trade Act and if you should think proper to favour my request. . . . I shall think myself infinitely in Duty bound to you, and shall thankfully acknowledge the Favour.

But he thought Bengal would be a better place to make money:

> When I was in England I remember you entertain'd Hopes, of removing me to Bengal, which would be much more Advantageous to me, as it wou'd not only reduce my Expences, as all Manner of Provisions are much cheaper, but also allows greater Liberty of Merchandizing, & trade is in a much more flourishing Condition than at Fort St George.

He therefore requested his father to 'make all the Interest you can to remove me'. He repeated this wish in a later letter.

Altogether, he declared, 'I shall let no Opportunity slip of improving myself in everything where I can have the least view of profit.' He also asked his father to use influence to have him promoted to the position of factor, but was somewhat sceptical. 'The World', he wrote, 'seems to be vastly debas'd of late, and Interest carries it entirely before Merit, especially in this Service, tho I shou'd think myself very undeserving of any Favour, were I only to build my Foundation on the Strength of the Former.'

He showed a strong sense of his obligation to his father and wrote:

> I think myself not only very happy, but infinitely oblig'd to you for my Education, and as it had render'd me in a fair Way of improving my Talent, I flatter myself with ye Hopes of enlarging tenfold. . . . I shall always make it my Duty to behave worthy & deserving of your Confidence, and Esteem, and am willing to give up all Pretensions to your Favour in case I don't behave with that Sobriety and Diligence which is expected.

He was also, within three months of his arrival at Madras, showing his loyalty to family and clan. He said that his stay at Madras was pleasant and satisfactory, 'as it is back'd with the Hopes, (if it please God to preserve my Life) of being able to provide for myself, & also of being of service to my Relations, and shou'd at this time as much as lies in my Power, be glad of serving You in this Part of the World'. In a more matter of fact way he wrote: 'If my Mother, sisters, or any of the Family, shou'd want any Silks, Stuffs, Tea, Callicoes, or any other Productions which the Country Affords, upon Notice given I will be sure to provide and send them by the first Opportunity.' He even suggested that his cousin Bobby might come over as a chaplain, and informed his father that the Company, which kept two, paid them £100 a year, besides 12 pagodas, or about £57 12s., more as a monthly allowance, and also allowed other perquisites.

As to other matters in this letter, there is only one sentence about his wish to read in order to pass the time. He wrote:

> As there is a great Part of the Year in which we have no Employment, and having no manner of Acquaintance, but with my Brother Writers, I find it a great disadvantage to me, however shall endeavour to employ my Time in reading, and all other Diversions, which may be of Service to me, & if you'll indulge me so far as to send some Books for that Purpose, I shall be very much oblig'd to you, a little News wou'd be also very agreeable to me.

With only petty money-making and economies to sustain him, he was naturally homesick and depressed. At the beginning of December, that is six months after his arrival in India, he wrote to his uncle who had been so kind to him in childhood:

> I must confess at Intervals when I think of my dear Native England, it affects me in a very particular manner, however, knowing it to be for my own Welfare, rest content and patient, wishing the views for which my Father sent me here, may in all Respects be fully accomplished. If I should be so far blest as to revisit again my own country, but more especially Manchester (the centre of all my wishes), all that I could hope or desire for would be presented before me in one view.

This homesickness made him wait for letters from home with impatience, and he felt heartbroken when he did not get any. In a letter to his cousin written two months later, he gave expression to his feeling that the worldly advantages which he thought of gaining by working in India were no compensation for the disadvantages which were present and very real. 'The Intemperence of the Climate together with the excessive heat of the Sun', he wrote, 'are very obnoxious to our Health, and I really think that the Advantages which accrue to us here are greatly overballanced by the Sacrifices we make of our Constitutions.' Then he declared emotionally:

> I have not been unacquainted with the Fickleness of Fortune, and may safely say I have not enjoyed one happy day since I left my Native Country; I am not acquainted with any one Family in the Place, and have not Assurance enough to introduce myself without being asked.

He felt that he could fall back only on one resource.

> If the state I am now in will admit of any Happiness it must be when I am writing to my Friends. Letters were surely first invented for the Comfort of such solitary wretches as myself. Having lost the substantial pleasure of seeing them I shall in some measure compensate this Loss by the satisfaction I shall find in their Writings; when you write me, I beg it may be carelessly and without study, for I had much rather read the Dictates of the Heart that those of the Understanding.

These confessions followed a moralizing introduction, in which he observed:

> The Bond of Friendship, especially when united by Ties of Blood aught not to be dissolved on any consideration whatever, and I believe you'll agree with me, that the only effectual Means to preserve it entire, must be by Letters, since the vast Ocean which divides us so far asunder won't admit of it by Word of Mouth, and which I heartily wish may turn out to the mutual Satisfaction of both of us. If there is any such thing which may properly be called Happiness here below, I am persuaded it is in the Union of two Friends who each love each other without the least Guile or Deceit, who are united by a real Inclination, and Satisfied with each others merits. Their Hearts are full, and leave no Vacancy for any other Passion.

Clive's unhappiness at being separated from his family became so acute that it broke out even in a letter written to his father a year and a half after his arrival. He wrote to him on January 31 1746:

> Hon^d Sir, — When I wrote my Last to You I was impatiently waiting for the long expected Ships from Europe, and on the 11th December

arrived here under convoy of two Men of War, five of the Company's Ships, viz., The Scarborough, Royal George, Lincoln, Kent and Admiral Vernon. I had for a long time Kept up hope with the pleasing Pleasure of what was to come, and I do declare never in my Life, did I enjoy such real Happiness, as upon Sight of the five above-mentioned Ships, not all the Riches of the Indies, could have satisfied my desires more fully than News from my Native Country, but it seems Fortune had elevated me to this high Summit of expectation, that I might in a greater degree experience so heavy a disappointment, in short I was the only sorrowful Person in Madras but as I cannot think You have forgot me, so shall I with Patience wait Arrival of the London and Princess Mary, by one or both of whom, I don't in the least doubt of being honoured with your Favour.

Yet this young man was to develop into the man who was denounced at the end of his life as a monster of high-handedness, greed and perfidy. That, simply, is the measure of the transition he was to make in India. Looking back from his final image in the eyes of his countrymen, one would see him in his first years in India not even as the chrysalis of that image, but as the caterpillar. But it was a very eighteenth-century caterpillar. If in his first letter to his father he showed himself as a typical son of the English bourgeois of the age, in his letters to his uncle and cousin he showed equally that he had in him the spirit of his age.

But the spirit of didacticism, which was given so typical an expression by Gray, was as foreign to India as was the kind of monetary ambition he had brought over from England. Both in his moral and worldly nature he became transformed, so that his exotic achievements, combined with his hypochondriac temperament, made him a Chatterton in the grand manner in his last days.

The process of Clive's transformation began with an incursion into military life after the capture of Madras by the French in September 1746, that is two years after his arrival in India. He was taken prisoner with the rest of the English, but as the treaty by which they could be ransomed was declared null and void, many of them refused to give parole, and Clive himself described what he did to Orme in a later communication: 'I made my escape, the beginning of October, disguised in the habit of a Dubosh [*dobhashi* – an interpreter; literally, 'speaker of two languages'] and black'd and arriv'd at St David the same month.'

He went there with two companions, one of whom was his future brother-in-law. Others had also gone there, and they were all without employment and money. As Clive described in a letter to the Court of Directors many years later (March 8 1755), they were 'for some time under the disagreeable circumstances of being unprovided for, till at last the Gentlemen of St David Offer'd a monthly writership to all those in our condition'. This offer was accepted by all the refugees except the three of them, who were 'of opinion that acting in a military sphere (tho' then at a very low ebb) was the most honourable of the two and most conducive to the Company's interest'.

After this Clive took part in the fighting to defend Fort St David and Cuddalore against repeated French attacks. There were in all five such attacks: the first on December 18 1746, closely followed by another on the thirty-first; the third was launched on March 11–12 1747; the fourth came later, on January 15–17 1748, and the fifth on June 27–29 1748. It has already been stated that the French failed to take St David. The attacks were foiled in different ways: the first by the intervention of the Nawab of the Carnatic under his sons; the second by a storm; the third and fourth by the arrival of an English naval squadron under Admiral Griffin; and the last by the small garrison of St David. The garrison also joined in the previous fighting. The threat to St David was definitely removed by the arrival there of Admiral Boscawen on August 4 1748, and the concentration of the largest British Naval force ever assembled on the Indian coast.

It was after the repulse of the third attack that Clive received his first commission as an ensign in the forces of the Company. It was granted by John Hind, the Deputy-Governor of St George, on March 16 1747, and in their despatch dated May 2 to the Court of Directors at home the Governor in Council informed them that 'Mr Robert Clive, Writer in the Service, being of a martial disposition and having acted as a volunteer in our late engagements we have granted him an Ensign's Commission upon his application for the same'. So Clive formally entered the military profession, though not as yet finally, when he was six months short of being twenty-two.

In reply to the letter from St David, the Court of Directors wrote on December 4 1747: 'Be sure to encourage Ensign Clive in his martial pursuits, according to his merit: any improvement he shall make therein shall be duly regarded by us.' There is, however, no contemporary record of what Clive did as a young officer defending St David. Many years later he himself described the actions in which he took part to Orme, but naturally he did not mention his share in them. Orme does not mention him either in his account of these attacks. But Clive's aptitude must have been noticed for him to be given his commission in March 1747, and in any case he had his experience of war, though it was on a small scale.

Clive took part in the siege of Pondichery which lasted from September 6 to October 17 1748. It was unsuccessful, but he distinguished himself during the operation. He described the siege to Orme, and the incidents in which he distinguished himself, particularly in rallying his men and foiling a French attack. After saying that, in the face of the advance of a French grenadier company before which the other troops had fled and only he and about 30 of the independent soldiers were left in the front trench, he added that they were 'received with such a heavy fire from Ensign Clive's platoon that they immediately went to the right about. In this affair Captain Le Roche and 27 French were killed upon the spot, of Ensign Clive's platoon, eight men were shot through the heart'.

But Orme, who must have had other first-hand information, wrote in his history:

> There now remained one platoon, of which two or three had been killed, and the rest were on the point of running away; when their officer, ensign Clive, reproached them sternly for their pusillanimity, and represented the honour they would gain by defending the trench, after it had been so shamefully abandoned by the rest of the guard. All the company's troops had an affection for this young man, from observing the alacrity and presence of mind which always accompanied him in danger; his platoon, animated by his exhortation, fired again with new courage and great vivacity upon the enemy, who now, perceiving the small number to which the defenders of the trench were reduced, resolved to storm it. They quitted the huts, and formed in front of them, and were scarcely got into order, when they received the whole fire of the English platoon, which was so well directed that it struck down twenty men, and the rest were in the instant so terrified by the shock of this extraordinary execution, that they ran back in disorder to the huts, which sheltered them until they were out of reach of the fire, and continued their retreat to the town in great confusion.

Clive was to emerge as a bold military leader in the fighting of the next four years, in the new phase of the Anglo-French conflict which began after the treaty of Aix-la-Chapelle. But already in the actions in which he had taken part he had shown that, although he was only a civilian volunteer making his début as a subaltern, he had the making of a good regimental officer in him. Even before he displayed his military capacity more fully it was noticed by Stringer Lawrence, a professional soldier, who had arrived in India in January 1748 and taken over the command of the troops at Fort St David.

Chapter Three

Young Military Leader

Dupleix's War
In the next four years Clive was to make a name for himself in India and England as an able and dashing military commander. The operations that gave him this position were part of a very strange war in the Carnatic. While it went on there, England and France were at peace. The two governments did not want the war, nor did the French company. It was not sought even by the English in Madras. Yet it was momentous, for it marked a serious departure from the previous policy of both the companies not to get involved in the political affairs of India and the quarrels of the native princes. This departure opened the drama that led finally to the establishment of British power in India.

The conflict, which was to have such far-reaching consequences, was brought to a head by a single man, Dupleix, who acted on his own, not only without the authorization of his company, but against its specific instructions. It may therefore be called Dupleix's private war. But even he could not foresee the course it would take, still less that it would lead to his own ruin.

In spite of the state of mind in which he was left by the war of the Austrian succession, Dupleix had no clearly conceived plan for such a war. In fact, he was contemplating to return to France, and have done with India. So on February 28 1749, one day before the discussion about the adventure was held, he wrote to Machault, a French minister: 'I venture to flatter myself that you will do me the favour of getting me retired to my country.' This was only a repetition of a previous request, and by a curious coincidence the very day he wrote the letter the Company in Paris granted him leave to come away after he had settled the affairs of India. His friends prepared to receive him, and Godeheu, who was sent later to replace him, wrote to him offering the hospitality of his house at L'Orient, and looking forward to having 'de bonnes causeries en bonnet de nuit et robe de chambre'. But the Indian maelstrom sucked him in.

The Greeks called such an eventuality *Anagkē*. Dupleix's ruin and the rise of the British Empire in India seem to have been predestined in the bizarre and almost grotesque intermingling of circumstance, necessity, temptation, fear and uncertainty which the political situation in that country presented at that juncture. Neither free will nor reasoning, except what was used *ad hoc* from day to day, had anything to do with the final shape of things that emerged out of this welter. This makes the interminable moral and intellectual argument about the establishment of the British Empire in India not only pointless, but almost flippant.

Dupleix's war was the beginning of the process that brought the Empire into being. It was preceded by an English adventure of the same kind but of smaller magnitude, which showed that without imitating each other both the companies were ready to fish in troubled waters in search of gain. But the English adventure was called off when its losses seemed to outweigh its profits. It was more tradesmanlike than warlike.

The English and the French interventions were in quarrels between Indian princes with which they as traders had no concern. Orme began his account of these events with the following words:

> The sword was sheathed; and it depended on the agents of the two Companies to re-assume in tranquillity their mercantile occupations: but the war had brought to Pondichery and Fort St David a number of troops greatly superior to any which either of the two nations had hitherto assembled in India; and as if it was impossible that a military force, which feels itself capable of enterprizes, should refrain from attempting them, the two settlements, no longer authorized to fight against each other, took the resolution of employing their arms in the contests of the princes of the country: the English with great indiscretion, the French with the utmost ambition.

The English intervention was on behalf of a native prince who had been driven out of his kingdom about ten years before and wanted to regain it. He was Shahaji, former Raja of Tanjore, a Maratha principality ruled by a dynasty related to that of the founder of the Maratha power, Sivaji. Towards the end of 1748 he sent his *vakil*, or agent, to seek the help of the English against the ruling prince who was his illegitimate brother, Pratap Singh. Charles Floyer, Governor of St David at the time, and some of his councillors as well as Admiral (also General) Boscawen considered the matter on December 8 1748, and Floyer wrote to Shahaji that they would be glad to help him, but that they also wanted to have a discussion with him personally. So he requested Shahaji to come to St David, where, Floyer added, he could stay in security and secrecy and as long as he liked. The pretender came, and was presented with the English terms, which were that the Fort of Devikottai, with enough land around it to yield a revenue of about ten to twelve thousand pagodas, would be ceded to the Company, and the expenses of the expedition should also be reimbursed. To these Shahaji formally agreed on March 17 1749. The expedition started on March 27.

The project was discussed thoroughly by one member of the Council, Prince and Admiral Boscawen. Lawrence, who was consulted afterwards, approved of it.

It was only on April 10 that the full Council was informed about it, and its sanction was required. Seven members, including the Governor, were present. The President explained that, after a consideration of all the circumstances, it had appeared to Boscawen, himself and Prince that 'great advantages might be made on behalf of the Hon'ble Company, by granting to him [Shahaji] the assistance he desired, which the easier might be done at this time, having so large a body of His Majesty's forces now in garrison, and the risk but small in comparison to the benefits that might be gained in the occasion'.

In spite of this two members wholly disapproved of the project and recorded their dissent in the proceedings of the Council; two agreed only because the expedition had already set out and could not be recalled. It would appear that Boscawen's was the decisive voice behind the expedition.

Both the Governor and the Admiral thought it necessary to inform the Nawab of the Carnatic, Anwar-ud-din Khan, who was the suzerain of the Raja of Tanjore. So Governor Floyer wrote to him, on the day that the Council considered the project, that he was going to assist the pretender in recovering his kingdom, saying he hoped the Nawab would be favourable to Shahaji.

The expedition was sent out both by land and sea. But a terrible storm in the night of April 13 wrecked three ships with the loss of almost all hands; among these was the Admiral's flagship *Namur*, a Seventy and the finest ship of her class in the

Royal Navy. The number of men lost was over 1,200. In addition to this disaster the land expedition also failed to take Devikottai and returned to St David. As such a failure was very damaging to the standing of the Company a second expedition was despatched under Lawrence. It took Devikottai on June 12. Even before that the general of the Tanjore forces had wanted to know on what terms a peace could be concluded. On their part, the British commanders also discovered that Shahaji had no popular support behind him. So the two sides met after the surrender of Devikottai. The British offered the same terms as they had to Shahaji, and in addition demanded a pension for him. The Tanjore general rejected the terms. His offer was cession of Devikottai with land to yield about 9,000 pagodas, and one lakh of rupees towards the expenses of the expedition. The Council considered this, and as it was regarded by all to be the best that could be secured it was accepted. The formal peace was concluded at the end of June 1749.

So ended the English company's sole intervention on their own initiative in the internal politics of India. It did not bring the English any military glory, but neither was it a failure. The English gained from it all that they had wanted for themselves, and, what was more, they kept these gains. The Raja of Tanjore, too, remained on the British side during the Anglo-French conflict that followed.

In the meanwhile Dupleix had decided upon and planned his own venture, which was more ambitious and in which the stakes, though indefinite and even unperceived at the beginning, grew larger and larger by stages. Even at its inception it was different from the English expeditions to Tanjore, for its aim was to install a nawab in the Carnatic who would favour the French. Chronologically, Dupleix's plan was finally decided upon before the English project, though it was not acted upon till the English expedition was over.

The pretender whom Dupleix decided to support was Chanda Sahib, who had been taken away by the Marathas as a prisoner to Satara in 1741, and who was the only surviving representative of the old dynasty of Dost Ali. His history from 1741 to 1748, when he appeared on the border of the Carnatic, is very obscure. His family was, however, living under French protection in Pondichery, and they learned about his freedom in July 1748. In February 1749, Chanda Sahib approached Dupleix through his son Raza Sahib to find out if he could have some troops of the

French company in order to overthrow Anwar-ud-din Khan. He offered to pay all the expenses.

It was a risky intervention, for Anwar-ud-din Khan had a large army, and he was also supported by the new viceroy or *subadar* of the Deccan, Nasir Jang, who had succeeded his father Nizam-ul-Mulk in May 1748. Besides, it was not unlikely that the English, who had been helped by the Nawab in the previous war, would come to his help. Nevertheless, Dupleix fell in with the proposal.

His main incentive was money, which would relieve him of the heavy expenses of maintaining the large force which he had still under arms. But Chanda Sahib himself had no money, and in the agreement concluded with him it was stipulated that for the present the French company would pay for the troops, and the cost would be reimbursed by Chanda Sahib after he had gained his kingdom. So even as a mercenary venture the project was speculation of a dubious sort, and even before Chanda Sahib began his march the amount due to the French had mounted to Rs97,651. Without some political *arrière-pensée* such a gamble could not have been undertaken. Dupleix had a motive.

He was distrustful of Anwar-ud-din Khan, and felt a grievance against him for what he had done against the French during the previous war. On the other hand, the previous dynasty had always been friendly to the French. As yet Dupleix had not received news of the final conclusion of the peace. Therefore he wanted to keep his troops without expense for the Company and himself, as well as to secure a nawab of the Carnatic on his side, in case hostilities broke out again.

Even so Dupleix would not perhaps have taken the risk if Chanda Sahib had not secured the collaboration of a more powerful prince who had higher pretensions of his own. This was Hidayet Mohi-ud-din Khan, a grandson of Nizam-il-Mulk by his favourite daughter, and better known under his title Muzafar Jang. Though a subordinate nawab, he claimed that his grandfather had designated him as successor to the subadarship of the whole of Deccan. He made common cause with Chanda Sahib, and they thought if they could gain the Carnatic their power and prestige would become so great that they might hope to be successful in the bigger task. So they prepared to march against Anwar-ud-din Khan towards the beginning of July 1749.

Dupleix had stipulated that the whole project should be kept secret until Chanda Sahib was ready to march. Now that he was, the sanction of the Conseil Supérieur at Pondichery had to be obtained. It met on July 13 1749, and was informed about the negotiations and the terms of the agreement with Chanda Sahib, and more especially about the reimbursement of the expenses. It agreed, finding that the project was to cost nothing and yet might be advantageous. So the Council resolved among other things: 'In order to show our gratitude to Chanda Sahib for it, it was agreed that M. le Gouverneur would continue to favour him with everything that depends on us, and he would consider proper, until Chanda Sahib is installed and becomes the indisturbed master of his government.'

The war that followed, and in which the English and the French fought each other indirectly as the auxiliaries of the native princes, lasted nearly six years until the fighting ceased with an agreement between the two companies at the end of 1754. Before that, however, Dupleix was recalled, and he left India on October 15 1754.

This indirect war was described in all its involved details by Orme in his Thucydidean manner, and the style of narration has been followed by modern historians, though with less elaboration. But all the operations in it were on so small a scale, relatively speaking – so scattered, so confused, so attended with unexpected ups and downs for all parties – and in the upshot so indecisive, that a plain chronological narrative cannot give a correct idea of its nature and results.

This method has been responsible, too, for a distortion of perspective by creating an impression that in this war the events followed each other closely and coherently, and moved to a climax as in a well-knit play or novel. Actually, the pace of the war was slow and its moves uncertain. The actions in it were divided by long periods of inaction and hesitancy, and the doldrums were as characteristics as the trade winds.

For all that, it has been regarded as the first act of the great drama – the founding of the British Empire in India – which itself shows how unedifying were its beginnings. There is a French saying: '*Il faut fumer les meilleurs champs*', which is capped by a Bengali one: 'Lotus blooms on the dung-heap'. The British Empire in India was to rise out of a very evil-smelling process of decomposition, and the compost for its later rank growth was not rotten enough to lose its stench even when

Warren Hastings took over the task of extending it.

Actually, it was the first act in a very restricted sense. It only made a complete break with the previous policy of the two Companies that they should not become involved in the affairs of the Indian princes, but also made the involvement irrevocable. It bequeathed to the companies ill-defined relations with two Indian princes, which made their principalities disguised protectorates, and this in itself left the situation incubating. Furthermore, it created a disposition to intervene elsewhere if an analogous situation called for it.

Also, it was not a development of Dupleix's local war which led to a renewal of the hostilities between the English and the French nations, and finally to the destruction of all French political power in the country: that result was the outcome of a new global war between England and France, the origins of which had nothing to do with India. That would have happened without Dupleix's war.

Therefore it would be enough to summarize its course, clearly demarcating its phases and taking note of the results achieved in each, only describing in greater detail Clive's participation in it, as well as considering those aspects of it that had a bearing on the establishment of British political power in India. To begin, then, with a summary of the course of the war.

The first phase lasted from July to October 1749. On July 28 the concentration of the troops of Chanda Sahib, Muzafar Jang and the French company was completed, and they marched against the camp of Anwar-ud-din Khan at Ambur. On August 1 the French contingent attacked and after heavy fighting killed Anwar-ud-din, whose army disintegrated. One of his sons was taken prisoner, but the other, Muhammad Ali, fled to Trichinopoly. Chanda Sahib proclaimed himself nawab of the Carnatic and occupied Arcot, the capital. At the end of September both he and Muzafar Jang went to Pondichery, where they were received with great pomp by Dupleix. They discussed future plans. Dupleix impressed on Chanda Sahib the need for urgency in driving out Muhammad Ali from Trichinopoly, and promised aid to Muzafar Jang to become the Subadar of the Deccan.

The second phase began in November 1749 and lasted until March 1750. After Boscawen had sailed from Madras and the possibility of a British intervention (in force) in support of Muhammad Ali had been removed, Chanda Sahib set out with a

French contingent for Trichinopoly. But he diverted the expedition to Tanjore, being in need of money and hoping to extort it from the Raja. Arriving before Tanjore on December 7, he laid siege to the fort. The French commander wanted to storm it, but Chanda Sahib would not allow this, for he feared that the troops might plunder the city and seize the treasures. The Raja on his part resisted as well as temporized, offering to submit. Months passed, and in March 1750 Nasir Jang appeared in the Carnatic. In panic Chanda Sahib's forces returned to Pondichery.

The third phase continued through 1750. Nasir Jang defeated his nephew Muzafar Jang, and took him prisoner. Then he drove the French forces to Pondichery. There were some negotiations between him and the French, but in July the latter took the offensive and in two battles at Trivady (July 31 and September 1) inflicted a check on Nasir Jang. All this was, however, indecisive. On December 16 Nasir Jang was treacherously killed by two Pathan chiefs of his own army. Muzafar Jang was liberated and proclaimed Subadar of the Deccan. Chanda Sahib was confirmed as the Nawab of the Carnatic, and Dupleix himself was made the Subadar's deputy or *naib* with powers to administer the territories south of the river Kistna.

This was the high point in the success of Dupleix. In January 1751 he sent Bussy with a contingent of troops to instal Muzafar Jang in his capital at Hyderabad. On the way Muzafar was killed by the same Pathan chiefs who had murdered Nasir Jang. But the French immediately proclaimed a brother of Nasir Jang, Salabat Jang, subadar and took him under their protection. From this time until 1758, Bussy controlled both Salabat Jang and the government of the Deccan. The English did not dispute this.

In May 1751 the fourth phase began, ending in June 1752. Chanda Sahib, helped by the French, now turned to Muhammad Ali in Trichinopoly. A large force besieged the fort, and though Muhammad Ali began to receive help from the English he was in a desperate position. But in order to relieve the pressure on him a diversion was made in the direction of Arcot. A small force under Clive took the city and fort. A large army was sent from Trichinopoly to retake them. But Clive defended the fort successfully, and forced the besiegers to retreat. This was the turning point of the war in the Carnatic. The English next turned to relieve Trichinopoly, which was invested by a French force under Law. After some reverses for the French

forces, Law surrendered to Lawrence on June 12 1752 (n.s.).*
Chanda Sahib was captured and beheaded. The news of this
disaster reached France in 1753. The French Government and
the Company decided at once to recall Dupleix, and they sent
Godeheu with instructions to replace him and conclude peace.
Godeheu arrived at Pondichery on August 2 1754.

The fifth phase, the longest of the war, was the least decisive;
it lasted from July 1752 to July 1754. Far from being discouraged by the capitulation of Law, Dupleix set himself energetically to recover power in the Carnatic. A number of engagements took place, and in them both sides had victories as well as reverses.

The authorities at home did not want this unofficial war, and
on the French side the disapproval was strong. Under pressure
from Paris, Dupleix met the English at a conference at Sadras,
but nothing came of it. After four months of discussions – which
for wrangling and chicanery can be looked upon as the prototype of the international dialogues of our times – it was called
off on February 6 1754. Trichinopoly was again besieged, and
indecisive clashes accompanied by *pourparlers* went on until
the arrival of Godeheu as the commissary of the French king on
August 2 1754.

August to December 1754 saw the sixth phase. Godeheu's
instructions were drastic. He was not only to take over from
Dupleix, but even to arrest him if he refused to obey the order of
recall. However, Godeheu did not wish to humiliate him, and
gave him the choice of announcing his own retirement. Dupleix agreed, and sailed away on October 15. Before that the
hostilities had come to an end with an armistice which took
effect from October 11. On December 31 a provisional treaty
was concluded between the two companies, by which the parties agreed to have parity in their advantages, and also to give up
all interference in the quarrels of the Indian princes. But no
cession, retrocession or evacuation was to take place and everything was to remain 'on the footing of *uti possidetis*' until the
treaty was confirmed from Europe. Therefore, in actual fact the
existing position was frozen, both the sides remaining dominant where they were already so. And before any confirmation
came the Seven Years' War broke out.

The purely military character of Dupleix's war is not of much
importance, but the diplomatic wrangling that accompanied it

*New style.

is significant, for it exhibited the emotional atmosphere of the Anglo-French rivalry in India, which Clive also absorbed. The war of words was carried on in a continuous and vigorous correspondence between Dupleix and the English governors of Madras, specially Saunders, and exhibited all the features of the so-called diplomatic exchanges of our times, namely, profession of the highest principles by each side, mutual accusation of cruelty and bad faith, specious apologia, and propaganda addressed to the world.

To begin with, each side accused the other of disregarding the treaty of Aix-la-Chapelle, the first article of which enjoined 'a Christian and perpetual peace by sea as well as land, and a sincere and constant friendship between the eight Powers above-named'. Quoting it, and accusing the English of utterly disregarding it, Dupleix wrote to Floyer and his Council:

> It would be to no purpose for sovereigns to make treaties like this if the first of their subjects might with impunity infringe them on pretences so frivolous and established with so little solidity as those you have heretofore made use of. Your masters at London and ours at Paris will soon discover the motives that urged you to act. Ah! how should they be kept secret when the whole Indies are acquainted with them. [July 21 1750]

This line of pleading was adopted by the English as well, and its most emphatic reiteration is to be found in a letter written by Saunders to Dupleix on August 22 1752. 'In what light will you appear', he asked, 'before so generous a Prince as His Most Christian Majesty? How can you ever show your face before so honourable a set of merchants as your Company?'

Dupleix's second charge was that the English were betraying fellow Europeans by siding with Asiatics. So, referring to the English active help to Muhammad Ali, he wrote to Floyer on March 14 1750:

> In the differences which the Nations of Europe may have with the people of Asia it has always been customary for other nations never to interfere in such differences or furnish any kind of succour to the enemy of such European Nation who may be engaged in a war with the said Asiatic government. This policy which is strong in itself has ever been strictly observed and the nations of Europe should rather hope for succour from the other European Powers than be apprehensive of furnishing the enemy with any assistance, a thing never practised till now and which may properly be said to be contrary to good policy.

Floyer replied that it was the intention of the English company

> ... to keep up to the good intentions of our separate Princes in maintaining peace [but] we shall never let our politics become so much refined as to let them in the least deviate from the strictest rules of equity. The laws of humanity oblige us to give protection to any people with us, except robbers and murderers for they are enemies to mankind and ought not to be protected. ... The succours we sent for the defence of Nazir Jing and Trichinopoly are in no ways contrary to the treaties of peace, but rather a duty incumbent on us to hasten a peace in the country which will be advantageous to your nation as well as ours. [21 March 1750 (n.s.)]

The desire for peace and the anxiety to restore it, accompanied by accusations about bringing ruin on the region and its people, were proclaimed by both parties with equal emphasis. At first Dupleix had the advantage, because after the death of Anwar-ud-din and the installation of Chanda Sahib he could reproach the English with supporting a pretender, and he did not spare words to bring their iniquity home to the English. On March 14 1750 he wrote to Floyer: 'The continuance of this war will be entirely owing to you as well as the ravages the necessary consequence of it.' Again, referring to their support for Muhammad Ali and their appeal to Nasir Jang to come down to the Carnatic, he wrote on July 21 1750: 'You have without the least resistance joined with an enemy to the name of Christian, with a rebel, to ruin, if it lay in your power, other Christians who are at peace with you.' About Nasir Jang's intervention he was even more severe. 'It is clear as the day', he wrote, 'that the desolation not only of this province, but of more than four hundred leagues of the country is owing only to you.'

Replying to all such complaints on August 7 1750, Stringer Lawrence gave instances of how the English company was suffering from the attitude of Chanda Sahib, and threw out the challenge: 'From all this let the world judge which of us is most zealously disposed for restoring the tranquillity of this country.'

To this Dupleix's reply was prompt and forthright. After declaring that not even a straw had been burnt after the victory of Chanda Sahib, he wrote on August 19:

> It were much to be wished that Nasir Jang's army, attended with the destruction of human kind, had had the same tenderness for the country. The footsteps of his march, are to be seen for more than four hundred leagues; wherever this army has passed it looks as if fire and madness followed it.

The tables were turned on Dupleix by Saunders after the surrender of Law at Trichinopoly and the death of Chanda Sahib. The English could now reproach the French with continuing an unnecessary and unjustifiable war, and Saunders took a high line. After referring to the troublous state of the country he wrote on June 2 1752:

> The source from whence these troubles, is in this country well known. Children lament their parents, parents bemoan the loss of what is most dear to them, all degrees of people, oppressed by every calamity that war can produce, in their last agonies groan out. Dupleix, I leave it to your serious hours of reflection to reconcile these truths. [Then he warns Dupleix that he would expose him and] leave it to the public to judge whether you, Sir, have not produced these terrible scenes. Strange! that one subject shall thus sport with the miseries of the most beautiful of all creation and turn a paradise into a desert!

Dupleix replied to this with an offer of peace on June 13 1752 'in order to put an end to a war which is equally ruinous to both parties'.

To this Saunders replied promptly on June 23 (n.s.): 'Be assured, Sir, I shall with you equally promote peace of the province and endeavour to put an end to this war, from whence the misery of thousands, as 'tis in my power by interesting myself with the Nabob.'

But Dupleix raised a new issue by saying that the soldiers and officers of the French company must be set free at once, otherwise he would not negotiate with Muhammad Ali.

This dispute about prisoners gave rise to another round of recriminations. Referring to the offer of peace in Dupleix's letter of June 13, Saunders wrote on September 2 1752 (n.s.):

> I am convinced you have forgot you ever wrote it. So ill your actions suit your words. Rise Ambition cursed, Avarice insatiable and Habit second nature! If with such qualities a Man there be, let him with pleasure grasp at countries unpossessed, the sport of fortune, view the costly strings of pearls, lacks [= lakhs] the value; purchase assassination; count over riches immense, often possessor's ruin; and endeavour by custom to make himself easy; vain pursuit! How many thousands already perished, how many more in misery – forbid it, time and reflection must convince him of it.

He did not take Dupleix's charges against the troops of the English company seriously and added: 'Certainly Mr Dupleix writes without reflection when he would insinuate that our troops ravage and plunder in towns and villages. Can this be meant for anything more than the Paris Gazette?' He referred to the boastful accounts of the defeat of Nasir Jang published in that newspaper, and observed:

> Ask anyone in this country they will tell you otherwise, even children lisp out Nasir Jang was cruelly assassinated, and to the natives we appeal whether wherever Mahomed Ally's [soldiers] have been, they have not always been loaded with the blessings of the people for humanity.

Dupleix had a particular dislike for Lawrence. He complained to Saunders on May 31 1752:

> His age and title of Commander-in-Chief of the English forces in India cannot engage Mr Lawrence to keep up the decency of his character. What will his superiors think? What will you yourself, Sir? and what end can be answered by the invectives which flow in abundance from him against my nation and me. What have we done to him?

He added that all French officers who had met him were 'stung by the haughtiness and contempt with which he affects to treat them on all occasions'. Then Dupleix commented: 'I see with pain how the poison of revenge spreads; will it be possible to stop it in time!'

Saunders replied: 'You remark that Mr Lawrence is, in conversation, extremely free with your name. I imagine the gentleman thinks he has been ill-treated by you.' This insinuation Dupleix passionately repudiated. He wrote on July 7:

> I am ignorant of the ill-treatment Mr Lawrence thinks he has received and which induces him to speak freely of me. When taken prisoner at the beginning of the siege of this place, I gave him up his arms, watch, ring, etc., in short everything he asked for. It's true I made good their value to the people who took him. During his stay my wife's and my whole attention was employed to give him satisfaction. My kitchen was his, and actually the best dishes were set before him. My purse, which he would not make use of, was offered him.

But Dupleix was not to get the best of this *argumentum ad hominem*. By the English hint he was touched on a specially sensitive spot – his wife's meddling in the war. When Dupleix complained about a conversation between Lawrence and Law, Lawrence replied that Law seemed to have reproduced the conversation in his own way to Dupleix, and had, to suit his purposes, left out certain parts. Lawrence reproduced these words of Law, who, according to him, said: 'Be assured, Sir, Mr Dupleix is a good man, a generous man, and it is not to him we owe our misfortunes, but to his wife whose violent spirit leads him to do things against nature and will always involve him in endless difficulties.'

Two years later, receiving a complaint from Madame Dupleix herself about discourtesy shown to her, Saunders wrote back (April 6 1754) that he wished Dupleix had written the letter and she had been 'plus gracieusement occupée'. Then he added (I quote his words in French to bring out the irony in its full force):

> Je suis toujours religieusement attaché au sentiment qui me fait croire que les plus fortes occupations des dame ne devraient tendre qu'à ajouter aux plaisirs de cette douce tranquillité pour laquelle elles sont faites et que c'est aux hommes qu'il faut laisser la fatigue des affairs et les travaux. Daignez, Madame, me permettre de discuter l'affaire en question avec M. le Marquis Dupleix.*

Clearly, Saunders wrote to Mme Dupleix in a style different from that which he adopted towards Dupleix, but in the war of words this must have wounded Dupleix more than his forthright anglicisms. And the worst of it was that when Godeheu arrived at Pondichery he also inclined to the view that Madame Dupleix might have been more 'graciously occupied'.

Clive as Military Leader
When Clive reverted to civilian life at the end of 1748 there was a relapse into the triviality of his previous life. He even became involved in a brawl with a clergyman in the service of the company, named Fordyce. Hearing that this man had lodged a complaint of assault to the Governor against him, Clive claimed to be heard, and both were summoned before the Council. Clive said that Fordyce had publicly declared that Clive was a scoundrel and a coward, and had shaken his cane over him. Besides this, Clive had also heard that Fordyce had threatened to break every bone in his body. Irritated by this abuse, Clive had struck

---

*Translated: 'I have always been religiously attached to the opinion which makes me believe that the highest occupation of ladies should tend towards adding to that a gentle tranquillity for which they are made, and that it is to men that the hardships of business and work ought to be left. Deign, Madame, to allow me to discuss this affair with the Marquis Dupleix.'

the man two or three times with his cane, upon which Fordyce closed with him, but the two were separated by a captain who was by. Clive added that he was not the only person to be abused in this manner by Fordyce, and that he was given to calumniating others, even the Governor. When questioned, Fordyce behaved obstructively and abruptly left the Council, which suspended him. The Council informed the home authorities about this and, lest Fordyce should lay his own story before the directors to the prejudice of Clive, thought it advisable to inform them that Clive 'is generally esteemed a very quiet person, and no ways guilty of disturbances'. Stories circulated later that at Madras Clive showed himself to be a quarrelsome and insubordinate person were wholly apocryphal.

However, release from the tedium of this life came very soon. He was appointed as a lieutenant of foot in the company's service and took part in the Tanjore expedition. When the bombardment of Devikottai by *cohorns* (mortars) was found to be ineffective, Clive proposed that the gates should be battered down and the place stormed. This was thought too risky, however, and the party came back.

But the operation was resumed under Lawrence, and Clive played an important part in the taking of Devikottai. The attacking force was subjected to fire both from a trench outside the fort and from its walls. It was decided to take the trench first. Clive volunteered to lead the attack. He advanced with 30 European soldiers and 700 sepoys, and after crossing a deep and muddy ditch he formed his platoon of Europeans for the frontal charge. But the sepoys had lagged behind, and there was a gap between his party and the sepoys who were to protect his rear. Perceiving this a body of the enemy's cavalry advanced into it, and killed all the Europeans, with the exception of three or four. Clive himself was on the point of being cut down, but avoided the descending sword by quickly stepping to one side. After that he ran back to the ditch where he found not only his sepoys but the entire force drawn up. The whole body then moved up, took the trench, and after that stormed the fort.

With the end of the Tanjore expedition Clive's military career was interrupted again. He took up a civilian post, or rather a civilian post which was at the same time concerned with military operations. He was appointed steward for supplying the stations, as well as commissary for supplying the troops. Though his actual salary was very small, it was from the perquisites of the post that he became possessed of wealth for the first time. In his quasi-military employment he also held the rank of captain.

His real chance to show himself as a military leader came when it was decided to send a diversionary expedition towards Arcot to relieve the pressure on Trichinopoly, and he was selected for the command on August 15 1751 (o.s.).* He is traditionally regarded as the man who inspired the diversion, but what part he played in its genesis is not definitely known.†

However, he set out with his troops, numbering only 200 Europeans and 600 sepoys, and three field pieces, on August 26. Arcot was sixty-four miles from Madras. In two days he reached Conjevaram, and hearing that the fort of Arcot had a garrison of 1,100 men, from there sent for two eighteen-pounders from Madras, and pressed on. On August 31, when only ten miles from Arcot, his forces came under a heavy thunderstorm, but, disregarding it, continued the march. Informed by their spies of this, the garrison at Arcot was not only impressed but even treated the incident as an omen. The commander abandoned the fort, and Clive entered it on September 1 1751.

Arcot, the capital of the Carnatic, was a large town of about 100,000 inhabitants, and the fort had a population of between 3,000 and 4,000. Its capture, and the subsequent siege of fifty days by the forces of Chanda Sahib under his son's command, is described by all historians – most vividly by Macaulay in his essay on Clive. But there is also among the Orme manuscripts a contemporary account, written by a sergeant who was present throughout these operations; Sir George Forrest has given long extracts from it in his life of Clive. What this man wrote about Clive's entry into Arcot is symbolic of the psychological atmosphere of all the British military successes in India. Clive's force, the sergeant wrote, marched without opposition into the town, 'amidst a million spectators whose looks betrayed them traytors notwithstanding their pretended friendship and dirty presents'. Orme wrote that the populace of Arcot 'gazed on them with admiration and respect'. But the simple sergeant had sensed their rancour and felt like the old Roman: *Timeo Danaos* (I fear the Greeks who bring presents). And he was right. Cringe and hate, which became the motto of the Indian people under

---

*Old style.
†See Appendix 2.

British rule, was given silent expression from the first day of British success in India.

The feat that made Clive famous in the weeks that followed was not the capture of Arcot, but its defence. He was young – only twenty-six, the age at which Napoleon got his Italian command. The eight officers under him were also young; six of them had never seen action, and four were, as Orme wrote, 'young men in the mercantile service who, inflamed by his example, took up the sword to follow him'. Two of them were to be shot dead by his side in the course of the campaign.

In the following few days he made two sorties with the object of preventing the garrison, which was still near the town, from organizing a counter-attack. Though these were partly successful they also involved losses which he, with his small force, could ill afford. So he employed his men in improving the defences of the fort and erecting new works. The enemy force was encouraged by the cessation of the sorties to advance within miles of the city, and it even tried to intercept the convoy from Madras which was bringing the eighteen-pounders. But Clive sent out a party and had these safely brought in.

On September 23 Raja Sahib, the son of Chanda Sahib, arrived before Arcot with a large force, and occupied the town itself, wholly confining Clive's small force within the citadel. Nevertheless Clive made another sortie on September 24. It was very costly. Fifteen of his Europeans were killed, and he himself was saved only because one of his officers, seeing a sepoy taking aim from a nearby house, pulled him aside, only to be himself shot through the body. But the moral effect of the sally was not negligible.

From the next day began the famous fifty days' siege of Arcot, justly regarded as one of the most memorable military feats of the British in India. With a few hundred soldiers Clive defended a perimeter a mile long against an enemy force of ten thousand, half of them well-trained and disciplined soldiers. A small force sent from Madras to relieve him was repulsed, and Clive, in his desperation, appealed to the Maratha chief Morari Row to come to his help. The Maratha agreed.

Learning about this, Raja Sahib sent an ultimatum to Clive to surrender, and threatened that, unless he did so, every soldier would be put to the sword after the capture of the city. At the same time he offered a very large bribe to Clive personally to induce him to give up the fort. Clive, of course, refused. At last, on November 14, an attack against the fort was launched in force. At that time there were only 240 men in the fort who were fit for duty. But in the desperate day-long fighting the enemy was repulsed from every breach, and once Clive himself had to aim a gun. There was a truce for burying the dead which lasted till the morning of November 15, and then the enemy suddenly abandoned the siege and withdrew. This must have been due to the approach of the Marathas as well as of a relieving force under Captain Killpatrick. The sergeant's account of the siege closed with these words:

> Thus did providence disappoint our fears, and relieve us from the dread necessity of starving or submitting to the terms of merciless barbarians. And Captain Kilpatrick's command joined us in the afternoon. We fully and unmolested enjoyed the fruits of the earth so long denied us, tho' every day in our sight, and solaced ourselves with the pleasing reflection of having maintained the character of Britons in a clime so remote from our own.

Though he had gone through great physical and mental strain during the siege, Clive was not the man to rest when something needed to be done. Within two days of the raising of the siege, he left Killpatrick with a small force at Arcot and set out in pursuit of Raja Sahib and his force. On November 18 he captured a nearby fort, and after some manoeuvring he found Raja Sahib at Arni, and gave battle in the middle of December. This was Clive's first battle in the field, and he was victorious, though Raja Sahib had been joined by a French force. According to Clive, the sepoys and the horse of Raja Sahib behaved much better in this battle than did the French. After this Clive expelled the French from the fort at Conjevarum, and went to St David to report the complete success of the operations.

But a new military task was given him there, which was to foil an attempt made by Dupleix to snatch a success like Clive's at Arcot by making an attack on Madras itself. He sent a force of 400 Europeans and 5,000 sepoys with a large train of artillery. Clive's force numbered about 400 Europeans and 1,300 sepoys with only six field pieces. But even with this inferiority in numbers and lack of cavalry, which hampered reconnaisance, Clive fought the French contingent at Caveripauk and completely routed it. All this took place at the end of February and beginning of March 1752, and this victory removed the threat to Madras.

After this Clive was getting ready to march with a large force to relieve Trichinopoly when on March 15 Lawrence arrived from England. He had been appointed commander-in-chief of all the company's forces in India, and at once took command. Naturally, Clive served under him, and accompanied him to Trichinopoly.

However, he remained with Lawrence only for a short time. At the beginning of April it was decided to divide the forces to put an end to the French siege of the fort at Trichinopoly. While Lawrence was to attack Law, the French commander, a detachment was to go north to prevent French moves to come to his aid. Clive was selected to command this force and conduct the ancillary operations. As Lawrence wrote later: 'Promising myself great success from the activity and vigilance of Captain Clive, I detached him with 400 of my best Europeans, 1,200 sepoys, and 400 horse to take post on the other side of the river Caveri.' Clive's operations were mainly against the French forces under d'Auteuil, and they were completely successful. In the end he captured this force with its commander at Volconda towards the end of May, and brought d'Auteuil with the French officers and soldiers to Trichinopoly. This, combined with the siege of Law's position at Seringham by Lawrence, resulted in the surrender on June 3 of the whole French force. The threat to Trichinopoly was wholly removed.

After this Clive, exhausted by the exertions in the hot weather and in poor health, returned to Madras, and did not take any further part in the military operations till the middle of September 1752. In the meanwhile, Lawrence was engaged in clearing the whole of the Carnatic of the French and establishing the authority of Muhammad Ali over the province. Two fortified posts, Chinglepat (about forty miles south-west of Madras and on the river Palar) and Covelong (also called Sadat Bandar, and on the coast) were strongly held by the French and were a threat to both Madras and Arcot. So Saunders decided to reduce both, and selected Clive to carry out the operation. He set out on September 15, and took first Covelong and then Chinglepat.

The capture of these two places was the last military exploit of Clive in the first phase of his military career in India. On his return to Madras he found his health to be so bad that he applied for home leave, which was granted on October 9 1752.

It was through the operations from Arcot to Covelong, and above all his defence of Arcot, that Clive established his reputation as a military leader. These have been praised by contemporary as well as by later historians. But, because they are diffused, even the plentiful superlatives scattered in the chronological narratives do not give a clear-cut impression of his achievement. So a more formal appraisal of his military capacity has to be given.

The very first thing that must be pointed out is that Arcot was the first British military success in India; and it put an end to a depressing record of either mediocrity or failure. With it the British military reputation began to rise in India, and the French to decline, until the idea gained ground that the British were invincible.

The raising of the seige of Arcot was also the decisive turning point in the war against Dupleix, and with the surrender of Law within six months the French lost the initiative completely, and were forced to the defensive. News of the surrender of Law made the Company decide to recall Dupleix, and this personal change gave a new character to the Anglo-French rivalry in India. From being an effort to establish French supremacy over the Indian princes, French military enterprise in India became merely an attempt to cause embarrassment to the English. Both during the Seven Years' War, when the French forces under Lally won some successes on land, and during the American War, when French naval forces under Suffren almost dominated the Indian Ocean, the operations were only secondary episodes in a world-wide Anglo-French conflict, and India was not a primary stake.

The psychological effect of the successes of Clive as well as of Lawrence was as decisive as the political. In the middle of 1751 Muhammad Ali's position was desperate, and his mood most pessimistic. From May onwards, in letter after letter to Saunders, Muhammad Ali entreated him to be energetic and not to abandon him. His anxiety increased after the relative failures of Gingen, and in a letter which was received on June 27 he wrote:

> You were pleased to undertake the entire management of my affairs.... Your union with me is well known to all our friends as well as our foes and your true regard and attachment to the interest of the Circar [authority of Muhammad Ali] has reached the ears of his Majesty the Great Mogul and Ghazi-ud-din Khan. You should therefore, agreeable to your promise and for the honour of your nation, be strictly inclined to assist me in such a manner that I may

obtain my desire which will gain you a good name and reputation throughout all Indostan, Deccan, Bengal, and Europe, where they will commend you. I also on my part shall gain great credit and be esteemed by the Mogul, Ghazi-ud-din Khan and the other great men of Indostan and the Deccan countries.

His tone became even more urgent a month later when he learned that Gingens had retreated, a decision he could not understand. And he wrote:

I must tell you that my whole dependence is upon your troops. I undertook the government of the Deccan country by the advice of the English and engaged in the present expedition by their assistance. I and my family remain in the fort of Trichinopoly and it is talked all over Indostan, Deccan, and Bengal that I am protected and assisted by the English who for their own honour should exert themselves to the utmost to support my reputation. Tho' it is improper for me to reflect upon the behaviour of your officers yet I cannot forbear writing freely to you, the Protector of my Affairs: I must desire you not to reveal this to your officers but to send them proper directions about the destruction of the enemy. With respect to my family write me what is proper to be done. Don't let the French and Chanda seize me. I depend upon God and you. Do whatever may be conducive to your honour and reputation regarding my affair. What can I say more!

In his next letter he even proposed negotiations with Chanda Sahib and the French with a view to leaving him with Trichinopoly and some adjoining territories. Realizing the urgency of the situation, Saunders at once wrote: 'The friendship of the English you may always depend on to the utmost of their power.' As to opening negotiations with the French and Chanda, he observed: 'It is a step we should not take till we are convinced we cannot succeed by any other means.' In the postscript to this letter the Governor informed Muhammad Ali that he had decided on the diversion to Arcot.

The low ebb of British prestige was no less revealed by the arrogance which Chanda Sahib showed to the Governor of Madras. On August 3 1751, the Governor wrote to him to say that Muhammad Ali had mortgaged Trichinopoly and its districts to the English company for a loan granted to him, and so Chanda Sahib should refrain from hostilities in this region. To this Chanda Sahib replied at once. Referring to the Governor's demand and the reason for it he said:

I look upon it as a joke because the said country and fort never belonged to Anerverdy Cawn [Muhammad Ali's formal name]. You are very sensible that this province is the property of the Great Mogul; Anerverdy Cawn has no business to mortgage it. What you write on this head is nothing but your invention to support you in your present proceedings. Your schemes and hostilities are well known to the world, and whatever you do is unjust.

All this was changed, and utterly so, in three months, by the success of Clive at Arcot. Even before the siege had been raised, in fact when Clive in his desperation appealed to Morari Row for help, the Maratha chief agreed to do so because he was impressed by the defence alone, which had convinced him that the English could fight.

On hearing of the retreat of Raja Sahib from Arcot Muhammad Ali wrote: 'Whatever advantages you may reap from this are entirely owing to the valour of Captain Clive.' In another letter, received by the Governor on December 10, he wrote:

> I was extremely glad to know that by the bravery of Mr. Clive the Enemy's son was obliged to raise the siege of Arcot fort and to fly towards Vellore. I must tell you that this is owing to God's mercy, good wishes of the elders and Your Honour's good conscience. As it is a great victory it is my wish that God may grant you, me, and all our friends joy on this account.

He went on to reiterate his appreciation of Clive: 'I am glad', he wrote, 'that Mr. Clive gave such proof of his valour and that your fame and reputation are talked of in the world as was requisite.' He further informed Saunders that it was his intention to secure a title, *mansab,* and jaghir for the Governor from Delhi. He also gave Clive the title of *Bahadur* (Brave) and requested Saunders to style him so in his letters, and, further, he said that he himself would send a mansab and jaghir for Clive.

In the next three months Clive established English dominance in the Carnatic; the turn of the tide was most significantly shown by the fact that after the battle of Arni, the first fought by Clive in the open field, the same sepoys who had tried to storm Arcot for Raja Sahib offered their services to Clive. Six hundred of them were taken and proved to be some of the best sepoys the English afterwards employed. Following the surrender of Law more enemy troops came over, and one of the most capable officers to do this was the future Haidar Ali. He came over with a large body of his horsemen.

Clive's personal position was now fully established. Muhammad Ali wrote to Saunders, in the same letter that has been quoted above: 'Let the fort of Arcot be delivered now to the care of Mr. Clive. . . . I desire you to continue him as the Head Commander; if you send anybody to him with a force let him act under him, for Mr. Clive deserves to be Chief.'

Another testimony to Clive's leadership was given by Muhammad Ali and the Maratha and Mysore commanders, when the commander for the detachment that was to be sent north of the Caveri to disrupt the French supplies and communications had to be selected. Clive was only a junior captain and there were other officers senior to him. Naturally, Lawrence could not give the command to Clive without reconciling them to it. But, apart from Lawrence's own preference, the question was virtually decided by the Indian commanders. As Orme wrote: 'The Nabob, the Marathas, and the Mysoreans demanded Captain Clive to command the army sent to Samiavaram.'

No less striking proof of his emergence was furnished by the notice that the French began to take of him, and during these months Clive became as much a *bête noire* to them as were Lawrence and Saunders. He was held to be the brain and instrument behind the more drastic actions of the English, like the hanging of four English deserters after the action at Samiavaram, the handing over of the French prisoners to Muhammad Ali in disregard of the assurances said to have been given to them, and, above all, for the refusal to give up Sheikh Hassan, who was known to have shot Anwar-ud-din Khan at Ambur and had become an officer in the French army. In respect of the prisoners, Clive was assumed to be the evil counsellor of Lawrence.

Law, after his surrender at Seringham, made a statement at Pondichery that when he was discussing the terms of surrender with Lawrence he demanded that Sheikh Hassan and other captains of the sepoys should be treated as French officers, and added: 'Mr Lawrence seemed inclined to accede to this demand concerning Sheikh Hassan till Mr Clive took Mr Lawrence apart, who after a moment's conversation came back and told him that Mahomed Ally Khan wanted Sheikh Hassan.'

This and other statements made by Law were referred back to Clive, who gave his version of the terms of the capitulation. This deposition was sent to Pondichery and on reading it Law blazed forth in anger. He addressed a letter to Clive and told him that his memory had failed him and he could not imagine that 'men of honour are forgetful enough of the care of their reputation to advance facts notoriously false, whatever advantage they may promise themselves'. He went on to say that Lawrence did not agree to his proposal to send the prisoners to Pondichery 'because you called him into a closet contrived in his tent and as you were the oracle he consulted for the pretended intentions of the Nabob', Lawrence did not agree to Law's proposal. As to Sheikh Hassan, he said that 'the Nabob refused me Sheikh Hassan or rather you for him'. He also said that Lawrence had assured him that, in spite of the Nabob's insistence on keeping Hassan, he would allow Hassan to escape in the night, but if this assurance was not kept afterwards 'it was owing to you, Mr Clive, who took Mr Lawrence aside'. Finally he apostrophized Clive:

> You take, Mr Clive, so deep an interest in this sending away the prisoners, that you go beyond all bounds to assert that it was my demand and all the officers; but which is a trifle with you: you have not been able to guard yourself against a reflection which betrays you.

In a separate letter to Lawrence, Law observed that in his deposition Clive wanted 'to throw a colour over my most simple discourses'.

Furthermore, after the surrender of Law, Clive had become so important in the eyes of the French that, in the hope of winning over the King of Tanjore and the Maratha Chief Morari Row, they sent an agent to them who told them that Clive had been taken prisoner. Giving this news to him, his friend Dalton wrote from Trichinopoly on July 29 1752: 'These reports only serve to do you honour, as it is manifest by 'em, how sensible the enemy are of how much consequence your life is to the cause.'

It was with such recognition from friends and enemies alike that Clive's first campaigning came to a close in 1752. He was twenty-seven, and Plassey was still five years away. But his military reputation was made, and it has now to be seen how much reality there was in it. Without attributing any extraordinary strategical or tactical insight to him, his military leadership is not to be underrated. It gave an illustration of the basic military doctrine that war is a contest of wills, and not merely of men, weapons and knowledge of the science of war. Clive demonstrated this at its simplest, perhaps also at its crudest. But a stark reality was there. It has to be pointed out that he was a leader rather than a general, and in that series of elemental, ferocious, and yet anarchical clashes what was needed was a leader with an inflexible strength of will.

Which is also saying that he was an amateur in warfare. In point of fact, the greatest British generalship was always amateurish, as it was in Cromwell, in Marlborough, in Wellington, who only evolved into a professional when in India. But even in Wellington's day an English general who had conducted operations in India was regarded in Europe as an 'admiral who has been navigating in the Lake of Geneva'. Clive remained throughout an amateur because there never arose any need for him to become a professional. From being an amateur soldier he made the transition to an amateur statesman quickly. But so long as he remained a soldier and conducted military operations, he showed that he had the making of a soldier in him. No one recognized that more generously than his chief Lawrence. In his account of the war published in 1761 he wrote about Clive:

> A man of undaunted resolution, of a cool temper, and a presence of mind, which never left him in the greatest danger. Born a soldier, for without a military education of any sort, or much conversing with any of the profession, from his judgement and good sense, he led an army like an experienced officer, and a brave soldier, with a prudence that certainly warranted success. This young man's early genius surprised and engaged my attention, as well before as at the siege of Devicottah, where he behaved in courage and judgement, much beyond what could be expected from his years, and his success afterwards confirmed what I said to many people concerning him.

Orme wrote of Clive's defence of Arcot:

> The achievement of a young commander with indefatigable activity, unshaken constancy, and undaunted courage: and not withstanding he had at this time neither read books, nor conversed with men capable of giving him much instruction in the military art.

His leadership was a personal quality, and its character, so clearly discerned by Lawrence, might be illustrated, among many that can be cited, by two incidents. In the night of April 15 1752, a large body of French soldiers and their sepoys made their way by a stratagem into the pagodas held by Clive. They had a number of English deserters with them who deceived the sentries by telling them in English that they were reinforcements sent by Lawrence and wanted to be taken to Clive, who was sleeping in a hut nearby. As soon as they were taken there they and all the French party began to fire. Their shots shattered Clive's escritoire at the foot of his bed, and killed the servant who was sleeping near it. Awakened, Clive jumped up in his shirt, and at first thought it was his soldiers who were firing from panic or false alarm. So he went among the enemy troops, and believing them to be his soldiers scolded them as cowards. One of these recognized him as an enemy, cut him in two places and ran away. Following him, Clive found himself surrounded by six Frenchmen who spoke to him in their language. At last he realized what had happened, and had the presence of mind to tell the Frenchmen that they were surrounded and would certainly be cut to pieces if they did not surrender at once. Upon this three did so. Clive then rallied his soldiers and drove the enemy out. Hearing of this incident Lawrence wrote: 'I rejoice at your success, as your wounds are not dangerous, and if they spoil the beauty of your face they raise your fame in having served your country when you got them.'

The other incident took place when he was attacking Covelong. The French brought their guns to bear on his troops, and neither the Europeans nor the sepoys could be kept at their posts. So, as Orme wrote:

> Captain Clive, judging that shame would avail more than severity to reclaim them from their cowardice, exposed himself continually to the hottest of the enemy's fire, and his example brought them in two days to do their duty with some firmness.

Clive never shrank from personal danger, and this made a great contribution to his reputation as a leader. He showed an indifference to danger which came from his nature rather than from any exercise of the will. Here an element of chance enters into military leadership. Military reputation is not always a matter of ability, but is almost equally dependent on luck. Frederick the Great used to ask before appointing anybody to a command: '*Est-il heureux?*' He knew that the confidence of the soldiers in their commander and their fighting spirit came largely from his successes. Though abstractly the quality of generalship is often judged by what a commander does in defeat, for practical purposes a run of victories is more important. And in the old days the personal survival of a commander in battles was as important a factor in his standing as were his victories.

From the first Clive had a series of miraculous escapes from death as he had successes, which was seen from Pondichery to Covelong. This made him a mascot, and a commander is not less valuable as a mascot than he is as a general. Those who follow him look out not only for ability but also for the sign. Clive became a leader on both the scores.

First Intermezzo in England
When Clive sailed for England on March 23 1753, he was a man who had arrived, in the eyes of the world. In position he was second only to Lawrence in India; his military ability was regarded as outstanding and his achievements indisputable; he had become rich; and he had also got married. Henceforth his life was to be divided between acts in India and *entr'actes* in England, and the alternating stages were to exhibit a curious contrast, for the English phases were as commonplace as the Indian were out of the ordinary.

Clive tried to make use of his exceptional career in India to live or rise socially in the most conventional manner in England. The conventionality was different in the successive stages, and could be seen in a rising scale. This meant that whenever he returned to England there was also a relapse in him from the extraordinary to the ordinary.

The relapse was most complete in his first intermezzo, which lasted only a year and a half. During those months he did nothing that any man of his social origins would not have done if he had suddenly become rich and famous. Though perhaps he added a touch of flamboyancy to what he did, the really striking feature of his behaviour after his return to his own country at the end of 1753 was his readiness to pick up the threads of life from the point at which they were broken off when he was sent out to India as the booby of the family. Though he had made good in a spectacular manner, he exhibited nothing of the upstart's resentment against his old life, nor even the successful but forgiving upstart's condescension to his modest antecedents. On the contrary, he showed unquestioning loyalty to his family and his old friends: he merely pulled out the thread from the unwound reel to go forward to a grander style of living.

But there was bound to be a clash, at first latent but increasingly manifest, between the two lives he was to have. This became more and more clear as his outlook, generated by his Indian career, was brought to bear on his life at home. A stable and static English society tried to digest this Englishman remade in India, and had Clive remained the normal East Indian nabob it would have absorbed him. But with each period of activity in India his achievements became more grandiose, his outlook more exotic, and his idea of what was due to him more over-pitched. On the one hand, he threw his Indian weight about, and, on the other, English society found him too big, too strange, and too intractable for reclamation. He would live among his countrymen only on his terms, and so, finally, England profited by his ability and achievements but destroyed him personally.

That, however, was still in the future, and the first relapse into English norms had begun even before he had left India. When he came back to Madras after the surrender of Law he plunged into the civilian life of that settlement, a life that attempted to reproduce the social life of the same class of men in England, with all its requirements, including women, imported from home. He was still engaged at Trichinopoly when his friend Boddam wrote to him from Fort St David to give news that eleven ladies were coming out by the next ship, and among them was the sister of his friend, Edmund Maskelyne, Margaret or Peggy. He also added: 'I would advise you to guard your heart well against these, when you think of the time of seeing us, as I do not doubt but after such a campaign as you have had, these beauties will have a wonderful effect upon you.'

Another friend, Dalton, also wrote from Trichinopoly after Clive had gone back to Madras:

Dr Beauty – By this time I reckon you are able to give one an account of the new arrived angels – by God it would be a good joke if your countenance was to smite one of them, and you were to court matrimony – I should however be concerned at it as it would put me out of all hopes of the pleasures I propose myself in company with you in Covent Garden Etc.

This also shows that Clive had not gone beyond the familiar in his anticipations of the *menus plaisirs* he would have at home. In the meanwhile, at Madras he was having the respectable form of the same pleasures, so that Dalton complained on July 26:

Dear Clive – What can be the meaning I can never have the pleasure of a line from you; you now and then favoured me with one when you had infinity of business on your hands and now you neglect me when you have no other employ than gallanting the ladies, and jovially entertaining your friends. I hear you keep one of the best houses in Madras – not in the least resembling our Bandipolem economy – however recollect at a leisure hour that you have a friend at Trichinopoly to whom the news of your health and welfare will always give infinite satisfaction and I am sure you'll write me a line.

All this was interrupted by the Covelong campaign and in October, after he had brought it to a successful end, Clive was permitted to lay down his command in the field and come back to Madras on grounds of ill health. Apart from exhaustion there was also a repetition of the fits (probably half mentally, half physically induced) he had in childhood. Lawrence felt anxious about these and wrote to him on November 30: 'I'm greatly concerned to find your fits continue which I sincerely hope will be removed by a change of climate, and shall be glad that you'll tell me yourself the last has not done much mischief and you are on the mending hand.'

In February Clive was finally given leave to return to England and to embark in the vessel *Admiral Vernon*. He did not do so, and instead was married in the church at Fort St George, on February 18 1753, to Margaret Maskelyne.

Nothing is known of his courtship, and throughout her life – from her marriage at the age of seventeen to her death at the age of eighty in 1816 – Clive's wife remained a shadowy figure. Later gossip tried to add romance to the marriage, but it conformed wholly to the Anglo-Indian pattern. In those days English girls, especially those who did not have money, came to India to seek husbands among the young men who were making money there. In England it was the young men who looked about for money, and in India the young women hoped to find it along with their husbands. As money was plentiful among the men, and women were scarce, falling in love was predetermined.

It is certainly curious that a brother in India should propose such a venture to a sister who was only seventeen, and belonged to a good family, and that so young a girl should fully weigh her chances, at first refuse to come over and then think better of it. But this is what happened. Edmund Maskelyne had been writing for some time to his sister that she should take a trip to Madras with a view to marriage, and was disappointed when she wrote to him to say that she would not. Thus, the brother wrote to the sister on March 28 1752:

Dear Peggy, – I was favoured with yours of the 20th August 1751, by the *Donnington*, on the 14th instant, and hope your declining my proposal for tripping it this way proceeds from some more agreeable views at Home, as otherwise I can't but blame you for it; matches in this country generally proving so vastly superior to what are made in Europe.

Before this chiding letter reached her the sister was already on her way to Madras, where she arrived in June 1752, to be married eight months later in the most respectable and conventional manner.

There was nothing uncommon in the fact of Clive's money-making in India. At first it conformed wholly to established practice, and had nothing spectacular about it. For a long time after this, young Englishmen of impoverished middle-class backgrounds, and also of impecunious noble families, were to come to India to make or repair fortunes. Arthur Wellesley, the future Duke of Wellington, went to India in 1796, heavily in debt, and came back in 1805 not only clear of all debts but with nearly £43,000. He made this money in ways that were considered wholly legitimate. So did Clive. The fortune of over £40,000 he amassed came from private trade, from the perquisites of his office of steward, and from presents or prize money, all recognized sources of money for the Company's servants in India.

In his trading, carried on in accordance with the regulations of the Company and in partnership with Orme, he did some lucrative business. The profits from supplying the forces and the establishments were like those of contractors. Once the Governor and his Council inquired of Lawrence whether the troops could not be fed at a lower *batta*, or *per capita* allowance, and he replied that they would be the best judges of that. But he also suggested that, instead of contracting for it, the steward might be paid a higher salary.

Everybody knew about Clive's money and his friends were glad for him. Repington wrote:

> You have deserved your money, Clive, and every honest Englishman will think so; besides I could prove that no man unless a soldier beloved by the country people and either in command himself or highly in favour with the commander can ever make half as much of the employ as you have done on the same terms.

On the eve of his departure Lawrence also wrote: 'May you have health to enjoy the fortune your merit has gained.'

Before he embarked for England some loose ends in his

affairs had to be tied up. He had learnt from the Governor that the Nawab of the Carnatic had made a present of Rs40,000 to him, but having heard nothing further about it he requested Lawrence to see to it after his departure. He also entrusted the management of his money by a formal document to Walsh, Vansittart and Maskelyne, and instructed them on March 21 that Rs50,000 was to be invested in diamonds, or, if diamonds were not to be had on advantageous terms, all his money in India was to be sent to England through the Company's bills. The amount of money he had made, though large for a man of his position, was not sensational as were his later gains or those of Napoleon from his Italian campaign.

He sailed away on March 23 1753 with his wife, not without expressing a small grievance against the authorities at Madras to Lawrence:

> I think in justice to the military in general I cannot leave this coast without leaving a paper behind me representing the little notice taken of people in our profession. I hope the world will not accuse me of vanity or be of opinion that I think too highly of my successes as I seldom or ever opened my lips upon the subject. All that I ever expected was a letter of thanks, and that I am informed is usual upon such occasions.

But Clive was not fair to his employers. They never underrated his services. They sent reports to England which made him a much-talked-about man, and from London the directors also wrote to India 'of the great regard they had for the merit of Captain Clive, to whose courage and conduct the late turn of our affairs has been mainly due'. And they added: 'He may be assured of our having a just sense of his services.'

On his arrival in England he found this to be so. He received a welcome from his employers and the public alike, which was greater than that given to Arthur Wellesley when he returned from India in 1805 after his brilliant military victories. In fact, the only other Englishman whose reputation travelled ahead of him from India to his country in this manner was young Kipling in 1889. The *Gentleman's Magazine* had already, in its historical chronicle for January 1753, reproduced from the *London Gazette* an extract about his military exploits described in a letter from Fort St George. It also reported in October that on the tenth of that month, 'Captain Clive who behaved so bravely in the East Indies, arrived at Plymouth, was dress'd, at the King's Arms Tavern'.

A year before, his father had written to him from London that on coming there he had had great pleasure in hearing 'the applause every one gives to your gallant actions and behaviour, and the success that hath attended you'. He added:

> You are compared to no less than some of those brave Generals who are gone but left their names upon record to their glory and honour. The Directors of the Company you have so bravely served, I hear, at a public entertainment drank to your health by the name of General Clive, and are pleased to say they are under a great obligation to you.

The whole family quite naturally was in a state of great elation. As his father informed Clive in the same letter, 'Your five sisters that are now most of 'em grown women and two little brothers, the one eleven and the other seven, all rejoyce at your welfare and are not a little proud of their relation.' His mother also wrote: 'I can't express the joy yours to your father gives me. Your brave conduct and success is the talk and wonder of the public, the great joy and satisfaction of all your friends.' These letters, written to him on December 15 and 16 1752, reached Madras after he had left for England.

After its call at Plymouth his ship berthed in the Thames on October 14 1753, and he went to the family's house in St Swithin's Lane in the City. On October 14 he went to pay his respects to the Court of Directors, and the Chairman, in the name of the Court, congratulated him on his arrival and thanked him for the signal services he had done the Company. He also expressed the hope that Clive would help the directors with his opinion on Indian affairs. The meeting directed the Committee of Correspondence to consider a proper present to Clive as a token of the Court's sense of his services.

The proceedings further reported that:

> Captain Clive then made his acknowledgements for the Court's favour, and desired leave to assure them, he should with the greatest readiness, offer any experience he may have gained, and embrace every opportunity for furthering their Service.

It would seem, however, that on the same occasion or immediately afterwards Clive gave an appraisement of the situation in India to the directors. For the *Gentleman's Magazine*, which reported this meeting, also gave a summary of a statement made by Clive. In it, according to this magazine, he assured the directors that the English had maintained themselves in all the posts which they became possessed of after the last engagement between him and the French; that though the French had made some new movements it was assumed that their intention was only to embarrass the English; and that the French seemed rather inclined to stand on the defensive than to act offensively, on account of the considerable losses they had sustained. The magazine also reported that Clive was to have 'a considerable pension during his life, as a recompense for his services'.

In February the Committee of Correspondence recommended that a sword set with diamonds to the value of £500 be presented to Clive. The directors accepted the recommendation, and at the same time decided to give a sword worth £700 to Lawrence. This is stated to have been done at the suggestion of Clive. In any case, without saying anything about his part in the decision, Clive informed Lawrence of it. The *Gentleman's Magazine* reported this as well, and informed its readers that Clive made a very handsome speech, acknowledging his obligation of the Company and assuring them of his future service whenever required.

It was to be expected that important political figures of the day wanted to meet him, and he saw Lord Hardwick, Lord Mansfield, Lord Holderness, the Secretary of State for War and also Lord Sandwich and Henry Fox, whom he came to know well.

All this was the aftermath of his achievements in India, and did not point to the future. But upon his return to his country and family after ten years he had occupations and interests enough to keep him from thinking about his future, and he also had enough capital, both in prestige and money, for him to be able to live on it for some time without being prodded by ambition. His most urgent object was to recoup his health, a process that was likely to take time. After that he seems to have formed definite plans to rehabilitate his family's position. His father was embarrassed financially and the estate of Styche was mortgaged. Clive at once paid it off, put his father on a comfortable footing, and also helped relatives and friends.

In all this he not only showed the most attractive side of his personality, but also the typical attachment to family ties shown by men who came from families of the impoverished gentry or nobility. Napoleon showed it on a grand scale; and, judged by his correspondence with his family, no one would have thought that art was a vocation with Michelangelo or that it had any other value for him except as the means, like any trade, of earning money to rehabilitate his family financially. Clive's early outlook on life had been formed by the relative poverty of his family, and after acquiring money it was natural for him to exhibit the generous side of that outlook.

But his father only became more assertively mercenary through the wealth of the son. His cupidity had been roused by the money that Clive had already sent from India, and he regarded his son's achievements as the means of making more money. When his mother wrote to him that his successes were a joy to her, she expressed the additional satisfaction of being able to expect that owing to them she would see him again sooner than she had hoped for. His father, on the contrary, wrote:

> As your conduct and bravery is become public talk of the nation and this is the time to increase your fortune, make use of the present opportunity before you quit the country [India], remembering that the interest of £20,000 in this country is no more than £500 per annum.

The old man had already, in December 1752, waited on three principal directors in order to find out what they proposed further for Clive, but, as he put it, 'perceive[d] they are desirous to have the account the next ship brings before they give me any positive answer other than a general one that they are very desirous to do you any service in their power'. All fathers dependent on a son who has become suddenly great are particularly anxious that the son should never suppress the sordid side of his greatness.

Clive at this stage was more concerned with spending than with safeguarding or increasing his money. There is a profound difference between those who become wealthy by following the beaten tracks of making money and those to whom wealth comes as a product or accompaniment of a larger self-assertion, or, to put it more abstractly, between those for whom money-making is a striving after security, and those to whom it is a pursuit of power in one of its forms. The latter class of men, as soon as they get money, want to rise to a magnificent style of living, making that another aspect of their self-assertion. Warren Hastings tried to do that, and also Burke with very limited means. If the rise is spectacular enough these men shed all money-mindedness because they can count on money running after them instead of running after it themselves. At that level they take any amount of money, however great, as due to them.

Clive was to come to this state of mind, but not as yet. Nevertheless, he was being tuned to that pitch.

He was also impelled to spend by the spirit of the age. Nothing was more characteristic of the decades of rising prosperity in the middle of the eighteenth century than the aspiration to live in style. As a didactic writer said in 1755, 'thanks to the foolish vanity that prompts us to imitate our superiors ... every tradesman is a merchant, every merchant is a gentleman, and every gentleman one of the noblesse. We are a nation of gentry.'

The same writer also moralized on the consequence of this levelling up:

> A kind of perpetual warfare between the *good* and *bad company* has subsisted for half a century last past in which the former have been perpetually pursued by the latter and fairly beaten out of all their resources for superior distinction; out of innumerable fashions in dress, every one of which they have been obliged to abandon as soon as occupied by their impertinent rivals.

As a revulsion from this competition, and also for the sake of greater simplicity and comfort, at this time gentlemen began to adopt the style of dress of the common man. As a writer said in 1739: 'There is at present a reigning ambition among our young gentlemen of degrading themselves in their apparel to the class of servants they keep.'

Clive fell in with these trends and belonged to the newcomers, and not to the established order. But in that century of taste no one was likely to sink to vulgarity by any kind of high living. The only perceptible difference could be between those who were in the manner born and those who were self-conscious.

Stories were told later of Clive's extravagance and ostentation during this period. But any expenditure by those who have been known to be poor is never viewed charitably, and the passage just quoted also explains the motivation. Clive certainly tried to live the life of a man of means, which he showed at the outset by taking a house in Queen Square, near St James's Park. The West End was expensive even in those days. In 1762 Casanova paid 20 guineas a week for a house in Pall Mall. Clive must have taken a bigger house, and lived in sumptuous style. After his return to India his coach was sold for £40, the pair of horses for £40 and a riding horse for £12 12s. This was taken by his first biographer, Sir John Malcolm, to indicate a very expensive style of living.

Clive did one thing that was typical of the wealth *novus homo* in England. He became a Member of Parliament. In the general election of 1754 he entered as a candidate in the interest of one of the factions of the Whig Party, that led by Lord Sandwich and Henry Fox, which was opposed to that of the Duke of Newcastle. With equal typicality he was elected by one of the rotten boroughs of Cornwall. But the result was contested by the defeated candidate. This was fought out with a factious unscrupulousness rare even in those days. After nearly a year a committee of the House upheld his election, but a few days later Newcastle got him unseated by the House itself. All this had nothing to do with Clive personally. With his money and record, he was only a pawn in the rivalry of the factions. The rejection took place on March 23 1755. A month later Clive sailed again to India with his wife, leaving two children behind.

The decision to do so has been attributed to the necessity of earning money again after his extravagance in England. That he should want money cannot be doubted, for he could live with only modest respectability in his country, and he could hardly have been reconciled to that. But there must have been other feelings. More through intuition than conscious reasoning he must have perceived that, even if he had the money to live according to his new view of himself in England, this would not satisfy him. For one thing he had exercised power in India, which he could never do here. Personally, far from being able to dominate those among whom he wanted to live, he would not even have been adopted by them as one of their own. Most important of all, he had discovered himself in the adventures, dangers and exceptional situations of his Indian career. That self could not survive in England.

All this is probable, but wholly speculative, for there are no documents to illustrate the state of his mind. One thing is, however, certain, and it is this – that in spite of all that he was doing to create a life for himself in his country, he never cut himself off from the East India Company. Towards the end of his stay he seems to have veered round to the idea that to be at home was profitable only to promote a career in India. He gave expression to this view in a letter to his friend Orme in which he said: 'I find *by experience* that a man is not further from preferment by paying a visit to his native country.'

Offers were being made to him to go to India soon after his coming to England, and he never rejected them. For instance, early in 1754 he wrote to a friend in Madras: 'My health would not permit me to accept the offers that have been made me of going abroad this year. If I can have the same next I shall be happy in the thought of seeing again all my old friends and acquaintances.'

At the same time he wrote also to Lawrence:

> The Company have made me some advantageous offers in a civil way. I am sorry my health will not permit me to accept them however. I hope the next year the same opportunity will offer again and that I shall have the pleasure of seeing you and my friends a second time in India.

On one occasion, dwelling on the possibility of a new war with France, he told the directors that 'for his own part he desired nothing better than to dispute the mastery of the Deccan with M. Bussy'. The opportunity came early in 1755. The idea of going back to India must have been strengthened in him by the uncertainty about his election. Even before it was decided, re-employment in India appears to have been proposed. He had agreed, and applied for a commission in the Army. Hearing that one might be given to him, his parliamentary patron, Lord Sandwich, wrote to him in panic:

> I heard last night for the first time that you was to have a Lieutenant Colonel's commission which surprised me greatly, as your seat in Parliament would thereby be vacated; I take for granted you are not unaware of this circumstance. Otherwise you could not have given in to it, and therefore will, I flatter myself, immediately prevent anything farther being done in it.

Lord Sandwich wanted an answer from Clive that he was not going to vacate the seat, so that with the help of such a letter he 'might possibly retrieve some of the ground this report [about his Commission] may have made us lose'. He added that about the election issue he was 'not at all diffident of success'.

This letter was not dated, but was obviously written before the election was finally set aside on March 23 1755. In anticipation Clive must already have decided on his future course. On the next day he signed the contract for the new post offered to him in India as a member of the Council with a seniority next to the Governor, and as deputy governor at Fort St David. He made immediate preparations for sailing. However, his father still urged a parliamentary career on him, and suggested that he should stand for an election which was going to be held at

Dover. Clive informed his father that he had already accepted his new post, and dismissed the idea with some jocular remarks. To this the father replied only five days before he sailed for India: 'Tho' you banter me abt. the Election at Dover I think as you are so near and the Electrs. so well disposed to oppose the M----y, you have a fair opportunity to disappoint the D. of N. [Duke of Newcastle] and after you are elected you may proceed on your voyage.' Clive did not change his plans, and sailed on April 23 1755.

Chapter Four

Gestation of the Empire

When Clive sailed to England, Dupleix's war, as I have called it, had not come to an end, but it had already established a definite pattern of relations between the two European Companies and the native princes of India. This was to be reproduced and extended in Bengal and it was this pattern of political relationship that was finally to take the form of the British Empire in India. For at least two decades after its inception with the battle of Plassey, its shape was very embryonic, and even those who were bringing it into existence seemed to be unwilling or unprepared to envisage its full potentiality. Even over the whole span of Clive's activities in India, when British political power became established and ineradicable in the country, its formal organization had not progressed very much beyond the pattern of relationship established by Dupleix and Bussy in South India. So, all aspects of the European involvement in India in those early years have to be considered in some detail.

Dupleix as Precursor
The first thing that has to be discussed is how far Dupleix can be looked upon as the precursor of Clive, and of the British generally, in respect of founding the Empire. In popular opinion, long accepted as the historical truth, he showed the example and the way, started the process, and inspired the British. And if he failed to forestall the British it was only because he was not supported from France.

The earliest contribution to this legend was made by Dupleix himself in the apologia he presented for his actions after his recall. Though he wrote it primarily to justify his claim for money on the French company, in its effect it was something like the creation of the Napoleonic legend from St Helena. The growth of the legend was fostered by later history: by the Anglo-French rivalry of the next 150 years, by the French chagrin at seeing a British empire in India, and by the growth of a French colonial empire in Africa and Asia – all of which made French historians dwell on and magnify what they regarded as their missed opportunity in India.

However, the English contribution to the legend was hardly less important, coming as it did from Orme, the first historian of the foundation of the Indian empire, whose authority was unquestioned. He showed the usual English admiration for a capable and brave and, of course, beaten enemy. In the first volume of his history published in 1763 (when French power in India was completely destroyed), he set down that the disadvantages, principally political, under which the French company had to carry on its trade in India convinced Dupleix that 'the trade of Indostan was no longer worth the attention of France, nor indeed of any other nation in Europe'. Then he observed:

> But discovering the unmilitary character of the natives, and the perpetual dissensions of their rulers, he was led to imagine that by joining some of these competitors he might gain by conquest more advantages than any other European nation had hitherto derived from trade. He therefore determined to prosecute this plan, by giving assistance to Chunda-Saheb.

He was more expansive in his comments on the recall of Dupleix. He remarked that Dupleix's 'conduct certainly merited a very different requital from his nation; which never had a subject so desirous and capable of extending its reputation and power in the East-Indies'. He asserted that, if Dupleix had been provided with sufficient forces after the death of Anwar-ud-din Khan and been supported from France, he would certainly have controlled Deccan and 'perhaps even the throne of Delhi itself; and have established a sovereignty over many of the valuable provinces of the empire'. Orme also thought that Dupleix would have expelled all other Europeans, and more especially the British, from India. Orme's final judgement on Dupleix was as follows:

> When we consider that he formed this plan of conquest and dominion at a time when all other Europeans entertained the highest opinion of the strength of the Mogul government, suffering tamely the insolence of its meanest officers, rather than venture to make resistance against a power which they chimerically imagined to be capable of overwhelming them in an instant, we cannot refrain from acknowledging and admiring the sagacity of his genius, which first discovered and despised this illusion.

But Orme explained Dupleix's failure by putting forward another reason besides lack of support from France. 'Military qualifications', he said, 'were wanting in his composition to carry effectually into execution projects which depended so much upon success of military operations.'

With such authority behind it the legend of Dupleix was accepted as history, and even British historians spread it. However, two modern French historians, Cultru and, even more exhaustively, Martineau, whose work on Dupleix is fundamental, have shown that he never put forward any plan to found a French empire in India, and that there is no evidence in his correspondence with the Company and other authorities in France that he had any such intention, although taking his political and military adventures at their face value both the French authorities at home and the English in India might have formed an impression that he had far-reaching and grandiose political aims.

It is, however, extremely difficult to ascertain from his correspondence what exactly was in his mind, because he was never frank and open with his masters. There was good reason for this. He knew that in principle the Company was completely against any involvement in the political affairs of India. The French Government was also opposed to it; it already had the heavy burden of defending Canada, and was not ready to accept additional responsibilities. So Dupleix knew that he would never obtain the consent of the home authorities to intervene in the quarrels of the native princes, not to speak of more ambitious ventures. Though the Company expressed its satisfaction at Dupleix's initial successes, and was not reluctant to profit by them, it never wavered in its basic policy – that it was in India only for commerce. From first to last, so far as it was consulted by Dupleix, it never went further.

In such a situation Dupleix sought to face the Company and the French Government with *faits accomplis,* and justify his ventures by their success. So he held out hopes, exaggerated successes, minimized failures, and never disclosed his full intentions, until the Company, informed by others and alarmed by reports, lost confidence in him and decided to recall him.

At last Dupleix decided to give a plausible exposition of his policy and measures within the commercial framework. This he did in a memorandum dated October 16 1753, when the failure of his policy was already evident and his recall had been decided upon. Receipt of the document in Paris did not make any difference to the Company's attitude.

What has to be noted is that this document did not contain any plan for establishing French political power in India; it only offered a justification of Dupleix's adventures in the light of a principle which he thought was the most effective one for maintaining and promoting the commercial interests of the Company in India. This basic principle was:

> No trading company, whichever it might be, could maintain itself on the sole profits of its commerce, and so it needed a fixed and assured revenue, especially when it had important establishments to maintain; that every company should avoid, as far as it was possible for it, exportation of gold and silver in specie.

Dupleix pointed out that the Portuguese were powerful only as long as they had such revenues, and the Dutch, who succeeded, owed their prosperity to the same policy pursued in Java, Sumatra and Ceylon. On the strength of this testimony Dupleix's military adventures could be described as commercial instead of being imperialistic, and ostensibly he was following Portuguese and Dutch precedents. As he himself put it:

> It is for this object that he had thought of winning a revenue for the Company. The events of the last war have served to disclose objects which had never been thought of before for the reason that no one could be persuaded of its feasibility. A chain of circumstances which it was difficult to foresee has nevertheless led to a goal which has been sought for a long time. All the opportunities which presented themselves were seized.

But in composing this document, the only one in which his policy is set down clearly and coherently, he was neither being perfectly frank, nor without mental reservations. It is hardly possible to assume that his involvement in the quarrels of the native princes had only a commercial motive. So it has to be assumed that in his memorandum he was trying to put his new political wine, which the authorities at home were bound to find heady, into the old and accepted bottle of commerce. That transformation was not, however, brought about by design. It had every appearance of taking place in an unforeseen chain of circumstances. None of the key events that formed the decisive stages of the unfolding of Dupleix's policy – i.e., the easy defeat and death of Anwar-ud-din Khan, the murder of Nasir Jang or the death of Muzafar Jang – could have been anticipated. But when these happened Dupleix was bold enough and ambitious enough, perhaps also enough of a gambler, to play for the highest stakes. And it has to be admitted that he played not only for himself but also for France.

But in doing so he passed the limits of prudence, and not only the limits prescribed to him by the Company. The intuitive *sens du possible* which makes for success in political as well as military enterprises was either absent in him, or was suppressed by his ambition, and the temptations offered to him, as well as his temperament, made him follow the siren's call. Even when a small stake was not fully secured he plunged for a higher one. For instance, when after the death of Nasir Jang the hold on the Carnatic had to be consolidated by eliminating Muhammad Ali from Trichinopoly, he most imprudently sent Bussy to Hyderabad, divided the French forces, and also removed the most able French commander from the most decisive theatre of operations. To him control of the Deccan and the subadarship of the whole of south India seemed so glittering a prize that he thought of the task in the Carnatic as one of merely tying the loose ends.

The gambler's spirit seized him again when Bussy was just established at Hyderabad. He thought he would send an expedition to Bengal, overthrow Alivardi Khan, and put Salabat Jang in his place. The Company, when it learned of the project, expressly forbade it. It asked Dupleix not to give any help whatever to Salabat Jang to that end and observed: 'The Company fears that so audacious a policy will create an implacable hatred against us without any gain, and our establishments in the Ganges basin will be its victim.'

Dupleix does not seem to have formed a clear conception of the European background of the French interest in India and did not realize that he could neither formulate nor control the grand strategy on which the success of his local adventures depended. He never took into account the relative naval power of England and France, which was bound to be the decisive factor for his policies, nor did he realize that the real opposition was not going to be local but would come from the centre of British power, London. Even in respect of the local situation he forgot that gains in the Deccan, a hinterland, would remain virtually useless unless it was based on the control of the coastal region of the Carnatic, through which alone he could maintain his hold on the interior. In a situation that demanded awareness of the sea, he acted like a landlubber.

In his memorandum of October 1753 he took a complacent view of the rivalry of other European powers. He declared that France need not fear the jealousy of other nations, and quoted the proverb that it was better to excite envy than pity. Other nations, he said, do not consider that they have to worry over French jealousy when they wish to extend their commerce, and a nation should not remain merely the spectator of the progress of other nations: she should disregard both jealousy from the outside and indifference within the country. He even reckoned on the decline of the British interest in India. 'Il faut, absolument,' he wrote, 'que sa decadence s'annonce; sa conduite dans l'Inde depuis la paix n'en laisse aucun doute.'

It is irrelevant to blame the French company for not supporting Dupleix in ventures of which they disapproved, and whose end they saw with perfect clarity even when Dupleix tried to mislead them. They were perfectly aware of the goal towards which his adventures were directed – not by any conscious intention but by the logic of facts – and would have none of it. Evidence on the opposition between their views and those of Dupleix is decisive. In fact, the issues were more clearly defined in the letters and memoranda of the French authorities at home than they were in the expositions by Dupleix. Only a few of their clear-sighted observations will be quoted here.

Even in January 1751, when only reports of operations against Tanjore had reached the Company in Paris, St-Priest, who was the royal commissioner with the Company, wrote a memorandum which he proposed to send to Dupleix. It is not known whether it was actually sent. But in any case, St-Priest wrote as follows about the war with Tanjore: 'It is not befitting that, after its success, the enterprise should be condemned; but at least it is permissible to say that this war should have its limits and these are set by the interests of the Company.' About the engagement with Chanda Sahib he observed: 'We are not, thank God, the principal parties, but only auxiliaries.' He added that the Company could remain allied with Chanda, but should not support the quarrels of Muzafar Jang, and then concluded: 'Let us be satisfied with the first step; let us not think at all of aggrandizing ourselves, and become great holders of territory – Tenons-nous en à être de grands commerçants,' because, as he saw it, 'Nothing is more opposed to commerce than war.'

Later in the same year Delaïtre, one of the directors of the French company, gave expression to the doubts and anxieties of the Company even more emphatically in a letter to Marchault, the Comptroller-General of Finance. He said that one could envisage the role of the Company in India under two systems: the first was that of peace and tranquillity, in which it would restrict itself to its old possessions or at all events to additions that could be obtained with the good will of the native princes; the other system was of domination and aggrandizement. If the last system was to be followed, he observed, Dupleix ought to be in charge, but for success in it the effort would have to be sustained by sending considerable numbers of ships and men, and a considerable quantity of money, from home for many years, and it would entail the risk of a war in Europe.

If, on the other hand, the first system was to be followed, someone other than Dupleix should be put in charge of Indian affairs. He gave the reason:

> Can anybody expect that M. Dupleix will abandon his domineering and insubordinate character which he has assumed everywhere – that after being absolute master since he had become governor, he would submit to what will be thought proper to prescribe to him, and adopt principles other than those on which he has acted since he has been in his post, and with which he is intoxicated?

Then he added: 'Enfin la Compagnie ne peut avoir la paix dans l'Inde qu'enne se melánt point des affaires des Maures. M. Dupleix a pris à cet egard de trop grands engagements pour pouvoir l'espérer de lui.'

In their official letter written on February 1 1752 the Company told Dupleix: 'It is time that the extent of our concessions in India were limited. The Company fears all increase of territory, its object is not to become a territorial power.'

Within a few months even more explicit a letter was written by Silhouette, who had become the Royal Commissioner with the Company, to Dupleix. He informed him that the ministry and the public in France were waiting for peace with impatience, and feared acquisitions that could involve the nation in wars with the Indian princes. Then he said:

> Truthfulness and frankness which I profess compels me not to conceal from you that any system which will depart from these views of neutrality will not have the approbation of the King, the Minister, and the public. Nobody wishes to become a political power; what is wished for is a small number of establishments, in

order to help and protect commerce; no victories, no conquests at all – plenty of merchandise and some increase of dividends.

Nothing could be clearer or more deliberate. It will be seen that the policy of the Company was the exact opposite of Dupleix's, and he had not obtained the successes that alone could have reconciled his masters to it. But that was inevitable. The Company was more realistic about the position of France in the world *vis-à-vis* England than was Dupleix. It should not be forgotten that England was not reconciled to French colonial expansion until France ceased to be a competitor for the hegemony of the world. One is tempted to think that Dupleix himself realized that he had failed when he decided to hand over authority to Godeheu. Some historians stated that had Dupleix's departure been put off by a few months the Company would perhaps have relented after receiving his memorandum of October 1753, and kept him in India. But as Alfred Martineau says: 'The *mea culpa* of the Company is a legend which does not rest on any foundation.' For some years Dupleix's adherents in India hoped for his return, but by 1758 these hopes faded away.

So, on the main question – whether Dupleix in any sense can be regarded as the precursor of the founders of the British Empire in India – one might say that this too is a legend. To see him as such is to impose a teleology on his adventures retrospectively, in the light of the British Empire. But certainly he showed the way by two means: first, he made the idea of involvement in the affairs of the Indian princes familiar, and also showed that the involvement could result in reducing these princes to the status of protégés. But the English did not intervene in these affairs in imitation of Dupleix. At first they intervened on their own initiative in Tanjore, and if they also intervened afterwards that was only to counteract Dupleix. As to imperialistic aims, Dupleix cannot be said to have had any such object except as an unanalysed emotional gravitation set in movement by his character and temperament. The English had none at all. Their aim in India was to safeguard their commerce by checking the French. It might be described as a commercial version of the American policy of our times to defend the 'Free World'.

Attitude towards Indians

In respect of two by-products of British rule in India, however, Dupleix can be regarded as the precursor. These are, first, the attitude of the founders of the Empire and their successors towards the Indian ruling order and the Indian people; and secondly the monetary gain of the founders. I shall deal with the first at this point. Dupleix in particular, and the French in general, were the teachers of the English in regard to what was finally to become the normal British estimate of the Indian character and the standardized attitude towards the Indian princes. The formulation of the view was a quick process.

Before the war of the Austrian succession, which brought the two companies in political touch with the Indian princes, both the French and the English had a very superficial knowledge of their character and behaviour. This war began the acquaintance, and Dupleix's war carried it much further. The resulting attitude was an illustration of the old saying that familiarity breeds contempt. But the really remarkable thing is that the growth of the contempt was very quick.

The loss of the old awe, the appearance of the contempt, and alongside this the development of confidence in dealing with the princes, are strikingly illustrated in a letter that Bussy wrote, apparently in 1754, from the Deccan. The relevant passage in it ran as follows:

> In order to appraise the present position of the French nation in India correctly it is necessary to recall those humiliating times when the French were compelled for the promotion of their commerce to go diffidently with their presents and their homage to the little village chiefs whom today we admit to our durbars only when our interests require it. I am not speaking of very far off times, it is only six years since the change began to come about. Then the Nawab of Arcot, quite the petty chief that he was in comparison with the Subadar of the Deccan – being only his revenue farmer – treated us as a sovereign does his subjects. In writing to our Governors he adopted a tone which was very humiliating to the French nation. We appeared before him only as suppliants and were always charged with presents which he expected as tribute. If any of his lower officials approached Pondichery deputations were sent out to receive him at a distance with tokens of high consideration. In short, whoever claimed to have been sent on his behalf was sure of being feared, respected, and loaded with presents from us. It was necessary, so it was argued, that everything should be done so as not to irritate these petty tyrants, whose displeasure could seriously harm our commerce. It was unheard of in those days that a Subadar of the Deccan should so lower his pride as to write to a Commandant General of the French. When Nizam-ul-Mulk, father of the present

reigning Nawab, came down to the province of Arcot to recover the town of Trichinopoly from the Marathas, all European nations hastened to show him marks of their submission and did everything to gain his goodwill. Did he write to any of those whom they represented? Certainly not. He did not even condescend to cast a glance at the rich presents which were placed with respect at his feet. What were the limits of the establishments of the Company before the expedition which is occupying me for four years? Pondichery, Karaikal, Chandernagore comprised almost all their extent. Could these limits be passed without stooping low and making presents in order to obtain permission from the Fauzdars or the Revenue-farmers of the country?

Bussy as the protector of Salabat Jang, son of the same Nizam-ul-Mulk, was not likely to overlook the change in the relative position of the two sides. Salabat was not, however, wholly reconciled to his dependent position, and was intriguing to reassert himself. So on September 22 1753 Bussy wrote to him: 'If today you are the Subadar of the Deccan it is to me that you owe it.' He then recalled how he had saved Salabat and added, referring to his attempts to assert himself:

> Apart from the frankness that you see in me I have the right to speak to you as I am doing, because all Deccan knows that I call you my son, and that you also treat me as your father. How does it happen that you do not speak in the same language to me as you did formerly? Who could have put these ideas in your head? . . . I hope you will recover from the blindness which can only lead to your ruin.

In fact, the subjection of the Subadar of the Deccan to Europeans had become irrevocable. When the French protection came to an end he passed under that of the English.

Of course, before finally accepting this position the ruler of Hyderabad and his court jibbed, and resorted to intrigues and double-dealing of every kind. Faced with all this Bussy enunciated his policy in very forthright language. He said in a letter written on July 22 1753: 'Among a people as doublefaced as are those with whom we have to deal, to show only straightforwardness and probity is, to my thinking, only to be their dupe, and we shall inevitably be that if we do not conform to the usages of the country.' Thus, with reference to a question that had arisen about whom to prefer between two claimants to some territory subordinate to the Subadar of the Deccan, Bussy wrote breezily: 'It is to our interest that these men should not come to an understanding. About all this I shall say with Hannon: "Parmi ce peuple faux, à qui garder ma foi? C'est aux événements à disposer de moi."'

The French, and following them the English, very soon discovered that the native princes understood only one language: that of force. If at any time any European did not command it – and very little of it was actually needed – only two alternatives, duplicity or defeat, would be left to him. Usually, the companies had enough of it to intimidate or crush their opponents. On the other hand, if at any time the Indian princes got an impression that they were not strong enough they would show an egregious insolence. This in itself cannot be condemned. But they never had the courage of their insolence. In the briefest time they passed from insolence to abject cringing. They excused themselves and submitted without any self-respect.

Nobody realized this in all its aspects more clearly than Dupleix, and throughout he was very outspoken on the subject, even more so than Bussy, to whom he wrote on August 22, 1752:

> The Asiatic, once he is taken up with an idea, acts on it without the least forethought, but he is also disconcerted more easily and can no more see what remedy to apply to the situation which his poor mental capacity has not allowed him to foresee. You know this scum [*canaille*] better than I do, and you saw the fright they were in before the beggarly Marathas. How grand it would be, my dear Bussy, to see you, after the reinforcements have reached you, laying down the law to these people, accursed of God.

From Dupleix downwards all French officers formed the worst possible opinion of the intellectual capacity and character of the Indian princes, as well as of Indians in general. For instance, the French Commander La Touche, who was helping Chanda Sahib and Muzafar Jang at Tanjore when they fled in panic at the news of Nasir Jang's coming down to the Carnatic, wrote on March 11 1750 to Dupleix: 'They were saved because we were there to rescue them. Otherwise, they would have been dead the day they heard that Nasir Jang had come through the passes. Judge their courage.'

Dupleix's judgements were even more scathing and contemptuous. About Chanda Sahib he wrote: 'Though more liberal and generous than other Indians, he is of the same character as all the Moors [the French term for the Indian Muslims], who, as you must be finding every day, are the greatest villains and the worst poltroons.' Of a notable at the court of Hyderabad he remarked: 'Sayyid Lashkar Khan is a very honest man, but an honest man among the Moors is only a rogue elsewhere. They are all possessed by avarice, and they have around them a band of rascals who always prompt a thousand chimeras and a thousand wicked calculations into them, so that one can never count on their constancy in being friendly.' Of yet another Muslim noble he wrote to Bussy: 'Beware of Shah Nawaz Khan as of others. You have greater experience than others of how little reliance one can place on the oaths and promises of these people. Your presence alone can make them carry these out.'

In his general judgements Dupleix was not less forthright, and some of his observations must be quoted. 'Honour is never a principle which governs the actions of Orientals.' 'None greater cheats than all the Asiatics; the more you cultivate them the more you learn of their badness.' 'What deceit is in the minds of these people! And it is a misfortune to be there with them.' 'Viziam Raja is Indian and nice – two adjectives which have always behind them deceit and falsehood.' 'All the Moors are rogues; so do not be surprised at what you hear them say, and at the same time there are none more cowardly.' 'Ingratitude is a vice which is almost natural in Asiatics, and above all in the Moors.' 'Be convinced, once and for all, that anybody who is black is a rogue; only, more or less.' 'All the Amuldars are black; that is saying all. Do not stop to notice all their lies. You will never have done with it.'

Dupleix's opinion of the intellectual capacity and energy of the Indians was also low. 'These people', he wrote, 'like all Asiatics think only from day to day and can never foresee anything of the future.' 'The Moors cannot foresee anything and are wholly absorbed in the present, and their reflexion comes afterwards.' 'Energy and exactitude are not common virtues in the Moors.' Dupleix's final advice to his subordinates was to have patience: 'You ought to provide yourself above all with patience among a people with whose ways you have not become familiar.' 'I see with pleasure that you are drawing on large funds of patience, and that is a virtue which is almost indispensable in this country.'

Let us turn now to the English attitude. As yet the English had not become king-makers; they were defending much smaller interests, and were less dependent on the Indian princes. Relying mostly on their own strength, which was adequate for their limited objectives, they had less reason than the French to feel bitter about the Indian princes. Even so their appraisal was not favourable, and the unfavourable first impressions grew until they crystallized into a set of codified axioms for dealing with Indians. This process began with their conquest of Bengal when they underwent the same kind of experience which Bussy had had in the Deccan.

The English, too, were under no illusions about the dependability of the Indian princes. For instance, in his history, published in 1763, Orme wrote:

> The governments of Indostan have no idea of national honour in the conduct of their politics; and as soon as they think the party with whom they are engaged is reduced to great distress, they shift, without hesitation, their alliance to the opposite side, making immediate advantage the only rule of their action.

Long before writing his history Orme had written a sketch giving 'a general idea of the government and people of Indostan'. It was composed in Calcutta in 1752 and revised in 1753. In it are to be found general remarks about the Indian princes, and there is a special chapter on the dissimulation of the Moorish princes and nobles. These give an idea of the impression the English were forming of the princes and peoples of India before they acquired any political power. Some of the judgements have to be quoted. On the Muslim princes Orme wrote:

> A domineering insolence towards all who are in subjection to them, ungovernable wilfulness, inhumanity, cruelty, murders, and assassinations, deliberated with the same calmness and subtlety as the rest of their politics, an insensibility to remorse for these crimes, which are scarcely considered otherwise than as necessary accidents in the course of life, sensual excesses which revolt against nature, unbounded thirst of power, and an expaciousness of wealth equal to the extravagance of his propensities and vices – this is the character of an Indian Moor, who is of consequence sufficient to have any character at all.

In fairness Orme singled out one or two exceptions, and he also emphasized that the Muslim princes and nobles observe the external forms of politeness meticulously. But he was distrustful of this, and gave his reasons:

> The politeness of other nations may have its rise from a natural ease and happiness of temper, a point of honour, the idea a man conveys

of himself by the respect he shows to others; but the decorum with which the common ceremonies and occurrences of life are conducted in Indostan, is derived from the constant idea of subordination, joined to a constant habit of the deepest disguise and dissimulation of the heart. In Indostan every man may literally be said to be the maker of his own fortune. Great talents, unawed by scruples of conscience, seldom fail of success: from hence all persons of distinction are seen running in the same course. The perseverance necessary to attain his end, teaches every man to bear and forbear contrary to the common instincts of human nature: hence arises their politeness. ... Let us carry these reflections a little farther. The general competition has put an end to mutual confidence; a sensibility capable of discerning everything, is soon taught a disguise capable of concealing everything. Where morality has no check upon ambition, it must form the blackest resolutions; and the dissimulation necessary to carry these into execution, will, amongst a people circumstanced as I have described them, be carried to excesses, which different manners and better morals will scarcely imagine human nature to be capable of.

Orme gave some examples, and observed that he could not 'ask credit for the multiplicity of facts of this nature' from his countrymen. Then he concluded his description of the mores of the Muslim princes with a sort of doxology: 'How grateful, how noble are the reflections inspired by such a retrospect, in favour of the cause of Christianity, and in favour of the cause of Liberty.' It was turning the moralizing of Montesquieu's *Lettres Persanes*, which was in favour of the Oriental, inside out.

Describing the Hindu princes, Orme said that they were not so violent as the Muslims, but they had their special badness. As he put it: 'It is a remark warranted by constant observation that wherever the government is administered by Gentoos, the people are subject to more and severer oppression than when ruled by the Moors.' He added: 'I have imputed this to intelligent Gentoos, who have confessed the justice of the accusation, and have not scrupled to give their opinions concerning it.'

Orme's explanation is that the Hindus when in power were less given than Muslims to luxurious living, ostentation and debauchery which enfeebled them, and were therefore more capable of giving continuous attention to affairs. A contemporary English writer describing the life of the Muslim princes said that when they were not at war they spent their time in luxurious indolence. 'As they sit for the most part (when they are not with their women) upon their sofas, smoking, and amusing themselves with their jewels, taking coffee or sweetmeats, seeing their quails fight, or such pastimes, nothing surprises them so much as to see a European walk about a room; and none but their very young people ever ride for amusement or exercise only.'

The Hindu prince, on the contrary, wrote Orme, 'retains in his durbar the same spirit which actuates him if keeping a shop.' Their dominant passion, Orme said, was avarice, and all their wiles, address, cunning and perseverance, of which they are such exquisite masters, were exerted to the utmost in fulfilling the dictates of this vice. Their religion, Orme explained, freed them from remorse over crimes; for whilst they were harassing and plundering their people by the most cruel oppressions they were making peace with the gods by denying nothing to the priests.

Orme gave a typical example of repentance and expiation by a Hindu prince, the Raja of Travancore. He was a cruel tyrant, but was suddenly seized with remorse from fear of divine retribution. So he consulted his Brahmin priests. They said that in order to be absolved from his sins he must be reborn, and be reborn out of the womb of a cow. To enable him to do that a golden cow was made, and the king was put inside it for some days. When the symbolic period had passed he was ceremonially brought out from the belly of the golden cow as a newborn and sinless man, and the golden cow itself was cut up to be distributed among the priests.

Now, the question inevitably arises whether these opinions set down by observant and acute Europeans were unfounded or unjust. This question has to be faced if the actions of the men who founded the Empire in India, for which they were attacked, is to be seen in their historical perspective. It has also to be taken up because the disparagement of the Indian character, which became a fixation with the British, stemmed from the opinions formed through these early contacts.

It is usual to dismiss this appraisal in retrospect as due to prejudice or racial arrogance. But no explanation has ever been offered for the appearance of these *a priori*. As late as the eighteenth century, if there were any preconceptions regarding India they were all favourable. India was the country of spiritual wisdom, of material splendour, of gentleness of manners and benevolent dispositions. For so thoroughgoing a revolution of opinion to have taken place as soon as direct contact was established there must have been a great shock from the first direct contact.

Furthermore, it should be kept in mind that the new attitude was shaped by empirical experience and the aims of the appraisal were severely practical. The men who formulated the opinions were neither moralists, nor theorists, nor idealists. They had come from eighteenth-century Europe, which had enough cynical immorality of its own, and they were cynical men. They had to deal with Indians in connection with political and commercial affairs. They had no interest in representing the Indian character as what it was not, for the success of their transactions with the princes and people of the country depended on the correctness of their estimate and knowledge. Dupleix and Bussy, more particularly, acquired a great reputation for their deep insight into the Indian character and their skill in dealing with those who mattered. The respect in which they were held was also due to this very clear-sightedness, for Indians do not admire those they dupe.

Thus, of these opinions about Indians one might say what is always said of scientific hypotheses: that, if they work, they have to be accepted as sound. There can be no doubt that they worked. If in that age and its peculiar circumstances there had been any belief in the goodness of the Indian princes, or any faith in the old formula *ex oriente lux*, the British withdrawal from India would have taken place in 1756, after the Black Hole, instead of in 1947.

However, there is one very important reservation to bear in mind, for without it the opinions would amount to an indictment of a whole people, and as such remain unacceptable. The important fact is that these views were not estimates of the character of the Indian people as a whole, but only of the ruling order, and of those others with whom the Europeans came into contact. In those days only Indians of the adventurer type, who wanted to exploit the Europeans in one way or another for worldly advantages, would care to cultivate them. So the intercourse between these two sides could not be anything better than a battle of wits. No European of those days had any opportunity of knowing the general masses of the Indian people, except as people who were suffering from oppression or fleeing from it.

The political moralists in England who denounced and even persecuted the founders of the Empire could not make this distinction. They were also the victims of another kind of imposition. Their moral indignation was usually kindled by the English adventurers who had been the unsuccessful rivals of the founders, or merely envious. In regard to facts, they were briefed by the same set of interested men. Of course, the political moralists took their stand on abstract principles, but the application of these principles had the paradoxical effect of favouring the men who neither professed nor practised them. So their condemnation of the founders for oppressing the Indian princes or dealing high-handedly with them had a disquieting aspect: it was in effect a defence of the most relentless oppressors of the Indian people.

Monetary Gains
Now the second aspect of Dupleix's legacy to the empire-builders, which concerned their monetary gains, has to be considered. Attacks on Clive in his later life were mainly on this score. These attacks, even when their real inspiration was personal enmity, were made in the light of the moral conventions about money-making – more especially by politicians and soldiers – current in England in those times. But money-making by the founders of the Empire has also to be seen in the light of the Indian conventions and practices of the period.

With respect to all methods of money-making, fair or foul, England and India stood at opposite poles. To consider corruption alone, there was in England a recognized and accepted form of it – which was to use money to gain or keep political power and position; in India, on the contrary, it lay in using political power for personal monetary gain. Far from being regarded as corruption, monetary gain from political position was universally regarded in India as the main use of political power. Statecraft had evolved in such a manner that for a long time politics, strictly so-called, had been thought of in terms of war against other kings or one's own king for the purpose of personal aggrandizement; and administration was the means of making money. To have political power and not to use it for making money was inconceivable in India. There was, even in the eighteenth century, a Muslim ruler who left no personal property of any magnitude when he died. But he was the only one. In a *Memoire instructif sur l'état politique des Maures et des Francais dans le Decan et sur leurs interêts reciproques*, which Bussy sent to Dupleix on July 10 1753, he wrote:

Homme de la patrie et de la nation, tous ces noms si sacrés chez tous les peuples ne sone rien parmi les Maures au prix de l'interêt particulier et des espérances d'un avantage personel. Aussi toutes ces grandes idées d'honneur de nation, d'interêt public qui lient tous les membres d'un état à son souverain et les arment pour la cause commune, sont des chimères dans ce pays, ou chaque particulier ne pense qu' à soi, ne cherche qu'à tirer parti des troubles et des revolutions qui arrivent.*

Indeed, this tradition is so deep rooted in India that it has reasserted itself after the withdrawal of the British from India – and this is well known to every observer of current Indian politics.

That public and private finance are distinct was a notion introduced into India for the first time by the two European trading companies, because they were public corporations and had to keep their corporate acquisitions separate from the private earnings of their employees. In Indian politics this distinction was not made because political position was wholly personal.

Money in Indian politics came either from plunder after a military victory, when it was intermittent, or steadily from land revenue and other levies. The regular taxes were assigned to a hierarchy of tenants or revenue-farmers of the rulers, and were extorted from the peasants, merchants and craftsmen without any regard for their welfare. If a ruler did not practise extortion, it was from enlightened self-interest. But such rulers were always exceptions. The general practice was to make hay while the sun shone. The rulers could never be sure when they would be ousted by a rival, and they could not think of long-term interests. So they became extortionate, and there was always a game of hide-and-seek between the exploiters and the exploited.

The Mogul military and civil administration was based on usufructuary grants of revenues and all kinds of taxes and levies to the subordinate governors, and there was an immense hierarchy of beneficiaries at different levels. At the highest level

---

*Translation: 'A patriot and servant of the nation – all these names so sacred among all peoples, are nothing to the Moors at the cost of private interest and hope of any personal advantage. So also all those grand ideas of honour of the nation, of public interest, which bind all the members of a state to their sovereign and fortify them for the common cause are chimeras in this country, in which each individual thinks only about himself, and only seeks to turn to his advantage the troubles and the revolutions which make their appearance.'

under the Emperor were the subadars, or provincial governors, and as long as they paid their quota of revenue, furnished military contingents and acknowledged the authority of their suzerain they were left free to make as much profit from their fiefs as possible. The relationship was repeated at every stage of the devolution of revenue and tax collection.

This pattern of money-making naturally made its impact on the servants of the European companies. But very soon the companies separated the gains of the companies from those of their employees. This separation was working satisfactorily in the commercial sphere when the European intervention in Indian politics began, but in the political sphere the distinction could not be introduced easily. At the initial stages of the intervention the agents of both the companies began to fall in line with the customs in India, instead of introducing European standards into the financial side of political activity. They felt that, in so far as they were participating in native politics, they were doing nothing wrong by acquiring money in the native manner through politics. They adopted two standards, one for commerce and the other for politics.

Nobody showed this dichotomy more, with a decided preference for the political side and therefore also for private interest, than Dupleix. If he was disposed to launch on exploratory political adventures he was not less disposed to look upon them as financial speculation on the part of himself and his subordinates. Some information about his previous financial enterprises and gains has already been given. But after he began to intervene in Indian politics these acquired a new character, and what he did is relevant to any judgement on what Clive and other British agents did.

It has been shown how Dupleix's decision to help Chanda Sahib was motivated by financial considerations for the French company. In fact, he was only providing Chanda with mercenaries with a view to recouping the expenditure on the soldiers, and neither overtly nor covertly did he have any political motive at that stage. Moreover, as a bid for money it was sheer speculation, for its recovery was contingent on Chanda's victory. Even after his victory he could not pay all the money due to the French company. But the scramble for personal gain began at once.

The battle of Ambur was fought on August 1 1749. On August 4 Dupleix wrote to his brother-in-law, d'Auteil, who was in command of the French forces: 'I am writing to the son of Chanda Sahib about a share in the plunder which should fall to our brave soldiers. I am also writing to him that it seems proper to me that he should send me my share of the elephants, horses, etc., and of everything he has captured from the enemy.'

The next day he wrote to say that d'Auteil was not to surrender the two important prisoners he had taken (one being a son of Anwar-ud-din) until satisfied about the share in the ransom, and cautioned him further: 'Take the utmost precautions in this matter, so as not to be the dupe of these people.' Whenever or wherever there were opportunities to make money, he pointed them out to his friends.

There was, however, no big plunder for some time. But the treacherous killing of Nasir Jang in December 1750 provided the next windfall. An immense treasure amounting to twenty-five million livres (in French money) in specie and fifty million in jewellery and precious stones was found in Nasir Jang's camp. The jewellery was handed to Muzafar Jang as his family possession. Of the cash, half went to the three Pathan chiefs who had betrayed Nasir Jang. Of the other half, two-thirds were given to Dupleix personally, and one-third was taken by Muzafar Jang. But Dupleix gave back his share to Muzafar, who distributed Rs400,000 (about one million livres) to the French officers. Some of it went to Dupleix.

Even before the reports of these immense private fortunes had reached Paris, the Company had set its face against such acquisitions by its servants. The occasion for laying down a rule for personal jaghirs and presents of money to them arose in connection with certain grants to Governor Dumas, the predecessor of Dupleix. A royal decree of June 6 1750 forbade all employees of the Company to receive gifts of any kind from foreign princes unless these were at once transferred to the Company. If this was not voluntarily done the transfer was to take place *ipso facto* and those who contravened the order were to be punished.

When Dupleix and others received their jaghirs and presents after the death of Nasir Jang this order had not reached India. The Company was disposed to be lenient at first. But in February 1752, it expressly reminded Dupleix of the decree, and Dupleix reacted very sharply. He wrote on February 16 1753:

> You have taken exception to the recompense given by Muzafar Jang to so many brave men and also to some of your principal employees, and you cite the laws of the kingdom. Not satisfied with what you

could indicate on the subject to the Council and myself, you have procured a decree from the King for the appropriation of the grants of revenue and perhaps even of the Jaghirs if that were possible. It is easy to see from the precautions you have taken on this subject that there is no other object but to appropriate to yourselves these lands and pensions without caring about the justice or injustice of the proceedings adopted in respect of them, and on the pretext that the laws of the kingdom forbid the subjects of the King to become pensioners of a foreign prince. The intention was to appropriate everything for the Company, and so the King was told what one intended that he should be told.

Naturally, the Company replied to this letter with great severity. But Dupleix and his associates regarded the acquisitions as legitimate, and any attempt to claim these for the Company as expropriation. But the question of Dupleix's personal income became bound up with the expenditure on the war in India, for which he was spending both his own and the Company's money. So upon his arrival at Pondichery Godeheu demanded an account of all moneys received and spent by Dupleix which were not entered in the Company's books from his agent. This agent, named Pariapoullé, refused to render them to anybody but Dupleix. Both he and Dupleix maintained that the income and expenditure from these sources were Dupleix's private affair. Godeheu had Pariapoullé arrested, and then Dupleix sent him a financial statement in which he showed the combined receipts of the Company and himself in his private capacity as 7,931,088 livres (Rs3,304,620), and the expenditure on all accounts as 7,931,088 livres (Rs3,271,965). This only covered the period from July 10 1752 to June 30 1754. Dupleix asked Godeheu to accept and endorse the statement, which the latter refused to do. He wanted to examine the original vouchers.

Nearly half the receipts thus shown were claimed by Dupleix as personal on the ground that he was the Nawab of the Carnatic under the Subadar of the Deccan. But Godeheu commented on Dupleix's claim to be independent of the Company as nawab, with devastating logic. On August 15 he wrote in his journal:

> It is indeed true that M. Dupleix regards himself as Nawab of the Carnatic. But at present I ought to be that, being Governor of Pondichery. Or, if M. Dupleix is the Nawab it would follow that a foreign power is in conflict with the Government of France. It is then as Nawab of Arcot and not as Governor of Pondichery that M.

Dupleix has been making war. If he has done that, then the Company is not responsible at all for the sums advanced to carry on the war; but if it is as Governor of Pondichery he has done that I must inquire into the sums spent on the war, for the position of Nawab ought to be combined with that of the Governor. It only remains to see whether it suits the Company that a Governor shall be Nawab or whether there shall be a French Nawab vis-à-vis the Governor of Pondichery.

In the next move Dupleix presented a new account on September 22 1754, covering the period from October 17 1749 to August 1 1754. In this he showed that he had received only 6,033,735 livres (Rs2,514,064) on the Company's account, and spent 13,536,735 livres (Rs5,648,621), so that the amount due to himself from the Company was 7,522,937 livres. Godeheu refused to accept this also. Finally, Dupleix slightly reduced his claim, and made it 7,126,927 livres. Litigation to recover this sum from the company was carried on even after the death of Dupleix (1763) by his heirs.

In spite of this huge expenditure on the war from what he claimed to be his personal money, Dupleix did not return to France a financially ruined man. He was able to leave India with personal effects valued at nearly three million livres, of which two million were in the form of jewellery and precious stones. When his belongings were loaded on to his ship there were in all 181 packages; in this ship, as part of his acquisitions, Dupleix took two camels, two asses, eight cats, thirteen cages of canaries and other birds, two parrots, one cockatoo and five monkeys. This precedent was followed by Clive, who even had elephants and very rare animals brought over to give as presents.

Thirteen more cases of Dupleix's were sent by another ship, and they comprised one case of tea, porcelain, pickles, etc.; one case of textiles, chinese fans and cotton thread; one case of tea services and dresses, one case of maps and plans, two cases of books, one trunk of cloths, handkerchiefs, etc., one case of handkerchiefs alone, one case of miscellaneous articles, one case of engravings and another of minor articles. The majority of these objects were sold by auction after Dupleix's death.

The spectacle of the wealth acquired by the French adventurers in India – Bussy's was also immense – was bound to create a sensation, if not a great scandal, in France. The *ancien régime* was still standing with its accepted conventions of making money by honest or dishonest means, and with its unquestioning obedience to the principle of remaining within the limits of opportunities offered by the station of life into which a man was born. In such a society neither the 'haves' nor the 'have-nots' were likely to be pleased with upstarts of the sort India was sending back to France.

In regard to acquisition of wealth, there is a basic difference between a society that is stable and one that is passing through rapid changes. The French people were to become quite used to upstarts of a more aggressive type and their wealth in the Napoleonic era. Although the unreconciled old nobility sneered at the wealth of Napoleon's mother or his marshals, even after the Restoration nobody thought any the worse of the upstarts of the previous decades: they became absorbed into the hierarchy.

In England the disapproval and scandalized shock were bound to be much more pronounced, because England did not go through any political or social revolution. In that period wealth in England was very largely the inherited privilege of the landed aristocracy, whose members disapproved of open pursuit of money even amongst themselves when it was not in the form of the pursuit of heiresses. The mercantile class with its norm of acquisitive methods was almost as conservative, and the industrial order had not as yet come into being. Thus to the entire established order in Britain, and in the eyes of all classes without reference to their wealth, the new rich from India were egregious and offensive parvenus.

The English Company's Policy
In giving all credit to Dupleix for being the forerunner and teacher of the English in certain matters, it should not be forgotten that British rule in India was established by a wholly different method and in different circumstances. It did not grow out of the process set going by Dupleix.

First, British rule was established in Bengal and spread to the rest of India from there. The war in the Carnatic was not the first chapter of its history, not even its prologue, though certainly the political and military experience gained in south India and the forces built up there to conduct the war with the French served to furnish the power to conquer Bengal. Nevertheless, after this initial contribution it was Calcutta that helped Madras, and not Madras Calcutta.

Secondly, the war in the Carnatic was primarily an Anglo-French conflict, in which the Indian princes were either proxies or pawns. On the contrary, in Bengal the English came into direct conflict with a Muslim prince who had occupied their settlement. The conquest of Bengal was thus the result of the direct employment of European military power against a native prince to recover and maintain an established commercial interest. Anglo-French rivalry was also there, but only as a minor feature.

Thirdly, neither the English influence over the Nawab of the Carnatic, nor the French influence over the Nizam in the Deccan can be compared with the new political status that the English attained in Bengal by overthrowing one nawab and installing another. Henceforward the Muslim ruler of Bengal had to be reconciled to the position of a puppet of the English, whatever his formal status; and if he showed any sign of aspiring after independence he was removed.

Thus the Carnatic must be regarded only as the stage on which the British acquired their experience of Indian affairs and their confidence in dealing with the Indian princes. But this confidence was not developed easily, only step by step. The French confidence was much quicker in growth, and sprang in full panoply out of the head of Dupleix. The gradual psychological transition of the English from timidity and opportunism to boldness and resolution has now to be described.

The character of the process comes out most vividly from the correspondence of the English at Madras with the native princes, which was carried on in the Persian language, the language of political and cultural intercourse throughout India in those days. In using this language the English not only fell in with the outward forms of the intercourse, but also with its spirit, and thus exhibited even a mental transformation. This is seen illustrated in the contemporary English translations of the letters from both sides, and would have been even more vividly seen if the Persian originals had been preserved.

Immediately after his victory over Anwar-ud-din Khan, Chanda Sahib gave the news to the Governor of Madras, saying: 'As you have been my old friend and well-wisher and still continue so, I thought it proper to write this joyful news to you.' The Governor at once replied:

> I must inform you that it was my constant prayer to the Almighty God to restore the Government of this province to the people of your

Cast as formerly and as it has pleased Him at present to hear my prayer and make you the Govr of the province I returned my thanks to Him and congratulate you on the same occasion and wish He may encrease your power and riches and destroy your enemies.

He also reminded Chanda Sahib of the mutual friendship between the English and his forefathers and hoped 'you'll look upon our Affairs in the same light as your own on all accounts and continue to write to me of your health and welfare'. With this letter he sent the usual present of some gold coins.

At the same time the Governor wrote a letter of condolence to Muhammad Ali:

It was an inexpressible grief and sorrow to me to hear of the death of your Father; as no one can resist the will of Divine providence and as all mankind must submit the same fate and as you are a Gentleman endowed with wisdom I hope you won't be griev'd. As God is gracious and merciful He will protect your Affairs. What can I say more?

After a few days Muhammad Ali asked for some guns, mortars and shells, together with some gunners so as to be able to defend Trichinopoly. The Governor at once agreed to this. Some time later Muhammad Ali wanted soldiers, and Madras agreed to this too. Both Muzafar Jang and Chanda Sahib came to know of it; they had, of course, learnt about the occupation of St Thomé. Chanda Sahib at once wrote complaining about seizure of the place, to which the Governor blandly replied: 'If such things are done, which I cannot yet believe, having no knowledge of it myself; it must be done by the King's forces under the command of General Boscawen whom I have no power over.' However, he promised to write to Boscawen and assured Chanda Sahib that 'for my part it is my desire to live in perfect friendship with you'.

Chanda Sahib was not impressed and replied: 'I know none of your King's people except yourself, nor have any business with them. In future you must answer this affair yourself.' The Governor only acknowledged this letter and repeated his previous statement that he had written to Boscawen.

Muzafar Jang was more imperious about the help to Muhammad Ali. After his accession to the subadarship of the Deccan he had been friendly and had asked the Governor to send him some velvet and broadcloth, an assortment of medicines and spices, and also ten bottles of brandy and six bottles of claret. But his tone later became different. He demanded that the soldiers sent to Muhammad Ali must be recalled, and added the following in his own hand to the formal letter: 'You did not do well in sending forces to the assistance of Muhammad Ali Khan. If you really sent them it will do no good to you as my vengeful army will march your way.'

The Governor did not reply, but began to incite Nasir Jang, the Subadar of the Deccan, to come down to the Carnatic. 'I must remind Your Excellency', he wrote, 'of the proverb which says that one must not neglect to punish an enemy tho' he may be weak.' After that the Governor explained the situation between England and France after the treaty of Aix-la-Chapelle:

> I think it necessary to inform Your Excellency about our affairs with the French that the English King in Europe is become conqueror and that the French King has desired a peace. Our ships of war which arrived hither fired against Pondichery 16,000 balls in one day both by sea and land but in the interim news of peace from England hindered us from taking the same town and the French were obliged to deliver up Madras to us. As Pondichery thus got clear from our hands, I suppose it will now fall into the hands of your brave army. I continue firm in a true regard and obedience to you.

This was a very one-sided account of the siege of Pondichery. But Nasir Jang came down, and for the time being the situation improved for the English. His death, however, brought about another change. Muzafar Jang, who had become subadar of the Deccan with the help of the French, wrote a threatening letter, first emphasizing his victory:

> It is impossible for me to express my thanks for the unbounded Mercy which it has pleased God to show me. I will praise him not once only, but a hundred, a thousand, nay a hundred thousand times for the extraordinary conquest he has given me, for by his assistance all the dust of troubles, which has been raised, is now laid by the waters of divine grace, and the air is made clean: praised be God all my adversaries are now destroyed, and I become sole ruler of the six Subahs under the Deccan country.

Then he made his demands:

> It was highly requisite for you to treat me with presents according to custom, in order to gain my good will. But you have not done it, which appears very strange to me considering your sincerity and obedience, and the understanding you are endowed with. However I now expect you to deliver back all the sea port towns and other places which you have been possessed of, during the time of the late

troubles ... and send me a satisfactory answer as soon as possible, if not I shall resolve upon a proper method to recover them.

To this was added in a different hand, assumed to be Muzafar Jang's own:

You should think it necessary to continue firm in the path of obedience which will gain you a good reward. On the contrary you meet with shame.

Madras did not take this seriously because Muzafar Jang was leaving for Hyderabad. On the way he was killed, and ceased to be a danger. The English went on helping Muhammad Ali, and the capture of Arcot by Clive wholly changed the aspect of affairs. After that the English, instead of obeying, dictated. Within days of the capture of Arcot the Governor of Madras wrote to the Raja of Mysore to remain on the side of Muhammad Ali in these words: 'As I have the greatest regard for the esteem of the Great Monarch [the Mogul Emperor] I shall continue to assist him [Muhammed Ali] to the utmost of my power. Do you the same and join him as soon as possible. Let me hear of your health.'

Hearing of some intrigues to make the Raja of Tanjore hostile to the English, the Governor wrote to him:

I have heard of certain people have lately made you great offers of friendship, I have heard of a snake that charms birds into his mouth and then devours them. I hope this won't be your case. But out of regard to the friendship I have for you I must tell you my opinion is that if the enemy should prove successful both yourself and the King of Mysore Country will be ruined. I can only add that you may depend on't the English will always be your friends.

The Raja of Tanjore had by this time fully realized whose star was rising and replied to this letter saying that the reference to the serpent was true, and explained that he had pretended friendship to the other side only to avoid molestation by their forces, but at the same time he had 'contrived some secret schemes against them'. 'As you are ingenious,' he added, 'I am certain that you are acquainted with state policy and that you know our above design. We aim at High Things.' Then he declared:

I need not be afraid of a Serpent while I have Garada* [meaning your honour] to protect me against injury. The Serpent can have no strength to hurt me, on the contrary will himself perish. My whole dependence is on you.

By that time Chanda Sahib had finally come to regard the English as his enemies, and had written a letter which did not have the usual politeness of expression. So, a week after the occupation of Arcot the Governor wrote to Chanda Sahib:

> I have receiv'd your letter which does not seem to be wrote in that fine style so peculiar to Musselmen.... My intention herein is the peace and good of the country. As to the Jageers granted to the English I shall keep them and oppose any that shall think fit to molest me. If you are an honest man and are in obedience to the Mogul desist from molesting Muhammad Ali and let him enjoy the districts of Trichinopoly and I shall not molest you in Arcot. By this means the people will be happy, the ground tilled, merchandize flourish and the Emperor receive his revenues. I have by my own Vakeel wrote to the Mogul that I am supporting his [Muhammad Ali's] interest and shall I doubt not receive a very very gracious answer.

The Pax Britannica was already in the offing under the name of the puppet Mogul's peace. Chanda was to perish soon, miserably, without the English commander intervening to save his life.

The stark fact was the psychological revolution by means of which the English became determined to defend their commercial interests in India against whomsoever threatened them. Their attitude could be defined in the words of the popular song which was sung more than a century and a quarter later:

> *We don't want to fight, yet by jingo if we do,*
> *We've got the ships, we've got the men,*
> *And got the money, too.*

The spirit of this song has been wholly misunderstood. It did not stand for what jingoism has since come to mean, that is, sabre-rattling and war-mongering. Its defiance was essentially defensive, the equivalent of the whoof with which a tiger wants to warn its enemy without any definite intention to charge. And if the whoof is heeded it never does. The song was a crude and illiterate version of the grander *'Le Dieu me l'a donné, gare à qui*

---

*Under the translated copy of the letter this explanation was given: 'The Garada is a kind of kite commonly called a Brahminy kite. Whenever a serpent sees him he loses strength and motion and sometimes dies in the instant. If the Garada perceives him he surely kills him with his beak.' This was, however, the popular notion of the Garada in the Tamil country. Actually, the Raja of Tanjore's reference was to Garada, the half-man, half-bird mount of Vishnu, the eternal enemy of all snakes.

la touche'. God, according to the English, had given them the right to trade in India and receive jaghirs, and if the French or the nawabs thought they could deprive them of that right both would have to take the consequences: the French would be driven out, the nawabs dethroned; and the English would not mind the nuisance of an empire in India.

War in India

The very first thing that has to be said about the foundation of the British Empire in India is that it was established by means of military power and military success. This would seem to be stressing the obvious if it were not remembered that as soon as modern nationalism made its appearance in India, under the impact of Western ideas, Indian nationalists sedulously spread the idea that the English overthrew the Muslim rulers and made themselves masters of the country by means of intrigues, trickery, cunning, bribery and the like, and never through any military superiority. Otherwise, the brave Muslim rulers could never have been overthrown.

Quite apart from contradicting such crudities, there is a case for stressing the role of military power in establishing British rule in India. Without it, the empire in India would never have come into existence, or been maintained. This was realized quite early in its history by the men who were creating it. I have found the role of military power very forcefully defined in a memorandum on military organization in India, preserved among the Strachey papers in the library of the India Office. The document is unsigned and undated, but internal evidence seems to indicate that it was written by Sir Eyre Coote and submitted to the authorities in London in 1771. The following passage occurs at the very beginning of the memorandum:

> **Fundamental Maxim**
> Before we enter further into this subject, we must lay down one fundamental maxim with regard to Indostan, which is, that as we acquired our influence and our possessions by force, it is by force we must maintain and preserve them, and that no neighbouring Subah, Nabob, or Rajah, will suffer us to remain in tranquillity except from fear and a thorough conviction that they cannot attempt to disturb us without danger to themselves.

This necessity had nothing to do with the fact that the British were foreigners, but arose from the very nature of politics in India, as it had been through the centuries both under the

Hindus and the Muslims, and the simple fact was that it was predatory.

But the application of military power in India was different from what it was in Europe, and its quality should never be judged by European standards. No one saw this more clearly than Alexis de Tocqueville when he was studying the phenomenon of the British Empire in India. In his notes and drafts he made some telling points: what the English did was nothing new – the Arabs, Afghans and Moguls had done it before them, as had the Portuguese and the French; it is always an advantage for a conqueror to come after others; India had always been a country most prepared for conquest and servitude; the conquerors never encountered a great nation but a multitude of small groups insufficiently united; it was not courage that was lacking in the Indian people, but the will to apply their courage to resist foreign invasion and tyranny; the natives were accustomed through the ages to see rulers of other races and religions dominating them; for the greater part the English did not have to fight any great nation in India, but only a foreign aristocracy.

Tocqueville was not less clear sighted about the role of generalship. In connection with Clive this question is important. The phrase 'heaven-born general', applied to him, has led both detractors and admirers to give a wholly unnecessary attention to the quality of his generalship. Actually, the standards by which generalship, that is, strategic and tactical ability, was judged in that age were wholly inapplicable to the wars between the English and the native powers in India. These wars were different from others in their scale and in the methods of waging them. Tocqueville wrote that the English victories were not due to the presence of great generals, and that, excluding the Duke of Wellington (who as Arthur Wellesley was in India for a short time), the British armies in India were commanded by officers of just ordinary merit. Then he made a very true remark: 'All this singularly diminishes the merit not only of the English but also of Alexander and of the Asiatic conquerors of India.' He added that something analogous to the conditions in the eighteenth century obviously lay behind the astonishing conquests of the men of the previous ages. In judging Clive, no question of military capacity in a professional sense should be raised at all, because it was not needed.

To make this clear some idea should be given of what warfare was like in India in that period. At first sight it did not seem easy to defeat the Indian armies. Tocqueville commented on this as well. He wrote: 'It could be seen that Clive himself, in spite of his audacity and perspicacity which were extreme, could not realize in advance how easy victory was. Many times he was seized with hesitations in the midst of his successes and tempted to retreat at the moment of seizing victory.' After writing this, Tocqueville made a note for himself: 'Re-read all that preceded the battle of Plassey.'

This fear of risk was due to the impression created by the immense number of men in the Indian armies. Modern historians have doubted the numbers given by ancient historians to the armies of the Persians which Alexander had to encounter. But there can be no doubt about the size of the armies of even minor Indian princes. Contemporary historians say that the army with which Nasir Jang came to the Carnatic in 1750 contained anything between 200,000 to 300,000 fighting men, and more like one million if all camp followers were included. They recorded that his camp had a perimeter of twenty miles.

The organization of these armies made these figures possible. Their effective combat strength was very much lower than the total. The main element was the cavalry, and each horseman had two servants, one for tending the horse and the other for foraging or cutting grass. The horsemen also took their families with them. The princes and their noblemen never took to the field without a train of women – wives and other female members of their families, and in addition there were the concubines, dancers and female entertainers of all kinds. All of them in their turn had their maidservants. After these came servants of all kinds, and among them the men who pitched the camps, *farashes,* were a very important element.

But these numbers reduced rather than increased the fighting capacity of the armies. Infantry was a minor part. It was made up by men assembled together without any regard to rank or file, and armed with swords, lances and bucklers, with a small number of matchlocks. These produced a very small amount of fire-power. But these numbers meant money for their commanders, as has been explained before. They received a fixed price for each man and paid out much less than this price.

It was the cavalry that was the main arm of these forces and the prince depended on it both for use and display. The Indian princes had a great respect for artillery, but could not employ it effectively. Their reliance was mainly on heavy pieces, which could not be moved or employed in the field easily. So the English and the French forces, with their lighter guns, marched round the artillery parks and put a shot or two among the train, at which the draught bullocks stampeded. Thus the Indian princes came to feel a great terror for European artillery, and later employed European gunners.

Strategy and tactics in any real sense of the terms did not exist. The fighting among the princes themselves was like rioting on a vast scale. As Orme put it, 'the rudiments of the military art in India can scarce be imagined but by those who have seen it'. The prince himself and his commanders led the soldiers into battle on elephants, which formed a very important part of the armies. This, however, made them very conspicuous targets, all the more so because if the soldiers lost sight of the commander on the elephant they concluded that he was killed and all was lost. Then they broke and fled. As a contemporary English historian wrote: 'these enormous beasts now seem to be brought into the field for no other end but to be a mark for our artillery.'

Superstitions of all kinds also made the effective use of armies difficult. The princes, Muslim or Hindu, would not move or fight without consulting astrologers about auspicious and inauspicious days, and this prevented their taking advantage of the opportunities of attack offered by an enemy. They also had great regard for omens. They looked for them, for example, from the wild animals which they kept, more especially from the great beasts of prey like tigers and lions: before engaging in battle the prince visited them, and if the beasts were seen to be dull and listless that was treated as a bad omen.

The habits of living also interfered with military enterprise. One habit was to eat a very large meal at night. This made the soldiers sleep so heavily that they would not attack at night and could also be easily surprised by a night attack. Here is a description and comment from a contemporary English writer who got his information from the English commanders in the early wars.

> At the close of the evening, every man eats an inconceivable quantity of rice, and many take after it some kind of soporific drugs; so that about midnight, the whole army is in a dead sleep: the consequence of these habits is obvious; and yet it would appear a strange proposition to an Eastern monarch, to endeavour to persuade him,

that the security of his throne depended upon the regulation of the meals of a common soldier: much less would he be prevailed on to restrain him in the use of that opium, which is to warm his blood for action, and animate his soul with heroism. It must fill the mind of an European soldier at once with compassion and contempt, to see a heap of these poor creatures, solely animated by a momentary intoxication, crowded into a breach, and both in their garb and impotent fury, resembling a mob of frantic women.

These armies had no morale; they were induced to fight only by the prospect of plunder, and were never inspired, as Orme said, by 'a real love to their country, or a real attachment to their prince – principles which are very rarely found to influence the people of Indostan'.

Indeed, after the first conflicts between the Indian princes and the European armies, these princes completely lost confidence in their capacity to resist Europeans. Tocqueville noted this as well and wrote: 'The princes of India themselves felt the impossibility of their being able to fight the armament of our civilization solely by themselves. Europeans could be expected to be defeated only with the help of Europeans – so said the brave and unfortunate Tipoo Sahib.' 'This prince', Tocqueville continued, 'had a troubled and confused mind, into which, however, there penetrated from time to time a ray of genius. He could never hope to defend himself except with the help of France. This idea had struck him, and it pursued him into his sleep.'*

Thus, in the course of Dupleix's war, both the English and the French became aware of the military inferiority of the Indian princes, and later experience only confirmed their opinion. They knew that, if provided with a minimum of forces, their commanders had nothing to fear from these princes and their armies. But at this stage the English had no idea of taking advantage of this weakness to establish their political power, no more indeed than had the French company. Their only object was to oppose the designs of Dupleix and make the French innocuous in India. To this end they were as ready to help an Indian prince as to oppose one, according to circumstances.

---

*Tipoo pondered over his dreams and attached a prophetic significance to them. He once dreamt that he was having an interview with a French leader who had disembarked in India with 12,000 soldiers. This was in 1799 when Bonaparte was in Egypt. One of the objects of the expedition was set down as helping Tipu Sultan.

Part II

Conquest of Bengal
1756–1759

Chapter Five
Loss and recovery of Calcutta

Prelude to Bengal

When Clive was reappointed by the company for service in India and sailed from England on April 23 1755, there was no problem in Bengal as far as the company was concerned. The old nawab, Alivardi Khan, was ruling the province with a firm hand, and he allowed the Europeans to carry on their trade freely, because that contributed to the prosperity of the province. As an endemic trouble, there were exactions by him or his servants, and occasional high-handedness, but the English company was very prosperous and could ignore both. The crisis that led to Clive's being sent to Bengal, and, finally, to the establishment of British power there, arose suddenly and unexpectedly.

For the time being what worried London was the continuation of the war with the French. The news of the provisional treaty concluded with them in India in December 1754 had not reached the directors, and so they sent out more troops with Clive. The dominant position of Bussy at Hyderabad was the great source of anxiety. Therefore a scheme was devised in London to remove the threat by sending an expedition from Bombay, which, in co-operation with the Marathas, was to attack Bussy and Salabat Jang. Clive was at first designated to command it, and was instructed to go to Bombay before joining his post at Madras. However, the Duke of Cumberland, as Commander-in-Chief of the King's forces, insisted that one Colonel Scott, who had been sent to India as chief engineer, should be the commander. Therefore instructions to Clive were made elastic enough for him to be with the expedition either as commander or in any other capacity according to circumstances, or to take up his appointment on the Madras council and as deputy-governor at Fort St David.

In respect of their position in India, whether commercial or political, the eyes of the British Government and of the directors of the company were always fixed on France. All those who were concerned with it, whether in India or in England, had come to the conclusion that there could be no security for their interests unless the French were removed from India, and Clive during his stay in England told the directors so. This remained the invariable principle of all their thinking about India for fifty years. Even though French power there was eliminated by the Seven Years' War, throughout the course of the American War and the French Revolutionary War approaches of French naval forces to the coasts of India, and the presence of French military adventurers as commanders or trainers of the armies of the Indian princes, were regarded as dangers to the English position. For instance, Arthur Wellesley (the future Duke of Wellington) wrote to his brother Lord Mornington (the future governor-general of India and Marquis of Wellesley) from Calcutta on July 12 1797:

> Mauritious [sic] ought to be taken. As long as the French have an establishment there, Great Britain cannot call herself safe in India. They must be particularly guarded against after the war, as it may be depended upon that swarms of them (aristocrats, democrats, modérés, etc., etc.) will come here to seek service in the armies of the Native princes, and all Frenchmen in such a situation are equally dangerous. They would shortly discipline their numerous armies in the new mode which they have adopted in Europe, than which nothing can be more formidable to the small body of fighting men of which the Company's armies in general consist and in the end they would force us to increase our armies and of course expenses to such a degree, that the country could not be kept, or indeed would not be worth keeping.

In fact, the only real battles that the British had to fight in India were against Indian armies trained by Europeans in the European manner.

In the epoch of Clive the French were not fighting by proxy; they were themselves in India, and it was their presence that had to be eliminated. In trying to do this the British showed great clear-sightedness. They realized that the French could not be made harmless simply by allowing them to remain in India and using the Indian princes to oppose them. In other words, they found that the traditional British policy, followed in Europe, of opposing their European rivals by helping the other European countries to fight them, would not work in India. For one thing, the Indian princes were incapable of fighting effectively. Next, they could not be depended on, because in the nature of things no oriental prince could be friendly to any European nation when in possession of real power. So they thought that attempts to fight their enemy indirectly would at best be waste of good money, good arms and good troops, and might in certain situations be dangerous. In short, they never entertained the illusion that prevails today in dealing with the Soviet Union. They took it for granted that whatever had to be done must be done directly by themselves.

Upon his arrival at Bombay at the end of October 1755, Clive found that Colonel Scott was dead, and so the command of the projected expedition devolved on him. But it was not sent, because there was a difference of opinion about its advisability between Madras and Bombay.

In the meantime, another combined operation was planned against a Maratha pirate chief, Tulaji Angria, who from two very strong forts and anchorages on the western coast of India was attacking the shipping of all nations in the Arabian Sea and had become a scourge to trade. Angria had a large fleet of small ships and rowing boats of forty to fifty oars, and operated mainly from two bases: Suvarnadrug, eighty miles south of Bombay, and Gheria, a hundred miles further down the coast. Early in 1755 Commodore James reduced the fort of Suvarnadrug, supposed to be impregnable, with its outlying forts, and compelled Tulaji Angria to take refuge in Gheria. After that the Bombay authorities decided to reduce Gheria, taking advantage of the presence of a powerful squadron of warships under Admiral Watson and Admiral Pocock. The attack was to be by land as well as sea, and as the operation was undertaken in co-operation with the Maratha chief, the Peshwa, a large Maratha force was also to assist in the reduction of Angria's stronghold. The English naval force was the largest ever assembled in these waters, there being twelve ships of the line, six belonging to the Royal Navy and six to the company's navy, with auxiliary vessels.

Before the expedition started the chief officers met to decide upon their share of the prize money, which was permitted by the regulations in force. It was found that, on account of his rank, Clive was entitled only to an amount equal to a naval captain's share, but Admiral Watson generously agreed to let him have as his share an amount that would be equal to that of the second-in-command of the fleet, Rear-Admiral Pocock. On their arrival the English commanders did not find the Marathas very keen to begin the attack. So the English fleet went into action and destroyed the entire fleet of Angria. The next day the fort itself was occupied by a naval contingent. After that Clive entered it with his troops. Seeing the strength of the English fleet Tulaji had already fled, leaving his brother in charge of the fort. The capture of Gheria by the English was a great disappointment to the Marathas, and they tried to have the place delivered up to them, even by offering bribes of Rs50,000 to two officers if they would let them go in. The officers at once informed Clive, and the Maratha attempt to seize the fort was foiled.

As there was nothing more for Clive to do on the west coast, on April 21 1756 he applied to the Governor and Council of Bombay to be permitted to join his own post at Madras. At the same time he offered to come back quickly if the expedition to Hyderabad was decided upon, which, on account of the rains, he did not think would be practicable before the next October. So he left. But just as two years earlier he had sailed from Madras with a grievance at not being thanked formally by the Governor and his Council, so he also sailed from Bombay with a grievance against the Governor, Richard Bourchier, for not being consulted about a court martial on an officer. He complained that the Governor, 'never thought it proper to ask my advice or opinion, or even to inform me himself or by any other person whatever with one syllable relating thereto; considering the rank I bear of Lieutenant-Colonel in his Majesty's service, of Deputy Governor of St David, and of a member of the Committee of this place'. He felt that the Governor had not treated him agreeably as to the intentions of the Hon'ble the Court of Directors, and he also added that he flattered himself that the Court would do justice to him when they came to know of the affair.

On behalf of the Governor and his Council the Secretary to the Council replied in a brusque manner. He informed Clive that the President and the Council did not think 'they were accountable to any officer of whatever rank, or the Governor of any other settlement, for what he shall think proper to lay before the Board'. They also informed him that they too would refer the matter to the Hon'ble Company in London.

Clive and Watson sailed from Bombay on April 27 1756, and anchored in St David's roads on May 14. Clive went to Madras and took his seat on the Council at Fort St George eleven days later. On June 1 he was formally appointed deputy governor at

Fort St David and given the salary of his post with retrospective effect from the date of his arrival in India. He took charge there on June 22 1756.

Expedition to Bengal
On July 14 news was received at Madras of a serious development in Bengal. The Governor of Fort William in Calcutta informed the Council at Madras that Siraj-ud-daula, the young Nawab of Bengal, had taken the field against the English and captured the fortified factory at Cossimbazar near his capital, Murshidabad, and appealed for reinforcements.

This faced Madras with a problem. At that time Salabat Jang, the Nizam of Hyderabad, had sought the help of the English in order to get rid of Bussy and his Frenchmen, and an expedition into the Deccan was being prepared. Even so, the Council at Madras decided to help Calcutta, and to send such troops as they could spare. So, on July 20 Major Killpatrick sailed with about 250 soldiers, mostly Europeans, in the Company's ship, *Delaware*.

Anticipating danger to Calcutta, the Council decided early in August to send further reinforcements to Bengal, and to suspend the Deccan project. By that time a greater calamity had come about. Calcutta had been lost to Siraj-ud-daula on June 20 1756. News of this disaster was received at Madras on August 16, and this wholly changed the aspect of affairs. The Council at Madras took a prompt decision in two days to send the whole naval squadron and all the available land forces to retake Calcutta, and asked Admiral Watson, commander of the King's ships, and Colonel Adlercron, commander of the King's men, for their co-operation.

Admiral Watson at once replied that he would readily give all assistance in his power, and sail with his squadron to Bengal. In the meantime, he added, he would send a frigate to Balasore roads, near the mouth of the Hooghly river, to have the pilots ready to take the ships up the river.

However, the decision to despatch a strong expedition to Bengal was not arrived at easily. There were adherents of the Deccan project who did not like to see it given up. But this view was not pressed. The more serious consideration was the possibility of a war with the French. News had been received from England that a general war with France was imminent, and that a powerful naval squadron and a large number of regular troops were being got ready to be sent to India in the event of a declaration of war. If that happened Madras and English interests in the Carnatic were bound to be seriously threatened, and in this situation the absence of troops and ships in Bengal might be disastrous for both.

The Council at Madras was fully aware of the risk, and therefore the question of what to send and when to do so was earnestly debated. Some members were inclined to play for safety, and proposed to send a small force to Bengal, which they thought would be able to retake Calcutta and intimidate the Nawab into coming to an agreement with the English. If he did not, they thought, the small force under Major Killpatrick could harass the Nawab by making raids. This was opposed by Robert Orme, the future historian of these events and at that time a member of the Council at Madras. He had resided for nine years in Bengal and, as he related in his history, he knew 'the strength and insolence of the moorish government in Bengal, believed that nothing but vigorous hostilities would induce the Nabob to make peace or reparations, and considered the force proposed as unequal even to the retaking of Calcutta'. Therefore he insisted on a larger land force and also on the despatch of the whole naval squadron to Bengal.

After much debate his opinion was accepted unanimously. The considerations that influenced this decision were both material and psychological: the English interests in Bengal were too large to be abandoned tamely, national honour had to be maintained, and humiliation avenged. There was also perhaps the sound strategic consideration that it would be advisable to settle with Siraj-ud-daula before a war with the French began.

But the execution of the decision was not easy, because the uncertainty about the war with France posed a serious problem. This was argued strongly by Admiral Watson. He pointed out the danger of going to Bengal with all his ships if war had already broken out with France, and in case a powerful French squadron arrived in those waters. He said that the last would go in search of him in the Balasore roads, and he would fall an easy prey to it, being without his full strength of men. He would thereby 'contribute to heap ruin on your affairs instead of being of any service'. He also proposed that the expedition should be put off till the end of the rains, so that the men might not fall ill after going to Bengal.

A number of alternatives were discussed, and at the end of August it was decided not to send any expedition until news of the situation in Europe was received by the two ships that were expected from England. At the same time it was decided to push on with the preparations, so that if no news of a war with France was received, the expedition could sail without delay. The two ships arrived on September 19 1756, and did not bring news of any war. So, on September 21 the Madras Council decided to send the expedition to Bengal.

The question of appointing the commander of the expedition then arose. At first Governor Pigot intended to go himself, but being without military experience he did not press the idea. Colonel Lawrence, the most senior officer in India, was suffering from asthma, and it was not considered advisable to send him. After that Colonel Adlercron was offered the command, but he would not accept the conditions laid down by the Council, and, besides, he had no experience of the special kind of warfare in India. So Clive, who had arrived at Madras on August 24, was appointed to the command on September 30.

This so angered Colonel Adlercron that he refused to allow any of the King's troops to proceed to Bengal, and insisted that the artillery and the stores that had been loaded on to the ships be immediately disembarked. This had to be done, and the expedition could not sail until the Company's stores could replace those of the King. Finally it did so on October 16 1756.

It was a powerful force. There were five of the King's ships of the line: one seventy, one sixty-four, one sixty, one fifty and one twenty, with auxiliary ships. There were three Indiamen, carrying a strong body of troops and some guns. In the end three companies of Colonel Adlercron's regiment also went, because they had served as a marine contingent before and were required to serve as such under Admiral Watson. Against the contingency of a war with the French, it was provided in the final instructions that the force would have to come back to Madras if recalled.

There was, however, an element of weakness for the expedition, in the form of divided authority and responsibility. Clive was in command of the Company's land forces, and Admiral Watson of King's ships and men, and the relations between them were dependent on good will between the two. But this was a standing feature of the organization of command in the early wars in India, and in the past it had worked with the

English, though not with the French. One possible source of trouble was eliminated by a previous arrangement between the Company and the King's forces regarding the share of prize money. It was agreed that when anything was taken which previously belonged to the Company, to English individuals or even to the natives who were tenants of the Company, these properties would be restored to their former owners, but whatever was taken which had not been owned by these classes of owners could, without the participation of others, become prize money for the squadron.

But apart from this division of military authority between the Company's and the King's commanders, political authority was also divided between a Select Committee in Bengal and the military commanders. As the Council of Calcutta was still in being, though as refugees at Fulta down the river, it was not thought proper to divest it of all authority. So a Select Committee on the lines of those at Madras and Bombay was constituted for Bengal, and it was to have the management of all political questions. But in certain circumstances Clive was empowered to act independently, 'to pursue such measures as you shall judge most conclusive to the Company's benefit'. In regard to military operations he was to be responsible to Madras and not Bengal. This was resented by the Bengal Council, and was disapproved of even by the directors at home when they learnt about it. Powers given to Clive as military commander went against their principle that in all matters the civil branch should be the supreme authority. So they wrote: 'Had we not the highest opinion of Colonel Clive's prudence and moderation, there would be no end to the disagreeable reflection we might make on so extraordinary a precedent.' Clive was, however, advised by the Madras Council to work with the Select Committee in Bengal and to endeavour 'to preserve good harmony throughout'.

The aim of the expedition was much more comprehensive and ambitious than the primary purpose of recovering Calcutta. As the Madras Council wrote:

> The mere retaking of Calcutta should we think by no means be the end of the undertaking; not only their settlements and factories should be restored but all their privileges established in full extent granted by the Great Mogul, and ample reparation made of them for the loss they have lately sustained, otherwise we are of opinion it would have been better nothing had been attempted, than to have

added the heavy charge of this armament to their former loss, without securing their colonies and trade from future insults and exactions.

This was also the view of individual members of the Madras Council, especially of Clive and Orme. From the very first Orme envisaged that in order to make Siraj-ud-daula respect the Company even Murshidabad might have to be taken. Clive on his part wrote to the Secret Committee in London on October 11 1756: 'I flatter myself that this expedition will not end with the retaking of Calcutta only: and that the Company's estate in these parts will be settled in a better and more lasting condition than ever.'

As to the success of the expedition, he said in a letter to the Chairman of the East India Company: 'I am not so apprehensive of the Nabob of Bengal forces as of being recalled by the news of a war with the French or checked in our progress by the woods and swampiness of the country which is represented as almost impassable for a train of artillery.' He repeated the same opinion in a formal letter to the Secret Committee.

It must be pointed out that neither the ambitious scope of the expedition nor the confidence about its success as felt by Clive and the Madras Council was based on any exact knowledge of the military power of Siraj-ud-daula. On the contrary, the ease with which the Nawab had taken Calcutta should have made them cautious and aware of the risks. But actually the spirit displayed by the commanders and the soldiers was almost exultant. Clive described it without minimizing the gravity of the disaster that had befallen Calcutta. His letters to his employers remind one of the speeches of Churchill in 1940. He wrote about the catastrophe:

> Providence who is the disposer of all events has thought proper to inflict the greatest calamity that ever happened to the English Nation in these parts – I mean the loss of Calcutta attended with the greatest mortifications to the Company and the most barbarous and cruel circumstances to the poor inhabitants. I have that sense of my duty to my country and of my obligations to the Company (be the event what it will) there is no hardship or risk consistent with common prudence I will not undergo to obtain the wished for success.

As to the spirit of the troops he wrote to London: 'Every breast here seems filled with grief, horror, and resentment. Indeed it is too sad a tale to unfold. . . . I am now on the point of embarking on board His Majesty's squadron with a fine body of Europeans full of spirit and resentment for the insults and barbarities inflicted on so many British subjects.'

He was also aware of the opportunity that had come for him personally. As he wrote to the Secret Committee in London on October 11 1756: 'Success on this occasion will fill the measure of my joy; as it will fix me in the esteem of those to whom I have the honour to subscribe myself with great respect their most obliged and humble servant – R. Clive.'

To his father he wrote in the same vein but more informally: 'This expedition if attended with success may enable me to do great things. It is by far the grandest of my undertakings. I go with great forces and great authority.'

The decision to send an expedition to Bengal and the confidence with which it was undertaken call for comment. The undertaking was not launched by statesmen of extraordinary genius and courage like Pitt the Elder or Churchill, but by men of ordinary stature, who were merchants turned for the moment into amateur politicians and soldiers. Their response to the calamity in Bengal must not be taken as if it was the only one that was to be expected. Worse things have happened and are happening in our times without evoking any reaction comparable to that which came from a group of English merchants at Madras.

For instance, in the last twenty-five years or so nations with a military power incalculably greater than any possessed even by the British government in India at its zenith, not to speak of the Council at Madras in 1756, have surrendered far larger commercial and financial interests without trying to defend them against seizure by countries which they could occupy in a week; they have also shown themselves ready to see their home economy strangled and their standard of living lowered by economy browbeating from countries which had no greater military strength; over and above, they have been acquiescing tamely in murders and other atrocities more cruel, deliberate and widespread than those perpetrated on the English at Calcutta, in their own cities, streets and public places; they are also swallowing continuous verbal insults, a single one of which would have brought about a war one hundred years ago.

There was no external circumstance to prevent the Madras Council from forestalling this 'modern' behaviour and to turn the other cheek to Siraj-ud-daula, so as to be able to proclaim their moral superiority over men of bygone ages. What stood in the way was the spirit of an age and the character of a people in that age. To moralize over the difference is utterly frivolous in the light of history, because causality in history is relative, and the same causes may produce wholly different effects in different ages. What has to be done is to recognize the historical particularity of the action of the English merchants at Madras. If history teaches us anything it teaches that all things are not possible in all ages.

This is, of course, due to the psychological element, which is variable. It is this element that makes economic interpretation of history an inversion of historical logic by putting effect before cause. To consider only empires, no empire was created by economic urges except as part of a far stronger urge in man – that of self-assertion. Motives of material gain accompany that urge because making money is the simplest, crudest and most easily understood form of self-assertion. If purely economic reasons could create empires the British people today should be founding even greater empires than any they possessed in the past.

Plato correlated different types of government with different states of the human soul. In the same way the creation or abandonment of empires is related to the national character at a particular point of time. One might even say that economic interpretation of history itself reflects a certain passing state of the human soul, in which this soul conforms to the teaching of certain schools of Hindu philosophy by regarding *itself* as totally inactive and only worked upon by the environment.

Siraj-ud-daula and Calcutta

If the character of the English in general at Madras made them send to Bengal what might be called their expedition to Troy, it was no less the character of a single individual there that provoked them to do so. Thus there was in this drama a clash of characters, and imitating the famous *bon mot* of Pascal about the shortness of the nose of Cleopatra, one might say that, had the character of Siraj-ud-daula been less unstable, the face of India would have been changed.

He came to the throne at the death of his maternal grandfather, Alivardi Khan, when he was less than twenty-five, and would not have become nawab if his capable father, Zain-ud-din, who was Alivardi's favoured son-in-law, had not been killed by the Afghan mercenaries. He has been represented as a ruler who was a monster of cruelty, greed, lust, violence, intemperance and wild caprices, mingled with an exuberant flippancy. But this emphasis on his individual wickedness has overlooked the fact that he was only an extreme example of an old and normal type in oriental dynastic politics, whether Hindu or Muslim.

The greatest poet of ancient India, Kalidasa, has left us the only political epic in Sanskrit, the *Raghuvamsa* (the Dynasty of Raghu), in which he described the full cycle of the rise and fall of a dynasty. It shows the power of a dynasty, beginning with a conqueror, being consolidated by a statesman, continued by progressively less able and less energetic kings, and ending at last with a feckless voluptuary. In the nineteenth canto of this poem is described the elaborate sexual orgies of King Agnivarna in such vivid details as are now enjoyed in England, in crude visual representations found in the debased modern erotic paintings bought in Rajasthan and other regions of India.

As it happens, many centuries later, the great Muslim historian and philosopher Ibn Khaldun, who has been previously cited in this book, described the Islamic counterpart of this type, which brought to a close the five stages of the history of a dynasty. The fifth and last phase, according to him was as follows:

> The fifth stage is one of waste and squandering. In this stage, the ruler wastes on pleasures and amusements the treasures accumulated by his ancestors, through generosity to his inner circle. Also he acquires bad, low-class followers to whom he entrusts the most important matters, which they are not qualified to handle themselves.... The ruler seeks to destroy the great clients of his people and followers of his predecessors. Thus they come to hate him and conspire to refuse support to him. He loses a number of soldiers by spending their allowances on his pleasures and refusing them access to his person and not supervising them. Thus, he ruins the foundations his ancestors had laid and tears down what they had built up.

This description can be applied without change of a word to many Muslim princes in India who brought their dynasties to an end, and especially to Muhammad Shah, the last effective Moghul emperor, who died in 1748. Basically, Siraj-ud-daula also conformed to the type, but he brought an unusual energy into his role as the last of his line. Ibn Khaldun described the normal type, who became a puppet in the hands of a strong minister who managed him in the following manner:

> He accustoms him [the titular ruler] to the pleasures of a life of luxury and gives him every possible opportunity to indulge in them ... he accustoms [the young ruler] to believe that the ruler's share in royal authority consists merely in sitting on the throne, shaking hands, being addressed as Sire, and sitting with women in the seclusion of the harem.

But Siraj-ud-daula, instead of being this kind of *roi fainéant*, became an active one. He was determined to rule, to be master in his house, and he displayed an energy that made him an eastern imitation of Caligula and Nero.

Two contemporary Muslim historians have left a description of him. The first, Ghulam Husain Tabatabai, author of the famous *Seir-ul-Mutakherin*, wrote:

> Making no distinction between vice and virtue, and paying no regard to his nearest relations, he carried defilement wherever he went, and, like a man alienated in his mind, he made the houses of men and women of distinction the scenes of his profligacy, without minding either rank or station. In a little time he became as detested as Pharaoh, and people on meeting him by chance used to say, 'God save us from him!'

The other historian is Ghulam Husain Salim, who wrote the *Riyaz-us-Salatin*, another important work. He wrote:

> Owing to Siraj-ud-daula's harshness of temper and indulgence in violent language, fear and terror had settled on the hearts of everyone to such an extent that no one among his generals of the army or the noblemen of the city was free from anxiety. Amongst his officers, whoever went to wait on Siraj-ud-daula despaired of life and honour, and whoever returned without being disgraced and ill-treated offered thanks to God. Siraj-ud-daula treated all the noblemen and generals of Mahabat Jang [Alivardi Khan] with ridicule and drollery, and bestowed on each some contemptuous nickname that ill-suited any of them. And whatever harsh expressions and abusive epithet came to his lips, Siraj-ud-daula uttered them unhesitatingly in the face of everyone, and no one had the boldness to breathe freely in his presence.

The two aspects of the character of Siraj singled out for emphasis by these two Muslim writers have to be considered historically. Licentiousness and pursuit of women by themselves would not have ruined him, for these were a normal activity for these princes. The strong rulers kept their sexual life as a secondary outlet for their energy, and were no more harmed by it than were Louis XIV, Louis XV or Napoleon by their amours. In India the princes could also collect women very freely, and even by violence, without arousing any dangerous opposition. This was owing to a recognized convention in respect of a king's right to pretty women. In India, land, by immemorial custom, belonged to the ruler, and his subjects enjoyed only usufructuary rights. In a similar manner, by a tacitly accepted usage, all the beautiful young women and the surplus wealth of the subjects could also be *claimed by the king*. So the subjects buried their wealth, but being unable to bury their women hid them as far as possible in the zenana. Nevertheless reports of hidden beauty always got abroad, and the king's procurers (and, if need arose, his armed retainers) tried to get hold of any woman who might be worth collecting.

This practice continued even after British rule was established firmly in certain parts of India. For instance, Tipu Sultan, the ruler of Mysore, who is admitted to have been an able ruler by all, and is even regarded as a hero by the Indian nationalist historians because he fought the British, seized such women as would be worth putting in his harem in the course of his campaigns. This gave rise to a bizarre problem for General Wellesley (the future Duke of Wellington) after the death of Tipu. Normally, after the death of a Muslim prince his harem was booty for the victor. The Europeans in India, beginning with Dupleix, had, however, wholly disinterested themselves in the women, and in the case of Tipu, the British had even taken under their protection his whole family and zenana, which of course included the concubines.

But after Tipu's death Père Dubois, the French missionary who was to write the famous work on Hindu customs and manners, wrote to Wellesley as the commander of the British forces in Mysore and military governor of Seringapatam, that the wives of about two hundred Christians had been taken away in the most indecent and tyrannical manner by Tipu, and their husbands now wanted them back. Wellesley did not consider this unjust, but felt compelled to refuse because, as he put it, 'the Company having taken this family under its protection, it is not proper that anything should be done which can disgrace it in the eyes of the Indian world, or which can in the most remote degree cast a shade upon the dead or violate the feelings of those who were alive'.

But after that Père Dubois made another request. He said that the Christian husbands wanted to marry again, but he could not perform the marriage ceremony until he knew that their wives were dead. Wellesley thought this reasonable, and requested that a list of the Christian women still in the harem should be sent to him. But difficulties were raised. This annoyed Wellesley and he let it be known that if the list was not furnished he would report the matter to the Government, who would no doubt compel Tipu's family to give up not only the Christian women but all the women retained in the zenana without their consent. Even so, Wellesley did not like to hold out this as a threat but merely left it to the good sense of the family, so inviolate did the harem of a Muslim prince seem to him!

If Siraj had remained within the recognized limits in his licentiousness these practices would not have harmed him politically. The permitted limits were the following: secret amours with women of one's own class who were willing; seizure of women in war; purchase of slaves, dancing girls and the like; purchase of young women from those who were ready to make money by selling their daughters, wives and sisters; or seduction of women who would meet him halfway in being seduced. An enormous variety and number of women to satisfy every sexual caprice could thus be collected by any Indian ruler.

But Siraj showed a complete disregard of conventions in this matter. As Jean Law, the chief of the French establishment at Cossimbazar, who had close personal relations with Siraj, related, 'Hindu women are accustomed to bathe on the banks of the Ganges. Siraj-ud-daula, who was informed by his spies which of them were beautiful, sent his satellites in disguise in little boats to carry them off.' What was worse, he violated the honour of high families. He even had a bride of the family of the great bankers, the Jagat Seths, who were the financiers of the State, brought to the palace so that he might have a look at her beauty – which was reported to be great. She was sent back without bodily outrage, but to be looked at like this was in itself a great dishonour. Even peasants and working men resented attention to their womenfolk.*

---

*I shall give an example of this from my personal knowledge. The lady of a well-known landowning family in a village near ours, and distantly related to our family, was once coming home in a palanquin, escorted by retainers. A Muslim peasant working on a field by the roadside asked: 'Who goes?' The retainers told him who she was. The peasant then insolently cried out: 'Open the palanquin door and let me see what your zamindar's lady looks like.' The

Siraj was also abominably cruel, and began to show it even during the lifetime of his grandfather. Again, Law relates: 'He was often seen, in the season when the river overflows, causing ferry boats to be upset or sunk, in order to have the cruel pleasure of seeing the confusion of a hundred people at a time, men, women and children, of whom many, not being able to swim were sure to perish.' Both Law and others have also related that he had the bellies of women in advanced pregnancy ripped open to see how the child lay in the womb. So people dreaded his accession and only hoped that, with it, he would become more humane.

He did not; he became even more violent and intemperate. By all this he particularly offended his Muslim noblemen. He raised a Hindu named Mohanlal, who is described by Law and others as the greatest rascal, to be his highest adviser and made the great noblemen show respect to him. This outraged them, and Siraj outraged them even more by his flippant and contemptuous remarks. There was nothing Muslims of high position resented more than verbal discourtesy, not to speak of insults.

In everything he did Siraj displayed a wild energy, which was not, however, sustained and was manifest only as spasmodic fits. This is what distinguished him from the familiar *spes ultima gentis*, 'the last hope of a line' in Muslim political history, who normally merely faded away.

One is tempted to see in this display of hysterical energy an illustration of Ibn Khaldun's theory of the decline of a dynasty. Siraj's dynasty was not even twenty years old. His grandfather had come from Turkestan as an adventurer in search of fortune. So the dynasty had not as yet undergone the natural decay of energy which, according to Khaldun, was a result of the transition from desert life to sedentary culture. Thus it had not lost the energy, cruelty and rapacious habits of desert life, though it had, by the self-assertion of the ruler, destroyed the group spirit which united the first rulers with their followers, who might be called his tribe. This was as important for Muslim dynasties, as united interests were necessary between a feudal king and his barons. Certainly, this was the case with the dynasty of Alivardi.

---

palanquin moved on. But the lady, as soon as she stepped out of it in her inner courtyard, said that she must have the head of that man and would not take a drop of water until it was brought to her. It was. The family had to spend an enormous amount of money to deal with the consequences of this vindication of honour. The incident happened about the time of my birth, and the lady was the great-grandmother of a Bengali who is now internationally known.

But the primary impulse behind Siraj's activities was that of a half-insane megalomania. His wild but unsustained fits of energy were brought about by the instability of his character, which in its turn was worsened by his excesses. His grandfather attributed it to drinking, and made him swear by the Quran that he would abstain from alcohol. Unfortunately, Siraj Sober was worse than Siraj Drunk.

Even so, if he had had to deal only with his own people, he would have continued for some time. In fact, he was doing remarkably well. He had succeeded to Alivardi without trouble to himself, which most observers, Muslim or European, did not expect. He had seized the wealth of his influential aunt by a trick. Encouraged by all this, he provoked a conflict with the English, who were not ready to stand any nonsense (as they saw it) from him. As it was, such a character as Siraj had no greater chance against the English than a drunkard against a sober man. By alienating his nobles and his people, especially the Hindus, he made his position worse, and the fact that in this conflict with the English he succeeded unexpectedly at the beginning, made his downfall all the more inevitable by producing a swift and powerful reaction from them.

The question therefore arises – why did he provoke the conflict? There is no uncertainty whatever about his reasons and motives. He stated them all clearly, and never shifted his ground. In a letter written to an intermediary he declared on June 1 1756, only twenty days before he took Calcutta:

> I have three substantial motives for extirpating the English out of my country; one is that they have built strong fortifications and dug a large ditch in the King's dominions contrary to the established laws of the country; the second is that they have abused the privileges of their *dustucks* [certificates which exempted British goods from tolls] by granting them to such as were no ways entitled to them, from which practices the King has suffered greatly in the revenue of his customs; the third motive is that they give protection to such of King's subjects as have by their behaviour in the employs they were entrusted with made themselves liable to be called to an account and instead of giving them up on demand they allow such persons to shelter themselves within their bounds from the hands of justice. For these reasons it is become requisite to drive them out.

In all this he was right. He was particularly angry about the fortifications, and had written four days earlier to the same agent that if the English wanted to remain in his country they must submit to having their military works destroyed, and to this letter Siraj added in his own hand:

> I swear by the Great God and the Prophet that unless the English consent to fill up their ditch, raze their fortifications and trade upon such terms they did in the time of Nabob Jaffeir Ali Caun [Murshid Quli Khan] I will not hear anything in their behalf and will expel them totally out of country.

In short, he required that merchants should remain merchants only. In all this he was perfectly logical, though from the practical point of view also suicidal. The English on their part asserted that they traded in India, and were entitled to maintain their establishments autonomously, by the same title by which Siraj-ud-daula himself ruled, namely, the permission of the Emperor of Delhi. They were right in this. The English would not concede that Siraj had more right to abrogate their privileges than the French.

In this quarrel no question of national independence arose for anybody, for all the parties to the quarrels were foreigners: the Turko-Mongol Emperor in Delhi, Siraj at Murshidabad, the English in Calcutta and the French at Chandernagore. The people of Bengal did not come into this struggle at all, except that they were terrified by Siraj and wanted his rule ended by anybody who could do it. Even if they did not have a positive aversion to him, they would have been passive in respect of his removal. In this they exhibited the fixed mode of behaviour of the Indian people when suffering from the struggles of power among their conquerors.

Behind these specific grievances of Siraj stood a general distrust and fear of the European traders which had also been felt and shown by Alivardi Khan. That ruler knew what had happened in the Carnatic and the Deccan, and saw plainly that in the former the English and in the latter the French had reduced the Muslim ruler to a puppet in their hands. He felt that they, or at any rate the English, would try to repeat this in Bengal. As Law related in his memoirs:

> Alivardi Khan was none the less jealous of his authority. He specially affected a great independence whenever there was question of any affair between himself and the Europeans. To speak to him of *firmans* or of privileges obtained from the Emperor was only to anger him. He knew well how to say at the proper moment that he was both King and Wazir....
> He saw with equal indignation and surprise the progress of the

French and English nations on the Coromandel Coast as well as in the Deccan. . . . He feared that sooner or later the Europeans would attempt similar enterprises in his government.

Alivardi was particularly sensitive about the fortifications in Calcutta and Chandernagore. The least repair or the pulling down of a house near the fort alarmed him. An order was immediately sent to stop any such work. Law has also written that he often said to the *vakils*, or agents of the English and the French: 'You are merchants, what need have you of a fortress? Being under my protection you have no enemies to fear.' But knowing that he was old and not liking to take risks, he did nothing to curb the Europeans.

Whether he told Siraj to take an aggressive line cannot be stated for certain. Law and Holwell stated that he did, whereas others have written that he warned Siraj against getting embroiled with Europeans. Once, when urged by his grandson to seize the wealth of the English, Alivardi is reported to have cried out: 'What have the English done against me that I should use them ill? It is now difficult to extinguish fire on land; but should the sea be in flames, who can put them out? Never listen to such advice . . . for the result would be fatal.'

Observing the character of his grandson, Alivardi is also reported to have said that when he was dead, 'the Hat men, i.e., the Europeans, would possess themselves of all the shores of India'. These speeches are found in the histories written after the event, and are too appropriate to the situation to be regarded as anything but Thucydidean. Alivardi *could* have said such things, for when Siraj began his march against the English he is said to have replied to the dissuasive pleas of one of his chiefs with this outburst: 'I will teach thee I am not Alivardi Khan, my grandfather, nor any other of my predecessors, but I am Siraj-ud-daula, and I do exactly as I please. . . .'

One thing is certain – he was determined to do exactly as he pleased with the English. His mind must have been made up before he ascended the throne, for he acted swiftly. Alivardi died on April 10 1756. By the middle of May Siraj had issued his orders to the English and the French to destroy their fortifications. At the beginning of June he took possession of the factory at Cossimbazar, and on the twentieth captured Calcutta.

The English on their part part gave him every provocation, by being arrogant and truculent. All along they had looked upon their trading rights in India as inviolable, and as far back as

1752, when Alivardi was in full control and there was some talk of his demanding a large sum of money from Calcutta, Orme, who was there, wrote to Clive at Madras: 'Clive, 'twould be a good deed to swinge the old dog. I don't speak at random when I say that the Company must think seriously of it, or 'twill not be worth their while to trade in Bengal'.

Governor Drake in 1756 showed the same spirit, though he was otherwise a mild man. He did indeed send a message of congratulations to Siraj, but his gift was so small that it was rejected. The English at Cossimbazar, too, would not admit Siraj to their factory or houses because they feared he would break or take away the furniture. There was no doubt that the English were hostile as well as contemptuous towards Siraj, and he on his part suspected them to be intriguing with all his enemies. The English were also reported to have treated the Nawab's messengers or spies badly. For instance, when Siraj wrote to Drake to deliver up Kissendas, who had taken refuge in Calcutta, Drake was reported to have torn up the order and thrown it in the face of the messenger.

Matters came to a head when Siraj-ud-daula demanded that work on the fortification of Calcutta be stopped, what was built be destroyed, and the moat filled up. Drake was said to have replied to the messenger that he would do so, provided he could do it with the heads of the Moors. Law, who reported this, did not believe that Drake could have made any such remark, but he thought that some young officer might have made it and that it may have been overheard and repeated to Siraj.

In any case, the formal reply which Drake sent infuriated Siraj, who received it at Raj Mahal on May 20 1756, when he was on his way to Purnea to put a rival cousin out of the way. No copy of this letter has been preserved, and Drake's version of it – representing it to be conciliatory – was given by him to the Council: it was stated that this version did not fully disclose the contents of the reply, which was much more offensive. What is definitely known is that it put Siraj in a rage. Law wrote, on the strength of the information given to him by trustworthy people, that on reading the letter Siraj jumped up in anger, drew his sword, and swore that he would go and exterminate all the *feringhis*. As this word included all Europeans, Law was alarmed for the French, and took military precautions.

But the English remained complacent even though they had behaved provocatively. They did not believe that Siraj would attack them, and treated his outbursts as bluff. They considered him a half-mad young man who was not to be taken seriously. Thus they took no precautions, and made no preparations to defend Calcutta. In fact, it was not possible to put it in a proper state of defence. The fort itself was weak, the approaches to it were sheltered by buildings, and there were not enough men. After the reoccupation of Calcutta Clive wrote that 'there never was that attention paid to the advice of military men in Calcutta as was consistent with the safety of the place when in danger – a total ignorance of which was the real cause of the loss of Fort William'.

Meanwhile, Siraj had not slept on his anger. He immediately gave up the plan to deal with his cousin and ordered the army to march back to Murshidabad with the intention of punishing the English.

This was done very easily; although eventually it proved to be his ruin, for the moment the English could do nothing. There were no plans, and everything was done haphazardly and in a panic. When retreat seemed inevitable, it was not organized properly, and such fighting as took place was simply an attempt to maintain honour. So it was foredoomed to failure. Holwell took a leading part in this hopeless defence, but Clive wrote to London immediately after retaking Calcutta that 'I am well informed there is no merit due to him for staying behind in the fort, nothing but want of a boat prevented his escape and flight with the rest'.

It is extremely difficult to apportion personal responsibility or blame in this débâcle. Afterwards there was recrimination on all sides among the English, one faction accusing another, and each putting forward its apologia. But the remark that may aptly be made is that the loss of Calcutta was the most discreditable episode in the history of the British in India, and unless redeemed, the reputation they had gained in India since Arcot was bound to be lost for ever.

The disaster was not expected by anybody – not by the British, the French, the Dutch or even the soldiers of the Nawab. It is said that they muttered fearfully when marching to Calcutta, and Siraj said to one of his chiefs – a Bengali Hindu – who brought this to his notice: 'I do not doubt that thou art afraid thyself. I am not astonished at it for thou art a Bengali coward.'

There was consternation among the other Europeans, and especially the French. All of them feared that, encouraged by his success against the English, the most powerful among the European traders in Bengal, Siraj would now turn against the rest. So they were very angry and felt that the English had betrayed them. One Frenchman wrote in August 1756:

> Would you believe it, my dear fellow, that these Englishmen, unworthy to bear the name of Europeans, gave themselves up without firing a single gun in their fort and that by common consent – excepting 4 or 5 men of distinction who did not wish to stain themselves by so black an action, and who preferred to sacrifice themselves to the fury of the Moors rather than consent to it, and who now actually have irons on their feet and hands.

The same Frenchman wrote about Governor Drake and his colleagues: 'In short whatever one may say, these gentlemen, especially Mr Drake, will never be able to deprive his nation of the right to hang him and all his Council.' Actually, eight months later Admiral Byng was shot for a failure far less serious and dishonourable, *pour encourager les autres*, as Voltaire put it.

Even Hindu Bengalis, who thought Siraj would destroy himself by pitting himself against the English, were shocked at what had happened. As another Frenchman wrote in a letter from Chandernagore twelve days after the capture of Calcutta by Siraj: 'They [the country people] hugged themselves in the expectation that the English would defeat the Nawab, and deliver them from his tyranny and oppression.' But after his victory their anger turned against the English and all Europeans. The Frenchman wrote: 'The country people here about, call the Europeans *banchots*, i.e., cowards and poltroons.'*

Siraj-ud-daula on his part was exultant. His successes justified all his self-confidence, and his low opinion of all Europeans. 'A pair of slippers', he used to say, 'is all that is needed to govern them.' He knew nothing about Europe and thought all Europe could not consist of more than ten or twelve thousand men. Even after taking Cossimbazar he cried out: 'Look now at those Englishmen, who were once so proud that they did not wish to receive me in their house.' He crowed even more loudly after taking Calcutta. He justified the fears of the French and the Dutch by demanding large sums of money from them on the charge of having helped the English. For instance, he said to

---

* The writer did not know the real meaning of the abusive word. *Banchot* is a Bengali corruption of the quite clear Hindi abusive phrase *Bahen chod*, which is usually preceded by the word *Sala*. The whole expletive sentence is *Sala, bahen chod* (O brother-in-law, f... your sister). It expresses extreme contempt and disgust.

one of the intermediaries: 'Tell the Hollanders they must bring me twenty *lacs* of rupees or I will ruin them as I have done the English.' Both the French and the Dutch in Bengal made it up with Siraj by paying large sums of money.

But in addition to the humiliation, the sufferings of the English were also great. They were ill treated and insulted, and, as is well known, a large number of them perished of heat and suffocation after being confined to a small cell for a whole night in the month of June. This was the famous Black Hole incident.

From the point of view of history it is regrettable that the interested accounts of the capture of Calcutta by Siraj-ud-daula, by the Englishmen who played a part in the episode, should have made it difficult to have a true idea of what happened. The inconsistencies and all too obvious special pleading in the different accounts have left room for the modern apologists of Siraj even to question whether the Black Hole incident took place at all.

It may, however, be accepted as a historical fact that a large number of prisoners of war did perish by heat and suffocation in the Black Hole. Aside from that, the English who were made prisoners were from the beginning grossly insulted and ill treated. But the historical significance of the Black Hole has not always been correctly appreciated.

First of all, some points of fact have to be noted. Siraj did not give the order for putting the English prisoners in the cell, and when he came to know about it it is reported that he was even 'affected'. The English women were not molested nor dishonoured at any time. The severity to the English prisoners was due to complete thoughtlessness. In India, and oriental countries generally, more cruelty is perpetrated and suffering inflicted through negligence, indifference and inefficiency than through deliberate brutality.

Moreover, death of prisoners of war through suffocation has happened elsewhere and on other occasions. In the course of the suppression of the rebellion of the Moplahs, a fanatical Muslim community of Malabar who rose in revolt in 1921, the authorities put one hundred prisoners in a railway wagon without opening the ventilating shutters. When the wagon door was opened at midnight to give them water it was found that they were in a state of collapse, and a total of seventy died. Again, in 1757, an English privateer was captured in the English Channel and its crew were put in the hold of their ship by their French captors and kept there for part of a day and a whole night without a drop of water and without sufficient air. In the morning twenty-seven were found dead. During the First World War a contingent of newly arrived English troops was sent by the British Indian military authorities to north India in the summer through the Rajputana and Sind desert. Many of them died of heatstroke.

As regards the historical importance of the Black Hole, there is no doubt that it inspired a deep resentment and produced a shock among the English of all ranks of the force. This gave the Bengal expedition its terrific energy. *Facit indignatio versus* (Anger makes poetry), runs the Latin tag: one may adapt it to: *Facit indignatio bellum* (Anger makes war). The expression of that indignation will be seen presently.

Retrospectively, the Black Hole incident served to throw a moral halo over the British conquest of India, as if it was God's punishment for iniquity, an illustration of theodicy, or of the Sanskrit saying: 'Where there is Righteousness there is also victory.' For this reason Indian nationalists on their part have tried to show that the Black Hole incident did not happen, as if by disproving its historical authenticity they could deprive the British Empire in India of its moral justification. Both standpoints are psychological products of history, but they do not belong to authentic history.

Calcutta would have been retaken, and if necessary Siraj-uddaula removed, even if there had been no Black Hole. This is made absolutely clear in the letter that the Council at St George (Madras) wrote to Bengal. They wrote: 'We could not have resolved to engage our Honourable Masters in the vast expenditure of fitting out this armament but with the hopes of obtaining equivalent advantages.' Then they explained what they had in view:

> Should the Nabob on the news of arrival of these forces, make offers tending to the acquiring to the Company the before-mentioned advantages rather than risque the success of a war, we think that sentiments of revenging injuries, although they were never more just, should give place to the necessity of sparing as far as possible the many bad consequences of war, besides the expense of the Company's treasures, but we are of opinion that the sword should go hand in hand with the pen, and that on the arrival of the present armament hostilities should commence with the utmost vigour.

The merchants had realized as clearly as soldiers that war is an instrument of policy.

The expedition found the refugees from Calcutta at Fulta – a village about twenty miles south of Calcutta as the crow flies. Drake had sailed down the river and arrived there on June 26 1756. It was a shipping station for the Dutch, but an unhealthy and dreary place, surrounded by marshes and jungles. As they were sailing down they found that orders had been sent to every headman of every village not to supply the English with food. The ships being short of it, they set ashore every person who was not European, and proceeded to Fulta. Drake reported: 'At this place we agreed to remain in hopes of expected succours from Madras and for intelligence from our servants or others who had been taken prisoners, and as it was represented as a place of safety for our ships and vessels and that we were supplied by stealth with small quantities of provision.'

On August 4 1756 the *Delaware*, which had been sent out from Madras with a small number of troops under Major Killpatrick, arrived at Fulta. As the ship's log recorded: 'Found riding here the *Fort William, Dodaly,* sundry other country ships and vessels, but the late inhabitants of Calcutta were greatly distressed and almost destitute of cloathing.'

Major Killpatrick reported at once to Madras. About the morale of the refugees he wrote:

> You may more easily imagine the conditions of those poor gentlemen, driven out from their habitations, driven out from all they have in the world, and what is worst, having lost all or almost all that had been committed to their charge; where many people around them who have also lost their alls, and are discontented and even troublesome, pretending to find fault and give their opinions without showing that respect which they ought.

Killpatrick hoped, however, he would be able to re-establish harmony and take such resolutions as would be 'most for the benefit for the Company'. For the moment he was very pleased that he himself had been made a member of the Council, which he had not been at Madras.

He found that any operation to recover Calcutta was impossible and decided to remain at Fulta, doing what he could. At Madras he had had his grievances and decided to return to England. But, he wrote in his letter: 'Affairs are in such a situation here that I have entirely given over all thoughts for the present of returning home as I intended.' He added that he would 'never let any private concerns sway with me where they [the Company] were at all interested'.

The place was, however, extremely unhealthy and grew worse as the season advanced. From August 6 the *Delaware*'s log began to have entries beginning with the words: 'Departed this life . . .'. Between this date and October 2 there were sixteen such entries. But on October 23 1756 the log recorded:

> In the morning had advice of His Majesty's ship *King Fisher* being arrived at Kedgeree from Admiral Watson. . . . At midnight the pinnace returned from the *King Fisher,* from whence we learn that Admirals Watson and Pocock with the whole squadron and a large number of land forces under Colonel Clive are daily expected to arrive in the Road, to our great joy and satisfaction.

Next morning a flagstaff was erected on shore and the British flag hoisted, which they saluted with nine guns. The spot was situated within Dutch grounds. But the place continued to take its toll. In the evening of October 25 'one of the Honourable Company's soldiers fell out of a boat alongside and was unfortunately drowned.' On October 27, 'Richard York, butcher, lying asleep in the starboard gangway accidentally fell overboard and was lost.' On October 28, 'Departed this life Thomas Clodd seaman.' On October 29, 'Departed this life Joseph Davies seaman.'

Nonetheless, on November 5 the ship fired nineteen guns to celebrate the anniversary of the Gunpowder Plot, and on November 10 the King's birthday was saluted with eleven guns.

Recapture of Calcutta

H.M.S. *Kent* – sixty-four guns, flying the blue ensign of Vice-Admiral Watson, and with Clive on board – anchored at Fulta on December 15 1756. Then followed the Two Hundred Days,* at the end of which the English became virtual masters of Bengal, and potentially the rulers of India.

The history of those days is perhaps the strangest that could be written on the foundation of any empire. Compared with the conquest of Bengal, even that of Mexico or Peru would make a tale of straightforward adventure. Looking back on the events in which he had played so decisive a role, Clive wrote to Orme at Madras on August 1 1757, showing a remarkable detachment even at the end of a month:

*Exactly two hundred days (both days being inclusive) from December 15 to July 2, on which last date Siraj-ud-daula was put to death.

I am possessed of volumes of materials for the continuance of your History, in which will appear fighting, tricks, chicanery, intrigues, politics and the Lord knows what. In short, there will be a fine field for you to display your genius in.

But it cannot be said that either Orme or the later historians have wholly brought out the true character of these events. The historical style inherited from Thucydides, Livy and Tacitus was quite inappropriate, and the polemical style of the early nineteenth century was no better. More misleading was the pseudo-imperialistic style of the late nineteenth and early twentieth centuries, which was only Henty made pedestrian; and the debunking style, which began to appear from the thirties, is perhaps the worst.

Yet it is very difficult to hit upon a style of narration that will convey an idea of the reality. There was in it a strident bravado which could be rendered in the style of the *Iliad* or the *Mahabharata*, but that would be too clean a manner for a story interwoven with baseness and squalor. On the other hand, if Machiavelli had had to write about it he would have been repelled by the kind of cunning, treachery and cruelty that was so inefficient and purposeless. Even the style of a picaresque novel would not be suitable, because there are farcical details in the story that would be appropriate only in *opera buffa*. So the best way to describe the events would be not to impose a style on them but to employ the language of the participants so far as is possible.

The commanders of the relieving expedition did not lose time in making their peremptory demands. They had brought letters to Siraj-ud-daula from Governor Pigot, from the Nawab of the Carnatic and from the Nizam of Hyderabad. Pigot referred to the seizure of Calcutta and the inhuman treatment of the English afterwards, and reminded the nawab that 'the English above all other nations enriched your province by a most extensive trade and importation of large sums of ready money'. He went on to say that he would have been willing to believe that the violence and cruelties exercised by the nawab's armies were without his knowledge, but he had found in fact that he was commanding in Calcutta in person. Then he told Siraj:

> The great commander of the King of England's ships has not slept in peace since this news and is come down with many ships, and I have sent a great Sardar, who will govern after me, by name Colonel Clive, with troops and land forces. Full satisfaction and restitution

must be made for the losses we have sustained.

Then came the admonition, *fortiter in re, suaviter in modo* – strongly put as to substance and suavely in manner:

> You are wise: consider whether it is better to engage in a war that will never end or to do what is just and right in the sight of God: a great name is obtained by justice as well as valour. You have heard that we have fought and always been victorious in these parts.

Last of all, he informed Siraj that the English had always acted in support of the orders of the Emperor of Delhi and closed his letter with the words: 'Mr Clive will explain all things to you. What can I say more?'

From Fulta both Watson and Clive wrote on the same lines. Clive informed Siraj that he had brought a larger military force than had appeared before in Bengal and advised him to be prudent both in his own interest and for the welfare of the country. He concluded with the following exhortation:

> Your power and personal bravery are universally known; my reputation in war is likewise established by being ten years continually in the field upon the Coast, in which time my undertakings have always been attended (by the blessing of Providence) with success; and I trust in God that I shall be as fortunate in these parts. Should necessity oblige me to proceed to those extremities one of us must be overcome, we cannot both be victorious and I leave you to reflect how uncertain the fortune of war is. . . . To avoid it you must make proper satisfaction for the losses sustained by the Company, their servants and *riots*, return their factories and invest them in their ancient privileges and immunities. By doing this piece of justice you will make me a sincere friend and get eternal honour to yourself, and save the lives of many thousands who must otherwise be slaughtered on both sides without any fault of their own. What can I say more?

It was almost the language of the barons at Runnymede. All the letters were sent to Raja Manikchand, who had been appointed Governor of Calcutta by Siraj, to be forwarded to his master. He replied politely, but represented that the letters contained some improper expressions. So he sent an alternative draft, in which the English were to appear as suppliants and say to Siraj: 'It is the praise of great men to behave with generosity and forgiveness towards those who have offended them.'

Clive answered at once, and said that he could not, consistently with his duty to the Company or its honour, accept Manikchand's draft. 'Such a style,' he explained, 'which however proper it might have been before the taking of Calcutta, would but ill-suit with the present time, when we are come to demand satisfaction for the injuries done us by the Nabob, not to entreat his favour, and with a force which we think sufficient to vindicate our claim.' However, on December 25 another letter was written with slightly more mellow phrasing. Siraj ignored the letters. Or at least no reply to them is preserved. But it was reported that they angered him.

At Fulta it was decided to begin the operations to recover Calcutta at once, though a substantial part of the troops had not arrived because the two biggest ships on which they were, the *Cumberland* and the *Marlborough*, had fallen behind. The plan decided upon at a council of war held on the *Kent*, the Admiral's flagship, was somewhat complicated. To begin with, the sepoys were to march up the river bank, while the ships were to go to a place named Mayapur and transport the King's troops and the Company's European troops, together with the guns and the train, for a rendezvous there. From Mayapur, the Company's troops, both Europeans and the sepoys, were to take their position north-east of Budge Budge, the most important of the Nawab's fortified outposts before Calcutta, in order to cut off the retreat of the garrison of the fort. Clive was opposed to marching on land because it would have inflicted great hardship on the men, and actually it involved a tiring march of sixteen hours in very difficult country. He would have preferred to be landed near Budge Budge. But he had to accept the decision of the war council. The movement from Fulta began on December 27.

On the twenty-ninth, Clive took his position north-east of the town of Budge Budge, and detached his sepoys under their Indian commander to make a foray towards the town. There they were joined by the English soldiers from the ships under Captain Coote, and were trying to take one of the forts when they learned that Clive was being hard-pressed by the army of Raja Manikchand, who had come down from Calcutta with two to three thousand horse and foot soldiers. Though their fire, directed from the cover of houses and bushes, was very harassing, Clive was keeping them at bay with brisk shooting, and a shot hit Manikchand's turban. When the other troops arrived Manikchand and his soldiers fled. Reporting the engagement to the Governor of Madras, Clive said that his losses in this skirmish were greater than could well be spared if such skirmishes were to be often repeated. One ensign and nine privates were killed, and eight wounded. But the enemy's losses were much greater, and the people of the country spread exaggerated rumours about the killed and wounded on the Indian side.

After that there were consultations about storming the fort. The ships had silenced the guns of the fort, and Captain Coote was eager to launch an attack. Clive, however, sent word that this was not to be attempted till the next morning. So, a strong body of sailors stood by. In the evening Coote went on board the *Kent* to ask if the Admiral wished the sailors to be sent back to the ships till the morning. In his absence a thoroughly drunk sailor named Strahan stole away from the party, entered the fort through a breach, and found a number of the Nawab's soldiers sitting on a platform. He fired his pistol at them and, flourishing his cutlass, rushed upon them with three loud huzzas and a shout: 'The place is mine.' He was attacked and began to fight desperately, though his cutlass broke off at the hilt. Hearing the noise the other soldiers rushed in and drove out the enemy. Coote took over command at once, and fired a salute at dawn.

Strahan was taken before the Admiral for gross breach of military discipline, and asked why he had behaved like that. He replied: 'Why, to be sure, Sir, it was I who took the fort, but I hope there was no harm in it.' Though the Admiral felt more like laughing than scolding, Strahan was severely reprimanded. In his injured innocence he muttered as he was being taken away: 'If I am flogged for this here action, I will never take another fort by myself as long as I live, by God.'

This was, however, the last and only resistance by the Nawab's army. Calcutta was reoccupied on January 2 1757, without fighting. Raja Manikchand, unable to forget his damaged head, went first to Hooghly and then to Murshidabad to tell the Nawab that the Englishmen who had come from Madras were very different from those he had defeated six months before. The terror aroused by English fighting was not only re-established but also increased. Clive reported that there was consternation at the quick recapture of Calcutta – accomplished in just a week's time. What impressed the people most was the dare-devilry of the sailors and the broadsides of the ships.

The comical feature of this feat was a quarrel, between Clive as the Company's representative and Admiral Watson as the King of England's, about the right to occupy Fort William. It was the soldiers under the Admiral who had first landed and occupied the fort. He had empowered Coote to garrison the fort of Calcutta with His Majesty's troops and 'not to quit your post, or deliver up your command till farther orders from me'.

So, when the Company's officers and troops arrived immediately after and wanted to go into the fort, they were ignominiously thrown out. Clive came down at once, either forced his way past the sentries or was allowed by them to pass (the point was disputed), and went to speak to Coote. When shown the Admiral's commission Clive denied that the Admiral had any authority to appoint a governor of the fort, and told Coote that if he disobeyed he would be placed under arrest. Coote yielded and went to report matters to the Admiral, who immediately sent an officer, Captain Speke, to find out by what authority Clive had assumed command of the fort. Clive replied that he had done so as lieutenant-colonel and commander-in-chief of the land forces.

There was a hot dispute between this officer and Clive about the manner in which Clive entered the fort. Speke wrote in a letter: 'I was much surprised to find you denied to Major Killpatrick having forced the sentinels – when to me you not only acknowledged it, but upon my taking the liberty to ask if it was a soldier-like action, you said much more so, than Captain Coote's making Mr Court a prisoner and driving out the sepoys.' But Speke wrote charitably: 'As you was then in heat, I have no doubt you did not much consider what you said. . . . I shall be glad to think this was, as I said, the language of passion.'

The Admiral upon hearing about Clive's action wrote angrily:

> I am extremely surprised to find you have not withdrawn the Company's troops, which puts me under a necessity of acquainting you, if you still persist in continuing in the fort, you will force me to take measures as will be disagreeable to me, as they can be possibly to you. I hope yet, after you have prudently considered this affair, you will not drive me to extremities I should be sorry to be urged to, for the plea you make of being commanding officer of the land forces, gives you not the least authority to enter a place (forcibly) conquered by me, and garrisoned by troops under my immediate command.

More mutual defiance followed, but at last Admiral Watson sent Captain Latham, commanding the *Tyger*, on a successful peace-making mission, Clive agreed to hand over the keys of the fort to the Admiral, and the Admiral in his turn agreed to hand them over to Governor Drake. This was done on January 3

1757. The party most pleased was the Governor and his Council and they passed the following resolution:

> Vice-Admiral Watson having taken Calcutta with His Majesty's ships of war, now delivers up the charge and possession of the fort and town to us the President and Council as representatives of the Honourable East India Company.
>
> Agreed likewise that we proclaim Fort William the seat of our Presidency, and publish our protection to the black inhabitants who are willing to return to the place.

The affair, though ending in a compromise, left Clive, a man of moods, with extremely bitter feelings, so that five days later, on January 8 1757, he wrote privately to Governor Pigot:

> Between friends I cannot help regretting that ever I undertook this expedition. The mortifications I have received from Mr Watson and the gentlemen of the squadron, in point of prerogative, are such, that nothing but the good of the service could induce me to submit to them.

He was also becoming suspicious of the conduct of the President and Council in Bengal, and wrote in the same letter:

> Added to all, the gentlemen here seem much dissatisfied at the authority I am vested with. It would be contradicting my own sentiments, if I was not to acknowledge that I still persevere in the opinion that the gentlemen of Madras could not have taken a step more prudent, or more consistent with the Company's interest: for I am sorry to say, the loss of private property, and the means of recovering it, seem to be the only object which takes up the attention of the Bengal gentlemen.

Actually, Clive had seen a letter of protest about his authority written by the Calcutta Council to Madras, and refused to add his signature to it.

This kind of behaviour is natural in those who are saved by the exertion of others. It would seem that the refugees at Fulta had begun to recover from their fright and demoralization when they heard about the approach of the relieving expedition from Madras, for an eye-witness who had come with the squadron from Madras wrote after seeing them upon his arrival: 'When we saw them first, to our great surprise, they appeared with as cheerful countenances, as if no misfortunes had happened to them.' From this state of mind to a mood of impudent self-assertion is only one step. So it is not surprising to find the Council of Fort William writing a letter of protest to the Council of St George on January 8 1757. In it, Calcutta objected to the action of the Madras Council in, firstly, giving independent powers to Clive, secondly, consigning all the money and military stores to that 'gentleman only', and thirdly, giving directions to Clive to return with his troops 'whenever you may call upon him'.

The language of the communication was extremely sharp. The Calcutta Council wrote:

> We cannot conceive by what authority you have assumed the right in giving that gentleman the powers you have done, and therein treating us in the light of a subordinate, notwithstanding you have admitted and addressed us Governor and Council. The incoherence of this proceedings is so apparent that we are astonished at your overlooking it.

So they warned Madras:

> Should any of the Colonel's plans therefore miscarry which deviate from our sentiments, we must esteem you Gentlemen responsible to the Honourable Company for the consequences.

And finally:

> Upon the whole we are of opinion, Gentlemen, the authority and trust invested in us by our Honourable Masters have been highly infringed by your unprecedented conduct.

Naturally, Clive felt disgusted, and he wrote to Pigot:

> My dear Sir, I would have you guard against everything these gentlemen can say: for, believe me, they are bad subjects and rotten at heart, and will stick at nothing to prejudice you and the gentlemen of the committee; indeed, how should they do otherwise, when they have not spared one another? I shall only add, their conduct at Calcutta finds no excuse, even among themselves; and that the riches of Peru and Mexico should not induce me to dwell among them.

Clive also informed Pigot that these men were trying to win over Admiral Watson to their side by the most assiduous attendance and respect. Actually, as Clive put it, 'in the Company's present distressed circumstances they propose giving the sailors 50 bales of broad cloth which I think might well be spared. . . .' He suspected Holwell to be the moving spirit behind these moves against him. This quarrel was to continue.

173

Chapter Six

War with Siraj-ud-daula

Formal Declaration of War
These family quarrels did not, however, affect the resolution to deal firmly with Siraj-ud-daula. On the very day the quarrel between Clive and Admiral Watson was made up, i.e. on January 3 1757, the Council at Fort William issued a declaration of war against Siraj-ud-daula, and requested Admiral Watson to issue another in the name of the King of England.

In so doing the Council took their stand on the firman granted by the Emperor of Delhi, and stated that it had not entered their minds that Siraj-ud-daula as the Subadar of Bengal, Bihar and Orissa should violate the said firman. Then they recounted all that had happened, and declared 'open war against the aforesaid Siraj-ud-daula and against the subjects of the said subadar, their cities, towns, shipping and effects, according to the maxims and rules of all nations until ample restitution was made'.

They assured the other European nations that they did not intend to molest them unless they assisted Siraj directly; to the people of Bengal they said that unless they took up arms for Siraj, whose conduct they must detest, they could rest assured of the company's favour and live in security, and no hostilities would be offered to them in their persons, habitations, grounds or effects.

The Admiral, in his declaration of war on the same day, asserted that the duty he owed to the King his master, whose honour had been insulted, and his subjects would not permit him to refuse the request of the Company to declare war. So he proclaimed: 'I do therefore in the name of His Britannic Majesty hereby declare war by sea and land against the Subah of Bengal, Bihar and Orissa and his subjects who hath so unjustly begun it.' He warned everybody that if they transported soldiers, arms or any contraband goods for the Subadar of Bengal their goods would be taken as booty.

Both Clive and Watson acted promptly on the declaration and sent the twenty-gun *Bridgewater* and the sloop *Kingfisher* with troops to raid and destroy the nawab's establishments at Hooghly, a town about thirty miles up the river. It was the seat of the nawab's *faujdar*, or military governor, and contained granaries and other stores. The expedition started on January 5; it took Hooghly and burnt the stores there on January 10. It was a very bold stroke.

But all this outward defiance did not have much real confidence behind it. Clive had very little information about Siraj-ud-daula's intentions and movements, and was worried about his own insufficient strength. He wrote formally to the Council at Madras on January 8 that 'from the slight trial we have hitherto had of the enemy we cannot form a judgement what success we may promise ourselves against them; deficient as we are of our complement of men, artillery and stores, the event must needs be doubtful'. He asked for reinforcements to make up at least two thousand sepoys.

To Governor Pigot he wrote informally: 'I cannot take upon me to give my sentiments about our future success against the nabob in the open field.' Indeed he feared that he would labour under many disadvantages if attacked by the nabob. He even doubted whether the expedition to Hooghly would succeed.

This was the first expression in the course of the war against Siraj of Clive's inclination not only to be prudent and cautious, but also to be pessimistic about his prospects. Uncertainty about most things is unavoidable in warfare, and it tends to make all prudent commanders somewhat hesitant. Even when they take what is called a calculated risk, from their point of view it is almost a gamble. Clive, however, had in him something more than this natural military diffidence. In fighting he was so temperamental as to be almost like an animal, whose fiercest attacks are provoked by fear. On most occasions he was prone to be cautious by calculation but desperate in action, as if he had read his Shakespeare and was always having a dialogue between the two sides of his self:

The purpose you undertake is dangerous.

Why that is certain: 'Tis dangerous to take a cold, to sleep, to drink; but I tell you (my Lord Fool) out of this Nettle Danger, we pluck this Flower, Safety.

The purpose you undertake is dangerous, the Friends you have named uncertain, the Time itself unsorted, and your whole Plot too light, for the Counterpoise of so great an Opposition.

Say you so, say you so: I say unto you again, you are a shallow cowardly Hind, and you lie.

Clive was only half a berserk: both the desperate courage and the pessimism were in his nature, and in a manner of speaking one might say that it was his successes that contributed most to the unfair judgements on his actions. In retrospect they appeared so inevitable that he was crudely represented as timorous.

At the moment of writing to Pigot, in any case, his pessimism was supported by the cooler judgement of the French at Chandernagore, who had more reliable information about Siraj and gave their appraisement of the prospects for the English in a letter written to their chiefs in Paris on January 18. After narrating the events up to the recovery of Calcutta, they observed:

> This is, up to the present time, the extent of their advantages, more brilliant than solid ... whatever pretence the English may make that they will maintain themselves in this town [Hooghly], there is little appearance of their doing so or that they will divide their force between this town and Calcutta at the risk of seeing themselves driven from both at once. What is certain is that they will speedily have on their hands all the troops of Siraj-ud-daula, who is always in the position to repair his losses and will not hesitate to sacrifice men to keep them ceaselessly on the alert, whereas the slightest check might deprive them of all resources and oblige them to withdraw.

So the French at Chandernagore thought that in spite of any successes the English might have in the fighting they would be forced to come to terms with Siraj.

There is no doubt that all appearances were in favour of this appraisement. For themselves, the French had great fear. Law had written to them that Siraj had left Murshidabad with rage in his heart against Europeans in general, and that he was a man of such ferocity that if he was defeated he might be guilty of the greatest excesses against the smaller factories, and cut the throats of all in them in order to avenge himself on at least some Europeans for the affront he received from others, even though of a different nation.

One of the Jagat Seths at Murshidabad whose intercession Clive had requested also wrote to him that he could do nothing if the English remained on the war-path:

In what manner then can I introduce an application for accommodating matters between the Nabob and you? What your intentions are it is impossible to find out by these acts of hostility. Put a stop to this conduct and let me know what your demands are. You may then depend upon it I will use my interest with the Nabob to finish these troubles. How can you expect that the Nabob will pass by or overlook your conduct in pretending to take up arms against the Prince or Subah of the country? Weigh this within yourself.

However ready Clive might have been to weigh his chances against Siraj within himself, he was not disposed to show any conciliatory spirit in his reply to the Jagat Seth brothers, which he sent on January 21. He drew their attention to the 'horrid cruelties and barbarities' inflicted upon the unfortunate English and referred specifically to the fact that no less than 120 people, 'the greatest part of them gentlemen of distinction', were put to an 'ignominous death'. Under these circumstances he asked: 'How can you expect we should no longer defer our resentment?' He said that the English had waited at Fulta without committing any hostilities; that the Governor of Budge Budge first declared war against the English by firing on the King's ships. Even so he added that he was ready to negotiate and sent his terms. But he accompanied them with the following concluding words:

> You should consider that the English are a great nation, and that a King reigns over them not inferior in power to the Padsha himself. What resentment will not His Imperial Majesty express when he comes to hear of the death of so many of his faithful subjects?

He reminded the Seths that on the coast of Coromandel the English had dealt with as powerful enemies as the Nawab and had been successful. He concluded with the warning:

> The like may happen here. However, I hope the Nabob will not reduce us to the cruel necessity of trying our strength, for after all success depends upon God alone, who will aid and assist the injured.

In the meanwhile, Clive and the Council tried to make Fort William stronger for defence, so that, as Clive stated, the place 'cannot be taken again by the Moors but by cowardice'. He also raised a small local battalion by enlisting the north Indian soldiers of fortune. He gave them not only European arms and equipment but also a modified European uniform – with a red coat, tall headgear, but scanty underclothing, and sandals – and it became the *Lal Paltan* (the Red Regiment), or the 1st Regiment of Bengal Native Infantry. In spite of that he found his strength to be too small, and on January 20 wrote to Admiral Watson that his whole military force, rank and file, would not exceed 300 Europeans. Therefore he requested the admiral to send him the King's troops and place them under his command. Watson at once agreed and wrote the next day: 'I cannot help thinking the number of your own troops are too few even to act defensively against the Nabob, therefore I have given orders to the captains of the several ships to discharge their troops, and have directed Captain Weller to join you, and put himself under your command until further orders.'

Siraj marches down to Calcutta
Siraj-ud-daula was already marching towards the south with a large force. After the capture of Calcutta he had marched back in triumph to Murshidabad, extracting his tribute from the French and the Dutch. He did not take the presence of the English refugees at Fulta seriously. People saw his reappearance in his capital with dismay. Everyone longed for a change, but saw no prospect of it. It would seem that some prominent persons at court were already hatching conspiracies against Siraj, and some of them, including Mir Jafar, were in touch with Shaukat Jang, Siraj's first cousin, who had already obtained a firman from Delhi appointing him nawab. Siraj decided to deal with this rival at once, and sent one of his courtiers to demand the surrender of some of the districts. Shaukat replied arrogantly that he was the subadar and he would allow Siraj to retire to Dacca and live there as a private person. Siraj marched against him, and in a battle near Rajmahal Shaukat was defeated and killed on October 16 1756. Upon his return to Murshidabad Siraj received his formal investment from Delhi. The mood of his subjects and of the Europeans in Bengal is best described in the words of Law, who was present at Cossimbazar (very near Murshidabad) and was in touch with Siraj through all these events. Law wrote in his memoirs:

> Behold him then, freed by this event from all his inquietudes; detested it is true, but feared even by those who knew him only by name. In a country where predestination has so much power over the mind, the star of Siraj-ud-daula was, they said, predominant; nothing could resist him. He was himself persuaded of this. Sure of the good fortune which accompanied him, he abandoned himself

more than ever to his passions, which urged him to every imaginable act of violence.

The predicament of the Europeans was no less humiliating. Law wrote:

> It can be guessed what we had to suffer, we and the Dutch, at Cossimbazar. There were continual demands on demands, insults on insults, on the part of the officers and soldiers of the country, who forming their behaviour on that of their master, thought they could not sufficiently show their contempt for everything which was European; we could not even go out of our grounds without being exposed to some annoyance.

But Law also made the amazing statement that 'the rash valour of the young Nawab of Purnea, in delivering Siraj-ud-daula from the only enemy he had to fear in the country, made it clear to all Bengal that the English were the only power which could bring about the changes everyone was longing for'.

But Siraj did not seem to be very eager to begin a new war with the English. In the latter half of January 1757 two important persons approached both the French and the Dutch with a view to bringing about a peace between Siraj and the English. This was believed to have been inspired by Siraj. Then he wrote himself.

While marching on Calcutta he sent a belated reply on January 23 to Admiral Watson's letter of December 15–16. He pretended that he had sent a reply at once but that it had been lost, and then complained about Drake. He showed himself ready to give the English the right to trade on the same terms as before. His formal letter closed with the words: 'If the English behave themselves like merchants and follow my orders, they may rest assured of my favour, protection and assistance.' But he added in his own hand: 'If you imagine that by carrying on a war against me you can establish your trade in these dominions you may do as you think fit.'

On January 27 the Admiral replied to his letter very politely. He laid the blame of the cruel acts of the nawab on his advisers – 'wicked men, who have misrepresented things to you through malice or private ends.' Then he made an appeal: 'Great Princes delight in acts of justice and in showing mercy. If therefore you are desirous of meriting the fame of a great Prince, and a lover of justice, shew your abhorrence of these proceedings by punishing those evil counsellors that advised them.' He also wanted restitution of property made to the company, and then added with his own hand, like Siraj:

> Although I am a soldier as well as you, I had rather receive satisfaction from your justice than to be obliged to force it by the distress of your innocent subjects.

The Admiral sent copies of both letters to his superiors in London and observed: 'What will be the event I cannot pretend to say, but I am afraid I will be under the necessity of continuing longer here than I would chuse to do, as I must not leave them till such time they are in a state of security against insults from the Country Power.' This, he added, would be harmful for the squadron, for the ships were in a bad state and men sickly. He said that he had lost more men since he had entered the river (i.e. in six weeks) than in a whole year before.

Siraj's next letter to Admiral Watson expressed great indignation for the capture and plunder of Hooghly and he observed that 'these are not actions becoming merchants!' However, he showed himself conciliatory and even assured Watson that for the sake of the friendship of the English he would make good the damages inflicted by his soldiery. He observed:

> You are a Christian, and know how much preferable it is to accommodate a dispute than to keep it alive, but if you are determined to sacrifice the interests of your Company and the good of private merchants to your inclination for war, it is no fault of mine. To prevent the fatal consequence of such a ruinous war I write this letter.

But certainly Siraj was not the man to mean what he wrote, or rather to realize what he wrote. He wrote on the impulse of the moment, according to the state of mind he was in. So when he was giving assurances of his good will to Admiral Watson, he also wrote to Renault, the French chief at Chandernagore, with a view to getting the French to help him. His letter, written on January 30, was most ingratiating:

> To the greatest of merchants, the model of true friends, M. Renault, Director-General of the French Company. Be always happy. I remember that between the greatest of merchants and the English, a people without faith, there is enmity and hatred.... I will never pardon their crimes except at your intercession.... I learn also by Raja Manikchand, my very beloved brother and sustainer of my grandeur and power, that it is certain that the greatest of merchants promises to assist me. This is why I notify you, that if you, who are the model of friends, employ your power to aid me, and if you

continue in this intention, you should prepare the ships of war you have in this country, put one of my people on each, and send them to punish this faithless people and chase them from the country.

In return he promised to abolish the imports on their commerce for ever, and to give them the right to establish a mint at Chandernagore. He also said that he would write to 'the high in honour and dignity, the very illustrious Nawab, M. Bussy'. However, two days later he wrote to Clive in the same conciliatory tone as he had employed in writing to the Admiral, though he also observed that 'your plundering of Hooghly was not like merchants'.

Clive replied two days later (February 3 1757) in the following words:

I thank God that I have found you so graciously inclined. I shall send a relation of my own and another person tomorrow morning to confer with your Excellency about our affairs, who will fully explain to you my inclinations, and may advise me in return of your pleasure.

Clive wrote about the situation to his father on either the same day or the next (February 4):

We are encamped with our little army; and the Nabob is at the head of forty thousand to give us battle. I am in hopes of everything will be concluded to the Company's advantage, though not in so glorious a manner as I could wish.

Previous to this Clive has established a fortified camp about five miles north of Calcutta, and decided to wait for Siraj-ud-daula there, instead of in Fort William, which was in his opinion 'in a wretched defenceless condition'. At first he was not sure that it might not be a hazardous step, but after reconnoitring he found a suitable spot which commanded a wide plain, where he could stand between Siraj and the town. The place is now a congested suburb of Calcutta, but it was a desolate spot then. A wild buffalo charged and gored to death a sepoy of his party, and then escaped, though shot. Clive also established two batteries, one on the river to the west and another to the southeast, to secure his communications. Admiral Watson had arranged for three of his ships – the fifty-gun *Salisbury*, the twenty-gun *Bridgewater* and the sloop *Kingfisher* – to support Clive's river flank, but he found that the bank was so high that the ships could not bring to bear the full power of their broadsides, and so they were withdrawn. But as it was, Clive reported on January 28: 'We are in a very good condition to act defensively against his [Siraj's] whole army, and when the other forces arrive hope to finish everything by a decisive stroke.'

He was not left in peace, however, to deal with military matters by the Council in Calcutta. Not satisfied with protesting to Madras about the powers given to Clive, on January 18 they formally summoned him to 'recede from the independent powers given you by the Committee of Fort St George', to 'strictly comply with and follow whatever plans the Select Committee of Fort William may judge proper to point out' and 'not to think of making any treaty of peace or accommodation with the subah without concurrence and approbation'. There were other peremptory demands.

Clive replied firmly on January 20 that he refused to give up his powers, and said that he could do so only to those who had entrusted him with them. But he assured the Calcutta authorities that his one interest was that of the Company, 'and as long as that is kept in view, I do assure you, Gentlemen, you shall always find me ready to follow your instructions'.

He wrote to the Governor of Madras on January 25: 'You will observe I was not mistaken in telling you the gentlemen here would not be wanting in their endeavour to possess themselves of the whole or part of my power. However, they have found themselves mistaken and Mr Watson has not been prevailed upon to look upon them in any other light than what they really deserve.' He added: 'The gentlemen seem well satisfied with my answer and I believe I may venture to assure you I shall meet with no further opposition.' But the Calcutta Council complained to London the next day.

There was also uncertainty about the Nawab. He was sending out proposals for a settlement through many channels and was also writing conciliatory letters himself, expressing his willingness to restore the Company's business. Clive believed that he was sincere, and told the Calcutta Council very plainly that 'if he [Siraj] will give such terms as are consistent with the interest of the Company, and no other, all private satisfaction must be laid aside'. Both he and the Admiral were of the opinion that the matter must be settled quickly, and if possible without fighting.

But neither he nor Clive could be sure whether Siraj really wanted a settlement or was only misleading them in order to be able to reach Calcutta without molestation and retake the town and fort. What was undoubtedly true was that he was coming down with a very large and apparently powerful force.

Nonetheless, Siraj made a formal proposal to have a discussion with Clive's representatives, and as has been stated before, Clive agreed. On the morning of February 4 he sent Walsh (his relative) and Scrafton. They had been asked to meet Siraj some miles north of Calcutta, but upon going there they found that Siraj had left the place. He was actually in Calcutta, and had pitched his camp in Omichand's garden on the outskirts of the city, within the Company's territory. His army was also there, encamped in tents stretching for miles around him. Siraj wrote to Clive to explain that the place previously mentioned was unsuited for encampment and so he had come to Calcutta. Then he wrote:

> Let not this give you any uneasiness. Your business is with me. Rest contented and send me your relation and the other person whom you shall depute to settle affairs with me as soon as possible. I swear by God and His Prophet that no evil shall happen to them.

When Walsh and Scrafton did not find him at the appointed place, they came down to the camp in Calcutta. What followed was typical of the drama throughout the conquest of Bengal. At seven in the evening they were introduced to the audience. Before that Raja Durlabhram Rai, a Bengali raised to the position of *diwan,* wanted to find out if they had any pistols with them, and also asked them to leave their swords behind; this they refused to do, regarding it as an indignity. However, they were introduced to Siraj, who, as Scrafton himself related, 'affected to appear in great state, attended by the best-looking men among his officers, hoping to intimidate them by so warlike an assembly'. Orme gave further details that

> many others of inferior degree, such as were of the largest stature, and bore the greatest marks of ferocity in their countenances, had likewise been selected to attend on the occasion; who, to appear still more terrible, were dressed in thick stuffed garments, with enormous turbans, and during the audience sat scowling at the deputies, as if they only waited the signal to murder them.

Siraj did not discuss the matter with them, and after the preliminary compliments desired them to retire and put their proposals to his ministers. Walsh and Scrafton first of all insisted that Siraj should go back to the previously appointed place, which was refused. On being presented with the English terms, the ministers shuffled around with them a little; dissatisfied, they asked to see the Nawab himself, privately. But Siraj was convinced that they had hidden arms with them and would murder him, and so would not see them. They were, however, asked to see the agent of the Jagat Seths, who, they were assured, would have something 'to communicate to them that would be very agreeable to the Colonel'.

Walsh and Scrafton were, however, suspicious. They were convinced that Siraj meant to detain them and attack the fort the next day. So instead of going to the agent they made their escape in the dark, and reported what had happened to Clive in his camp. It was late in the evening, but Clive decided to act at once and attack the Nawab's camp.

Siraj retreats from Calcutta

It is necessary to have a very precise idea of the strength of each side. At the camp Clive had 800 European soldiers, 1,300 sepoys and 100 artillery men with 14 six-pounders. Against him, according to rough estimates, were at least 20,000 horsemen and 30,000 infantry with 25 pieces of heavy artillery. So Clive went to Watson and asked for a contingent of sailors. From midnight a total of 569 sailors began to be landed from the ships. The concentration was completed by about 3 a.m. (February 5 1757), and the whole attacking force, consisting of approximately 500 British infantry, 800 sepoys, 600 sailors, 6 fieldpieces and 1 howitzer, began its march a little later in the dark.

At dawn the force came down to the nawab's camp and was challenged. They repulsed attacks and continued the march in thick fog. A little later they were attacked by a large body (estimated at 300–500 men) of horsemen. These approached to within ten yards of Coote's soldiers, who fired at very close range, killing nearly all of them. When the fog cleared they had passed south of the Nawab's camp, and were being fired upon by both guns and matchlocks. It was not possible to turn back to attack the nawab's camp. Therefore the force continued to march southwards, and, reaching the point where the railway station of Sealdah now stands, turned right and reached the fort before noon. In the evening they marched back into their camp. For a force of its size, the losses were heavy – 27 British soldiers, 12 British sailors and 18 sepoys were killed; and 70 British soldiers, 12 British sailors and 55 sepoys were wounded.

Among the dead were two British officers and Clive's secretary, Belcher. Their bodies could not be recovered, because the dead were so barbarously mutilated that they could not be identified. The enemy's losses, by reliable reports, were placed at 1,300, including some of their best officers. Clive wrote to his father on February 23: 'The last attack was the warmest service I ever yet was engaged in.' In fact, the English losses were higher than at the battle of Plassey – where 20 were killed, 45 wounded and 2 were missing.

This action has been criticized. Orme even wrote that 'the troops, as well as common men, dispirited by the loss which had been sustained, and the risques to which they had been exposed, as they thought, to very little purpose, blamed their commander, and called the attempt rash, and ill concerted.' The French at Chandernagore thought that the attack was bungled. Even Clive wrote to his father: 'The expedition is attended with nothing but reputation.'

But Law, who was in close touch with the events, gave a wholly different complexion to the second attack on Calcutta by Siraj and the calculations of the English. He wrote in his memoirs that the English

> ... wished for nothing better than to see the nawab precipitate himself upon them. It was their interest to decide the quarrel in the quickest way, for fear we [the French] should resolve to take part in it. Accordingly, as soon as they saw the enemy they purposely spread alarm in Calcutta. All the women were ordered on board the ships. The country merchants and people who had entered Calcutta with the English left it, all with the intention of giving confidence to the nawab and encouraging him to approach so that they might be more certain of the blows they struck him. The nawab fell into the snare. He imagined his mere presence sufficed to put the enemy to flight, that the present attack would differ in nothing from that of the month of June in the preceding year.

Law even asserted that Scrafton and Walsh were sent with peace proposals only for the purpose of examining the position of Siraj's camp so that they might carry out an attack which would be premeditated.

This was, however, too subtle an explanation for the facts; when the two representatives were sent the English thought that the nawab was still twenty miles to the north. On February 3, they found the nawab's troops trying to enter Calcutta and

185

repulsed them in the afternoon. On the morning of the fourth they learned that the nawab himself might be with his main army, which appeared in sight. They got certain information about his presence only when Scrafton and Walsh returned. So the decision taken by Clive to attack Siraj in his camp was impromptu, but its purpose certainly was, if possible, to capture or kill Siraj in his camp. This was never clearly admitted, but the account in Clive's journals says that 'an unlucky fog prevented an attack upon the nabob's headquarters, which if successful, would have made the action more decisive'.

It is established by all the documents that both Clive and Watson wished the dispute to be settled by negotiation rather than by military action. For instance, even after learning that Siraj was within Calcutta, Admiral Watson wrote to him on February 4 that he was still inclined to peace, 'notwithstanding the little prospect of its taking place'. So he concluded his letter to Siraj with the following words:

> If you really and sincerely mean to treat of peace, listen to the proposals which will be made by the gentlemen who are now with you. They are for nothing but justice, nor mean anything more than the mutual good of both nations. If you refuse it, remember, that princes are only placed at the head of mankind to procure their happiness, and that they must one day give a very severe account, if through ambition, revenge or avarice, they fail in their duty.

He added that he had done his duty by giving his advice and explained that he was writing the letter 'to take away all blame from me, both in the eyes of god and man, and to convince the world how much rather I wish to see the happiness of mankind than their misery'. But the return of Scrafton and Walsh convinced both Clive and Watson that Siraj wanted war, and they took the decision to forestall him.

The attack on his camp brought Siraj round, and he made an offer of peace, while breaking up his camp and moving northwards. Both Clive and Watson wrote to him on February 6, justifying the attack on the score of his treatment of the envoys and, as the Admiral put it, 'to shew you what an army of Englishmen was capable of doing'. Clive said: 'I therefore made a tour through your camp to show you what I was capable of effecting.' Watson wrote that unless Siraj acceded to the reasonable proposals that were being offered for the last time, 'the sword is going to be drawn that never will be sheathed again'. Clive wrote that he was going to have reinforcements sent, and 'if these should not prove sufficient to procure satisfaction from you... the great King of England... will certainly send forces sufficient to destroy the whole province'.

On February 7 the Admiral wrote to Clive that he felt that Siraj's offer to make peace was a feint, to cover his retreat and gain time till he was reinforced. He thought that the Nawab's rear should have been attacked, and set down his advice:

> Till he is well threshed, don't, Sir, flatter yourself he will be inclined to peace. Let us therefore not be overreached by his politics, but make use of our arms, which are more to be depended on.

He further requested Clive to consult his officers, with an apology for the liberty he was taking. But Clive at once agreed to call a council of war. No military action was, however, necessary. Siraj accepted the English terms and signed a treaty of peace on February 9 1757, with the following preamble by him:

> God and His Prophets are witnesses, that I never will deviate from the terms of the treaty I have now made with the English company, and that I will on all occasions show them my favours, relying on your faith to observe inviolably your part of the treaty.

In considering the conflict between the English and Siraj it must never be forgotten that it was more a psychological than a military war. That war was virtually decided by the night march through Siraj's camp on that marshy plain north-east of Calcutta. One very early morning nearly fifty years ago, standing at the extreme end of this plain, not inhabited even then, I saw the moon setting across the dreary salt lakes and casting a wan light on the desolate countryside. That light must have come down from that night in February 1757 which decided the fate of Muslim rule in Bengal.

Intimidation and Intrigue

The significance of this event was not, however, realized at the time. Indeed, it is not realized even now, and the battle of Plassey, fought on June 23 1757, in spite of being only a skirmish from the purely military point of view, is thought as one of the decisive battles of the world, judged by its result. In reality, this battle was only a military demonstration which was the last push in a game of intimidation and intrigue played with cynical thoroughness against the ruler who had provoked it, yet could only meet it with an imbecility made worse by his cunning. What gave a military complexion to the battle was a paradoxical situation in which, on the face of it, Siraj had overwhelming superiority in numbers and weapons against the small army of his antagonists. This superiority was, however, completely nullified by the disloyalty created by his own conduct and by his terror of English military power. But until Plassey revealed this situation fully these facts could not be perceived or relied on.

After the conclusion of the treaty on February 9, the English in Calcutta envisaged two possibilities, without being sure of either: the first was that there might be peaceful co-existence between the Company and the Nawab, and the second that further military action might be necessary. As things turned out, the goal afterwards reached was only just round the corner, but the path was winding, jungly, muddy and dark. The only circumstances that could have given a military character to the overthrow of Siraj was a collaboration between him and the French – a circumstance that might have occurred because war had been declared between England and France in Europe, and the news had reached Bengal by the beginning of 1757. But Siraj was afraid of openly siding with the French, though he secretly sought their help. He would not take their help, nor come to their aid, until he knew that the French were winning by themselves. The French, too, at the beginning were more afraid of Siraj than of the English, and missed their opportunity. So both were destroyed, one after the other, by the English. Even so the only real military operation in the conquest of Bengal was the capture of Chandernagore. The rest of it was tortuous intrigue punctuated by sabre-rattling.

Intrigue began on the very morrow after the treaty. But before narrating the course of these political moves it would be helpful to the understanding of the events to review the character and intentions of the dramatis personae and describe the methods employed.

Of course, the main character was Siraj-ud-daula. The curious thing was that, though his character was well known, it could never be predicted what it would lead him to do. However, it became evident to all observers that after his failure to take Calcutta a second time his behaviour and outlook changed. It brought to the surface his real character, which, although not wholly suspected, was hidden by the arrogance created by his position, apparent power and successes. All these had made him appear as the typical Muslim prince, haughty and intoxicated with power, whose ambition would make him repeat: 'Ten dervishes can sleep under one blanket, but two kings cannot reign in one kingdom,' and incite him to patricide or fratricide without hesitation. But the English in Calcutta gave him such a fright that after this he emerged into a type very common in the East – desperately timid or wildly bold, everlastingly greedy, and full of cunning which never did him any good. But even this erratic character he exhibited in a demented form during these months.

Jean Law, who was in close touch with him during this period and tried his best to give him good counsel, has left a description of Siraj's feelings after the treaty. 'The anger of the Nawab against the English', he wrote in his memoirs, 'was naturally inflamed by all that had happened. To his first reasons for dislike there were now joined disgust, the shame of his inability to avenge himself, and the rage caused by his seeing his enemies dictate the law to him.' Soon after the treaty Law had a talk with Siraj in a private place, to which he was expressly sent. There Siraj began to question him about the forces the French had in Bengal, why their ships did not appear, why Bussy did not enter Bengal with his army. 'Then, passing to the English,' Law related, 'he said many things to me about them which made me understand that the peace he had made with them was nothing less than sincere. Fire flashed from his eyes as he spoke.'

But abject fear of the English had taken hold of him. To quote Law again:

> Fear and greed are the two chief motives of Indian minds. Often they combine to produce the same result. . . . When in 1756 Siraj-ud-daula determined to expel the English, fear and greed combined to make him act. As soon as the Nawab had experienced himself the superiority of the English troops fear took the upper hand in his mind, strengthened itself day by day, and soon put him in a condition in which he was unable to follow and often even to see his true interest.

He could not, on the other hand, lie low. As Law put it:

> Siraj-ud-daula was not a master of his temper; it would have needed as much firmness in his character as there was deceitfulness to make this last quality useful to him. His natural disposition overmastered him at certain times, especially in his harem, when he was surrounded by his wives and servants.

These were not the words of an enemy, but of a man who was

trying to be his friend and helper. Law was seeking to persuade Siraj to make common cause with the French, but doubts passed through his mind. As he wrote later, 'I ask in all good faith, if we could expect any advantage from his friendship? This person, cowed by fear, irresolute and imprudent, could he alone be of any use to us?'

Watts, who had been intolerably humiliated after the capture of Cossimbazar the previous year, now accompanied Siraj as the representative of the Company at the durbar. He was equally aware of the state of Siraj's mind. As early as February 25 (i.e. only sixteen days after the treaty) he wrote to his friend Walsh: 'As the predominant passion in the Nabob is fear, the more powerful we make ourselves the greater compliance we shall meet from him.' He repeated the same opinion in a formal letter written to the Council at Fort William on the same day, in which he also suggested the practical application of the view he took of the Nawab's character and observed:

> Therefore if we attack and take Chandernagore every part of our agreement will be fulfilled and more indulgence granted us. If we are unsuccessful we shall get nothing, and if a neutrality is concluded with the French no artifice, no chicanery, or cunning will be left untried to delay putting us in possession of what the Nabob has assented to.

Watts wrote emphatically in his letter to Walsh: 'For by what I can learn there is no faith to be put upon either his word or oath. This is the current opinion of all degrees and orders of people.' Law, also, wrote: 'The English, knowing the character of Siraj perfectly, relied very little on his promises, and expected him at the first opportunity to take his revenge. His whole conduct favoured the idea.' This became the fundamental assumption of English policy and actions.

From the day of the treaty, Siraj began to shower letters on Clive as well as on others, sometimes sending even ten letters in one day. He wanted to disarm their suspicions but overdid the persuasion. On February 9 he wrote to Admiral Watson:

> As long as I have life I shall esteem your enemies as enemies to me, and will assist you to the utmost of my power whenever you may require it. Do you likewise, and the Colonel, and Chiefs of the English Factory swear in the presence of the Almighty God to observe and perform your part of the treaty, and to esteem my enemies as your own, and always be ready to give me your assistance against them.

Two days later he wrote to Clive in almost the same terms and assured him: 'When you write to me that you stand in need of my assistance I will give it to you.'

Ten days later he wrote again. He had heard that five or six more English ships had arrived and was afraid that the English might attack again. So he wrote to Clive that he understood that the real intention of the English was to make war on him during the rains, and apostrophized:

> This is not acting like a soldier or a man of bravery, who should be the same thing in heart as in profession. . . . After having made peace to begin war again, no religion can justify. The Marathas have no Book of God, yet are just to their contracts. You have the Book of God, if you are not just to your contracts it will be astonishing and unaccountable.

To the Admiral also he wrote in the same language:

> Is it becoming or honest to begin a war after concluding the Peace so lately and solemnly? The Marathas are bound by no Gospel, yet they are strict observers of treaties. It will therefore be a matter of great astonishment and hard to be believed, if you, who are enlightened with the Gospel, should not remain firm, and preserve the treaty you have ratified in the presence of God and Jesus Christ.

But a few days later or about the same time – the letter is undated – he wrote to Bussy:

> These disturbers of my country, the Admiral Watson and Colonel Clive, Sabut Jang, whom bad fortune attends, without any reason whatever are warring against Zubdatoo Toojah, Monsieur Renault the Governor of Chandernagore. . . . I, who in all things seek the good of mankind, assist him in every respect, and have sent him the best of my troops . . . and if it becomes necessary I will join him myself. I hope in God, these English who are unfortunate, will be punished for the disturbances they have raised. Be confident. Look on my forces as your own.

When the English attacked Chandernagore, he again wrote to Bussy telling him of his satisfaction on receiving the news that he was approaching Orissa in order to help in the defence of the French settlement. Encouraged by the French resistance at Murshidabad, he openly threatened to cut off Watts's head or impale him. But when the news of the fall of Chandernagore reached him he wrote to Clive:

> The particulars of your victory at Frankedongy [the place of the French. The popular Bengali name of Chandernagore is Farash

(Français) Danga], which I had long been impatient to hear, gave me inexpressible pleasure. I thank God that your enemies so easily fell into your hands, and that their great place is fallen into your hands. You have no longer any uneasiness on their account. It has pleased God to make you and all your friends happy in this great victory.

At the same time he wrote to Bussy: 'What can I write of the perfidy of the English, they have without ground picked a quarrel with Monsieur Renault and taken by force his Factory?'

On April 11 Siraj received Luke Scrafton with very great good humour. In the morning he had inquired who Scrafton was, and when he was described, he at once recalled that he had met Scrafton in his camp in Omichand's garden. He cried out: 'That's the garden chap, let him come.' When in the evening Scrafton appeared – as he reported – Siraj laughed and shook his head, as if to say 'It was a damned comical trick, but I shall remember you for it.' The trick was the flight at night. Scrafton returned the Nawab's laugh 'to the no small surprise of the solemn faces at his durbar'. Siraj then cried out: 'Give him a horse and a dress; no, let it be an elephant.' He was given the dress, and had to go to another room to put it on. Somebody dissuaded Siraj from the elephant, and Scrafton got a horse. Siraj also complimented Scrafton on his appearance in Muslim dress, and asked him if his health was good. Two days later, however, he got into a temper with Watts and in front of the entire court said again that he would cut off his head. Watts knew his man and wrote to Walsh:

> I write this for yours and the Colonel's notice alone, and desire no public affair be made of it, for I despise what the Nabob can do to me, and would not have you desist from any vigorous measures you may intend to pursue on my account.

Clive and Watson, who were fully informed of what was passing at Murshidabad through their spies by the interception of the Nawab's letters, and through the letters of their representative, took nothing seriously except the Nawab's bad faith. At about the time Clive and Watson were busy eliminating the French from Bengal, Watts was informed about the line to be taken with the Nawab. Clive wrote to Watts: 'The bent of our politicks hitherto has been by haughty and by submissive letters such as occasion required to persuade him to abandon the French to us. We must in pursuit of that system now endeavour to convince him that what we have done is best for him and us.'

This alternation of threats and cajoling was generally followed as a method of dealing with Siraj on all questions. However, generally speaking, the haughty line was given to the Admiral and the submissive to the Colonel. Two examples may be quoted. On March 6 1757, Admiral Watson wrote to Siraj:

> Is it thus that soldiers and men of honour never violate their words? But it is now time to speak plain, if you are really desirous of preserving your country in peace and your subjects from misery and ruin. In *ten days* from the date of this, fulfil your part of the treaty in *every article*, that I may not have the least cause of complaint: Otherwise, remember, you must answer for the consequences: and as I have always acted the open, unreserved part in all my dealings with you, I now acquaint you. . . . I will kindle such a flame in your country, as all the water in the Ganges shall not be able to extinguish. Farewell: remember that he promises you this who never yet broke his word with you or with any man whatsoever.

It should be kept in mind that there was nothing of which Siraj was more terrified than the great ships with their guns. His representatives were shown the thirty-two-pounder guns and spread wild tales about them.

Clive on his part employed as unctuous a language as Siraj himself. He also summoned the Nawab to fulfil the terms of the treaty but in the following language:

> I now call upon Your Excellency in the name of God and His Prophet to fulfil the articles, and I further call upon Your Excellency in the most sincere manner to put an entire confidence in the English, and to believe that they will never forsake you. . . . I conclude this letter with declaring before God and His Prophet Jesus, that if you comply with the contents of this letter and be a true friend of the English, I will in all respects act conformable to your wish and join against all your enemies.

There is no doubt that at this stage the best policy for Siraj would have been to fulfil every term of the treaty and gain the friendship of the English. But if his fear of the English kept him from siding openly with the French, the same fear, combined with his pride, made him incapable of trusting the English. He was not the man to forget his humiliation. What influenced him more was the fact that his judgement of the English led him to believe that they would never forget what had happened in Calcutta in 1756 and would try to take their revenge. So he evaded the commitment and thus drew more suspicion upon himself.

Apart from this, his general antipathy to Europeans was not to be overcome. Clive tried to incite him against the French by reminding him of what they had done in the Deccan. He wrote to Watts at Murshidabad: 'Represent to him in the strongest light what a state they have reduced Salabat Jang to; that they have extorted whole provinces from him.' In writing this Clive certainly did not consider that this might be precisely the position to which Siraj thought the English would reduce him.

The Court of Siraj
At all events, his fears deprived Siraj of the capacity to take any decision whatever, and made him resort to tergiversations in which he was only too cunning by half. As Law realized, Siraj needed a strong man with a clear judgement to guide him. But virtually none was to be found at his court. He had totally alienated all his natural supporters, i.e. the Muslim commanders of foreign origin holding the highest ranks and, above all, Mir Jafar, the ablest and most eminent among them. So far as this was the result of policy, Siraj gave offence by continuing his grandfather's practice of giving the highest posts of the state to the natives of the country, especially Hindus, in preference to the Muslim commanders of foreign origin. Being a foreign adventurer himself, Alivardi had been afraid of them as possible rivals, and he had also suffered from the disloyalty of his foreign mercenaries. But he kept the natives in their place and employed them as tools. Siraj preferred the natives out of pride, because they would be more servile, and he became more and more dependent on them. In addition, as has been already stated, he insulted his Muslim commanders from sheer frivolity. They were also afraid that he might have them assassinated out of greed or suspicion.

It has been mentioned that Siraj raised a particularly low Hindu adventurer, Mohanlal, to one of the highest posts, and made him his favourite. This man at least was loyal to him. Law regarded him as 'the greatest scoundrel the earth has ever borne, worthy minister of such a master', and still Siraj sought his help because he knew him to be resolute and clear-sighted, and besides bound to be true to Siraj because, hated as he was, he knew that the ruin of Siraj would also be his own ruin. But at this critical period he was seriously ill, supposedly having been poisoned. He recovered from it, but was never his old self again. The other Hindu ministers and high officials were all cowards and opportunists, ready to go over to the winning side as soon as they felt sure about the winner – which of course took them time to work out.

Siraj had also frightened and offended the house of Jagat Seth, the bankers and financiers of the state. After the army, such houses were the strongest support of the Muslim rulers. The Jagat Seths' honour had been wounded, but they were even more influenced by their fear of Siraj's greed for money. Though cautious at first, from the time of the treaty they seem to have become convinced that Siraj must go, and threw all the weight of their money and influence against him. They were the initiators of the final intrigue against him, and the most powerful movers. In order to see Siraj removed by the English, who were the only people who could do this, the Jagat Seth brothers even inflamed him against the English and persuaded him to reject any conciliatory proposals coming from Calcutta.

So Siraj was left with his unreliable Hindu advisers. Leaving aside their character, the mere fact that all the important offices of the state, including military commands, were held by natives had a deep significance. No foreign ruler of India has Indianized the upper stratum of his government without paying the price. As it was, all foreign rulers of India had to depend on three classes of natives in order to maintain their power and carry on their government. These were: the indigenous soldiery who were always ready to serve as mercenaries; the Hindu officials in the lower administration, especially in the collection of revenue; and the bania, or trading class, on whom the economic life of the country depended. These groups invariably passed from one set of foreign rulers to another as a legacy or as spoils of war. Their adherence to the foreigner depended on the power and stability of his rule. Towards the end of the nineteenth century a Russian officer wrote about the Indian soldiers under the British that they were like cats, more attached to the house than to the owner. But at that time the soldiers believed in British power, and so they said:

Khalk-i-Khuda
Mulk-i-Sarkar
Hukm-i-Sahiban Alishan
or translated:
Mankind to God
The country to the Government
The imperium to the great Sahibs [White].

This might have been the motto of the other two classes as well. But their support always depended on full foreign control at the top level of government, to dilute which was to undermine the whole fabric of foreign power. This was why Lloyd George called the Indian Civil Service the steel frame of the Empire in India. There is no doubt that Indianization ate into it, and contributed to the disappearance of British rule in India. No native of India can serve any foreign ruler without being a thorough opportunist, ready to leave the ship when it begins to sink.

This had happened to the Muslim government of Bengal at the time of Siraj, and the natives who were serving him were of an even lower order than the Indians in high office during the last days of British rule. To take only one man, there was the Bengali Durlabhram Rai or Rai Dullub: a worse coward, liar, and timeserver could not be conceived. There were others, among them another Bengali, Nandakumar, who was to come into greater prominence during the governor-generalship of Warren Hastings, and to be hanged for overplaying his hand. He had begun his rascally and double-dealing career under Siraj.

Contest in Bribery
The immediate aim of all these men was to fish in troubled waters and make as much money as possible out of all sides. So all moves against or for the English and the French became a contest in bribery. Both sides resorted to it cynically, and yet charged each other with greater unscrupulousness. Certainly, in this game the English were better placed. Law, who thought that he had secured a reliable intermediary with the Nawab by liberal gifts, found later that the man was taking larger bribes from the English. In his memoirs he stated the case very fairly:

> It would appear from the English memoirs that we had corrupted the whole Durbar of Murshidabad in our favour by the presents and false statements. I might with justice retort the reproach. In fact, except Siraj-ud-daula himself, it may be said that the English had, throughout, the whole durbar on their side. . . . Without insisting on this point, let us honestly agree, since the English themselves confess it, that we were much engaged in opposing corruption by corruption in order to gain the friendship of scoundrels, so as to place ourselves on equal terms with those opposed to us.

He observed that such was the nature of the government of Siraj that in it 'a man succeeds only by what he puts in the balance of iniquity', and he added: 'Right or wrong, it is certain the English were always in a position to put in more than we could.'

Watts, who appears to have been the agent of all this corruption at Murshidabad, did not lack humour in handling this dirty business. Nandakumar, who was at this time at Hooghly in the *de facto* position of *faujdar*, or military governor, wanted a bribe of some ten or twelve thousand rupees to mislead the Nawab about the intentions and movements of the English. So on February 18 1757 Watts wrote to Clive: 'If you approve of giving this present, all that you have to say to the bearer of this letter is, *Goolab-ki-phool*, or a "rose flower"; with which message Nuncomar will be satisfied that you comply with the agreement. . . .'

Apparently, Clive agreed and Nandakumar began to send reassuring reports to Siraj, who was nervous. On April 5 Watts wrote to Clive from Murshidabad:

> By bribery all the Nabob's *hircarras* [messengers] are our enemies, and are continually writing and giving false intelligence, which would be entirely successful if Nuncomaur's letters did not contradict those reports; therefore if you think proper when he comes to you again, you may tell him the *Goolab-ki-phool* is fresh and flourishing. Omichund and I are of opinion it is better not to let him smell it yet, but keep him in hopes, and acquaint him if he keeps firm to his agreement made with Omichaund, he may depend on your fulfilling your promise.

But Nandakumar was too thorough a rascal to be a traitor on credit. He got tired of waiting, and turned against the English.

It would be a mistake to think that the language of this diplomacy was always so delicate and flowery. Scrafton, who was more lively and inquisitive, was at Murshidabad, and his activities roused the suspicion of Siraj and his minions. So one of his high ministers (a Hindu) called on Walsh, a more discreet person, again and again and asked him: 'Why does not that *beti chod* of a Garden Chap go to Dacca?' Walsh had been posted to the English factory there. The *vakil* of the English replied gravely: 'Sir, he is only waiting to get the balance of his Dacca affairs.' 'Let him have it immediately,' was the reply, 'that I mayn't have that fellow here.' Scrafton added that Siraj could not bear the mention of his name.*

---

*Beti chod means 'a man who f - - - s his daughter', a term of abuse. From the way Scrafton reported the speech, it is not clear who actually made the remark, and it is possible that he was reporting Siraj's language as repeated to him by the Minister. From what is known of Siraj's manners that is quite possible.

With all this treachery and intrigue around him Siraj would not even be warned by friends. On this point Law wrote:

> In India it is thought disrespectful to tell a great man clearly the evil which is said of him. If anyone knows that designs are being formed against his life, the subject or inferior must use circumlocutions, suggest the subject in vague terms, and speak in enigmas. It is for the Nawab to devine what is meant. If he has not the wit, so much the worse for him. As a foreigner, I was naturally more bold, and said what I thought to Siraj-ud-daula.

This, however, was disapproved of by Law's native intermediary, who blamed him for his plain speaking. Normally, a ruler did not like to be told such things because he resented any expression of doubt about his power and position. But in the case of Siraj the unwillingness was caused mainly by fear. Knowing that he could not meet a really dangerous situation, he would turn his eyes and ears from it. But he was restless. Scrafton gives a vivid account of his state of mind in his letter of April 21 1757, when the conspiracy against him was just hatching.

> The horse frets and bites and cannot bear the bit. How glad would he be to fling his rider, and give him a kick that might give full swing to his unruly passions uncontrolled. What farther proofs would we have? The army is daily increasing. In the fit he was in ten days ago he ordered Meer Jaffeir to march, and promised him six *lack* the instant he advanced beyond their present encampment, and to make it ten* if he was victorious; the next day he starts at the danger, countermands the march, sends for the English *vacqueel* and gives him *beetle*.

But there was also danger from Siraj in spite of his cowardice. He could suddenly do something out of desperation or panic without regard for consequences. What was most to be feared from that kind of outburst was not so much military or political danger, as personal risk for those who had to do with him. He could at any moment order somebody to be assassinated. This was what prevented most of the prominent persons who were conspiring against him from acting so as to reveal their intentions until a military victory for the English had made it safe for them to do so.

Even Watts, the English representative at Murshidabad, fled before the march against Siraj began. Moreover, he could not

---

*Rs600,000 or 1,000,000. *Beetle* is, of course, *betel – pan*, given as a token of amity and regard.

leave openly. He and a friend pretended to go out for a ride in the evening, and even took their greyhounds with them to create the impression that they were going for coursing. The syces and the dog-keepers were sent back; they were told that Watts and his companion were coming back 'after taking a small circuit on the plain on their way home'. Most Englishmen in India kept greyhounds in the country and regularly went coursing. So this ruse was not suspected. As things turned out, Siraj, though urged to do so, did not take the life of anybody. He was too afraid. But whether his fear would not be suddenly suppressed by his anger could never be foreseen.

Chapter Seven
Plassey

Phases of the Campaign

The treaty with Siraj-ud-daula, which pledged friendliness between him and the Company, was concluded on February 9 1757; on June 23 the battle of Plassey, which resulted in his overthrow and death was fought. In retrospect, the clash and its outcome seemed inevitable, but at the time nothing at any moment between these two dates was certain. So, if philosophizing is permitted in history, these events might be drawn on to illustrate the unresolved debate between free will and predestination. All along free will in the person of Alice appeared to be asking predestination the Cheshire Cat:

> Would you tell me, please, which way I ought to walk from here?
> That depends a good deal on where you want to go to.
> I don't much care where –
> Then it doesn't matter which way you walk.
> So long as I get *somewhere* –
> Oh, you're sure to do that if you only walk long enough.

The English did not have to walk long to get to Plassey, but even on that day of battle, as will be seen later, they did not know where they wanted to go, or even to what point exactly they had progressed. As to policy, there was no agreement among the three parties concerned – namely Clive Watson and the Council in Calcutta. Yet they all acted, or were made to act, in concert at every critical juncture, and, without consenting, consented to what was in effect a course of aggressive action against Siraj.

It is not easy to narrate what happened. The discussions and decisions on the English side were confused by the disagreements among them, and also by the first and second thoughts of all the persons concerned. In addition, there were complications introduced by the vacillating manoeuvres of Siraj, which, though intended to be cunning, were more like the figures-of-eight made by an angry and frightened snake than like the dodges of a fox. Therefore, to give a chronological narrative of these events would be like throwing the pieces of a jigsaw puzzle at the reader without giving him the picture, and to destroy the perspective. A better method would be to define the phases clearly, say briefly what exactly happened in them, and then illustrate the happenings from contemporary accounts, bringing out the shifts in acting and thinking.

In the first phase the past was discussed – i.e., whether it had been right policy to make the treaty with Siraj instead of continuing the war in order to extort greater concessions from him. Over this question there was difference of opinion between the Calcutta Council and Clive.

The second phase, which began almost simultaneously, saw the question of the French in Bengal coming to the fore. The news of the war between England and France had been received both in Calcutta and Chandernagore, and the English had to decide whether to have a treaty of neutrality with the French in order to keep Bengal out of the European war (as had been done at the time of the war of the Austrian succession) or to eliminate the French from the province by attacking them. On this question the Calcutta Council and Clive on one side and Watson on the other held opposed views at first. When finally an attack was considered right, it could not be launched in Siraj's territory without his consent. He refused to give it. The French at first tried to secure neutrality and then, finding that the English would not agree to it, sought to have Siraj on their side. There was a good deal of intrigue at Murshidabad, but the English at last obtained the tacit consent of Siraj, and attacked Chandernagore, which was taken on March 23, 1757.

In the next phase the English were concerned with two questions: first, getting the remnants of the French forces eliminated and obtaining all the French settlements; secondly, making Siraj fulfil the terms of the treaty. This was not easy, for Siraj continually shifted his ground until the English finally came to the conclusion that he was not dependable.

The fourth phase saw the conspiracy to depose Siraj. In late April news was received in Calcutta from Murshidabad that some prominent persons there wished to replace Siraj with another nawab. The person finally fixed on was Mir Jafar. After discussing the matter the English decided to join the conspiracy and help Mir Jafar. A formal treaty was drawn up and signed by the Calcutta Council on May 19 1757. After some delay Mir Jafar swore to it on June 5.

The final phase began with the march towards the north and concluded with the death of Siraj. Calcutta learnt about this on the tenth, and on the thirteenth Clive began his march northwards, to reach Plassey on the night of June 22–23. But even on the morning of the twenty-third, when the battle began, Mir Jafar showed no signs of joining the English. However, it ended in the rout and flight of the Nawab's army.

On June 29 Clive entered Murshidabad and installed Mir Jafar as nawab. On July 2 Siraj was brought as prisoner to the city and killed. He was buried the next day.

It may indeed be said that as the events unfolded the English illustrated the saying: *'L'appétit vient en maneant'*. But it has to be added that they were fully convinced of the justice of their claims. They were also conforming to the Indian style of pursuing self-interest, according to which even now this is justified by the formula: *Mera roti ki bat* – It's a question of my daily bread. The Indian does not pray for it, he preys on it. But it also has to be noted that, even when they had installed Mir Jafar, the English did not realize that they were on the way to becoming the rulers of Bengal, but only thought that for the time being they had secured their commercial position there.

Discussion of Policy

These five phases have now to be described in some detail so as to bring out their peculiar character.

In the first phase, immediately after the treaty was signed, the Calcutta Council sent a note to Clive. They asked that he should call a council of war to consider whether the present strength of the Company was not sufficient to force the Nawab to better terms, and if new advantages should be insisted upon as they might well be granted. Clearly, with the repulsing of Siraj, Governor Drake and his colleagues had recovered their courage. After holding the Council, Clive and his colleagues jointly replied on February 12 that additional advantages might be requested but not demanded. Someone well acquainted with the language and customs of the country might be deputed to see the Nawab, who might be able to grant these and also discuss matters both public and private which could not be put in writing. But as to the treaty, they thought the conditions highly honourable and advantageous to the Company. In the treaty Siraj had not agreed to compensate private losses from the capture of Calcutta. Clive and his associates said that as they had suffered such losses themselves it would give them pleasure if private persons could be compensated. But they did not think that it was practical policy to make more demands for three reasons: first, their 'present insignificant strength'; secondly, the situation in the Carnatic, with the possibility of war with the French; and, last of all, possibility of the recall of Clive with his troops to Madras. Their final opinion was that 'by insisting upon terms still more advantageous we expose the Company to the risque of losing those already granted them, having neither time nor the means of making the Nabob comply, should he retreat.'

Apparently, the criticism continued and Clive had to put forward an emphatic justification of the peace to the chairman of the directors of the Company in London in a letter written on February 23 1757.

> If I had only consulted the interest and reputation of a soldier, the conclusion of this peace might easily have been suspended. I know, at the same time, there are many who think that I have been too precipitate in the conclusion of it; but surely those who are of this opinion never knew that the delay of a day or two might have ruined the Company's affairs, by the junction of the French with the Nabob, which was on the point of being carried into execution. They never considered the situation of affairs on the Coast [the Carnatic] and the positive orders sent me by the Gentlemen there, to return with the major part of the forces at all events; they never considered that, with a war upon the coast and in the province of Bengal [both with the French] at the same time, a trading company could not subsist without a great assistance from the Government [of the country]; and, last of all, they never considered that a long war, attended through the whole course of it with success and many great actions, ended at last with the expense of more than fifty *lacs* [Rs5,000,000] to the Company.

This argument of Clive's not only established the case for making the peace, but also indicated all the complex and shifting circumstances in which he had to act. Moreover, even up to the beginning of March, in spite of the warnings given by Watts about the unreliability of Siraj, Clive was not convinced of it. On March 1 he wrote to Watts: 'I cannot be of your way of thinking that the Nabob will not abide by any part of the agreement so solemnly sworn to, as it does not appear that such an opinion is backed by any proofs.'

So, for the moment Clive thought that his task in Bengal was nearly over, and he wrote to London on February 22: 'All operations therefore are now over, and I may hope in a few days to take my passage for the Coast [Madras] with the satisfaction of having left your affairs well re-established and general tranquillity in the province.'

But, in a letter written on the twenty-third, he complained privately to the chairman of the Board of Directors about his associates.

I never undertook an expedition attended with half so many disagreeable circumstances as this: the natural jealousy subsisting between sea and land services has given me much uneasiness; I have suffered mortifications, the independent power given me by the Gentlemen of the Committee at Madras has created me many enemies; and lastly, that attention which, by my public station, I owe to the interest of the Company in preference to that of the private, has not passed by unreflected upon.

Yet, he said, 'nothing harsh, ungenerous or uncharitable shall fall from my pen'. But he could not avoid expressing his concern at the future prospect of the affairs of the Company from such bickerings. He also set down even at this early date the basic consideration which had to remain, and did remain, the keystone of the Company's policy towards the native princes.

It cannot be expected that the princes of this country, whose fidelity is always to be suspected, will remain firm to their promises and engagements from principle only. It is therefore become absolutely necessary to keep a respectable force in this province for the future. How far this is agreeable to the Company's circumstances, you, Sir, are the best judge.

As regards his own career – he was not yet thirty-two, the age of Napoleon as First Consul – he was in an elated mood. He wrote to his father on February 23 (on the same day he wrote the letter just quoted to the chairman in London):

As this success has saved the Company, this is a proper time to push my interest. I have written to my Lord Chancellor [Lord Hardwicke], the Archbishop [of Canterbury], Mr Fox, and my Lord Barrington, Secretary of War, to desire their interest. I have likewise written to Messrs Marbot, Drake [the Elder in London], and Payne [all on the Board in London]. I am desirous of being appointed Governor-General of India if such an appointment should be necessary. I have opened myself a little to Mr Mabbot; however I would have you manage this affair with great prudence and discretion and not mention the word Governor-General without finding it hinted at by other hands.

In speaking about a governor-general in India in 1757 Clive was anticipating what had to be done later for Warren Hastings. His letters to Hardwicke and the Archbishop of Canterbury were identical in language, but to the former he added the following request: 'As Your Lordship honoured me with your favour and protection I flatter myself with the hopes of a continuance of it and that if Your Lordship thinks me deserving Your Lordship will recommend me to the Court of Directors.' In those days and continuing till much later nobody in England could rise in the world without 'interest' behind him. Even Nelson and Arthur Wellesley had to go to the anteroom of Lord Castlereagh and were kept waiting.

Capture of Chandernagore

In the second phase, in which the English took Chandernagore (the French settlement in Bengal) on March 23, Admiral Watson was the principal figure, because this was part of a war between the Kings of England and France, and Watson was the representative of the former. As soon as the peace with Siraj was concluded he turned his attention to the French. He had received the declaration of war between the two countries on January 16, and it was incumbent upon him to act. After he had arrived in the Hooghly, the French at Chandernagore, who knew vaguely about the possibility of a war, were anxious to know his intentions. When Calcutta was recaptured they sent deputies to him to find out whether, according to precedent, he would observe neutrality in Bengal. They themselves had received advice that for the present the war was only to be maritime.

Watson consulted the Council in Calcutta on January 13 1757, and they replied on the fourteenth that they were in favour of neutrality. The Admiral's own view was that he would not leave the French in peace unless they joined the English against Siraj. The Council was against that, but, seemingly, Watson communicated his views to the French deputies. As the French would not act against Siraj the talks led nowhere.

The French let things drift. They were in an extremely difficult position, between two fires – they were as afraid of the English as of Siraj. So apart from making an ineffectual attempt to act as mediators between Siraj and the English they did nothing, though Law at Cossimbazar suggested to Renault at Chandernagore that the French should actively join Siraj against the English. The treaty between the English and Siraj, in which they were not included, surprised them disagreeably, for they had not expected the rout (psychological rather than military) of Siraj. So they made a new offer of neutrality to the English on February 23. Before this Watson had prepared plans and got his forces ready to attack Chandernagore. But on the same day that he received the communication from the French he also got one from Siraj, warning him against attacking the French. This letter, addressed to Clive and Killpatrick as well, forbade the English to commit any hostilities within his dominions. Siraj went further and declared that he would regard an attack on the French as an open and direct violation of the treaty with himself and that it would lead him to help the French with his forces. After that there was no alternative for Watson and the others except to call off the operation against Chandernagore and enter into negotiations with the French for a treaty of neutrality in Bengal. A draft was drawn up, but at the last moment the Admiral refused to sign it because the French deputies told him that they did not have the final authority to bind Pondichery to neutrality.

The Admiral's refusal annoyed and upset Clive. Anxious as he was about the intentions and conduct of Siraj, he did not want a combination of the Nawab and the French against himself and his small forces. So he wrote angrily to the Council in Calcutta on March 4 1757 that the refusal of the Admiral to sign the treaty, which was considered satisfactory by all sides, might provoke Siraj to hostile action. He asked:

> What will the Nabob think after the promises made him on our side and after his consenting to guarantee this neutrality? He and all the world will certainly think that we are men of trifling, insignificant disposition or that we are men without principles.

He thought that, after the rejection of the offer of neutrality, the French would immediately assist the Nabob 'in all his designs against us'. As the commander of the land forces, he was aware that the most difficult task would fall on him. He wrote:

> Our future operations against the Nabob will chiefly depend upon the land forces, and the officers of such forces must certainly be the best judges of what can be effected by land; and I do take upon me to give it as mine and my officers' opinion that success against the Nabob and the French together will be very precarious, notwithstanding the arrival of Bombay troops.

He therefore asked the Council to request the Admiral for a third time either to ratify the treaty or to attack Chandernagore immediately by water. On his part, he added, he was ready to do the same by land with all his forces. 'If he refuses,' Clive finally set down, 'he becomes responsible for every misfortune that may happen to the East India Company's affairs.'

On March 6 Watson wrote to Clive to say that he would not attack the French if the Nabob did not give his consent, and also that he would not commit any hostility against the French unless the French Governor-General and the Supreme Council at Pondichery refused to consent to a treaty of neutrality. But on March 10 1757 Siraj-ud-daula's consent to an attack on Chandernagore was secured. This was the result of the manoeuvres of Watts at Murshidabad. On that day returning after an audience with Siraj-ud-daula, he wrote to Calcutta:

> The Nabob said he could not write, but desired I would inform you that if you was [sic] determined to attack the French, he would not intermeddle or give them the least assistance, he only requests to be informed of your sentiments three or four days before you begin upon action.

But Siraj did write on the same day to Admiral Watson. He expressed satisfaction that the Admiral had refrained from attacking Chandernagore, and noted the Admiral's explanations about not signing the treaty of neutrality. He then wrote:

> It is true, if it is the custom of the French that one man makes an agreement, another will not comply with it, what security is there? My forbidding war on my borders was because the French were my tenants, and upon this affair desired my protection: on this I wrote to make peace, and no intention had I of assisting or favouring them.

After that came what was virtually permission from Siraj to the English to attack Chandernagore:

> You have understanding and generosity, if your enemy with an upright heart claims your protection, you will give him his life, but then you must be well satisfied of the innocence of his intentions; if not, whatever you think right that do.

Both what Watts wrote about Siraj and what Siraj himself wrote in that letter were contrary to all his expressed intentions before that date. Furthermore, all that he did after this, up to the day of the capture of Chandernagore by the English, confirmed that Siraj did not sincerely mean what he said or wrote. How he came to write this letter will be told later. Here it is only necessary to say that Clive and Watson took the letter as Siraj-ud-daula's permission to attack the French and at once began their operations.

Clive marched to Chandernagore and took up his position near the city. Watson summoned the Governor of Chandernagore to surrender on March 13. Upon his refusal the siege began on March 14. Clive did not press his attacks on land very hard. His reasons were obvious. As Law explained: 'Being quite sure that the fort could not hold against the fire of the ships he was in no hurry to sacrifice his men, whom he could not replace and whom he needed for the execution of his projects.'

In fact, the fort was reduced by the ships. The *Kent* and the *Tyger* carried out a terrific bombardment of the main fort and silenced its guns, killing most of the gunners. Finding resistance useless, the Governor hoisted the white flag. But the ships also suffered terribly, and were never fit for service again. Admiral Watson exposed himself recklessly on his ship, the *Kent*, and Admiral Pocock, his second in command, was also slightly wounded. Upon their surrender the French were given generous terms. But here again, as after the reoccupation of Fort William on January 2, there was an exhibition of jealousy between Clive and Admiral Watson. The Admiral, contending that the naval forces had taken Chandernagore, would not at first consent to Clive's being a party to the capitulation and signing the document. But he did not maintain the objection. Clive on his part pointed out that it was impossible that the fort could have been taken without the assistance given by his troops. He said that he had been attacking the place six or seven days before the ships came up; that his troops had destroyed eleven enemy batteries, including a heavy one on the riverside which was intended to prevent the passage of the ships; that he was keeping up constant fire on the French with guns as well as musketry. In any case, this childish dispute did not go on for very long.

Coaxing of Siraj

The capture of Chandernagore eliminated the French as a possible source of trouble for the English in their dealings with Siraj. Their aim was to make him fulfil all the conditions of the treaty of February 9, and furthermore to make him surrender all the remnants of the French forces as well as the French settlements, factories and goods that still remained in Bengal. For the present the second aim was the more pressing one. On March 29 Clive wrote to Pigot: 'Our stay till August, which is now become inavoidable, will, I hope, settle everything here in the most advantageous manner for the Company, and perhaps induce the Nabob to give up all the French factories. This will be driving them out root and branch.' To the Nawab he wrote in more diplomatic language:

> It was almost impossible that there could be lasting peace in your kingdom while there are two such powerful nations in it, because whenever a war breaks out between our two Kings they would not fail to extend the effects of it to these parts, endeavouring to drive each other from their settlements in Bengal. . . . All these circumstances make it absolutely necessary that Your Excellency should deliver up to us persons and effects of the French at Cossimbazar, and their other outsettlements, as being our enemies. We shall then be without rivals, and our whole force ready to obey your commands, and assist you in punishing all those who dare to molest the peace of your kingdom.

This was almost like the Norman Bohemund's request to the Byzantine Emperor Alexius Comnenus to make him the Grand Domestic of the East. Indeed, in his dealings with Siraj, Clive, normally taciturn, became as loquacious and florid as Bohemund. Unfortunately, at the court of Siraj there was no Anna Comnena to admire him.

Perhaps it would have been wise for Siraj to have worked with the English from that stage, for at that time the English had no desire to come into conflict with him, provided he complied with the terms of the treaty and did not protect the French. This was shown by all the letters Clive wrote to him after the capture of Chandernagore. He followed up the letter already quoted with another the next day (March 30 1757) in which he said:

> I once more swear by the God that made me, that I ever will be true to all that I have promised, and that I have nothing more at heart than that the friendship between Your Excellency and the English may last for ever. I hope I shall find Your Excellency's heart the same, and that you will shortly fulfil all your engagements, and that the English from your goodness and justice will have ample restitution of all their losses, and by once more sitting themselves down to trade, contribute to the increase of the revenues and to make your kingdom flourish.

This was not trying to wheedle Siraj. Clive showed that he meant it sincerely by his expectation of going back to Madras soon, and more especially by what he wrote to the Madras Council the same day. He informed them: 'I have the pleasure to acquaint you that the nabob has wrote me a letter of congratulation on our success; and that this enterprise [the capture of Chandernagore] so far from enraging him, has served to attach him more firmly to us.' Admiral Watson, too, as late as April 14, when Siraj's evasions were becoming plain, wrote to London: 'Unless we can establish a lasting friendship and alliance with him [Siraj], notwithstanding our late success, it will be impossible for the Company to preserve their rights and privileges granted them in this country.'

But both Clive and Watson were mistaken in expecting from Siraj even interested friendship. Hatred, fear and distrust of the English had become ineradicable in him. Besides, some of his courtiers, who were in the pay of the French, were telling him how much power the French had and also that large French land and sea forces were soon coming to Bengal. His tacit consent to the English attack on Chandernagore was given under what he must have regarded as some sort of compulsion if not actual duress. He was frightened by the reports of the invasion of Ahmad Shah Abdali, King of Afghanistan, who had made the Emperor of Delhi his captive. He thought Abdali would come down to Bengal, though the fear was chimerical. The English used it as a handle. Both Clive and Watson agreed to help Siraj against the Afghans, but the Admiral represented to Siraj that it would be imprudent for the English to send their forces so far inland, leaving their French enemies behind. 'This', the Admiral reported to London on March 31, 'wrought such an effect on the Nabob that though he could not be brought to give his full consent in writing to our attacking the French, yet he explained his sense of the matter sufficient to be understood he would not interfere or know of anything done between us and them.'

But even then he was playing a double game. To the French he wanted to give the impression that he was on their side, and was going to forbid the English from attacking them. Law in his memoirs has left an account of what happened in his presence on the day Watts sent his message and Siraj wrote his letter, i.e. March 10. In the evening both he and Watts were before the Nawab, who told Watts that 'he was not in the humour to allow our two nations to make war in a country under his rule and he was determined that the neutrality treaty should be preserved as it had always been'. According to Law, Watts replied that he was ready to do whatever the Nawab wished.

Siraj then wanted to know the real reason why the treaty of neutrality was not signed. Watts gave the English version, and Law replied that the plea was false, and that the real reason was the arrival of fresh troops for the English. Siraj then proposed to write two documents which Law and Watts should sign, promising in the name of their respective nations that the treaty would be ratified. Both agreed, but Law asked whether the Admiral would be bound by the promise. Watts said that he could not answer for what the Admiral would do. Siraj at once said he would himself write to Admiral Watson. Law remarked that the Admiral would not pay more attention to this letter than he had done to the previous ones. Siraj looked angrily at Law and cried out: 'What! who then am I?' The servile courtiers at once asserted in one voice that all possible regard would be paid to the Nawab's orders. It was then decided that Siraj would write a strong letter to Watson and also send a representative to help in the negotiations. As they left the durbar Watts remarked to Law that it was the first time the Nawab had spoken so firmly in reference to the troubles in question. Law was much inclined to believe him.

How then did it happen that both the message and the letter carried the opposite meaning? Law inclined later to the view that Watts bribed a secretary to write the letter in a manner to suit the English. He explained that the Nawab never read the letters which he ordered to be written; besides, he said, the Moors never sign their names; the envelope being closed and well fastened, the secretary asks the Nawab for his seal, and seals it in his presence. Often, Law added, there is a counterfeit seal.

Though not improbable, this explanation is not satisfactory. There must have been a previous meeting between Watts and Siraj or a subsequent one, at which Siraj's indirect permission was given, and at the meeting with Law he was only maintaining his public stand, so as not to forfeit the friendship of the French if the English attack on Chandernagore miscarried.

Throughout the period of attack on Chandernagore Siraj wavered. Law went on urging him to intervene with his army. But he ordered and countermanded the orders according to the news he received about the progress of the English. At last Durlabhram Rai, the Bengali commander of the Nawab's forces, set out towards Chandernagore. But he was so afraid of finding himself under English fire that to encourage him Law gave him Rs 15,000 in cash and a promissory note for Rs25,000 more. But the town was taken when Durlabh had gone only ten or twelve miles. Nonetheless, he advanced further to stop the English in case they wanted to march on Murshidabad. Clive wrote a warning letter to him the day before Chandernagore surrendered:

> I hear you are arrived within 20 miles of Hughly. Whether you come as a friend or an enemy I know not. If as the latter say so at once, and I will send some people out to fight you immediately. If as the former [i.e. friend], I beg you will stay where you are, for we can conquer the enemies we have to deal with here if they were ten times stronger.

Then Clive declared his friendship for the Nawab and recalled that, by writing that the enemies of the English were also his enemies, Siraj had made his agreement to co-operate with the English in removing the French from Bengal a part of the treaty, and that Durlabh and other high personages had also set their seal on the treaty. So, if the Nawab went back on the agreement, the fault would be his. Finally, Clive wrote: 'I now declare to you the French are our enemies, and I will destroy them. It would give me great concern to see these troubles begin again, which must be fatal to one party, which God alone knows. Now you know my mind.' Durlabh remained where he was.

But Siraj was not the man to take a straight course. It has already been mentioned that he asked Bussy to come to Bengal. In dealing with the English, he temporized after the capture of Chandernagore, agreeing to what they suggested, and yet trying not to. When the English asked him to hand over the French factories to them he parried with two arguments. First, he said that by the English seizure of Chandernagore and other places he would lose the revenue which the French were paying. So he wrote to Clive: 'Whatever they paid into the treasury, write to Mr Watts to make good here, and it is very well then you keep possession of the factory.' But he also recommended generosity: 'But if it be agreeable to you,' he observed, 'it will be showing yourself a man of great mind to give it up to them that they may carry on their trade as before.'

The English were ready to compensate the Nawab for the loss of revenue. Siraj then raised a second objection. 'The French', he wrote to Clive, 'are indebted to my subjects *lacs* of rupees. If I act as you desire what answer can I give to their lawful creditors? Do you who are my well-wisher consider this well, and write me that I may act accordingly.'

But the most important and urgent English demand was that Siraj should hand over Law and his soldiers at Cossimbazar to them. He replied that the French were in Bengal by virtue of the firmans of the Emperor of Delhi, and he could not deliver them up unless they surrendered voluntarily. He could not do it 'without hurting my character and exposing myself to trouble hereafter', and added, he was sure Clive would make him do nothing by which his fame would suffer.

Clive replied that the French were his enemies, he would destroy them, because he did nothing by halves. As regards Law, he wrote, if the Nawab had scruples, he would send a body of troops and make him surrender. But Siraj took his stand on the tradition in the East of never betraying those who sought protection. As he wrote to one of his commanders: 'Concerning the French the case is this. It is not the custom of the head of the kingdom of Hindostan to bind and deliver up the weak, because by so doing I shall have a bad name through the whole world.'

Nevertheless, by threats and cajolery Watts at Murshidabad brought Siraj round to agreeing, up to a point, to make Law surrender.

It had already been agreed that Law should leave Cossimbazar, provided Siraj gave him passport and money, and go towards Patna. But on the twelfth he was surprised to learn from the intermediary that the Nawab wanted to speak to him. He anticipated trouble, and he was right. On April 13 he went to the palace, and found that the Nawab had not yet come to the audience hall. But Watts and some officials were there. One of the latter asked Law if he had anything particular to say to Watts. Law replied that he had not. Upon this Watts said to him in English: 'The question is, Sir, whether you will resolve to hand over your factory to me and go down to Calcutta with your people. You will be well treated and obtain the same terms as the gentlemen of Chandernagore.'

Law replied that he would do nothing of the kind, and if forced to leave Cossimbazar would surrender the factory to the Nawab and to no one else. Watts turned to the ministers, explained what had been said, and observed that it was impossible to do anything with Law. The officials tried to persuade him to do what Watts suggested. They and Watts went to the Nawab and came back to tell him that the Nawab had ordered him to do what Watts demanded. He replied that he would not, and would see the Nawab himself. At last the Nawab consented to see him, but only if he came alone, for by that time a party of French grenadiers had arrived at the palace to protect him. The officer commanding them would not agree to Law's going alone, but was at last persuaded.

When he went in and saluted, Siraj received him kindly, but as soon as he was seated said to him in a shamefaced manner that either Law must accept Watts's proposal or he would have to leave Siraj's territories. He explained:

> Your nation is the cause of all the importunities I now suffer from the English. I do not wish to embroil the whole country for your sake. You are not strong enough to defend yourselves, you must give way. You ought to remember that when I had need of your assistance you always refused it. You ought not to expect it from me now.

Law replied that he would be dishonoured if he accepted Watts's proposal. He would leave for Patna, as had been previously arranged, but do no more. All the courtiers cried out that he must not refuse, that the Nawab would not allow it. The argument went on. At last Law turned to the Nawab and asked him if it was his intention to place him in the hands of his enemies. Siraj replied: 'No, no, take what road you like and may God conduct you.' Law returned to the factory and made his arrangements for a march westward. On April 16 he started with his troops.

The English were furious. On April 19 Admiral Watson wrote a strong letter of protest to Siraj and told him that, while one Frenchman remained in the kingdom, he would not cease pursuing him. Clive wrote the next day: 'Your highnese's not delivering up Mr Law and his people to me and suffering him to go away is not very kind.' Siraj assured him with specious words, but kept in touch with Law. However, he showed an amazing vacillation in these communications. One day he inquired why Law was going so slowly, on another why he did not go fast. At last, when he was at Bhagalpur, a town about 120 miles from Murshidabad, a messenger arrived from Siraj on May 3 with a letter in which he was asked to return to the capital at once and join him in attacking the English.

By this time the English had lost faith in Siraj, and were

already involved in the conspiracy to replace him by another nawab. On April 10 Clive had written a conciliatory letter to Siraj asking him to comply with the terms of the treaty. On April 19 Admiral Watson wrote a very stern letter asking him to do so without delay; this was the Admiral's last communication to Siraj. His concluding words were:

> If you would have me believe that you wish peace as much as I do, no longer let it be the subject of our correspondence for me to ask for the fulfilment of the treaty, and you to promise and not perform it, but immediately fulfill all your engagements: thus let peace flourish and spread throughout all your country, and make people happy in the re-establishment of their trade, which has suffered by a ruinous and destructive war. What can I say more?

Clive, however, continued the correspondence till June 13, the day he began his march on Plassey. He did this in the graceful manner of the snakecharmer playing his weird pipe before the swaying snake. His last words in his last letter, when he was setting out to fight Siraj, were bland. He wrote:

> The rains being daily increasing, and it taking a great deal of time to receive your answer, I therefore find it necessary to wait on you immediately, and if you will place confidence in me no harm shall come from it. I represent this to you as a friend. Act as you please.

On June 15 Siraj wrote his last letter to Clive. He said that, with the exception of some little things, everything stipulated in the treaty had been done. But just as matters were being rapidly settled, he had learnt that Mr Watts and his companions at Cossimbazar had left on the pretext of a party of pleasure. This, he wrote:

> ... appears to be done with a very deceitful design and intention to break the treaty. For certainly without your orders and directions Mr Watts would never have acted in this manner. It was the consideration that something of this kind was contriving that hindered me from recalling the army from Plassey, for I knew some trick was intended. I thank God, however, the treaty has not been broke on my part, and as it was so solemnly sworn to before God and His Prophet, He will doubtless punish him who has first violated it.

The Conspiracy

It would seem that the idea of replacing Siraj with another nawab was being discussed even before the attack on Chandernagore. Law wrote in his memoirs that on April 9 or so he went to see the Jagat Seths to find out their attitude to the French (who were indebted to them). Afterwards the conversation turned on Siraj, and Law said casually that he understood they wanted to make another nawab. Omichand was also present at this meeting. The Seths, instead of denying it, contented themselves with saying in a low tone that this was a thing which ought not to be talked about. Law remarked in his memoirs that 'if the fact had been false, the Seths would certainly have denied it and would have reproached me for talking in this way'.

At the same time, Scrafton, who was at Murshidabad (i.e. Cossimbazar), sent to Walsh on account of what he had learnt about the situation in a letter written on April 9 1757:

> I passed the day with Watts yesterday. The character he gives of the Nabob and his Court is this – that the Nabob himself has but an indifferent understanding, timorous as a hare, yet loves to boast and consequently relishes flattery: that the Camp affair of 5 February [the night attack on his camp] urges him to resentment, his dread of our force on the other hand makes an eternal contrast in his mind with regard to us.

He added that Siraj's 'mind is a slave to a set of low rascally fellows who never look further in the advice they give him than for their immediate pecuniary advantage'.

As to the Court, in describing it Scrafton drew on his knowledge of Roman history:

> I think on the whole his Court may be compared to that of Ptolemy's that reigned in Egypt when Pompey fled there after the battle of Pharsalia, that is that the head and members are all as corrupt and treacherous as possible, and the Colonel [Clive] should be the Caesar to act as Caesar then did, take the Kingdom under his protection, depose the old and give them a new King to make his subjects happy.

He considered the English approach to him as improvisation, and urged well thought-out moves.

> As in a building, unless the plan whereon to build be first formed in the builder's mind, it can have neither elegance or strength, so in politicks unless we proceed on some fixed principle, some well planned system, affairs can never be brought to a happy conclusion. How glorious it would be for the Company to have a Nabob devoted to them!

It was from Scrafton again that a hint was to go to Walsh in Calcutta on April 20 that a conspiracy to get rid of Siraj was afoot.

There was, however, to be no elegance in the manoeuvres to depose Siraj. As Renault wrote to Dupleix (who was still keeping his eyes on India) on September 4 1757, reviewing the whole course of events before and after the capture of Chandernagore, of which he was the governor:

> Never was there a conspiracy conducted so publicly and with equal indiscretion on the part of the English and the Moors. Nothing else was talked about in all their Settlements, and what will surprise you is that, whilst every place echoed with the noise of it, the Nawab, who had a number of spies, was ignorant of everything. Nothing can prove more clearly the general hatred which was felt for him.

Clive was the principal actor on the English side in this conspiracy. Therefore its progress and conclusion will be described mainly from his point of view. After Scrafton had hinted at it, Watts wrote more clearly about the idea of replacing Siraj by one of his commanders, Khoda-i-Yar Luft Khan (referred to as 'Laitty' or variants in the English correspondence). Watts was of the opinion that Siraj at heart was the bitter enemy of the English, would never support their interests and would attack them, uniting with the French to do so, whenever he felt safe from other dangers. He also informed Clive that at his request Omichand had seen Yar Lutf Khan, and this commander had given his word that he would join the English on condition he was made nawab, and that in return he would give the Company substantial advantages. This was written on April 23 1757.

On April 26 Clive took Admiral Watson into his confidence and wrote:

> ... there is such confusion and discontent at Muxadavad [old name of Murshidabad] from the Nawab's weak conduct and tyranny, that I have received certain advices of several great men, among them are Juggut Seat and Meer Jaffeir, being in league together to cut him off, and set up Murgodaunyer Cawn Luttee, a man of great family, power, and riches, supported tooth and nail by Juggut Seat. I must request you, Sir, you keep within your own breast this intelligence. By this you will judge I cannot stir from hence. We are all ready for fear of the worst.... You may be assured, Sir, some great revolution will happen before long and I hope much to the advantage of the Company.

Two days later Clive wrote to Watts:

> If the Nawab is resolved to sacrifice us, we must avoid it by striking the first blow. You should inquire if Luttee be a man of interest. Is

he a Moorman? May not all be overset by the Afghans if they come? Has Luttee any interest there? You should consider the honour of the nation, and if possible avoid engaging us in any executions. I hear Mir Jafar wants to get rid of the Nabob. I hope it is true.

By that time there had been a change of candidate for the throne at Murshidabad. It was now Mir Jafar, the most important person in Bengal, next to Siraj. He was supported by the Jagat Seths, and there could be no question that he was infinitely superior to Yar Lutf Khan. On April 26 Watts informed Clive that Mir Jafar had sent an emissary to tell him that, if Clive was willing, he and other prominent commanders were ready to seize Siraj and set up another nawab.

On April 30 Clive wrote to Pigot at Madras that Siraj was 'a compound of everything that is bad, keeps company with none but his menial servants, and is universally hated and despised by the great men'. Clive continued:

> This induces me to acquaint you there is a conspiracy carrying on against him by several great men, at the head of whom is Jagat Seat himself, as also Cojah Wazeed. I have been applied to for assistance, and every advantage promised the Company can wish. The Committee are of opinion it should be given as the Nabob is secured. For my own part, I am persuaded, there can be neither peace nor security while such a monster reigns.

The choice of a new nawab had by that time fallen on Mir Jafar.

The Calcutta Council acted promptly. On May 1 1757 the Select Committee at Fort William held a meeting to discuss the project. It was formally recorded in the proceedings that 'the arguments in favour of such a step and the objections against it were maturely weighed and debated'. The Committee was unanimous in the opinion that there could be no dependence on the Nabob's word, honour or friendship and that a revolution would be advantageous for the Company. But the Committee also thought that 'a proceedings of this nature ought to be supported with good and substantial reasons'. Then the main reasons were formally set down in the proceedings.

1. It was evident that Siraj had made peace with the English merely to extricate himself from the danger which at the time had threatened him – his life and government having been exposed to imminent peril.

2. The Committee did not believe that he would abide by the treaty he had made; on the contrary, it had reason to believe that

he would break it upon the first possible occasion. Therefore common prudence obliged the Committee to prevent the ruin of the English by divesting Siraj of any power to do them mischief.

3. Siraj was so universally hated by all sorts and degrees of men, the affection of his army was so alienated from him by his ill-usage of the officers, that the Committee thought that a revolution might be attempted whether the English joined it or not.

It is unnecessary to describe how this conspiracy was being managed at Murshidabad. There was such ambition, greed, suspicion, fear, cowardice and treachery on all sides that nobody cared to take a decisive step. Yet it was being talked about everywhere. Historically, it would be true to say that the conspiracy ran its own course, and it was this quality of inchoateness which put a severe nervous strain on Clive. This lasted down to the day of battle. In his anxious mood he was startled to learn in a letter from Watts written on May 14 and received by him at his camp near Chandernagore that Omichand, who had so far been the trusted agent or intermediary of the English in dealing with the Nawab as well as other notables, was demanding a very large sum of money as his share of the spoils of the conspiracy if it succeeded. Watts informed Clive that Omichand wanted five per cent of all the Nawab's treasures, and other large sums and concessions besides, from which his monetary gains from the conspiracy would amount to many millions. 'These and many other articles of the proposed treaty with Mir Jafar,' Watts wrote, 'in which his own ambition, cunning, and avaricious views were the chief motives, he positively insisted on, and would not be prevailed upon to recede from one article.' Mir Jafar had expressed his utter distrust and disgust of Omichand. Watts clearly saw that Omichand's insistence might ruin the plot and seems to have included an article in the treaty ensuring a large sum of money for him.

The question as to whether Omichand employed any threats to levy this blackmail has been discussed. It was afterwards stated by Clive and others that he threatened to tell Siraj about the conspiracy and get Watts and others murdered. As no threat is mentioned in the contemporary documents it has been held by certain historians that Omichand did not threaten. But it requires very little knowledge of human nature to understand that such demands are not made unless a man has a trump card.

Watts, Clive and the Committee in Calcutta all thought that they were facing a dangerous man, and set that down in letters and other documents written at the time.

Before describing their action it is necessary, however, to say something about the antecedents of Omichand because he has been given quite an important place in the history of the British Empire in India.

He was an immensely wealthy merchant who had lived in Calcutta for many years. It is generally believed that he was a Punjabi. He could not have been a Sikh, as some have regarded him. He was of the bania order, either a *khatri* or an *arora*, and a Hindu. He was believed by the Calcutta Council to have played a very treacherous part in the capture of Calcutta by Siraj, and by some even to have been the instigator of the Black Hole.

However that might be, after the recovery of Calcutta the Calcutta Council passed a formal resolution, on January 19 1757, saying that his conduct at the time of the siege of Calcutta and afterwards, as well as commonly held opinion about him, allowed room for suspecting that he had been directly or indirectly concerned with the calamity for the English; therefore the Committee sequestered all his properties. Where he was at the time is not known. But on January 28 Clive received the following letter from him:

> God be praised that Calcutta is again restored to its former splendour by your happy arrival. Most fortunate is their lot who serve you, but how unhappy is mine who am secluded from your presence by my confinement, which you must be acquainted with. I hope that when I shall have the honour to be called to attend you I shall be able to find means to procure my liberty. At present I understand I lie under your displeasure by means of some evil persons who have misreported me to you. But I doubt not of being able to wipe off the stain. I have made it the subject of my constant devotion that God would bring back my masters into the country. God has granted my prayers. How little I am deserving of blame will be evident when I appear before you, and then I shall have justice done me. A man who can wish ill to those from whom he receives his bread will be branded with ignominy in the world. How can he hope for success or happiness? God grant that I may get free from my confinement, that I may throw myself at your feet and lay my whole conduct before you, who will grant me justice, and then I shall be delivered from all my misfortunes.

It is enough to place this letter against his demands four and a half months later to get a fair idea of Omichand's character. It is not known who had put him under confinement, or even whether he was actually under restraint. Afterwards it was said that he was in Siraj's camp in his own garden in Calcutta on the night of February 4–5. But it is certain that at the time of the treaty with Siraj Clive wrote to him asking him to come and see him. He also assured Omichand: 'No harm shall happen to you, and you shall be at liberty to return whenever you please in safety.'

He then became associated with the English, and accompanied Watts when he was going to Murshidabad with Siraj. When on February 19 the Nawab complained about the aggressive designs of the English, Omichand played his part. He reassured the Nawab with a characteristic antic. As Watts reported to the Committee in Calcutta:

> Omichand then told the Nabob that he had lived under the English protection these forty years, that he never knew them once to break their agreement; to the truth of which Omichand took his oath by touching a Brahmin's foot: and said that if a lie could be proved in England upon any one, they were spit upon and never trusted.

Upon hearing this Siraj was very reassured.

On reaching Murshidabad, Omichand acted as an intermediary between the English and the Nawab and all other dignitaries, and carried on negotiations, along with enriching himself at the expense of everybody, including the Nawab. He encouraged the English to attack Chandernagore, assuring them they need fear no opposition from Siraj. He hatched the plot to install Yar Lutf Khan as nawab because he thought this man would be a tool in his hands. When, therefore, Mir Jafar was decided upon at the instance of the Jagat Seths, Omichand became hostile. It was he who, by his intrigues with Rai Durlabh, caused the delay in securing Mir Jafar's agreement to the terms of the English. Just before he made his final demand to Watts he had even secured Clive's sympathy. On May 5 Clive wrote to Watts that 'Omichand in consideration of his services should have all his losses made good by an express article in the treaty.' Watts, who then became distrustful, had all along been sending glowing reports about the ability and usefulness of Omichand. But when Omichand was on the point of getting what he had never deserved he overplayed his hand, as most crooks do. His intrigues after the treaty also confirmed the

English in their distrust of him.

It is certainly one of the great ironies of history that the treatment of Omichand became the most serious count in the later indictment and persecution of Clive, and also that the conscience of England, including that of the historians, ranged itself on the side of this man against Clive. For the present, however, Clive and the Calcutta Council decided to deal with him at once in the manner they thought he deserved.

On getting the letter from Watts and the articles of the treaty with it, Clive immediately went down to Calcutta to discuss the matter with the Committee. He made the suggestion that Omichand's blackmail should be resisted and his cunning defeated by making two versions of the treaty, one real and the other fictitious. Only the fictitious version was to contain the clause about remunerating Omichand and to be shown or given to him. The Committee discussed this question at a meeting on May 17, at which both Admiral Watson and Admiral Pocock were present. They followed Clive's suggestion, and decided that the article on the remuneration of Omichand should be totally left out, as his behaviour merited rather disgrace and punishment than reward.

They then considered how Omichand might be deceived to prevent discovery of the whole idea. They thought they ran that risk if they refused to comply with Omichand's unreasonable demand for a reward; that it would be highly improper to ask Mir Jafar to agree to this remuneration for a person who could be of no service in the intended revolution. At the same time they realized that it would be dangerous to provoke a man of Omichand's character by seeming to be indifferent to his interest and slighting his weight and influence. They thought this might prompt him to make a sacrifice of the English and ruin their affairs.

So they deliberately set down their intention to deceive Omichand in these words:

> For these reasons we think it will be necessary to form a double treaty, both to be signed by Meer Jaffeir and by us; in one of which the article in favour of Omichand is to be inserted, in the other to be left out, and Meer Jaffeir is to be informed of that which we design to abide by and esteem authentick with our reasons for taking such a step.

So it will be seen that the whole Council took the decision to deceive Omichand, and at the meeting of the Council Admiral

Watson was present, together with his second-in-command. The treaty was drawn up and was signed in the authentic version by Charles Watson, Roger Drake, Robert Clive, William Watts, James Killpatrick and Richard Belcher. In this version clause eight of the draft treaty, stating 'That Omichand shall receive the sum of twenty lack of sicca rupees', was omitted.

Clive prepared the real and the fictitious treaties and sent them to the Council for signature on May 18. In the forwarding letter he wrote: 'The Admiral promised to do the same by the real one, but not the fictitious one; if he makes any scruple send it without and we will sign it for him in such a manner that Omichand shall not discover it.' The two versions of the treaty were formally signed on May 19, and in forwarding them to Watts Clive wrote on the same day:

> Both the Admirals Watson and Pocock and Gentlemen agree that Omichand was the greatest villain upon earth, and that he now appears in the strongest light what he was always suspected to be, a villain in grain; however, to counterplot this scoundrel, and at the same time give him no room to suspect our intentions, enclosed you will receive two forms of Agreement, the one real and to be strictly kept up to by us, the other fictitious; in short, this affair concluded, Omichand shall be treated as he deserves; this you will acquaint Meer Jaffeir with.

He also gave the advice:

> Flatter Omichand greatly, tell him the Admiral, Committee, and self are infinitely obliged to him for the pains he has taken to aggrandize the Company's affairs, and that his name will be greater in England than ever it was in India. If this can be brought to bear to give him no room for suspicion, we take off 10 *lacks* from 30 demanded for himself, and add 5 per cent upon the whole sum received, which will turn out the same thing.

Certainly, Omichand acquired a great name in England. Even after this he played fast and loose and delayed the final signing of Mir Jafar, trying to get more from everybody.

Clive never throughout his life felt any qualms about this transaction. Fifteen years later he declared before the Parliamentary Committee investigating all these affairs that 'he made no secret of it; he thinks it warrantable in such a case and would do it again a hundred times'. This defiant statement would recall the equally defiant one from Napoleon about the shooting of the Duc d'Enghien.

There was delay of over two weeks before the treaty could be sworn to by Mir Jafar. During this interval the nerves of everybody were on edge, and almost everybody lost his temper. There was jealousy between Watts and Scrafton, and Clive had to reassure Watts by writing: 'I desire that in this you will be persuaded that there is not the least intent to take from you any part of the reputation of conducting this affair, Mr Scrafton having orders to follow your instructions.' Then on the very eve of getting the affair concluded Watts lost his patience and wrote bitterly that all that he could hope from Mir Jafar and others was that they would remain neutral, and then commented:

> If we are successful they will reap the benefit, if otherwise they will continue as they were without appearing to have been concerned with us; if you think you are strong enough I am of opinion we had better depend on ourselves, and enter into no contract or have any connection with such a set of shuffling, lying, spiritless wretches.

Finally, Clive turned on poor Watts. On June 5 he wrote angrily to Watts: 'Surely, you are deceived by those you employ, or you have been deceiving me.' In another letter written on the same day he observed: 'I find you have been duped throughout the whole.' Watts firmly replied on June 8: 'I have not been deceived and have more honour and generosity of temper than to deceive any man. I hope you will now be convinced that you have been too hasty in your suspicion of me. I wish Omichand's insinuations and addresses may not have prejudiced me in your favour.' In another letter he wrote: 'I have not been duped as you must know by this time, and be convinced Omichand has been the occasion of the delay.'

Before this he had secured Mir Jafar's signature and oath to the treaty. On June 5 Clive wrote to Watts: 'I will not embark in any undertaking with such a set of cowardly rascals.' On the same day Watts wrote that Mir Jafar had signed the treaty, and he was going to get it sworn to. As the treaty had been sworn to, on the English side, on the Bible, Mir Jafar had to swear to it on the Quran. But it was extremely risky for Watts to visit Mir Jafar. So in the evening of June 5 he got into a covered *dooly* (litter used for women) and saw Mir Jafar, who swore upon the Quran and the head of his son – an awful oath for Hindus and Muslims alike in India – 'to keep firm to the agreement made between him and the Company'. On the next day the treaty as signed and sworn to by Mir Jafar was sent to Clive.

Some military plans were discussed. But as Watts wrote:

> Regarding the operations of war Meer Jaffeir can form no farther

resolution at present than that if the Nabob took the field and Meer Jaffeir was in the van he would on your approach beat his drum, shew his colours, march off and join you to the right; if placed on either of the wings he will then endeavour to secure the Nabob; if in the rear the same, which when performed the signal will be a white flag; if the Nabob should keep the city he will then endeavour to seize him on our army's approach.

Siraj's behaviour during the last stage of the conspiracy only illustrated the truth of the saying, 'Quem Jupiter vult perdere dementat prius' (Jupiter first drives to madness the man whom he wishes to destroy). At first he would not give ear to the warnings that came to him. The Frenchman Sinfray (who was left at Cossimbazar when Law left, and who at Plassey commanded the French gunners who alone really fought) obtained an interview with him with great difficulty. After telling Siraj about the conspiracy against him he asked the Nawab to arrest the conspirators. Siraj replied that it could not be and he was sure of the fidelity of those whom Sinfray was accusing.

Others also advised Siraj to put Mir Jafar and his associates to death. But Siraj dared not. Though almost insane with suspicion and fear, he wavered. He dismissed Mir Jafar from his post of commander-in-chief, but tried to get reconciled with him afterwards. It was reported at the time that Siraj sent men to arrest Mir Jafar after the flight of Watts, but Mir Jafar's men beat off Siraj's men. Mir Jafar described what happened in a letter to his confidant Mirza Omar Beg written on June 19:

> Monday and Tuesday [June 13–14] it was in agitation to destroy me. The guns and fire arrows were all ready against me, and the people were in arms day and night. Mr Watts's news was known early on Monday. This startled the Nabob; he thought it absolutely necessary I should be soothed; he came to me himself. On Thursday eve [evening of June 15] the Hughly letter arrived that they were marched. I was to be with him. On three conditions I consented to it. One, that I would not enter into his service; 2ndly, I would not visit him; lastly, I would not take post in the army. I sent him word that if he agreed to these terms I was ready. As he wanted me he consented.

But in order to ensure the safety of his family and himself Mir Jafar took a written guarantee from all the commanders of the army and artillery that if they were victorious in the battle with the English they would see him and his family safe wherever he chose to go. He added that he had sent his answer to a letter from Clive 'sewed up in slippers'. On the same day he wrote to Clive that he was afraid to send him news. He also said that Clive's letters came too openly to him, and advised him to be careful until the affair was publicly declared.

Plassey*

On the day Mir Jafar wrote this letter, i.e. June 19 1757, Clive reached Katwa, a fortified town on the western bank of the Hooghly or Bhagirathi river, about forty miles from Murshidabad and under fifteen miles from Plassey. Following the period of extreme anxiety and uncertainty about the success of the conspiracy, there was continuing uncertainty and anxiety for Clive. From an objective appraisal of his situation he could not feel confident. In fact, when the preparations for the northward push were being made Admiral Watson had written to him: 'I do not think your letters carry the most promising appearance of success; you cannot therefore be too cautious to prevent a false step being taken, which might be of very fatal consequence to our affairs.' Clive knew this fully, and as he was the man responsible for the venture a heavy responsibility rested on his shoulders.

On the previous day he had sent forward Eyre Coote to occupy Katwa, and on the morning of June 19 he had taken the fort without much resistance from the garrison. Clive came up later, took stock of the situation and at once wrote to Calcutta. He said that, though the town and fort of Katwa were strong, he felt the greatest anxiety at the little intelligence he had received from Mir Jafar, and feared, even if he was not treacherous, that his 'sang-froid' (meaning perhaps lukewarmness) or want of strength might ruin the expedition. He added that he was sending a messenger to Mir Jafar to prevail upon him to march out, and also to tell him, that, unless he gave Clive sufficient proof of his sincerity by coming to Plassey – given as the rendezvous – or some such action he, Clive, would not cross the river. He hoped that the Council in Calcutta would approve of this.

He also explained clearly why he was acting in this manner: 'I shall act with such caution', he wrote, 'as not to risk the loss of our forces, and whilst we have them, we may always have it in our power to bring about a revolution, should the present not succeed.' His idea was to keep his army intact, as an army 'in being' to be employed as circumstances allowed.

*The authorities on which the account of the battle is based are given in Appendix 3.

He informed Calcutta that there was enough food for his forces at Katwa to enable him to remain there till the end of the rains, which might in itself induce Siraj, by making him anxious, to agree to dependable terms. Alternatively, Clive thought in the interval he might be able to secure allies – either a local prince or the Marathas, or even the Grand Vizir in Delhi. In fact, the very next day he wrote to the local prince, the Raja of Birbhum, to send him a body of 200–300 good horsemen, promising to help and recompense him. (It should be remembered that Clive was wholly without cavalry, so necessary for reconnaissance and pursuit.) Furthermore, he requested the Council to tell him their sentiments freely, especially about how he should act if Mir Jafar gave no assistance.

Receiving no communication from him till June 21, Clive held a council of war in the morning of the same day. There were seventeen officers in all, and the question put was 'whether in our present situation without assistance and on our own bottom it would be prudent to attack the Nabob, or whether we should wait till joined by some other country power'.

A majority of ten officers, headed by Clive, voted against immediate action, while seven, led by Eyre Coote, voted for it. At the council Coote gave his reasons, which were quite sound from the purely military point of view, especially from a consideration of morale. Clive had to consider the wider background, in which the political issues were combined with the military. Nonetheless, after the meeting Clive said to Coote that in spite of the vote he intended to march the next morning. Clearly, he had decided that he did not want to lose the initiative in movement in case a battle was forced on him. So he gave orders for the troops to hold themselves in readiness to march.

After the meeting Clive forwarded the proceedings to Calcutta and informed the Council: 'I wait only for some encouragement from Meer Jaffeir to proceed, which must be the issue unless the Nabob makes very fair offers of accommodation.' Next morning part of the force crossed the river and stationed themselves on a hillock about two miles away. In the afternoon the rest of the army crossed over, and the march to Plassey began at 4 p.m.

What finally decided him was that at last, at 3 p.m. on June 22, he received the eagerly awaited communication from Mir Jafar. He had remained hesitant up till then. After forwarding the proceedings of the war council to Calcutta, Clive got a verbal message from Mir Jafar, which was of no importance. So he wrote another letter to the Council on the same day:

> I am really at a loss how to act at the present situation of our affairs, especially should I receive a confirmation by letter of Meer Jaffeir's resolution to stand neuter. The Nabob's forces at present are not said to exceed 8,000 men but a compliance with their demands may easily increase them.* If we attack them it must be entrenched, and ourselves without any assistance. In this place a repulse must be fatal, on the contrary success may give the greatest advantage. The Nabob's apprehensions at present are great, and perhaps he may be glad to grant us an honourable peace. The principle of fear may make him act much against his private inclination and I believe that has been the case ever since the capture of Chandernagore. There still remains the expedient of sending an embassy either to Gazoody Cawn [Ghazi-ud-din Khan, the Grand Vizir in Delhi] or the Morattoes to invite them in. I beg you will let me have your sentiments at this critical juncture.

On June 22 day, before he received Mir Jafar's letter, he wrote to him again:

> I am determined to risque everything on your account, though you will not exert yourself. I shall be on the other side of the river this evening. If you will join me at Placis, I will march half way to meet you, then the whole Nabob's army will know I fight for you. Give me leave to call to your mind how much your own glory and safety depends upon it. Be assured if you do this you will be Subah of these provinces, but if you cannot go even this length to assist us I call God to witness the fault is not mine, and I must desire your consent for concluding a peace with the Nabob, and what has passed between us will never be known. What can I say more than that I am as desirous of your success and welfare as my own?

These two letters are extremely important as revealing the mind of Clive on the eve of Plassey. Though he had committed himself to make Mir Jafar Nawab of Bengal, he was still keeping the chance of an understanding with Siraj open, and he informed Calcutta that Siraj might be brought round to this. The next point that the letter to Mir Jafar establishes is that Clive had decided to cross the river in any case on the afternoon of June 22, irrespective of any news from Mir Jafar. The communication only confirmed him in the decision.

Mir Jafar's communication, undated, was very curious. He said that he was glad to learn about the capture of Katwa, and informed him that he had started from Murshidabad on June 19

*Siraj's troops were wanting more pay.

and had reached Moncurra, and meant to start from there on Tuesday (June 21) – which indicates that the letter was written on June 20. He gave the information that Siraj intended to entrench himself at Moncurra, and advised Clive to descend upon him there and forestall his moves. Then, curiously, he urged action, and not merely planning, on Clive. He wrote:

> As yet you are only designing, but it is not now proper to be indolent. When you come near I shall then be able to join you. If you could send two or three hundred good fighting men the upper road towards Cossimbazar the Nabob's army would of themselves retreat. Then the battle will have no difficulty.

He also promised to send more intelligence privately when he had arrived near enough.

The main body of Clive's troops began to cross the river at once, and at 4 p.m. the march towards Plassey began. At 6 p.m. Clive sent his reply to Mir Jafar: 'Upon receiving your letter I am come to a resolution to proceed immediately to Placis. I am impatient for an answer to my letter by the trusty man.' The difference between this and Clive's previous intention was that, instead of merely crossing the river and going *towards* Plassey, he now decided to go to Plassey itself, though he had not received any assurance from Mir Jafar that he would join forces there.

The advance body of troops began to arrive at Plassey before midnight, but the rear did not join till 3 a.m. on June 23. It must be made clear that when the march to Plassey began Clive and his officers did not know why they were going there – to fight a battle, to meet Mir Jafar or to make it up with Siraj – nor did they know more when they arrived there. Furthermore, they had no information as to where Siraj was, or what the strength of his army was.

At daybreak they saw a very large army on the plain in front of them towards the north, advancing upon their position as well as marching southwards at some distance beyond their extreme right. The troops were at once moved from the stations they had taken up at night and deployed in a thin line from the river to the west to the outer edge of the grove of Plassey to the east, slightly in advance of the grove. The European infantry, divided into four groups, was placed in the middle, the sepoys to their right and left, with the guns at suitable points along the front.

Even the sight of the disparity of the two sides was disquieting. The whole plain was full of the Nawab's troops, elephants, cavalry, foot and the white bullocks drawing the artillery. The strength of the Nawab's army was learned afterwards by the English commanders from information given by his commanders, and the figures vary. But all agree in giving a general estimate that the force had between 15,000 and 20,000 cavalry, 35,000 to 40,000 infantry and nearly 50 guns, mostly twenty-four- and thirty-two-pounders. Against this army Clive had less than 1,000 European soldiers, about 2,000 sepoys, 8 field-guns (six-pounders) and 1 howitzer.

Naturally, he had misgivings about the situation and could not come to a decision. So at 7 a.m. he sent a note to Mir Jafar:

> Whatever could be done by me I have done, I can do no more. If you will come to Daudpur I will march from Placis to meet you, but if you won't comply even with this, pardon me, I shall make it up with the Nawab!

During the previous few days these were the alternatives he had always kept in mind. If the sight of the Nawab's army made him revert to them there was nothing discreditable in it. Such hesitations are common among commanders of armies, even the greatest, at critical situations, because they are responsible not only to their troops but also to their country or cause. Napoleon was undecided at Mantua before the battle of Castiglione, Lee at Gettysburg and Ludendorff before Tannenberg. But the battle was begun by the Nawab's forces, whose advanced parties had come to within two hundred yards of Clive's line and occupied a strong position around a water tank. Behind them in support could be seen a larger force of horse and foot. A heavy shell fell, and this made clear what had not been seen before – that the Nawab's artillery was also in position.

The lighter English guns were outranged and could not deal with the Nawab's artillery. So, in order to prevent his soldiers from being exposed to its fire, Clive withdrew the whole line behind an embankment which was a part of the grove at Plassey, and reformed them in the previous order. In this position the troops were relatively safe, and indeed they suffered very little. But Clive's guns kept up brisk fire, and the howitzer was even advanced half-way towards the water tank in a position where it was safe.

This cannonade went on till about 2 p.m. and there was no closer fighting. Besides the guns in the advanced position, which they could see were manned by white men – Sinfray and his forty Frenchmen – Clive and his officers could also see, in front of the Nawab's main force, his artillery moving in such a manner that the whole plain seemed covered by the bullocks drawing the guns. Occasionally the artillery soldiers halted, unlimbered and fired on the English line. But the Nawab's horse and foot were kept at a distance by the firing of the guns and, at times, musketry. Clive's idea was to do nothing during the day that might endanger his army, but to attack the Nawab's camp at night as he had done in Calcutta.

At about midday Clive thought of calling a council of war, but changed his mind. At the same time there was a heavy shower. The English officers feared that, finding the English guns silent, the enemy's cavalry might charge. But nothing happened and only the desultory cannonade continued.

At about two Clive went to the brick house at the extreme left of his line, where he had his headquarters, to change his clothes which had become drenched. During his short absence Killpatrick saw that the party round the water tank was retreating. He at once advanced with two guns. When Clive saw this on his return, it is reported that he was very angry and rebuked Killpatrick for endangering the army. But instead of ordering a withdrawal, he himself joined in the forward movement. The water tank position was occupied.

At this the enemy advanced to dislodge the English detachment. It was only at this point in the course of the battle that the Nawab's large force of cavalry and foot made any attempt to intervene actively. They were kept at a distance by the fire of guns and musketry. But some of the Nawab's troops and guns took up a strong position round a second water tank to the north of the first and harassed Clive's troops. So an attack was ordered on this position, and it succeeded. Then the English troops charged, at which began a general flight of the Nawab's troops.

While this fighting was going on, the very large body of troops that were to the east of the British position began to advance towards the grove. They were fired at and fell back. Afterwards it was learned that these were Mir Jafar's troops, who had no intention of attacking the English troops. By that time there was a general rout of the Nawab's army on the fighting front, and by the evening the Nawab's camp was occupied, and a large booty captured. Siraj had by then fled to Murshidabad. The English losses were small: 4 European soldiers killed, 9 wounded, 2 missing; and 16 sepoys killed and 36 wounded. The losses in the Nawab's army too were small, and were estimated at 500. But many important officers were killed.

Thus ended the battle of Plassey. Though it was not much of a battle, yet it can be compared to another decisive battle in history, also not much of a battle: the famous cannonade of Valmy on September 20 1792, by which the Austro-Prussian attack on revolutionary France was checked, and the French conquests of the revolutionary and Napoleonic epoch began. But at Valmy 34,000 Austro-Prussians faced 52,000 French, of whom 36,000 were engaged in actual fighting.

Even from the military point of view Plassey must not be dismissed. Much has been made of the inactivity of Mir Jafar and his collaborators. But even without them Siraj had, according to contemporary estimates, 15,000 good troops – in fact his best – engaged in battle, and an overwhelming superiority in artillery. Yet this force made no attempt to close in on the English, and the guns were effectively used only by the forty Frenchmen. This has been attributed to the depressed mood of the army and of Siraj himself. But if Clive with his 3,000 men was not depressed by the complete non-co-operation of Mir Jafar and the other conspirators, there was hardly a rational reason for Siraj to be depressed, with his 15,000 faithful men. His depression was produced by his terror of English arms and the name of Clive. It was also due to the death of Mir Madan at an early stage of the battle. But the general influence was that of the telekinesis from Clive. If this could demoralize an army there could be no sense in getting men killed in fighting. The greatest soldier that exists, tactically – the tiger – never charges if he can scatter his enemies with a roar.

It was only when the rout of Siraj's army began that Clive came to know what had happened in Siraj's camp from a letter from Mir Jafar, which was brought to him at 5 p.m. From it he learned about Mir Madan's death, and of the effect it produced. The letter was Mir Jafar's reply to Clive's letter of the morning, and it must have been written when the withdrawal of the Nawab's army began in the early afternoon. It ran:

> Your note is arrived. I was in the Nabob's presence on this plain, and observed that everybody was intimidated. He sent for me and flung his *turband* off before me, and one day he made me write on the side of the Koran, so that I cannot come over to you. By the blessing of God you have the better of the day. Meer Madan was wounded by a ball and is since dead. Buxshee Hazarry is killed, and

ten or fifteen horsemen are killed and wounded. Roydullubram, Luttee Codair Cawn, and myself are moved from right to left. Make a great and sudden discharge and they shall run away and we shall do our part.

Mir Jafar did not know that on perceiving the falling back of the Nawab's troops the English had already pushed forward. So he wrote:

The commanders of the foot and the swordsmen have left the entrenchments, leaving the guns there. I have mentioned but a small part of the loss of that part of the army commanded by Meer Madan has sustained. Had you taken that opportunity to advance with your army there had been nothing more to do. It grieves me that I was then at a distance.

This shows that Mir Jafar's judgement of the situation was right. But since he was ignorant of what had been done by the English, he gave the following advice to Clive:

Attack him at 3 in the morning; they will run away, and then will be my opportunity. The forces want to return to the City. Attack him in the night by all means.

In this too, Mir Jafar was agreeing with Clive's alternative. But the English did attack in the afternoon. It is possible that after writing his letter Mir Jafar perceived that they were doing so, and may have assumed that Clive had got his letter. He must have advanced towards the grove under this impression, but, finding that his move was not understood, withdrew.* After the battle he wrote again:

Your note is arrived, Your trusty man is taken. I congratulate you on executing your design. Mirza Aumar Beg, or Mr Watts, or Coja Petrus send one of them to me. I am here on the banks of the lake agreeable to your desire.

It is interesting to note that such was the atmosphere of suspicion that Mir Jafar, when he gave his account of what had happened in Siraj's camp, thought it necessary to say: 'I swear by my Prophet that the above is fact.' Clive, however, understood his position.

*The importance of this letter from Mir Jafar has not been realized. It is explained in Appendix 3. Here it is only necessary to point out that there is no real contradiction between Mir Jafar's suggesting the attack at '3 in the morning' in one sentence and 'in the night' in another. In the original Persian the '3 in the morning' must have been *tin ghari*, three hours, which by Muslim reckoning would be three hours after nightfall, because the Muslim day begins in the evening, after sunset.

Though in his very first announcement of his victory to Calcutta he had written that Mir Jafar, Rai Durlabh and Yar Lutf Khan had given no assistance except by standing neutral, he also added that they were with him with a large force. He was even more generous in his reply to Mir Jafar's congratulations. He wrote on the morning of June 24 1757:

> I congratulate you on the victory, which is yours and not mine. I should be glad if you would join me with the utmost expedition. We propose marching tomorrow to compleat the conquest that God has blest us with, and I hope to have the honour of proclaiming you Nabob. Mr Scrafton will congratulate you on my part. From him you will learn how much I am yours.

They met later in the day, and Clive reported to Calcutta: 'I have the pleasure to inform you Meer Jaffeir came to me this morning, and made many expressions of gratitude to the English, and assured us he would be faithful to his treaty.'

Death of Siraj and Accession of Mir Jafar

It is now necessary to follow Siraj. At about midnight on June 23–24 he arrived at Murshidabad. The next day he threw open his treasury to induce the soldiers to support him. But people merely took away the money, and no one would support him. Late in the night of the twenty-fourth he heard that Mir Jafar had entered the city, and he took to flight. Next morning Mir Jafar informed Clive that Siraj had fled at 11 p.m. and a party of soldiers was being sent after him. A large part of Siraj's treasures and his women had, however, been sent away by a different route with Mohanlal. Mir Jafar hoped 'in God to take them all'. Mohanlal and his son were brought to Murshidabad the next day.

Siraj, after many wanderings, arrived on June 29 near Raj Mahal, whose *faujdar* or military governor was Mir Jafar's brother. He sought refuge at the house of a man called Dan Shah Pirzada. This man had formerly offended Siraj, and had had his ears and nose cut off. He recognized Siraj in his disguise, detained him under the pretence of preparing food, and sent word to nearby Raj Mahal to the military governor. He came immediately, took Siraj into custody and sent him to Murshidabad.

Clive was informed by Mir Jafar on the evening of June 30 that Siraj had been captured. He was taken to Murshidabad on July 2. One Muslim historian relates that Mir Jafar held a council to decide what to do with him, and was in favour of clemency. But the meeting could come to no clear decision, and for the night he was kept in custody in charge of Miran, Mir Jafar's son. This young man had Siraj murdered the same night. Collusion in this between father and son was suspected, but never proved. On July 3 his mutilated body was carried through Murshidabad on the back of an elephant, so that it might be known definitely that Siraj was dead.

The truest and saddest comment on Siraj's fate came from Law, who was marching at great speed to come to his help. He and his troops were only two days late in their attempt to rescue Siraj. He wrote in his memoirs:

> If we had saved Siraj-ud-daulah we should have had something to boast of [like Hitler's rescue of Mussolini], but possibly he would have been saved for a short time only. Wherever he might have presented himself in the countries subject to him he would have found enemies and traitors. No one would have acknowledged him. Forced by the pursuit of Mir Jafar and the English to fly to a foreign country he would have been [more] a burden to us than an advantage. In India no one dreams of standing by an unfortunate man. The first idea which suggests itself is that of despoiling him. Besides a man of Siraj-ud-daulah's character could nowhere find a real friend.

But ghastly as his fate was, the fate of his mother Amina Begum and his aunt Ghaseti Begum (who was despoiled by him), was even more ghastly, cruel and tragic. They had been living in Dacca for safety. One day they were put in a boat by Mir Jafar's agents, rowed out to the middle of the river Buri Ganga, and told that the agents had orders to drown them. The two women held their copies of the Quran, and went down in each other's arms, cursing, it was said, Miran and calling God's justice on him.

In all this the Muslim historians saw the working of the Evil Eye, rival of Allah and co-existent with Him, with his malevolence. So Ghulam Husain Khan Tabatabai, the author of the famous history *Seir-ul-Mutakherin,* wrote: 'Siraj-ud-daula had attained the zenith of power and opulence, and therefore a declension was inevitable according to the laws of nature.' Another historian saw in it God's punishment for Alivardi's teachery to the family of his master. This, as it happened, was visited on the third generation.

To go back to Clive and Mir Jafar. On June 27, on his way to

Murshidabad, Clive had two unpleasant experiences. He got a letter from Calcutta in reply to his requests for the views of the Council to clarify his situation of suspense. The reply was evasive: it disapproved of any understanding with Siraj, suggested an immediate attack, and yet left it to the judgement of Clive to decide whether this course would lead to success. This infuriated Clive, who was not slow to lose his temper. He wrote angrily:

> I have received your letter of the 23rd instant, the contents of which are so indefinite and contradictory that I can put no other construction on it, than an intent to clear yourselves at my expense, had the expedition miscarried. It puts me in mind of the famous answer of the Delphic oracle to Pyrrhus, *Aio te Claude Romanes vincere posse*.

At the same time he got a letter from Watts and Walsh at Murshidabad to the following effect:

> Rugeet Roy is despatched to us by Juggutseat to desire that you will not come into town this afternoon for treachery is intended you. A consultation was held last night between Meerum, Roydulup and Cossim Hussain Cawn about cutting you off at your visit to the Nabob. You may return on pretence of illness if you are on the road, but it will be necessary to write of it. Juggutseat will then visit you tomorrow morning. He begs you will not mention a syllable of this intelligence as you value your life.

Clive had already come to know of the intrigues of Rai Durlabh and had written to Calcutta: 'The chicanery and villainy of Roy Dulub obliges me to go tomorrow to the City to prevent the ill consequence that attends the great power lodged in his hands, so prejudicial both to the Nabob i.e. Mir Jafar and the Company.'

On June 29 he entered Murshidabad with 200 European soldiers and 300 sepoys and took up his quarters in one of the palaces. As he reported to the Council in Calcutta:

> In the afternoon I waited on Jaffeir Ali Cawn, being escorted to him by his son. As I found he declined taking his seat on the *musnud* [the cushioned seat on which kings in India sat] I handed him to it; and saluted him as nabob, upon which his courtiers congratulated him and paid him the usual homage.

Clive then wrote how he had explained the policy of the Company towards the Nabob and his government to those present:

As this was a visit of ceremony, we could enter very little upon business. I only attempted to convince them, that it was not the maxims of the English to war against the Government, but that Surajah Dowlat not only would not fulfill the treaty he had entered into with us, but was taking measures by calling in the French to destroy us; but it had pleased God to overthrow him, and that as the present Nabob was a brave and good man, the country might expect to be quiet and happy under him; and for our parts we should not anyways interfere in the affairs of the Government, but leave that wholly to the Nabob; that as long as his affairs required it, we were ready to keep the field, after which we should return to Calcutta and attend solely to commerce, which was our proper sphere and our whole aim in these parts.

This was the view taken of the conquest of Bengal by those who brought it about. The Calcutta Council was even afraid it might not be approved in London. So on July 14 1757, they wrote a long despatch to the Secret Committee in London justifying and explaining their action. They gave the same reasons for their part in the 'happy revolution' as they called it, as they had recorded in the proceedings, and observed: 'Motives so interesting and founded upon the prime law of self-preservation determined us to embrace the proposal made by Jaffir Aly Khan.' Then they sought the approval of their masters in the following words:

> Having given you, Honourable Sirs, a very particular detail of our transactions since engaging in the confederacy to set up Jaffir Ali Cawn, we have reason to flatter ourselves you will approve of our conduct through the whole of this nice but necessary step.

The exact point reached both politically and psychologically in the creation of the British Empire in India when the battle of Plassey was won should be obvious to anybody who reads the contemporary records of the doings, thoughts and feelings of those who were concerned with it. Unfortunately, it is the historians who are most responsible for the distortion of history in the light of later developments. They try to represent the unfolding of great historical processes as a straight course to make their job easy. And if the men concerned do not navigate the historical process in this manner the historians accuse them of incompetence and every other failing.

There is indeed teleology in history, but it is only perceptible in retrospect, and is never controlled by free will. There can be no doubt that after the battle of Plassey the course was set for the

Proclamation of Queen Victoria in 1858. But those who won the victory saw only the solution of a commercial problem for the time being. They were not certain that even this solution would be lasting. For instance, in the letter from the Calcutta Council just quoted, this fear was expressed. After pointing out the advantages of the treaty with Mir Jafar, the Committee in Calcutta thought it necessary to add:

> But we must take the liberty to recommend to your serious consideration, the preservation of the grants and privileges acquired by this revolution, which can be done only by keeping up a large body of troops in the country. As it is in the Company's interest to exert themselves on this occasion, we make no doubt you will immediately enlist and send out a sufficient number of recruits to make a respectable garrison in Bengal, which should consist of a body of two thousand Europeans at least; which expences we think will be overpaid by the advantages of our acquisitions.

They finally added:

> This, we are of opinion, will be the only method of preventing in future the encroachments of the country government, to make our friendship and alliance courted, to carry on our trade on the securest footing, and to oppose the resettlement of the French in these provinces.

This was all that the Company wanted in July 1757, a month after Plassey.

Chapter Eight

Settlement in Bengal

Implementation of the Treaty

The installation of Mir Jafar as Nawab of Bengal (formally, of the three *subas* of Bengal, Bihar and Orissa) was an easy matter. For the present his position was also undisputed. As Clive wrote to London on July 26 1757:

> The present nabob has every appearance of being firmly and durably seated on the throne. The whole country has quietly submitted to him, and even the apprehension of an inroad from the side of Delhi is vanished, so that this great revolution, so happily brought about, seems compleat in every respect.

But Mir Jafar's assumption of the subadarship had to be legitimized by a firman from the Emperor of Delhi, who at that time was Alamgir II. Clive wrote to him on July 30:

> ... by the consent of all the greatest men of the City, Meer Jaffeir Caun Bahadre [Bahadur = brave] succeeded him [Siraj], a man just and merciful as his predecessor was wicked and cruel. He therefore beseeches your Majesty that you will grant him a *sunnud* for the Subaship of these three provinces.

To add weight to his request Clive added: 'I have joined him with 25,000 matchless *seapoys*, and if it please God there shall be nothing wrong to make the country flourish and subjects happy.' But lest the reference to his troops should disquiet Delhi he was careful to say: 'I kept my army out of the City nor permitted them to plunder the least thing.' In respect of his own position he was as correct to the Emperor as he had been to Mir Jafar. He wrote: 'I am always ready with my life to obey your Majesty's commands.' Clive also wrote to the Vizir Ghazi-ud-din Khan saying that he hoped that, by the Vizir's favour Mir Jafar would obtain the Emperor's sanction. Of course, it was granted.

Then came the question of prompt fulfilment of the terms of the treaty, especially the monetary ones. The political and territorial clauses offered no difficulty. There was to be an offensive and defensive alliance between the Nawab and the Company against all enemies, native or European; all Frenchmen within the Nawab's territory were to be delivered up to the English with their goods, factories and effects and they were never again to be permitted to settle in the provinces; the Nawab was not to fortify any place below Hooghly; the Company was to receive substantial extension of territory round Calcutta and south of it as the Nawab's tenant, but all of it was to be under the perpetual government of the Company; the Company was to come to the military assistance of the Nawab if required, but the extraordinary expenses for such help were to be paid by the Nawab.

The monetary clauses were about compensation to be paid to those who had suffered by Siraj's capture of Calcutta – 10 million rupees to the Company, 2 million to the native inhabitants, 700,000 to the Armenians. Omichand's 2 million were not, of course, in the genuine treaty. All these sums were to be paid within one month of the accession of Mir Jafar.

But difficulties arose about the payments. Even before Clive went to Murshidabad, Watts and Walsh had written to him: 'Rai Dulabh with his whole stock of Gentoo [Hindu] rhetoric endeavoured to persuade us that the treasure had been examined and it appeared that the money available was not above 15 million or so.' They added: 'In short he appears to pride himself in shuffling and tricking, and we are persuaded, whilst he is Minister [*diwan*] our affairs will meet with all the interruption that Gentoo cunning can raise.' But there was no means of circumventing Rai Durlabh.

Clive on his arrival found this to be so. The jewellery and other treasures that Siraj had sent off with his women had been looted, together with the women, by those who had seized them. So only what was left in the public treasury was available. Watts had suggested that Omichand should be questioned about the treasures. Clive was convinced that large sums of money had been taken away and concealed by the ministers. But, as he wrote to Calcutta, 'it would have been both a difficult and insidious task for me to have sifted into this affair'.

In a private conversation in the morning of June 30, Mir Jafar suggested a consultation with the Jagat Seths. They went to the bankers, who, after 'a long and friendly debate', suggested that half of the English demands should be paid immediately, and the rest within three years, in three equal yearly instalments.

Because of the circumstances Clive agreed. But he had also to agree to give Rai Durlabh a commission of five per cent, because 'it was absolutely necessary to satisfy Rai Durlabh, who is the principal minister, and through whose hands our affairs must pass' (letter from Clive to the Select Committee in Calcutta, June 30 1757). The amounts agreed to were paid at once, and were sent down in boats and under military escort to Calcutta. There, after the victory of Plassey, not only were guns fired from the *Kent*, the *Tyger* and the fort, but 'the ladies were getting footsore with dancing, and bumpers were going to Clive's health'.

It was at the meeting with the Jagat Seths that Omichand discovered the trick that had been played on him. Orme gave a sensationalized account of it. Clive's version, given in his evidence before the Parliamentary Committee, was more matter-of-fact and probable. As recorded in the Report of the Committee:

> At this meeting [with the Jagat Seths on June 30 1757] was Omichand, and when the real treaty came to be read the indignation and resentment expressed in that man's countenance bars all description. He said, 'This cannot be the treaty; it was a red treaty that I saw.' His Lordship replied, 'Yes, Omichand, but this is the white treaty.'

Whether he was told about this in the manner described by Orme cannot be corroborated from any other account. But that he did not become an idiot after his disappointment – as stated by Orme – appears to be certain. For one thing, crooks do not take their punishment tragically, and besides there is a definite statement of Clive's about him in a letter written to the Secret Committee in London on August 6 1757. In it Clive wrote:

> Omichand likewise had merited well while acting in concert with Mr Watts, but I had reason to think his intriguing disposition was carrying him too far in the pursuit of private interest, therefore recommended to him a visit of devotion to Malda. He is a person capable of rendering you great services while properly restrained, therefore not to be wholly discarded.

It would seem that for some time Omichand was very upset, for on July 6 Scrafton wrote to Drake in Calcutta: 'Omichand shams sick and swears he has lost faith in man.' The Calcutta Council wrote to Clive on the same day: 'It would be better that Omichand was in Calcutta lest he do prejudice to the cause.'

But Clive did not agree. On the contrary, he requested the Council to support him in the contract he had secured to supply saltpetre.

Thus Omichand faded away in India, only to acquire a great name in England among English moralists as a martyr to the villainy of Clive, and to be re-exported to India more than a century later – there to become a stick in the hands of Indian nationalists with which to beat Clive and the British Empire. A fiery book on Clive was written in Bengali with the title *Jaliat Clive – The Forger Clive*.

Besides the payments noted above, the members of the Council and the officers of the Navy and Army, including Admiral Watson and Admiral Pocock, received large sums of money as private gifts. This was to create a very unpleasant sequel for Clive in his last years. Why these presents were made, and the considerations that made the recipients accept them, have therefore to be set down. But before doing so it is necessary to see what sums were involved, and the only full and systematic statement that is to be found is a table given in the third report of the Select Committee, 1773. It included all the sums that were proved or acknowledged before the Committee to have been distributed by the princes and other natives of Bengal from 1757 to 1766 (both years inclusive). This table did not include the presents to the two admirals. The following were the sums:

	Rupees
Roger Drake as Governor:	280,000 = £31,500
Clive as second in the Council and Commander-in-Chief, and also from purely private donations:	20,80,000 = £234,000
Watts as member of Council and from private donations:	10,40,000 = £117,000
Killpatrick:	540,000 = £60,750
Manningham:	240,000 = £27,000
Becher:	240,000 = £27,000
Six members of Council 1 lakh each:	600,000 = £68,200
Walsh:	500,000 = £56,250
Scrafton:	200,000 = £22,500
Lushington:	50,000 = £5,625
Grant:	100,000 = £11,250

In addition, under a special stipulation, all members of the Army and Navy received five million rupees (approximately six hundred thousand pounds); Clive's share in this was Rs200,000, which is included in the amount shown in the table.

The acceptance of these gifts was not contrary to the regulations then in force for the King's Army and Navy, nor were they forbidden by any rule laid down by the Company. On the contrary, when the directors in London heard about these large gifts of money they expressly wrote that they did not intend 'to break in upon any sums of money which have been given by the Nawab to particular persons by way of free gift or gratuity for their services'.

In a letter written to Payne, chairman of the Court of Directors, Clive explained these gifts so that there might be no misunderstanding. As to the gifts of money made to the members of the Calcutta Council, he made a point worth noting. He wrote that Payne might think they were not deserved by the members, but 'I may venture to assure you, what is no secret, that without some such provision I should have found it difficult a task to have executed the late glorious expedition.' In simple words, the Calcutta Council would not have co-operated without the assurance of personal profit for its members.

In the same letter, Clive wrote about his own share:

> If I had been disposed to grow rich by receiving presents from any other hands but those of the Nabob, surely no one had ever the like opportunity; but there is not that man living among the daily temptations which offered who can accuse me of receiving anything of value but from the Nabob himself.

He frankly told Payne why he was writing about these acquisitions of his: 'I have troubled you with these particulars because among some it may be computed a crime my being rich: if it be a crime, you, Sir, are truly acquainted with the nature of it.'

In fact, Clive made no secret of his acquisitions at any time, either immediately after receiving them or later. Fifteen years afterwards, when Parliament was looking into this matter, Clive repeated the justification he had put forward in a letter to the proprietors of the East India stock, which was circulated as a printed pamphlet in 1764.

First, he said, such presents were customary. 'The Nawab,' he stated, 'agreeable to the known and usual custom of Eastern Princes, made presents, both to those of his own Court and to such English who by their rank and abilities had been instrumental in the happy success of so hazardous an enterprise, suitable to the rank and dignity of a great Prince.' He was only one amongst the many who benefited by the Nawab's favour.

Next, he argued, this was not depriving the Company of its due. 'What injustice', he asked, 'was this to the Company? They could expect no more than what was stipulated in the treaty; or what injunction was I under to refuse presents from him, who had the power to make me one as the reward of honourable services? I know of none.' He added that he thought he had a particular claim, because, devoting himself wholly to the Company's service, he had neglected all commercial advantages. He pointed out what the Company had gained through his efforts, and asked another question: 'What would the world have said had I come home and rested upon the generosity of the present Court of Directors?'

Lastly, he asserted that it was known to everybody in Bengal, that he had put the honour of his country and the interest of the Company first, and had he taken advantage of all the opportunities which offered themselves he would have had so much money that his jaghir (of which more will be said later), great as it was, would have been an object scarce worth his attention.

He explained that Murshidabad was as extensive, populous and rich a city as the City of London with this difference – that there were individuals in it who possessed infinitely greater amounts of property than any in London. In this he was wholly correct, for in India more money is made by individuals favourably placed during imperial interregnums than when a strong imperial regime is in being, because in these interludes public power is used for private profit, and profiteers are ready to give a generous brokerage to those who wield public power.

So, Clive said, many men of property came to gratify him. But he asserted in his statement, 'preferring the reputation of the English nation, the interests of the Nabob, and the advantages of the Company to all pecuniary considerations, I refused all offers that were made to me.' He was telling the truth in this.

An incident characteristic of the times took place over the distribution of the money given to the British land and naval forces. In order to settle the principle and method of distribution, Clive held a council of war at Murshidabad on July 3 1757. There, as Clive wrote to Watson, 'several warm and selfish debates arose'. By a majority, consisting of the officers of the land forces, it was decided that the men belonging to the naval squadron would not get a share of the money set apart for the troops, though they had formed part of the expedition. This Clive considered gross injustice. Furthermore, the officers clamoured for the money at once, before it was properly allocated and the agents of both the parties could be present.

At this, Clive dissolved the war council, whereupon some officers sent a letter of protest to him. He at once had the officers who brought the letter arrested, and sent down one of the ringleaders, a captain, to Calcutta. He also wrote a severe letter to the officers, making very telling points: firstly, that the money was a gift from the Nawab, and could not be claimed as a matter of right; secondly, that they had not found the money by storming towns, nor was it found on the plains of Plassey; thirdly, that if they were getting this money it was entirely due to the care Clive took of their interest; lastly, that if he had not intervened for them they would at best have received six months' pay as bonus from the Company.

Despite all this, he said, he had been treated with the greatest disrespect and ingratitude, and what was worse his authority had been flouted. He therefore said that he would send the money to Calcutta to be accounted for, and then leave it to the whim of the Nabob whether to pay them or not.

This had its effect, and the officers withdrew their protest with apologies. Clive, who was pleased as easily as he was roused to anger, wrote a generous letter in reply, saying that he had ever been desirous of the love and good of his officers and added that what had passed would be forgotten.

One comment on this affair would not be out of place. When money flows in abnormal amounts in abnormal circumstances, and comes as a gift from others, the recipients always complain. Napoleon, exasperated by the discontent and grumblings of his brothers and sisters, to whom he was always over-generous, once remarked that they behaved as if they had received their crowns and wealth from '*feu notre père*'. In India, even now, any impudent claim is rejected with the words: '*Tera bapka . . . ?*' (thy father's?). Clive might have said to those who tried to grab the money he had gained in Bengal: '*Tomara bapka . . . ?*' (your father's?).

Guardianship of Mir Jafar
The hope Clive had expressed when he put Mir Jafar on the

masnad, that the Nawab would give good government to his people, and the English would be able to devote themselves solely to commerce, was not fulfilled – perhaps in the very nature of things it could not be.

It was not simply that the dynastic revolution had left loose ends, mental reservations, discontents and unsatisfied ambitions. Such things are left by all political changes, and in Islamic history troubles broke out not only at the establishment of a new dynasty but also at the accession of almost every prince. But as long as the Islamic body politic retained strength and soundness, the disturbances were suppressed quickly by a capable ruler, and were not more serious than teething troubles for a child.

In contrast, throughout India in the eighteenth century – a period of general political decadence – not one capable ruler was seen either in Delhi or elsewhere. In that century, even in the three provinces in which an energetic and able subordinate governor asserted *de facto* independence, competence disappeared with the death of the founders – in the Deccan with that of Nizam-ul-Mulk, in Oude with that of Shuja-ud-daula, in Bengal with the deaths of both Murshid Quli Khan and Alivardi.

It was as if India was seeing the fulfilment of the words of the Hebrew prophet; he said that Sheol, the dim abode of the Jewish dead, was stirred and those who were once leaders on earth, but were living in it as shadows, said to those who were still reigning: 'You too have become as weak as we! You too have become like us' – all gliding shades. There seems to be some influence arising out of the general social ambience of decadence which prevents the emergence of any outstanding personality in periods of political decline. This is being seen as clearly in Europe today as it was seen in India in the eighteenth century.

So it is futile to dwell on Mir Jafar's feebleness: he was almost predestined to be a *roi fainéant,* unless propped up by Clive and his successors, and to collapse when unsupported. That the Company was the real sanction of any Muslim prince who ruled in Bengal before it assumed government directly was realized soon enough by Clive. He referred to the power he left behind him in the letter which he addressed to the proprietors of East India stock in 1764. His words were:

> By the services rendered to the Nabob, the Company not only recovered the misfortunes sustained from the late Nabob [Siraj] with

the possessions I have already mentioned, but also acquired, and delivered into their hands, the absolute power over the three provinces of Bengal, Bahar, and Orissa, whose ordinary annual revenues produce three millions and a half sterling; insomuch that they were enabled to set up and establish in the Soubaship any person they thought fit.

(This was a reference to the deposition of Mir Jafar and installation of Mir Qasim in his place in October 1760. It should also be recalled that even the deposed Mir Jafar chose to reside in Calcutta and would not go there except under English guard.)

But while Clive remained in India, he was able to protect Mir Jafar. As he related in the same letter: 'The unfortunate Meer Jaffeir was a stranger to distress until I had left the country.' But it was a sore trial for him to save Mir Jafar from his own weakness and *amour-propre* and also from his evil counsellors and enemies, and this experience certainly made Clive realize that it was an easier task to fight an Indian prince than to have to help and protect him.

The first thing that Clive had to face was Mir Jafar's sense of combined guilt and humiliation at being raised to the throne by the English—*feringhees,* or the *gora log* (white people). This was behind his attempts to evade the execution of the unfulfilled parts of the treaty and his desire to maintain a large army of his own at ruinous expense and considerable risk from the insubordinate soldiery. Clive said that Mir Jafar's policy was 'to appear, in the eyes of his subjects, as maintaining himself by his own strength, and not by our support'.

Behind this was also the influence of his son Miran, who was another Siraj and hated the English. The Muslim commanders and notables also resented the protection and the veiled power of the English. This feeling made the Muslims forget the oppression of Siraj and look back to him with sympathy.

Curiously enough, this Muslim resentment against the English and sympathy for Siraj was acquired in the last quarter of the nineteenth century by the new Bengali Hindu intelligentsia created by British rule, who could admire Siraj with impunity, being immune from his oppression. This was first exhibited in literature, with the publication in 1874 of a long poem in Bengali entitled 'The Battle of Plassey', by a Bengali Hindu poet, Nabin Chandra Sen. Reviewing it, the great Bengali novelist Bankim Chandra Chatterji, the creator of the new

Hindu nationalism, wrote: 'When Nabin Babu's patriotism flows out, he does not speak in a restrained manner; it gushes out like lava. . . . If those who are Bengali by birth will not read the heartfelt lamentations of the Bengali people, they have been born Bengali in vain.' By that time, the Bengali Hindus had identified themselves with Siraj. The Muslims, who had been delivered from Siraj, were bound to do so from the time of his death.

Another fact that rankled with Mir Jafar and his fellow Muslims was that the plot to raise him to the throne was hatched and made successful by the Hindus. Clive had to depend on Durlabhram and other Hindus because at that time they were carrying on the administration, especially in fiscal matters; also, knowing the hatred the Muslims at Siraj's court felt for them and all Hindus generally, they felt safe to be with the British, and would not be faithless to them except in attempts to cheat them out of money – an activity perfectly consistent with political co-operation.

But in dealing with the situation created by Plassey, Clive's main handicap was lack of such overwhelming military superiority as would have made him independent of all rival cliques and individuals, and of their manoeuvres. Nevertheless, it was not till about two years after Plassey that he began to think of direct rule as a possible policy for the Company in Bengal.

It was inconceivable to replace Mir Jafar so soon after setting him up. So what Clive did was to suppress the active revolts against Mir Jafar, repel the invasions of his territory from outside, make up the quarrels at court and press the claims of the Company on the strength of the services rendered. In short, he employed whatever military strength he had in favour of Mir Jafar instead of against him. Clive defined the basis of his action quite consciously. He wrote to Calcutta early in November: 'The less occasion he has for us, the more unwilling he will be to comply with any of our requests.' Even so, Mir Jafar continued to play fast and loose until in 1759 he was delivered by Clive from two very great dangers to himself.

During the months after his accession, Mir Jafar was confronted by two active rebellions and one incipient one. All were by Hindu chiefs. The former two were in two outlying districts to the south-west and north-west of Bengal, and were very minor affairs. They were suppressed by Clive, through diplomacy and military demonstration combined.

The third rebellion, which did not break out openly, was potentially more dangerous, because the chief concerned was the deputy subadar in charge of Bihar, the westernmost province of Mir Jafar's kingdom. It was adjacent to Oude, which was under Shuja-ud-daula, a powerful prince, reported to have his eye on Bengal. The deputy subadar's name was Ramnarayan. He was supposed to have been more sympathetic to Siraj than to Mir Jafar, and to be in touch with Shuja-ud-daula. He had also incurred the suspicion of the English, because he had allowed Law (who was retreating before his pursuit by an English force under Coote after his his failure to rescue Siraj) to pass through Bihar into Oude. Being in a strong position, Ramnarayan showed every inclination to defy Mir Jafar, and was virtually independent.

After the other rebellions had been suppressed Mir Jafar marched with a large army against him. At first he was not very willing to let Clive go with him; but was induced to do so because he was more afraid of leaving Clive behind at Murshidabad. Rai Durlabh also joined them afterwards. This operation kept Clive occupied from November 1757 to May 1758. It was accompanied by all the tortuous intrigues, double-dealings and unwillingness to bring matters to a head which marked the relations between a ruler of this age with his subordinate chiefs. Ramnarayan was as distrustful of Mir Jafar as the latter was of him. Clive, who was at first against Ramnarayan, came round to the view that it would be necessary to keep in Bihar a man who was relatively capable. So, at his insistence, an understanding was arrived at, by which both sides were willing to maintain peace, if it suited them.

Meanwhile, at Murshidabad there was incessant intrigue. Mir Jafar and Rai Durlabh, who was the *diwan*, or chief minister in charge of revenues, were at loggerheads. The minister was trying to keep all power in his own hands, while the Nawab wanted to get rid of him. He was also suspected of inciting the rebellions. Clive intervened to bring about a reconciliation. It was not, however, an easy thing to do. In December 1757, when Rai Durlabh remained behind at Murshidabad and showed no eagerness to join Mir Jafar, Clive gave his account of the trouble to the Secret Committee in Calcutta:

> It is very certain that Roy Dulup had a powerful party in the State, and more than probable that he took measures to strengthen it, according to the common policy of all Duans: However that might

be the Nabob's jealousy of him was carried to such a height, that Surajah Dowla's brother, a young lad and almost an idiot, was suddenly cut off, on a surmise of Roy Dulup's intending to make him Nabob, and having sent his own brother to Chandernagore to engage me in the business, which is altogether groundless. Roy Dulup no sooner knew of his sudden execution and motive for it, than he began to fear for his own life, and open hostilities might possibly have ensued if we had not been a check to each party.

Mir Jafar excused himself of all knowledge of this murder, and blamed his son Miran for it. Clive did not wholly believe this. Rai Durlabh on a pretence of sickness remained behind. But at last Clive brought about a reconciliation between the two.

Before setting out on the expedition to Patna, Clive also insisted on the strict fulfilment of the terms of the treaty and prompt settlement of all arrears of payment. Clive's own account of this was given in his letter to the holders of East India stock, already quoted. He wrote:

> At our first meeting [November 1757] I reproached him with the duplicity of his conduct, and insisted on his immediately paying down all arrears, and that he should give secure assignments for the rest of the treaty-money.

His special advice was about the army Mir Jafar was maintaining.

> I freely gave him my opinion of his keeping up such a vast army, which drained the treasury to no manner of purpose; that the example of his predecessor might be a lesson to him how little such troops were to be depended upon; and that when danger pressed, he he would find the English his only true and firm support.

But, as Clive wrote:

> In his exaltation to his new grandeur, and seeing himself at the head of such a numerous army, my advice made little impression; so I concluded with telling him, he might amuse himself with his own ideas, but in the meantime, that I was neither to be trifled with nor intimidated; and after some struggle, I obtained immediate payment of the arrears, amounting to several thousand pounds, and an assignment of certain districts, the revenues of which be collected by the Company as a security for the rest.

'From this instant,' Clive concluded, 'the Nabob may have been said to comply literally with his treaty.'

By the middle of 1758, Mir Jafar's affairs had been so settled that Clive could write:

> All domestick troubles are now happily ended and the Nabob seems so well fixed in his government as to be able with a small degree of prudence to maintain himself quietly in it. For ourselves we have been fortunate in the course of these transactions to attach to us the most considerable persons in the kingdom.

He added that friendship of the English was solicited on all sides.

The lull lasted for some months. But it was broken early the next year by an invasion from outside, which frightened Mir Jafar almost out of his wits. This was attempted by the son of the reigning Emperor of Delhi, whose personal name was Ali Gauhar. He was to become Emperor as Shah Alam II, to confer the *diwani* of Bengal to the Company, to be blinded and to reign afterwards under British protection. At this time, he had been driven out from Delhi by the Vizir Ghazi-ud-din, and was living as an adventurer at Allahabad, trying to get a kingdom. But he was not a capable man, having ambition and vainglory as *shahzada* (son of the Emperor) rather than any following. He was supposed to have been encouraged by Shuja-ud-daula, and to be in collusion with Ramnarayan.

In January 1758, news was received that he was approaching Bihar, and in February he was near Patna. Warren Hastings, who was at that time the agent of the Company at Murshidabad, informed Clive that Miran had come to him in a panic to request Clive to come at once to the help of the Nawab against the Shahzada. Clive assured the Nawab of his support. Some days later he heard that the Nawab was trying to buy off the invader with a large sum of money. He immediately wrote to Mir Jafar:

> If you do this, you will have Shuja-ud-daula, the Mahrattas, and many more come from all parts to the confines of your country, who will bully you out of money, till you have none left in the treasury.... What will be said, if the great Jaffier Ali Khan, Subah of this province, who commands an army of sixty thousand men, should offer money to a boy who has scarce a soldier with him? I beg Your Excellency will rely on the fidelity of the English and of those troops which are attached to you.

The important factor in this situation was the attitude of Ramnarayan. He was certainly wavering, either genuinely so or merely to gain time in negotiating with the Prince. Finally, however, he decided to resist him. The Shahzada summoned

Clive to his presence 'to pay your respects to me like a faithful servant'. Clive replied firmly that he was under the strictest engagements with the subadar of the provinces, and it was not the custom of the English nation to be guilty of insincerity.

In the early days of March 1759 Clive reached Murshidabad in order to march to Patna. Mir Jafar's troops were discontented at not having received their pay, so he could not accompany Clive. Only Miran, with a small force, went.

In the meanwhile, the Shahzada was laying siege to Patna with an army of 40,000. Ramnarayan held out, and on April 4, at the mere approach of Clive, the Prince raised the siege and retreated. He was pursued vigorously, and his forces melted away. At the end of April, Clive wrote: 'We have now dispersed all his followers and he is himself in great distress wandering about with a few men, not knowing whom to trust to.' In fact, the Prince wrote a letter seeking the protection of Clive. After having consulted Ramnarayan, who advised that the presence of a prince of Delhi in Bengal would be a source of intrigue and danger, Clive refused the Shahzada's request and even wrote:

> I have received repeated orders from the Vizier, and from the King [the prince's father], not only to oppose Your Highness, but even to lay hold of your person. I am sorry to acquaint Your Highness with these disagreeable things, but I cannot help it. Were I to assist Your Highness in any respect, it would be attended with the ruin of this country. It is better that one should suffer, however great, than that so many thousands should be rendered unhappy. I have only to recommend Your Highness to the Almighty's protection.

As things transpired, the Shahzada got that protection later, so as to become Emperor. After settling everything at Patna, Clive returned to Murshidabad in July. But Mir Jafar was in great trouble there on account of the mutinous behaviour of his troops who wanted the money due to them. They would have killed him, but were deterred when they heard of the success of Clive at Patna.

At last, Mir Jafar felt sincerely grateful. So, as Clive related later:

> On my return from the north he came to meet me, and after many obliging expressions, that I had saved his life, and made him a second time Soubah, he reproached himself with ingratitude in never having appointed me a Jaghire. On taking his leave he told me, Jaggerseat (a man of great note in that country) was entrusted with his orders on that subject.

This was the conferring of the famous or notorious jaghir, which became a source of wealth as well as vexation to Clive.

The troublesome Jaghir

A jaghir was the assignment of the revenue derived from a certain amount of land (large or small) to a person who had received a commission from the reigning monarch to command a special number of men. The assignee of the revenue was called a *jaghirdar* (holder of a jaghir) and the holder of the commission (which was also an honour and a status) a *mansabdar*. A jaghir was given to a commander as the means of fulfilling his commission, for he had to raise and maintain the number of troops which his *mansab* specified. The numbers were as low as twenty or as high as seven thousand or more. The revenue assigned would be from Rs1,000 a year for the commander of twenty to Rs350,000 for a commander of seven thousand. The higher commanders became the most important officials and supporters of the State. Collectively, they were called the *umarrah* (plural of *amir*), and the jaghir was a necessary apanage of their command, but afterwards it became an entitlement to revenue without any military responsibility.

As it happened, Clive had become a mansabdar in December 1757. When Mir Jafar applied for his firman, or *sanad*, as sabadar of Bengal, he also recommended a mansab for Clive. This was granted to Clive formally by an order of the Emperor of Delhi, which said that 'Colonel Clive, an European, be favoured with a *Mansab* of the rank of 6,000 and 5,000 horse, and the titles of "Zabdat-ul-Mulk, Nasir-ud Daulah Colonel Clive Sabat Jang Bahadu". This order was received at Patna in April 1758. But Clive received no jaghir to support this dignity. So he pleaded his inability to pay the large fee demanded, and directed his representative to pay the usual *nazar* (or present of money).

The matter rested there for the year 1758, but he addressed a letter to the Jagat Seths in January 1759, to which the Seths gave an evasive reply on behalf of Mir Jafar. However, after the repulse of the Shahzada, Clive received a letter from the Seths that the Nawab had finally decided to give him a jaghir. The following is Clive's version of the gift, given in 1764, which tallies with what can be learnt from the letters written at the time. He said:

> From the time of my receiving my honours from Delhi... to this time [middle of 1759] nothing had ever passed on the subject but one letter from me to Jaggerseat, in January 1759, informing him, that the Nabob had made me an Omrah, without a Jaghire, which I understood did actually accompany it and to desire he would apply to him on that occasion; to which letter he returned answer, that he had applied to His Excellency, who ordered him to acquaint me, that he never granted Jaghires in Bengal; that Orissa was too poor, but that I might have one in Bahar.

But, Clive continued:

> Looking on the Nabob's answer as an evasive one, and that he was not inclined to comply with my request, I never wrote or thought any more on the subject, until I received a second letter from Jaggerseat in an answer to my first, after our success against the King's son, that the Nabob had turned the thing in his mind, and was willing to grant me a Jaghire in Bengal; but the nature of it, where, and of what value it was to be, I was entirely ignorant, till the patent explained it, and I confess it gave me the greater pleasure to find it to be lordship of the Company's lands, because the Company was thereby freed from all dependence on the government.

The order for this was handed to Clive after the meeting referred to above. As Clive said:

> Jaggerseat soon after put a paper roll into my hands, in the presence of Mr Francis Sykes, Mr Luke Scrafton (both now in England) and Major Carnac, which proved to be a patent for the lordship of lands rented by the Company, in consequence of our treaty with him. This patent was soon followed by an order to the Governor and Council of Calcutta to pay me the rents of the said lands, instead of paying them as before into his treasury.

The value amounted to approximately £30,000 a year.

The validity of this jaghir began to be questioned in England even before Clive came to Bengal a second time in 1765. It is necessary, therefore, at this point to give Clive's justification of it. In his letter to the holders of East India stock he dealt with the question exhaustively. His case, in his words, was as follows:

> It is to be observed that the lands ceded to the Company by the IXth article of the treaty, were only ceded to them as perpetual Jemindars, or renters, the Nabob reserving the Lordship and quit-rents, which amounted to near £30,000 yearly; and the Company could never be lawfully dispossesed, so long as they continued to pay that quitrent. It was, then, the Lordship and the rents so re-

served that he made over to me; no prejudice resulting to the Company who had farmed out the same to a very considerable yearly amount, with a prospect of great increase of rents, and only this difference, that they were to pay the quitrent to me, instead of the government; to this nation a profit of £30,000 a year.

This, in simple words, meant that the jaghir to Clive made no difference either to the title of the Company or to any profit it could make out of the lands; only what was due to the Nawab, and would always have remained due to him, was made over to Clive.

The second question was whether the Nawab could make such a transfer of his own dues to another person. On this Clive said:

With regard to the validity of this grant, I shall only say, that the patent passed all the usual forms of the Country, and was founded on the very same authority that the Company had for their acquisitions, the power of a Soubah.

There can be no doubt that both arguments were irrefutable on legal grounds.

The Elimination of the French and the Dutch

During the Seven Years' War the French were completely eliminated in India as a political and commercial competitor. In Bengal the elimination was carried out by Clive and Watson by their capture of Chandernagore. But the main political power of the French was in the Deccan, although Bengal was more profitable to them commercially. Bussy's influence at Hyderabad remained unimpaired despite all the intrigues of Salabat Jang, and when Lally landed on the coast in 1758, war for the domination of the Carnatic was renewed. In this war Clive from Bengal played an indirect part.

After the recapture of Calcutta, Madras repeatedly wrote to Clive asking him to come back, but he pleaded his inability in view of the situation in Bengal. This displeased Madras, but Clive could not oblige them.

When early in 1758 it was learnt that Lally had arrived on the coast of the Carnatic, and a powerful French naval squadron under Comte d'Aché was in the Bay of Bengal, there was temporary anxiety in Calcutta lest the French ships should attempt to come up the Hooghly river and attack Calcutta. The work on the new fort had not progressed far, and the older defences of Calcutta were very weak. So batteries were erected down the river and ships sunk to make the passage of large vessels difficult. But after an indecisive first engagement with d'Aché, Admiral Pocock fought a second battle which ruled out the possibility that any French squadron would go to Bengal. The entire strength of the French had to be concentrated in the Carnatic. Fort St David was taken by them, and Lally besieged Madras. Bussy in the north had occupied the English factory at Vizagapatam soon after the revolution in Bengal.

Clive was angry when he learned about the surrender of St David. He wrote to Pigot: 'I cannot express to you my resentment and concern at the infamous surrender of St David.' He even suggested a court martial to try those who were responsible for the surrender and observed: 'For the future, I would not leave it to the power of a commanding officer to forfeit his trust; but give him positive orders not to surrender any fort, till a breach were made in the body of the place, and one assault at least sustained.'

As to Madras, despite the undoubted danger to which Fort St George was exposed, Clive was not very worried. In a letter to Pigot written on August 14 1758, he expressed doubts about the military ability of Lally. He wrote: 'From the several accounts I have received of Monsieur Lally, I do not entertain that high opinion of him that seems to have gained upon the Coast, and indeed his late behaviour has confirmed me in this opinion.'

In the same letter he also showed his awareness of two factors which were likely to be decisive in the war in the Carnatic, namely sea power and money. As to the first he wrote:

> By this time the superiority of our force at sea I take for granted is beyond dispute, and of consequence our resources must be more than those of the French: this will be another inducement for us to hazard an engagement whenever we can do it with the least probability of success.

In respect of money, the English position in Bengal was most advantageous. Clive wrote that:

> Bengal is in itself an inexhaustible fund of riches, and you may depend upon being supplied with money and provisions in abundance; in the meantime what must become of the French, if they cannot raise money sufficient to pay their forces – they must disband their Blacks and the Whites will disband themselves.

Clive's confidence about the war in the Carnatic was expressed again and no less strongly in his famous letter to the

Elder Pitt, written a few months later – on January 7 1759, to be precise. In it he put forward the same grounds for his confidence as he had given to Pigot. He also made a forecast:

> Notwithstanding the extraordinary effort made by the French in sending out M. Lally with a considerable force the last year, I am confident, before the end of this year [1759], they will be near their last gasp in the Carnatic, unless some very unforeseen event interpose in their favour.

This prediction was wholly fulfilled in a year's time. It has to be noted that, though the scale of warfare in India was relatively small, the basic strategic factors were the same as in a large war, and in grasping them Clive really showed himself to be a born general, as Pitt described him. Hesitations entered his mind only when, in dealing with the native princes, he could not be sure of the data on which to form a judgement.

In respect of military operations, Clive decided as soon as he learned of the recapture of Vizagapatam for the English by the Raja of Vizianagram, to send an expedition to that area under the command of Colonel Forde, a very able officer, at that time under him in Bengal, in order to deprive the French of all support from the northern Circars. This was done in spite of the unwillingness of the Calcutta Council, whose attitude Clive characterized in these words: 'Self-preservation for the present seems to possess every breast, without any regard for the future, or the good of the service in general.'

The force reached Vizagapatam in the fourth week of October 1758, but owing to delays in organization the combined forces of Forde and the Raja did not come in contact with the French till the beginning of December. The troops under Forde consisted of 470 Europeans, about 1,900 sepoys, and 6 field-pieces. The Raja's contingent was of no military significance. The French force was very much larger. On December 7, a battle was fought at Condore, at which the French, under the Marquis of Conflans, an able officer, were decisively defeated. After some minor operations Forde attacked Masulipatam on March 7 1759, and took the important city and fort. The result of this victory was the permanent cession by Salabat Jang of the rich territory of the northern Circars. Forde came back to Bengal in October 1759 and Eyre Coote, who had arrived at Madras in July, took the field against Lally and defeated him totally at the battle of Wandewash on January 22 1760. This destroyed

French power in India. Clive learned of this on board his ship as he was sailing home.

In the meanwhile, there was a brief military clash in Bengal with the Dutch, as a result of which they too were eliminated as political competitors. This conflict had been incubating ever since the English had recaptured Calcutta in January 1757, developed further after Plassey, and could not be averted in 1759. The Dutch ambition to play a political role in Bengal led them to attempt clumsily what Renault and Law at Chandernagore had failed to do when Siraj was in conflict with the English. Viewing the Dutch action in the light of the extremely unstable equilibrium that he was maintaining in Bengal, Clive took a serious view of it, and said later before the Parliamentary Committee that 'he knew the fate of Bengal and of the Company depended upon it'.

He was certainly somewhat exaggerating the importance of the episode; he was making war on the Dutch when they were at peace with Britain and were not involved in the Seven Years' War. This aspect of the matter was seriously considered by him and some of his friends, who told him that he was taking a grave responsibility on himself. To this he replied that 'a public man may occasionally be called upon to act with a halter round his neck'. To the Parliamentary Committee he said that 'he risked his life and fortune in taking upon himself to commence hostilities against a nation, with whom we were at peace'. His reference to his fortune was made because at that time he had sent the greatest part of his ready money by Dutch ships, and if the Dutch wanted to retaliate they could seize about £180,000 of his which was in their hands. Apart from this personal risk, to which he attached no importance, there would be both political and military risks if Mir Jafar made common cause with the Dutch, as he was being urged to do. But though Mir Jafar was involved in a sort of intrigue with the Dutch, and his son Miran was ready to join them, both were careful to see who won before committing themselves.

The Dutch certainly thought that they could repeat the English achievement. After Plassey they wrote to Mir Jafar that their nation was as great as, if not greater than, the English, and they also had many ships. But publicly they only pleaded their concrete grievances against the English in regard to trade. The English also had some against them.

Matters came to a head when a number of Dutch ships with

European and Malay troops entered the Hooghly river. Then the Dutch sent a long list of grievances to Clive and said if the Dutch boats were searched and the advance of their troops to the settlement at Chinsurah obstructed, they would retaliate. Clive replied by saying that he was simply acting under the orders of the Emperor of Delhi and the Nawab, which, he privately remarked, 'savoured a little of audacity'. He was throughout kept informed by Warren Hastings from Murshidabad about Mir Jafar's equivocal attitude.

The Dutch seized some small English craft and began to move their ships and troops up the river. Clive on his part prepared his defences along the whole line of the river from near Budge Budge to present-day Barrackpore, and sent down three ships of the Company, the *Dorset,* the *Calcutta* and the *Hardwicke,* to stop the eight vessels.

On November 27 1759 the Dutch vessels landed the troops opposite the southern point of Calcutta, and dropped down the river, while the troops marched northwards. The English ships, though outnumbered, attacked the Dutch fleet and forced them to surrender. One ship that attempted to escape was captured further downstream by two incoming English men-of-war.

On land Forde, who had come back from the coast, was ordered to attack the troops at Chinsurah (the Dutch settlement just north of Chandernagore) as well as the troops coming up from the south. On November 24, he chased the Dutch, who had advanced from their settlement, back to Chinsurah but did not go into the town. He then marched south for a few miles and on November 25 met the Dutch force at Badarah, south of Chandernagore on a wide plain. The English had 240 European soldiers, 80 artillerymen with 4 field-pieces, 800 sepoys, and about 100 horse from the Nawab. The Dutch had 700 European and 800 Malay soldiers, besides some sepoys. The battle, as Clive said, was 'short, bloody, and decisive'. In half an hour the Dutch force was routed. Thus ended the so-called battle of Badarah.*

The Dutch at once made peace, acknowledged themselves aggressors, agreed to pay a large compensation and met all the other British demands, upon which their ships were returned to

---

*The place-name Badarah is certainly a corruption of the Bengali 'Bhadreswar', a village south of Chandernagore. Between it and Champdani, a little further south, there was a plain called 'the fields of Champdani', which must have been the plain of Badarah.

them. But now Miran came down to chastise them for disturbing the peace. Clive interceded very firmly and a new treaty was signed between the Dutch and the Nawab, by which they were permitted to continue their trade but were totally forbidden to retain troops and fortifications or to make war. Peace was formally restored on December 5 1759. After that Clive prepared to leave for England.

Clive's Personal Position
During the time Clive was engaged in making war and peace in Bengal, he was acting as a virtual dictator. Of course, he consulted the Calcutta Council and formally obeyed its decisions. And as long as Admiral Watson lived, he had a collateral status. But for all practical purposes Clive's authority was untrammelled. The real responsibility for the decisions as well as their execution rested with him.

Yet he had no regular official status. His only legal position was that of a member of the Select Committee in Calcutta. His independent powers, especially as military commander, were derived from the Madras Council, which had no jurisdiction over Bengal.

As has been seen, the Calcutta Council at first resented these powers. But very soon it accepted his leadership. Thus from the time of the recapture of Calcutta till a year after Plassey he managed the Company's affairs and dealt with the country's powers only on the basis of a personal and *ad hoc* authority.

In June 1758, however, he became the president of the Calcutta Council, i.e. the formal head of the Company's affairs in Bengal. But this position did not come to him from London, with whom the legal power to appoint a governor lay, but from his fellow-members of the Calcutta Council. They had received a very unworkable order from London by which the presidentship of the Calcutta Council was to be exercised by its members in rotation. How and why this direction was issued will be explained later. Here it is only necessary to see how Calcutta reacted to it.

After getting their instructions from London, on June 20, they wrote to Clive on the twenty-sixth that after considering the order for a rotation of governors they had arrived at 'a sincere conviction of its being in our present situation and circumstances repugnant to the true interests of our Hon'ble Masters and welfare of the Settlement', and they believed that if the directors had 'been apprized of the state of their affairs in this Kingdom, they would have placed the Presidentship in some one person as the clearest and easiest method of conducting their concerns, as well as preserving and maintaining the weight and influence the late happy revolution has given us with the Subah of these provinces'.

They referred to the difficulties of acting by rotation, and very wisely and handsomely asked Clive to act as president and governor until the directors made their further pleasure known. They said that this was no time to think of personal honours and advantages and, waiving aside all those considerations, thought only of Clive. They added: 'Your eminent services, abilities, and merit, together with your superior weight and influence with the present Subah and his officers, are motives which have great force with us on this occasion.'

The letter was signed by all the six other members of the Council. Clive accepted the offer and thanked them heartily, saying: 'I have received your letter of this day's date; and cannot sufficiently express the grateful sense I have of the favourable opinion you are pleased to entertain of me.'

However, he expressed his dissatisfaction at finding that in the instructions of the directors there was no mention whatever of his name. This he took as a deliberate slight, but observed that the public spirit which his colleagues had shown induced him to brush aside all private considerations where the general good was concerned. He also remarked that 'the government of a single person, involved as we now are with the Country Powers, must have infinite advantages over that complicated form of government established from home'.

Clive expressed himself more strongly to Pigot at Madras. 'The absurd system of government,' he wrote, 'ordered from home, and the fatal consequences likely to attend it in these parts have induced me, at the particular request of the Gentlemen of the Council, to accept of the management of affairs for the present much against my own inclination.'

What Clive did not realize was that the directors were not aware that he was in Bengal. On the contrary, getting his despatch after the recapture of Calcutta, in which he had written of going back to Madras, they had concluded that he was there. Neither had they got the news of Plassey. They learned about that only in February 1758, and at once issued new orders appointing Clive governor of Bengal. This order reached Calcutta only in November 1758. Clive was very pleased and wrote to the Calcutta Council:

> I find the Court of Directors have done me the honour to appoint me to the Presidency of Bengal, accompanied with such marks of regard and esteem as have induced me to continue 14 or 15 months longer in India, by which time I persuade myself the treaty with the Nabob will be fulfilled, the fortifications in a state of defence, and such a force arrived from England as may secure to the Company their valuable acquisitions.

These three, he added, were the objects he had much at heart, and if they could be completed, he thought, 'the Court of Directors will think I have answered their expectations, and will approve of my returning to Europe, to enjoy the fruits of war which has been carried on for upward of eleven years almost without intermission'.

This showed once again Clive's usual readiness to take offence at any slight unwillingness of others to co-operate with him, real or imagined, and his equal readiness to forget and be happy if his work was appreciated. He had also showed this when he received the congratulations of the Calcutta Council after Plassey, and forgot the anger he had felt when he received their non-committal reply to his inquiries before the battle. These inclinations must have been implanted in him by the neglect to which he was subject when he was a child, but which also made him very grateful for any sympathy or love when he received it.

As it happened, his angry reaction was again seen when, before he left India in February 1760, he and his colleagues received despatches from the Court of Directors in which there were criticisms of him and his colleagues, the style and tone of which deeply offended him. This made Clive decide to leave the Company's service. In any case, in a general letter, addressed to the Court of Directors on December 28 1759, he protested against the

> ... general reflections thrown out at random against your faithful servants of this Presidency – faithful to little purpose, if breath of scandal, joined to private pique or private personal attachments, have power to blow away in one hour the merits of many years' services, and deprive them of that rank and those rising benefits which are justly a spur to their integrity and application.

The despatch closed with the words:

> The little attention shown to these considerations, and in the indis-

criminate favours heaped on others, will, we apprehend, lessen that spirit of zeal so very essential to the well-being of your affairs, and consequently, in the end, if continued, prove the destruction of them.

This letter was signed by four other members of the Council besides Clive. It began Clive's feud with a clique in the Company's headquarters in London that was to become a vendetta against him. Its origin and motives will be discussed in the next chapter.

In Bengal, however, there was both grief at his departure and appreciation of his achievement. 'It appeared', one contemporary wrote, 'as if the soul was departing from the government of Bengal.' The Nawab himself inquired of Warren Hastings if he thought Clive could be persuaded to put off his intention to return to Europe. The European citizens of Calcutta presented him with an address in which, besides setting down their appreciation and gratitude, they requested him to remain in Bengal.

> Our apprehensions are greatly alarmed by the reports which are now current and publicly asserted that you intend to withdraw your presence from us, and take your passage to Europe this season, and we cannot from the present face of things, but feel real concern in the knowledge of what must be the consequence of the want of that influence which is derived from it.

So they humbly requested him to reconsider his decision. But Clive sailed for England on February 21 1760.

Clive's Political Testament: 1758

More important than the impending quarrel with the directors is the view that Clive arrived at, less than a year and a half after Plassey, of the future of the Company's position in India. It was first set down in a letter written on December 30 1758, to Lawrence Sulivan, who had become the chairman of the Court of Directors that year, but much more elaborately to William Pitt on January 7 1759 – i.e. eight days later.

The letter to Sulivan dealt with general policy as well as particular recommendations. He said that 'every well-wisher to the Company' must hope that 'every thing in India may be reduced to its first principles'. So he attached more importance to Bengal than to the coast of Coromandel, and observed that a speedy peace with the French would be attended by solid advantages for the Company.

He enclosed a statement of the revenues of Bengal for Sulivan, and wrote that from his first-hand knowledge of the province he could assert with some degree of confidence that 'this rich and flourishing Kingdom may be totally subdued by so small force as two thousand Europeans, and the possession thereof maintained and confirmed by Great Mogul upon paying a sum – the sum of 50 Lack per annum, paid by former subahs'. He did not anticipate any resistance from the inhabitants. 'The Moors, as well as Gentoos [Hindus], are cowardly beyond all conception.'

Turning to the military aspect of holding Bengal he said that the country was full of great and navigable rivers, wooded and surrounded by hilly regions with narrow passes. This terrain favoured infantry and made cavalry, chief strength of the armies in India, a mere burden.

The soldiers in India, he explained, if they at all deserved the name, did not have any attachment to their prince, and served those best who paid them best. He set down the deliberate opinion:

> After the battle of Placis I could have appropriated the whole country to the Company and preserved it afterwards with as much ease as Meer Jaffeir the present Subah now does, through the terror of the English arms and their influence.

The Mogul Empire, he went on to say, was breaking up and the Delhi court would be happy if it could only get money regularly from Bengal. 'There is not the least doubt that he [the Vizir in Delhi] would much rather grant the Royal Sunud to a nation famed for the success of its arms and for their strict adherence to treaties, than to one who is scarce master of any other influence or authority but what he enjoys under the wings of the English reputation.' (This 'sunud', or sanad, was obtained by Clive in 1765 with great ease.)

Clive was careful to explain that he did not intend any disloyalty to Mir Jafar. 'I do not want', he wrote, 'to aggrandize the Company at the expence of all equity and justice; long may the present Subah [Mir Jafar] enjoy the advantages gained him by our arms, if he abides strictly by his treaties.'

But he asked Sulivan, who had experience of India, to remember the conditions obtaining in that country:

> You are well acquainted with the nature and dispositions of Mussulmen, gratitude they have none, bare men of very narrow concep-

tions, and have adopted a system of politick more peculiar to this country than any other, viz, to attempt everything by treachery than force. Under these circumstances may not so weak a Prince as Meer Jaffeir be easily destroyed, or influenced by others to attempt destroying us? What is it then can enable us to secure our present acquisitions or improve upon them, but such a force as leaves nothing to the power of treachery or ingratitude?

He concluded with some personal recommendations, especially for Watts. He made a very shrewd remark about Holwell: 'Mr Holwell has talents, but I fear wants a heart, therefore unfit to preside where integrity as well as capacity are equally essential.' He assured Sulivan that he had no other attachment to particular persons than to what their capacity for serving the Company entitled them.

In his letter to Pitt, Clive made the same points, but amplified them further. For instance, he described the contingent need to take the place of the present Nawab as being more immediate. He was old, Clive wrote, and his son was a worthless young fellow, and apparently such an enemy of the English that it would be virtually unsafe trusting him with the succession.

To the attitude of the people of Bengal he gave a more positive colour. The natives themselves, he wrote, had no attachment whatever to particular princes; and since under Mir Jafar they had no security for their lives or properties, they would rejoice in a change which would give them a mild instead of a despotic government.

As to a grant from the Emperor of Delhi, he said in this letter that he had actually been approached, and could have been entrusted with, the collection of the revenues as *diwan*, but he declined the offer for fear of offending Mir Jafar, and also because the Company did not have a large enough force in Bengal to back up this heavy responsibility. The number of troops required, he stated, would be only 2,000 Europeans: with them the Company could even take up the sovereignty for themselves.

But Clive's main object in writing to Pitt was to tell him that the task that faced the English in India was too big to be borne by a mercantile company, and needed the nation's assistance. He put his suggestion before Pitt as follows:

> I have therefore presumed, Sir, to represent the execution of a design, that may hereafter be still carried to greater lengths, be worthy that may hereafter be still carried to greater lengths, be worthy of the

of the Government's taking it into hand. I flatter myself I have made it pretty clear to you that there will be little or no difficulty in obtaining the absolute possession of these rich kingdoms, and that with the Mogul's own consent, on condition of paying him less than a fifth of the revenues thereof. Now I leave you to judge whether an income yearly of upwards of two millions sterling, with the possession of three provinces abounding in the most valuable productions of nature and of art, be an object deserving the public attention; and whether it be worth the nation's while to take the proper measures to secure such an acquisition, – an acquisition which, under the management of so able and disinterested a minister, would prove a source of immense wealth to the kingdom, and might in time be appropriated in part as a fund towards diminishing the heavy load of debt under which we at present labour.

There was another inducement:

Add to these advantages the influence we shall thereby acquire over the several European nations engaged in the commerce here, which these could no longer carry on but through our indulgence, and under such limitations as we should think fit to prescribe.

Finally, the expense would not be heavy:

It is worthy consideration that this project may be brought about without draining the mother country, as has been too much the case with our possessions in America. A small force from home will be sufficient, as we always make sure of any number we please of black troops, who, being both much better paid and treated by us than by the country powers, will very readily enter into our service.

He sent the letter by hand with Walsh, who was his secretary in Bengal, and who, he added, would be able to explain the matter more fully.

At this stage of the establishment of British power in India, this was as far as it was possible to see. In fact, practical action did not go much further in the next twenty years. But even when Clive's ideas seemed to be acted upon they were not in fact being followed by deliberate plan. The actions contemplated by him were forced upon the British authorities in India and at home. From first to last British action in India remained a series of improvisations under pressure. Whatever was done never caught up with what was needed. It was always too little, and always came too late – even the abandonment of the Empire. The whole development of British policy in India seemed to be an illustration of what Burke wrote in 1770: 'The generality of people are fifty years, at least, behindhand in their politicks.'

Part III

Clive Against England

1760–1774

Chapter Nine

Victor of Plassey in England

Anticipations of Home
It is curious that within thirty-eight days of his greatest achievement in India Clive should be thinking of going back to England. The battle of Plassey was fought on June 23 1757, and on August 1 he wrote to Orme: 'I only wait to see everything firmly settled before I steer my course for old England.' Thus, after Plassey, he showed in a more strengthened form the dichotomy that had made its first appearance after his early successes in the Carnatic. Henceforth it was to become unresolvable. It became the source of all his later troubles. In a manner of speaking, even with Plassey he began to live 'with dirge in marriage, in equal scale weighing delight with dole'.

This dichotomy sprang from his aspiration to reap in England the exotic crop he had raised in India – which in its turn stemmed from his incapacity to forget England and live away from his country, and the still greater incapacity to break with the lower middle-class antecedents of his life. Even his body and India did not agree. After every bout of demoniac energy and spectacular achievement he fell seriously ill, and seemed to say to his real vocation: 'The spirit is willing, but the flesh is weak.' So he had to go back to his country to regain his health. But to do so was also to fall into the clutches of the ambition derived from his social origins, which was to live the life of an opulent English gentleman. This would not have been impossible, but unfortunately the ambition had become inflated to the scale of his achievements in India. So magnified, given the social and political conditions in England of that age, it could never be satisfied. Clive would keep the old bottle but pour heady new wine into it, and the bottle was bound to burst.

The ambition was revealed in an exuberant form, though not in a manner unrealizable, in the same letter to Orme:

> I must now trouble you with a few commissions concerning family affairs – Imprimis, what you can provide must be the finest and best

you can get for Love or Money; 200 Shirts, the wrist bands worked, some of the ruffles with a border, other in squares, and the rest plain; socks, neck cloths and handkerchiefs in proportion, 3 large of the finest stockings, . . . several pieces spotted Muslin and plain 2 yards wide for aprons, book Muslin cambricks or a few pieces of the finest dimity and a compleat set of table linen of Fort St David diaper made for the purpose – You will have 5 months for these matters, and tho' there may not be time to get a compleat set of chintz furniture for a room, bed, chairs, etc., it may follow. Mrs Morse is a great connoisseur in these affairs. Excuse this trouble from a friend.

At that time, as will be seen from the time limit of five months given to Orme, he looked forward to sailing for England in January. On August 19 he also wrote to his father about this, adding the qualification '. . . if I can but leave this country in peace'. After giving an account of the political revolution in Bengal he informed his father that Mir Jafar's generosity 'has been such as will enable me to live in my native country much beyond my most sanguine wishes'. In this letter he also showed his loyalty to family, relatives and friends, which is characteristic of men from poor families who find themselves suddenly enriched and elevated. He wrote: 'I have ordered £2,000 each to my sisters, and shall take care of my brothers in due time: I would advise the lasses to marry as soon as possible for they have no time to lose.' To his father also he said: 'There is no occasion for your following the Law any more; but more of this when I have the pleasure of seeing you, which I hope will be in 12 or 14 months.'

At the end of the letter he referred to the ambition that had remained unfulfilled during his previous visit to his country: 'If I can get into Parliament I shall be very glad, but no more struggles against the Ministry; I chuse to be with them.' But in spite of his unwavering devotion to his father he had no great faith in the latter's discretion. What distinguished Clive above everything else was his capacity to calculate rationally his chances in any project, and then exhibit a daring amounting to recklessness in execution. In his political aspirations at home, in so far as he pondered over them, he wanted to go forward carefully. This discretion he could not expect from his father, and he therefore wrote to a friend.

I wait for nothing but the settlement of these provinces to begin my voyage for old England which I hope will be some time in January. All this good news may set my father upon exerting himself too much and upon paying too many visits to the Duke of N[ewcastle], Mr Fox, and other great men; I desire you will endeavour to moderate his expectations, for altho' I intend getting into Parliament and hope of being taken some notice of by his Majesty, yet you know the merit of all actions are greatly lessened by being too much boasted of. I know my Father's disposition leads this way, which proceeds from his affection for me.

It must be set down here that Clive's father was no asset to him. He remained the petty attorney, officious and always sniffing around for advantages. Brought into undeserved prominence by the achievements of his son, and admitted to a company which otherwise would never have been his, he behaved in a manner likely to bring his son into ridicule. Therefore wits made use of him to have a joke against Clive, or even others. To give one instance here, in 1763, when the ministry of the day had proposed a settlement of the question of his jaghir, Horace Walpole wrote: 'Just after the bargain was made, his old rustic of a father was at the King's levée; the King asked where his son was; he replied, "Sire, he is coming to town, and then your Majesty will have another vote".'

But Clive could not set sail for England till February 1760. By that time his position and reputation had grown much beyond what they were even after Plassey.

Clive would have had no trouble if he had decided to live as a wealthy private individual in England. Then perhaps even the question of the validity of his jaghir, a trumpery issue over which the conscience of the biographers of Clive and historians of the British Empire in India has been so much exercised, would not have arisen. The directors would have left him in peace to enjoy it. But in the England of that period, and for a long time afterwards, the social ambitions of a man could never exclude Parliament, because it was not simply a political body, still less a mere legislature, but the grand club of all Englishmen of any significance. Even if a member of that club had no political inclinations he was bound to be drawn into the grim political game.

Clive was bound to be political, because he could never disinterest himself in the future of British power in India, which was his creation, and which in his judgement was not as yet firmly established. It was also dependent on the issue of the general war between England and France. Clive could not be sure how it would end, and during 1759 nothing was known in India about what was happening in Canada. In fact, the victory at Quebec was won only in September 1759. Clive was indeed in favour of a peace with France, but he wanted to be sure that in any peace treaty the position and interests of the Company in India should be fully safeguarded. So on August 20 1759, he wrote to Vansittart:

> If a peace should be upon the tapis I may be of some use likewise, for convinced I am the Directors are not masters sufficiently of the subject and will probably conclude a peace in Europe which cannot be abided by in the East Indies.

The French in India had not been decisively beaten as yet, and he did not want the kind of situation that had been left in the Carnatic by the treaty of Aix-la-Chapelle. He also wanted to be in England so as to be able to raise the status of those who were responsible for upholding the British position in India, and to help those who had been his capable and devoted colleagues in establishing that power in the country. So he wrote in the same letter:

> All things considered my design is to get with the utmost expedition to England, for which purpose I am particularly desirous of having the *Royal George* sent here that I may run thro'. Supposing I set out in January I may arrive the beginning of May, and an answer to my proposals may come to hand by the latter end of the same year. My intentions are to get you fixed in this Government and to have Forde and Caillaud at the head of the military and if possible prevail upon the Directors (for it entirely depends upon them) to apply to his Majesty for Commissions of Major Generals for the Governors for the time being of the three Presidencies. If my interest prevails I flatter myself I shall have rendered the Company more service by my return to England than by my stay in Bengal. If not, I shall be very glad to have quitted the service.

He was also very much annoyed that the directors had appointed Eyre Coote instead of Forde to command the Company's forces in Bengal. On August 25 he wrote to Forde as well:

> I assure you [the news of the appointment of Coote] has affected me greatly and is one of my principal motives for wanting to push home with the utmost expedition on the *Royal George*. I flatter myself the request I have to make will not be denied me, which is that you will stay in Bengal all next year, provided Coote remains on the Coast. If within that time I do not get you a Colonel or a Lieutenant Colonel's Commission and an appointment of commander-in-chief all

the forces in India I will from that instant decline all further transactions with Directors and East Indian affairs.

This championing of those who had rendered good service was a part of Clive's character. It was never due to favouritism.

However, Clive was certainly mistaken in thinking that he could render a greater service to the Company by going to England than by remaining in Bengal. In respect of his own position and that of his friends, he was still more in error. The Company's position in India and the changes in it were the products of an interaction of local circumstances with the men on the spot; the result was wholly dependent on who the men were. If Clive had remained in India he would perhaps have put through what he did during his second governorship from 1765. It was likely that the salvaging work of that term of office would not have been needed at all, because had he remained, he would not have allowed the Company's position and administration to deteriorate. Thus the whole transition between himself and Warren Hastings would have been accomplished by himself.

Personally, he would have had the happiness that comes from the fulfilment of a mission, and, far from being persecuted, his power would have remained unchallenged. Even if the home authorities had sent him orders these would have been left so far behind by events that there would have been no question of reversing the *faits accomplis*. If they disapproved all that they could have done was to impeach him – as they did Warren Hastings and thought of doing in the case of Wellesley. But it is doubtful whether such a thing would have happened. All these antics in the British people's dealings with India were due to the see-saws in the growth of the power and the slowness of the process. If the establishment of British rule there had gone forward in more of a rush the critics would have been silenced by the force of the current.

Of course, this is one of the might-have-beens of history, but not an irrational speculation. The absence or presence of Clive in India mattered both for Britain and himself. His presence there helped both, whereas his sojourns in England harmed both. But he could not resist the gravitation towards his country. For one thing, his constitution was not fit to cope with the Indian climate. While other Englishmen came through thirty years of grilling in India unscathed, even two years were enough to reduce Clive to physical wretchedness.

Over and above this, his mind was always harking back to

England. Kipling in one of his stories pointed out the permissible relation between India and England in the life of an Englishman who went out to that country. Home on leave, he looks out from the terrace towards the round-bosomed woods and the white pheasant boxes, takes in the air, which is golden and full of a hundred sacred scents and sounds, and cries out in ecstasy: 'Perfect! By Jove, it's perfect.' But he has enough realism to add that there is no place like England – when one had done one's work. The father replies: 'That's the proper way to look at it, my son.' But neither Clive nor his father could think in that way.

And behind the gravitation towards England as such, to which Clive was certainly subject, there was also, as mentioned, the compulsion of his social origins. The poor boy and the son of a petty attorney wanted to show in England the prizes he had won in India, as any schoolboy does. The temptation to which the same boy of lowly origins was exposed, to play the lord in England, was also irresistible. He wanted to go home, where only an English 18th Brumaire could leave him unmolested. But that was out of the question. So even the temporary victory he obtained over the tradesmen of the East Indian directory before he went back to India in 1765 created renewed trouble for him in England.

Reception in England
Initially there was, however, no persecution. He was treated as the prize boy, with some awe as well as amusement, and with the recognition that he had served his country well in India. Clive landed at Portsmouth on July 9 1760. His reputation had preceded him. One conclusive piece of proof of this is a reference to him by Lord Chesterfield. In a letter written to his son on June 13 1758, he described the improvement of the position of England all over the world, and after telling his son about Africa and America, came to Asia and wrote: 'Captain Clive has a long since settled Asia to our satisfaction, so that three parts of the world look favourable to us.'

Even before that (March 21 1758), Horace Walpole had written to a friend: 'I forgot in my last to say a word of our East Indian hero, Clive, and his victories: But we are growing accustomed to success again!'

His interest in the 'hero' continued. Three months before Clive's arrival in England, Walpole put the following news in a postscript to a letter written on March 4 1760 to Sir Horace Mann:

> P.S. – There is some big news from the East Indies. I don't know what, except that the hero Clive has taken Mazulipatam and the Great Mogul's grandmother. I suppose she will be brought over and put in the Tower with Shahgoest [correctly shiyagosh], the strange Indian beast that Mr Pitt gave to the King this winter.

The animal was a kind of lynx, which Mir Jafar presented to Clive because it was both a rare and a beautiful animal. Clive in his turn sent it to Pitt, and he with the King's permission had it lodged in the Tower of London. Both the *Gentleman's Magazine* and the *Annual Register* recorded the coming of the *shiyagosh*.

To be able to interest Chesterfield and Horace Walpole was to be somebody as well as to have done something. In a different but no less significant way a cousin, Miss Sarah Clive, has left her testimony to the position of Clive. In a letter which bears no date but must have been written in 1758, the young lady wrote to Mrs Clive, who was in India with her husband:

> As to the name of Clive, the Colonel has made it so famous that it is the only comfort I have in still being Clive. I begin to fear that the Colonel will not bring me the Eastern Prince till it is too late: The bushel of diamonds runs strongly in my head. . . . I wish I had been the Colonel's sister; not to detract from them; certainly he is a great advantage to his family; and I believe, after my aunts and myself, that horrid name of old maid will be extirpated out of the house of Clive.

It is a pity that nothing more is known of this charming cousin.

Upon Clive's arrival the *Gentleman's Magazine* published the following poem in its July 1760 issue:

To Colonel Clive on his Arrival in England

Great, as from Peorus' conquest, Philip's son,
Glorious Cortez from New Indies won,
'Midst trumpets' loud acclaims and cannons' roar,
Welcome, illustrious Clive, to Britain's shore.
From eastern dawning, swift as Phoebus's rays,
We now behold thy full meridian blaze.
Proud of that chief, at whose impetuous course
Old Ganges trembled to his distant source,

Who, like fam'd Warwick, master of crown,
On loftiest Nabob, look'd superior down,
And made fierce Mogul with conscious fear
Startle, and deem a second Nadir near.
To thee, her safety twice Bengalia owes,
Alike from Indian and Batavian foes;
Hence no dungeon now her sons remain,
Nor of a new Amboyna's fate complain.
And see! with wreaths by glorious toils acquired,
Kind heav'n rewards the genius inspir'd;
Bestows thee all thy fondest wish could claim,
Unenvy'd fortune, and unspotted fame;
Thy aged Sire's, embrace, thy sov'reign's praise,
And from a stranger-muse unpurchas'd lays.

CRITO

In this poem there is allusion not only to the Black Hole, but even to the massacre of Amboina in 1623. The writer is also anxious to put on record that he is wholly disinterested in praising Clive.

The arrival was, however, recorded in a different style by Horace Walpole. He wrote on August 1 to Sir Horace Mann: 'General Clive is arrived all over estates and diamonds. If a beggar asks him charity, he says, "Friends, I have no small brilliants about me".'

On Monday July 14 Clive, accompanied by his father, had an audience with the King – George II, who was to die on October 25. On September 2 the University of Oxford conferred the degree of Ll.D. on him, upon presentation by Dr Vansittart of All Souls College. On September 24 Clive received, together with Admiral Pocock and Colonel Stringer Lawrence, the formal thanks of the Court of Directors and proprietors of the company, 'for their many, eminent, and signal services'.

The peerage he certainly expected was somewhat delayed, perhaps owing to the accession of a new king, and also to his own illness. Soon after he arrived in England the gout he had developed in Bengal became very much worse. In other ways too he was very poorly. So he went to Bath to take the waters, and came back restored to health. Towards the end of 1761 he got his title. It was an Irish one. He chose the name of Baron Clive of Plassey, County Clare, in the Kingdom of Ireland. The Plassey in Ireland was his estate of Ballykitty, which he renamed for the title, yielding £2,000. He thanked the Duke of Newcastle for it, regarding him as 'the first cause and principal promoter of this honour', though received formally from George III. He was not, however, wholly satisfied, and wrote to his friend Carnac:

> If health had not deserted me on my first arrival in England, in all probability I had been an English peer, instead of an Irish one, with the promise of a red riband. I know I could have bought a title (which is usual), but that I was above, and the honours I have obtained are free and voluntary. My wishes may therefore be accomplished.

Against this feeling of his might be set the revealing comment that Macaulay made on the recognition and honours Clive received. 'At home,' Macaulay wrote, 'honours and rewards awaited him, not indeed equal to his claims or to his ambition, but still such as, when his age, his rank in the army, and his original place in society are considered, must be pronounced rare and splendid.'

There was, however, no reserve in the view the people in general had of him. Even the sophisticated Horace Walpole shared this, and gave expression to it in a characteristic manner. He wrote:

> For, as this age is to be historic, so of course it will be a standard of virtue too; and we, like our wicked predecessors the Romans, shall be quoted, till our very ghosts blush, as models of patriotism and magnanimity. What lectures will be read to poor children on this area! Europe taught to tremble, the Great King humbled, the treasures of Peru diverted into the Thames; Asia subdued by the gigantic Clive! for in that age men were near seven feet high. . . .

This letter was written to the Hon'ble Seymour Conway on October 29 1762. It is remarkable, for it is another illustration of the point I have emphasized, that it makes a difference to the position and image of a man according as he appears before or after a revolution. In 1804, after the French Revolution, the position as Emperor of the son of a poor provincial lawyer was accepted as a natural phenomenon, whereas in England, where no revolution had taken place, Clive, with no comparable rise but of the same origins, became a legend. In this, however, there was a risk. When a man becomes a legend he may be looked upon as a hero one day and a monster on another to people who see him only from the outside. No view of him is quite incredible.

Even Clive's money, which was the most concrete of his possessions, became a legend. It was a subject of general conversation and speculation. The *Annual Register* for 1760 (then edited by Burke) recorded: 'It is supposed that the General can realize £1,200,000 in cash, bills, and jewels; that his lady has a casket of jewels which are estimated at least at £200,000. So that he may with propriety be said to be the richest subject in the three Kingdoms.' Actually Clive's fortune yielded him an income of about £13,000 a year, and if the £27,000 or so from the quitrent of his jaghir was added he had approximately £40,000 a year – not an exceptional sum even for a merchant.

But it attracted notice for many reasons. Whereas a rent-roll of £100,000 did not, because it was traditional, Clive's money was obtained in exceptional circumstances. It was the free gift of an eastern ruler, and what was worse, the gift was to the son of a country attorney. What this meant in that age and later must not be forgotten. When Elizabeth Bennet, urged by Lady Catherine de Bourgh not to quit her proper sphere by trying to marry Darcy, spiritedly replied that she would not be quitting that sphere because 'he is a gentleman; I am a gentleman's daughter; so far we are equal', Lady Catherine retorted: 'True. You *are* a gentleman's daughter. But who was your mother?' She was the daughter of a country attorney.

Moreover, Clive spent his money, instead of living like a miser, and spent it in a manner not thought decorous in a parvenu. He gave away £50,000 in gifts to friends and relations; settled an annuity of £500 on his father, the same amount to his old commander, Lawrence, £150 a year on his aunts, and so on. He took a house in Berkeley Square, and not satisfied with repairing Styche, his old home, acquired Walcot Park at the inflated price of £92,000, and had a house built there. even if he had not gone into politics or tried to dominate the Company all this would have been held against him. On the other hand, if he had hoarded the money and left it to his son, educated him at Eton and had a daughter to become the mistress of either the Prince of Wales or one of his brothers, Clive's style of living would have been considered natural in the second generation.

What began to make its appearance soon after his return to England was the relationship, which must be stressed in any biography of Clive, between the two parts of his career – before and after Plassey. Most men who achieve greatness leave their personal struggles behind when they have reached their peak, though they may be destroyed by the public conflicts they set going – as were both Napoleon and Hitler. But there is a minority whose personal struggles begin after their rise and achievement. Clive belongs to this minority. His rise was steady and relatively smooth. But this very rise made for the rough going of his later years.

It is certainly strange that the similarity between his life and that of the ancient Roman hero Scipio Africanus has never been pointed out. Yet it could have furnished a theme for an English Plutarch to write at least one set of parallel lives. After saving Rome from the greatest threat to her existence, Scipio was subjected to a perverse vendetta. Of course, Scipio has to be rated as one of the greatest soldiers of history. Nonetheless, he was an amateur general who had found his opportunity. To Clive that opportunity never came. Again, Scipio commanded greater moral prestige than Clive, because people have a greater sense of obligation to a soldier or statesman who saves them from a great peril, and in praising him they do not think they are bragging vulgarly. Those who make gifts of empires to their people are spoken about with a certain amount of reserve, for such acquisitions are never free from some suggestion of wrongdoing by those who acquired them.

Despite all this, the parallel between Clive and Scipio is very close in essentials: both fought their most significant battle in early life – Clive, that of Plassey at the age of thirty-two, and Scipio, that of Zama at thirty-four; both died early – at forty-nine and fifty-two respectively; both were persecuted by narrow politicians or party leaders in spite of their services to their nations; and both were indicted over money.

Along with this similarity, a contrast should be noted. Cecil Rhodes added immense territories to the British Empire by way of personal financial ventures; quite anachronistically, these were governed by a chartered company till 1923; Rhodes was not less wealthy than Clive. Nonetheless, a moral halo surrounds his memory – or at least it did. Though ironic, this contrast is truly historical. In the age of Clive the English people were falsely anti-imperialistic; in the age of Rhodes, falsely imperialistic.

The influence of Clive's social origins in relation to his career is also seen asserting itself in a very unexpected way, which has hardly been noticed. He always showed a submissiveness, which almost amounted to obsequiousness, to those whom he considered his social, political or official superiors. It was not simply the polite self-abasement of the times, or self-interested flattery. It was the natural deference to a superior in life which was then unconsiously imbibed by all of the lower classes. But in Clive's case, if this clashed with his urge for self-assertion, the latter prevailed. So at any rebuff or opposition his pugnacity was aroused. This was the original form of the two-sidedness of his nature which also found expression in the extreme caution of his military appraisals and the equally extreme daring which he showed in execution.

All this is stated at this point because the conflicts that began to appear in his life after his return to England in 1760 and were to embitter his last years had their seed-bed in a general psychological situation created at that juncture by an interaction between his social antecedents, character and achievements on the one hand, and the social structure and outlook of the age on the other. The deciding factor in the final tragedy of his life was not the opposition of his rivals and enemies, but an alienation between him and the popular mind which developed gradually, to become quite plain when he finally returned to his country in 1767.

In this he presented a striking contrast to Napoleon, who remained emotionally identified with the French people in spite of being rejected as ruler on account of his military failures. On the face of it, the alienation for Clive was created by the calumnies which were unscrupulously spread about him by his enemies. But these would not have stuck unless there had been the alienation, which again would not have been so complete if he had been an aristocrat born, instead of being an upstart from the lower middle-class.

Nevertheless, it must be added that, at this stage of his career, the psychological situation was incipient and embryonic rather than full blown. In 1760 and the years immediately following, the prestige gained by his achievement and the power of his money were too strong to make it possible for anyone to ill-treat him, except from a very protected situation. Yet it is really surprising that, in spite of these advantages, it was possible for a clique in the Company's headquarters to harm him seriously in respect of money. This injury would have become permanent if a serious situation in Bengal had not made his services indispensable and restored his influence in the Court of Directors and proprietors.

The Government, the Company and India

This tussle has now to be described. But before doing so it is necessary to describe the relationship of the British Government of the day to the Company, the internal history of the Company and its leadership, the place India held in the public mind and Clive's relations with the Government as well as the Court of Directors before the clash.

It was unfortunate that just when, with the prestige of his achievement fresh in the public mind, and with his own awareness of the problems that had arisen for the Company in India, Clive could have performed his highest function in England – first by creating a public, as distinct from a private, concept of England's interest in India, and then by shaping a practical policy based on the concept – this very opportunity was denied him. That was due to the instability, unrest and lack of purposiveness in politics which marked English public life for at least ten years, if not more, after the accession of George III.

There was a good deal of contemporary discussion and speculation on the causes of these disorders. Of some of the diagnoses, Burke said that if they were to be accepted as true the disease would appear to be without remedy and therefore likely to reduce those who wanted to cure it to despair. So he offered his own diagnosis. Some recent historians have not accepted either his or the traditional historical view of the political troubles. Their interpretation has again been contested. But what remains uncontested is the fact of the instability in action and thought. This resulted in the greatest setback for the British people in their progress towards becoming a world power, namely the loss of the American colonies. If India did not go that way too, the escape was due to a very special situation: first, neither the home government nor the Company had any power to control local and immediate action in India, which was dictated by the day-to-day events there; secondly, during this period the affairs of the British people in India were in the hands of two autocrats, Clive and Warren Hastings. Without the dictatorial position of these two, the political confusion in England between 1760 and 1784 could well have brought about an extinction of British power in India.

At this point it is interesting to note Tocqueville's recognition of the achievement of Clive. He believed that purely general causes would have brought India under the power of a European nation in the eighteenth century, but added that there were happy accidents in favour of the English people, of which the happiest was the appearance of Clive. He set down the definite view: 'In my opinion, even if Clive had not presented himself, India would have fallen under the same yoke. The force of events pushed towards that.' But he qualified the statement by saying: 'However, the task of the conquest would have been longer and more arduous. Perhaps it would have been renounced before being brought about.' This is quite a handsome recognition of the practical significance of Clive against a speculative conclusion.

But the instability and confusion were not the worst things in English politics of that time. They were also vitiated by the predominance of private over public interest in political life. Nobody seemed to care to conduct politics *rem publicam sustinere* – to sustain the public interest. The most detailed description of this aspect of English politics in these years is to be found in the works of Sir Lewis Namier and his school. The picture which they have painted with their so-called structural analysis is perhaps one-sided, and it has indeed been put down by Sir Herbert Butterfield to the 'occupational disease' of the historians of structure. But it is also true that this historiographical method is very apt for the politics of the period That sordid motives wholly swamp the idealistic or ideological can never be wholly true of any age, however squalid. But what does matter is whether sordidness occupies the first or the second place. Certainly, in English domestic politics of those times it predominated.

This state of affairs harmed Clive personally, and was basically responsible for creating his alienation from the affections of his people to which I have referred. As I have also said, it interfered with the impinging of his personality on public affairs at its highest level. This was a greater misfortune for him, because it was on that plane that his character and conduct showed themselves at their best. Three and a half years after his death Dr Robertson, the historian, said to Dr Johnson:

> He would sit in company quite sluggish, while there was nothing to call forth his intellectual vigour; but the moment any important subject was started, for instance, how the country is to be defended against a French invasion, he would rouse himself, and shew his extraordinary talents with the most powerful ability and animation.

Robertson considered him to be 'one of the strongest minded men that ever lived'. Dr Johnson demurred with an objection which showed him as the typical English moralist of the eighteenth century. Of this more at its proper place. What has to be noted here is that Boswell's anecdote is a testimony to the strongest side of Clive's personality, which remained obscured in England through the political circumstances of his day.

Impact at this level would have given him the status of a statesman among his people. But without the continuation of such an impact, it was not possible even for the greatest figures in English politics, whose work and achievement the English people could watch with their own eyes, to retain for long a position created for them by past services. The greatest of those who passed into ineffectiveness in this way was Pitt. He was completely eclipsed, and at first even became insane; when he came back for a time he was not his old self, nor did he have his old authority.

Clive was the second victim. The state of politics after the accession of George III compelled him to show himself both in Parliament and to the Company as a fighter for his private interest, and nothing lowers a man more in the public eye than to see him engaged in pursuing private interest in a public role, however just or necessary that pursuit might be. And in Clive's case, the private interest was created by such un-English means as to seem undeserved, and even unjustifiable.

To pass on to the specific features of the situation, the British Government of the day had no power to control the activities of the Company so long as they were conducted according to the provisions of the charter granted to it. There was one vital nexus between the two – public finance of the country was dependent partly on the Company for both long- and short-term loans. There were also Members of Parliament who had East Indian interests. But neither the one nor the other created any urge on any of the sides to exert power on each other.

This situation did not change even when the Company began to intervene in Indian politics. The only serious issue that arose was due to the employment of the King's soldiers and ships in the wars in India, which made them wars of the Crown and of the Company in co-operation with the Crown. Owing to this the wars with the French, which should have been wholly the King's wars, also became the Company's. On the other hand the wars with the Indian princes, which should have been only the Company's affair, also became the King's.

This created the need for a formulation of the rights and

duties of the two parties in regard to territorial and other acquisitions in the course of the wars. Thus, in 1757 the directors of the Company thought it necessary to obtain a clear definition of their right to make war and peace, and submitted a petition to have confirmation of their right to cede or restore fortresses and territories taken in war; and, in addition, they asked for the right to retain all the booty captured by the combined forces of the Crown and the Company. Legal opinion was against giving such rights in a general way. But for reasons of practical convenience the rights were given, with the reservation that possessions taken from European powers should not be restored without royal consent. This position was laid down formally in a charter granted to the Company on January 14 1758.

It was on account of this arrangement that Pitt could not consider the proposal that Clive sent to him in his letter of January 7 1759, written from Calcutta. Walsh, who was entrusted with the letter, wrote to him on November 26 1759 that, owing to pressure of business, Pitt could not see him 'till six days ago', but when he did he received Walsh with great politeness and had a private conversation for an hour and a quarter. Walsh wrote in his letter (Clive did not receive it in India but only after his return to England):

> He began by mentioning how much he was obliged to you, and for the marks you have given him of your friendship; and then began on the subject of your letter. I said I was apprehensive, from my not having had the honour to speak with him before, that he looked upon the affair as chimerical: he assured me, not at all, but very practicable; but it was of a very nice nature.

Pitt mentioned the rights given to the Company in two recent charters. Walsh wrote: 'He spoke of this matter a little darkly, and I cannot write upon it with precision.' According to Walsh, Pitt also said that it was not proper that either the Company or the Crown should have a yearly income of upwards of two million sterling for 'such a revenue would endanger our liberties'. Finally Walsh reported:'He said the difficulty of effecting the affair was not great, under such a genius as Colonel Clive; but the sustaining it was the point: it was not probable he would be succeeded by persons equal to the task.'

From 1760 onwards, however, officers and other persons from India began to approach the Government directly and to give a minute account of what was happening in India to prominent and influential persons in England with a view to persuading them to take a more active interest in the Company's affairs. This was not liked by the authorities in the Company. But there was no practical interference. That began in 1766, when, after the grant of the *diwani* of Bengal to the Company, the Government wanted to have a share of the Indian booty.

Thus, when Clive came back to England the control of Indian affairs and the appropriation of the gains derived from India rested with the Court of Directors, in which the voice of the chairman naturally had the greatest weight. During the conflict with Siraj the chairman was John Payne. He was, however, ousted in 1758 by Lawrence Sulivan. The rise of this man was due to the administrative ability he showed both at Bombay, where he made a moderate fortune, and afterwards in London, when he became a director in 1755. Owing to this he rose to the position of deputy chairman of the Court of Directors, which carried with it the membership of the committees in which was transacted the most important business of the Company.

But he did not become chairman by virtue of his capacity; he did so as the leader of one faction in a faction fight which had arisen among the directors as a result of the Company's political position in Bengal. The quarrel was over patronage, and, more specifically, over the succession to Clive as governor at Fort William. Holwell had returned to England in 1757 and was trying to secure the post for himself, if not permanently, at least in rotation. He was favoured by John Payne, the chairman, and it was Holwell's arguments that appear to have been responsible for the unworkable instruction sent to Bengal about a rotation of the presidentship among the members of the Council.

Sulivan and his followers were opposed to Holwell, and supported the claims of those servants of the Company who had been involved in the loss of Calcutta but had not behaved in an unworthy manner. Among them were William Watts and Charles Manningham, with whom Sulivan had close personal and business relations. When the news of Plassey reached London, the governorship had, as a matter of course, to be given to Clive. But the dispute continued about the reversion.

When a decision was taken by the Court of Directors, Sulivan and his supporters were found to be in a minority. They at once appealed to the General Court of Proprietors, who normally did not intervene in such details. Sulivan's influence prevailed, but the General Court did not name a successor and restricted itself to the laying down of a principle. When the matter went again to the directors, the Payne faction won. Upon this Sulivan and his supporters contested the election of the chairman in April 1758. In the voting Payne lost, and Sulivan was elected chairman. This inaugurated a period of four years of domination of the Court of Directors by Sulivan.

He was an Irishman, and twelve years older than Clive. His great administrative ability was useful for the Company, but with it he combined love of power of a narrow kind, that is, a determination to impose his will on the management of the Company's business, and above all to control patronage. He might be called the Newcastle of the Company. With interruptions for short periods, he remained powerful in the Company till the time of Warren Hastings. Towards the end of Sulivan's career, R. Atkinson, who was a vigorous debater on Indian affairs from the time of Fox's India Bill, wrote about him:

> Mr Sulivan has great experience and some talents – great cunning; will go through thick and thin with his party while he remains attached to it, but not to be trusted for a moment when his own views lead him to be faithless; clean handed I really believe as to money or unfair profits himself, but careless to how great a degree he supports the job of any of his connections. I think the *ruling passion* with him is the vanity of being supposed the head of the India Company and the power of giving protection to his friends in the Company's service.

It is curious that such a man should have become the enemy of Clive and succeeded in inflicting a good deal of injury on him. Sulivan belonged to a type which must be found all over the world, but which has always been very common in India and has recently become dominant in every public body, political, economic, social, educational, cultural and even philanthropic. Whenever men of this type see that an organization has been made profitable by the ability and exertion of others, they take possession of it, if its control is determined by voting, by creating a clique of their own. They create voters, offer inducements like office or money, and at times even employ violence to gain and consolidate their power. They are, of course, men with a certain amount of ability and strength of character, but both are of a restricted order, and effective only where self-interest is the driving force. They are like the young of cuckoos which push out the young of their foster-parents. They themselves can be pushed out only by bosses of a worse type, and never by those who are only public-spirited.

Sulivan was such a man. But he seems in addition to have the traits of another type, which has also appeared in India after independence. To it belong the Indians in the bureaucracy, who under British rule would have retired after reaching a post of minor importance but whom the withdrawal of the British officials has raised to the highest positions. They are men of narrow minds and narrow abilities, but have an overweening self-conceit derived from their unexpectedly high position. They have just enough intelligence to perceive real superiority of other kinds, and are intolerant of it. If they find that superiority in their offices, and especially in men subordinate to them, they show a violent rancour against it. They would humiliate those who possess it out of resentment at their status in the outside world and even to persecute them. Unfortunately, on their special terrain it is impossible to beat them on the strength of any external position.

Sulivan stood on such an impregnable terrain because in the central direction of the Company in those days nothing but the monetary incentive had any power to influence men. Clive had to employ the same means because his situation was like that of a battleship which cannot use its main armament and has to fall back on its secondary armament in which its enemy is fully its equal.

No one has described the position more vividly, yet with complete truth, than Macaulay in his essay on Clive. He said that the interest taken by the public of England in India was far greater in the days of Clive than it was in his day, i.e. the 1830s. The lack, according to him, was due to the restrictions on the opportunities for making money quickly. In his days an English civil servant started life in India young, and if he was fortunate he could retire with an annuity of £1,000 a year and savings amounting to £30,000 at the age of forty-five. No single person could make a fortune except what was made slowly, painfully and honestly, nor could any talents, however splendid, or any influence, however powerful, obtain any lucrative posts for a person who did not enter by the regular door and mount by regular gradations.

'Seventy years ago,' Macaulay wrote, 'less money was brought home from the East than in our time. But it was divided among a very much smaller number of persons, and immense sums were often accumulated in a few months. Any Englishman, whatever his age might be, might hope to be one of the lucky emigrants.' With luck he could return to England in three or four years as rich as Clive or Pigot. Macaulay continued:

> Thus the India House was a lottery-office, which invited everybody to take a chance, and held out ducal fortunes as the prizes destined for the lucky few. As soon as it was known that there was a part of the world where a lieutenant-colonel had one morning received as a present an estate as large as that of the Earl of Bath or the Marquess of Rockingham, and where it seemed that such a trifle as ten or twenty thousand pounds was to be had by any British functionary for the asking, society began to exhibit all the symptoms of the South Sea year, a feverish excitement, an ungovernable impulse to be rich, a contempt for slow, sure, and moderate gains.

But such a scramble for money also generates an implacable rancour in those who fail to make money or do not have it. Sulivan was able to exploit this rancour against Clive, because he could say with perfect truth that he had never received as much as £20 as a present from anybody, and thus lay claim to disinterestedness in respect of money.

There was another advantage for Sulivan. Whenever a great passion or a great national danger fails to lift politics out of its rut, the able and adroit party man who is otherwise mediocre can always keep out a man of uncommon ability and insight. He also does it without any sense of guilt, for it is one of the privileges of mediocrity to be able to despise the genius. As La Rochefoucauld said: 'Mediocre minds usually condemn what is beyond their understanding.' Moreover, this condemnation is often pronounced with an insolence that is stupid, as exemplified in a remark of Neville Chamberlain's about Churchill after Munich. 'If I am asked', he said, 'whether judgement, the greatest quality in a statesman, is one of the qualities of the Right Honourable Member for Epping, I hope the House will not press me too far.' But Chamberlain was not the only political mediocrity to air this perversity with perfect composure.

As for the common people, they no more remember their great men in normal times than they do God when they are prosperous. They see the great man only as the neighbour they have known or as the neighbour's son, and exclaim: 'Is not this Jesus, the son of Joseph, whose father and mother we know? How is it then he saith, I came down from Heaven?' And biographers and historians, too, in dealing with the quarrel between Clive and Sulivan, have set down sententiously that between two men equally greedy of power a clash was inevitable. To quote La Rochefoucauld again: 'It befits only very great men to have very great faults of character.' Sulivan did not have that greatness.

Months of fretting

Clive had come to England in search of health and recuperation. But he was the last man to enjoy rest. Such men must be active or they fret. He complained that, but for the state of his health, which compelled him to seek treatment, he might have been an English peer. The normal delays in giving formal recognition to his achievements irked him so much that he provided a naïve instance of self-revelation by writing to Newcastle on May 3 1761: 'If less had been said I should have been less ambitious and consequently less unhappy.' For a man of his temperament the period of relative inactivity from the time he returned to England (July 1760) to his first attempt to supplant Sulivan, in the spring of 1763, was a period of mental torture. Compared with it, even the year that followed, in which he was nursing a sense of injury at being undeservedly deprived of his jaghir, was a time of enjoyment because he could act.

This period of doldrums for him, during which he also had some minor frustrations in connection with his friends and colleagues, certainly added to the violence of his quarrel with Sulivan in 1763. Biographers often slur over the periods in which nothing notable happens to their subjects, and forget what these becalmed spells can generate in ambitious men. There is nothing such men are more impatient of than to find prolonged beyond the limit of tolerance those periods in which they cannot do anything spectacular. They are irked by them because of their temperament as well as from the fear that they will lose the place they hold in the public mind. So one kind of ambitious man – whose power is commensurate with his ambition – deliberately plans and executes impressive ventures in quick succession, as did both Napoleon and Hitler, until they were driven to go beyond what was possible for them.

But there is a second category of ambitious men who are not self-sufficient, and for whom others have to provide opportunities. Clive belonged to this type. The most significant fact about his life is that he was never able to create himself the opportunities that made him great. They had always to be provided for him by others. This kept his ambition vulnerable all his life, gnawing at his heart and making him prone to fretting.

To enable them to keep their mental balance, such men have to be given their rewards timely, and assigned a new job before their enjoyment of the rewards for a previous achievement has dropped to zero. The Latin maxim, *Bis dat qui cito dat* – He who gives quickly gives twice – is particularly true of these men. The alternation of a quick reward and a new assignment maintains the normal rhythm of their ambition, which is like the alternation of the gorged slumber of a great beast of prey and his resumed hunting. What the beast does if the hunting is denied him can be seen by watching a tiger in a zoo as his feeding time approaches. If he does not see or hear the meat-cart at the end of the path at the exact time, his hunger-driven fury bursts out in a dazzling exhibition of wavy motion and fire shooting out of his eyes. Clive was this man-tiger from Bengal, locked up for a time in the English zoo.

The slow march of the events in Clive's life may first be illustrated by his election to Parliament. He first wrote about it at the end of 1757; it was raised as a practical proposal in 1759, when he was absent; and he was elected on March 21 1761. Moreover, in spite of his personal fame and wealth, his candidature became a contest of patronage between the parliamentary interests of two great landed magnates, the Earl of Bath and the Earl of Powis, with the Duke of Newcastle poised between the two.

The canvassing for the seat – Shrewsbury, a borough which had two members – began in June 1759, two years in advance of the election year. When the sitting member declined to stand, Clive's name, supported on his behalf by his father, was put forward by the Powis interest, and accepted by the Corporation. Lord Bath at once angrily protested, because he wanted the seat for his son, Lord Pulteney. The tussle went on for a year, and to support his claim Pulteney even raised a volunteer regiment for the King. Newcastle was generally for Powis, but would not offend Bath either.

The remarks about Clive made by his supporters and enemies at the time show what position he held in their estimation. Lord Bath himself wrote: 'Mr Clive is a very worthy man, as well as a dangerous antagonist.' Nevertheless, he pressed the claim of his son to the Mayor of Shrewsbury, who wrote back: 'The Colonel being of a family of great antiquity and merit amongst us, and having so remarkably distinguished himself in the service of his country, was agreed by all to be a proper candidate.' Bath still persisted, reckoning on Clive's absence from the scene. He wrote to Newcastle that Clive would not be a 'warm friend of your Grace's', described Powis as 'this little mortal' and Clive as a 'Nabob worth half a million'. Newcastle could not, however, abandon the Whigs of Shrewsbury. Finally, Clive's return clinched the matter. On August 31 1760 Powis reported that things at Shrewsbury stood 'on the part of Mr Hall [the second candidate] and Colonel Clive as well as their own hearts can desire'. On September 25 Bath himself gave up, observing that it was 'in vain to contend with the power of the Corporation and the wealth of the Indies'. So Clive was returned uncontested six months later, on March 21 1761.

Sure of his own seat, he intervened on behalf of his relatives – his father Richard, his cousin George, his brother-in-law Edward Maskelyne and his friend John Walsh. He had no difficulty about his father. Lord Powis had already, at Clive's request, got him returned in 1759 in his pocket borough of Montgomery (where the voters numbered about seventy), and he was again returned in 1761 without a poll. John Walsh also got returned in Worcester, though on account of his previous commitment Newcastle could not support Walsh. However, he failed over his cousin George and brother-in-law Edward Maskelyne, whom he set up at Penryn in Cornwall against the interest of Lord Falmouth, behind whom stood Bute. Attempts were made to induce Clive to withdraw their candidature, at first through Lord Powis and then through Lord Hardwicke. One of the election managers wrote to Bute: 'Mr Clive is Lord Powis's election bull-dog; and the master can certainly call him off.' This the master did not do, and Lord Hardwicke too failed. But both George Clive and Edward Maskelyne were rejected, though they cost the other candidates, one of whom was Admiral Rodney, a great deal of money. However, after Clive had acquired the main interest at the rotten borough of Bishop's Castle in Shropshire by buying the estate of Walcot, he got George returned in 1763.

So in the House of Commons in 1761 Clive had only his father and Walsh with him, and did not control a large number of votes. But in those days of personal and factional groupings in the House – the party system as operated later being non-existent – even one vote counted, and the personal support of a man of Clive's standing and wealth was bound to be valued. Attempts were thus made soon after his election to wean him away from his adherence to Pitt and bring him over to Newcastle. On April 24 Lord Sandwich wrote to the Duke that this was a favourable moment to secure the friendship of Clive 'as he is dissatisfied with the person [Pitt] to whom he seem'd most inclin'd to attach himself'.

Lord Sandwich proposed sending an emissary to Clive to assure him that Newcastle was ready to serve his interest, and added that Clive 'will carry at least two Members besides himself; and will never have anything to ask beyond the present favour'. This was a peerage, which was also sought for him by Lord Powis and the Duke of Devonshire. As has been stated before, he got his peerage, an Irish baronetcy, at the end of 1761. It has, however, been suggested that this was given to him not so much for his Indian achievement as to prevent him from going over, with his three votes, to Pitt.

Pitt, however, resigned in October 1761, and Newcastle in May 1762. During these months Lord Powis, presumably at Clive's instance, sought the patronage of Newcastle for Walsh and Maskelyne. The post of commissioner of taxes was asked for the latter. But at that time Newcastle was giving up office, and he did not think that the King would accept his recommendation. So he wrote to Powis:'I beg you would shew my Lord Clive that it is impossible for me to do it.'

At the end of 1762 another attempt was made to enlist him in a faction, this time that of Bute. Lord Sandwich had by that time gone over to the Court party, and Henry Fox wrote to him about Clive on November 12. He hoped to win over Clive and gave his reason for thinking so: 'I am told Lord Clive's great love to the D[uke] of D[evonshire] in new and not fix'd. To your Excellency it is neither new nor weak. And I hear the whole family were, not long ago, vastly pleased with a letter Lord Bute wrote to his Lordship.'

But nothing came of this overture. Clive preferred to remain independent. As he wrote to Carnac on November 23 1762:

> Now that we are to have peace abroad, war is commencing at home amongst ourselves. There is to be a most violent contest, at the meeting of Parliament, whether Bute or Newcastle is to govern this kingdom; and the times are so critical that every member has an opportunity of fixing a price upon his services.

Then he defined his own attitude. He wrote:

> I still continue to be one of those unfashionable kind of people who think very highly of independency, and to bless my stars, indulgent fortune has enabled me to act according to my conscience. Being very lately asked by authority, if I had any honours to ask from my sovereign, my answer was, that I thought it dishonourable to take advantage of the times; but that when parliamentary disputes were at an end, if his Majesty should then approve of my conduct by rewarding it, I should think myself highly honoured in receiving any marks of royal favour.

By that time, however, the negotiations for a peace treaty with France were coming to a close and its terms were to be submitted to Parliament. This took Clive's parliamentary activity on to a public plane, and also brought to a head his relations with the Company, with which so far he had been in touch mainly over patronage. Within a few months the period of doldrums in Clive's life came to an end with a quarrel between him and Sulivan, in which his parliamentary activity also became entangled.

These details about Clive's parliamentary life are being given in spite of their utter triviality, to show the falsity of the trite but traditional view that Indian politics of the day made Clive depart from the high moral standards obtaining in England. On the contrary, any comparison between Clive's activities in India and in England shows that India raised and England lowered him. Whenever he participated in the public life of England he was compelled by its lowness to exhibit himself as an adventurer out to serve self-interest, and this was made worse by his insistence on the purity of his motives, because it made him seem hypocritical as well. India, on the other hand, made him rise to the highest potentialities of his nature. Clive's moral tone. like a snake's temperature, varied with the environment in which he had to act.

It must never be forgotten that Clive's personality had no elevated moral element in it. Neither his social origins nor his education had moored him to the highest moral traditions of English life, which, moreover, in that age exerted no influence on politics. Until the French Revolution made its impact and produced a reaction, English politics in the whole of the Hanoverian age was a series of personal struggles for power, and if it was immoral occasionally, the immorality too was insipid – *fade à faire vomir*. It was only the attempts at asserting the royal prerogative, the question of the American colonies and issues of abstract justice raised in connection with the establishment of British rule in India, that made some politicians, and especially Burke, infuse some moral fervour, though ineffectually, into politics. So, apart from his eloquent preaching of principles, even Burke would be seen only as an adventurer, hanger-on, factionalist and a man of faulty judgement, riddled with prejudices and not above mercenary motives.

Clive had no interest in the theories of political ethics. He was a man of action, interested in thought as a means for action. He always thought correctly when some practical course of action had to be determined. Thus, how he would show himself depended wholly on the situation he was in. That is to say, the environment governed his behaviour. The Indian environment of his life was stark, elemental and challenging, and India always raised the level of his capacity. The English environment of his life was petty, and it always degraded him – with the one exception already referred to. Then, too, it was India that raised him to a grandly tragic plane.

However, it has to be mentioned that during this period he showed his best side in the memoranda he submitted to the politicians about the Company's position and affairs. In these he could give an exposition of the larger aspects of the Company's affairs in India. But when he tried to formulate a view of English politics, he could see in it only the power of money. Thus, contemplating it in his uneventful months of parliamentary life, he wrote to Vansittart on February 3 1762:

> Believe me there is no other interest in this kingdom but what arises from great possessions, and if after the Battle of Placis I had stayed in India for myself as well as the Company and acquired the fortune I might have done, by this time I might have been an English Earl with a Blue Ribbon instead of an Irish Peer (with the promise of a Red one). However the receipt of the Jaggeer money for a few years will do great things.

This letter is of great significance for understanding his tenacity in clinging to his money and his ferocity when being deprived of it for a period. He had come to feel that without money he would be nothing in his own country, because he could not claim a position through birth. Either he had to be reconciled to be nobody in England, where his heart was set on being somebody, or he had to defend his money by every means in his power. One extremely important point to note in this letter is that Clive regarded the income from his jaghir as only second best for maintaining a position in England.*

---

*Clive emphasized the importance of money to others as well. On February 27 1762, he wrote to Amyatt (a friend in Bengal), warning him against retiring before he had acquired an ample fortune. He said that he had noticed the disappointment of many friends by the discovery of inadequate means, and added that he himself since his return to England in July 1760, i.e. in about eighteen months, had already spent upwards of £60,000. This could not have included his gifts and investments in property.

Chapter Ten
Tussle for Power in the Company

The Factions

The quarrel between Clive and Sulivan was over obtaining control of the central direction of the Company in London. For this it was necessary to be in a majority in the Court of Directors (which consisted of twenty-four members); this in its turn depended on the election of the directors by those proprietors of East India stock who were entitled to vote – the qualification being the ownership of £500 of the stock. Thus the power of any person or group in the Company's management rested on the choice of the proprietors entitled to vote. The election took place in a General Court of Proprietors, i.e. a meeting of them, held usually in April of each year.

Before describing the factional fighting, which had two rounds in 1763 and 1764 respectively, it would make for a clear grasp of the complicated manoeuvres if the results were set down at the outset. In the first contest in 1763 Clive and his adherents fared very badly, and Sulivan was able to take his revenge on Clive for challenging his power and position. But the next year it was the turn of Sulivan to lose, and to be put in a minority, which meant loss of power. In 1765, when Clive was in Bengal, his followers further consolidated their position, and Sulivan was not even elected a director.

The whole contest was personal and factional. No principle or policy was at issue. In the first round India did not come into the picture at all. In the second the troubles that had broken out in Bengal and led to a war with Mir Qasim influenced opinion in Clive's favour. But his victory was ensured only by a ruthless manipulation of the election of 1764 on factional lines. Neither the election of 1763 nor that of 1764 took any account of the merits of the candidates.

For instance in 1763 Saunders, who as governor of Madras had conducted the war against Dupleix, and with Stringer Lawrence and Clive had saved the Company, was a candidate but failed to be elected as a director because he was in Clive's group. Again in 1764, when the state of affairs in Bengal called for a man of outstanding ability and prestige and with experience in Indian affairs to be sent there – and Clive was the most obvious choice – Sulivan's faction, according to Horace Walpole, intended to make Colonel Isaac Barré governor of Bengal if they won. Now Barré had no experience whatever of India and was at best a parliamentary gladiator who was capable of attacking even Pitt scurrilously, though in very classic and eloquent diction. In 1765 he made a speech in the House of Commons pointing out the danger of making the Company a fighting instead of a trading concern, thereby giving its servants motives for avarice and ambition and the natives a knowledge of war, and exposing Englishmen to cruel incidents. He also opposed Lord Clive's party and their schemes, yet artfully contrived to give him his due praise personally. This man could only have been an opportunist. But in the party warfare of those days a man's standing rose or fell according to the faction to which he gave his allegiance and its power to demand a scalp or give a share of the spoils.

Clive did not invite any quarrel with Sulivan. On the contrary, after Sulivan's election as chairman he even asked his father, in a letter written on December 29 1758, to make use of all his interest (i.e. influence) and that of his friends to support Sulivan. He added that should there be any occasion for laying out money for this, his attorney had his instructions to advance it.

He also adopted a very ingratiating manner in writing to Sulivan. For instance, when recommending some of his associates in Bengal to the Company, he addressed Sulivan in the third person: 'I should never have given Mr Sulivan the trouble of reading this letter, if I was not convinced he would look upon every syllable of it as proceeding from the dictates of a heart full of zeal and gratitude for the Company.' It is interesting to compare this sort of fawning on a mere official superior, on the part of a man who had dethroned one nawab and created another and recommended the son of an emperor of Delhi to the mercy of God because he himself could not help the unfortunate prince, with the young Napoleon's tone to the Directory when he said that he had not won his victories in Italy to oblige the Avocats du Directoire in Paris. After all, Napoleon came from a Tuscan-Corsican noble family, made all the more proud by poverty, whereas Clive could never shed the servility learnt by him in a family which, though old, had come down in the world and had acquired behaviour like that of a bailiff to his lordship. He could not just treat Sulivan as the Irish financial adventurer he was, risen to power in a very superior counting house somewhere in the East End.

Thus, when the quarrel began it had the character and complexion of one upstart's rivalry with another upstart. Clive's distrust of Sulivan was first roused by the despatch from the Court of Directors dated March 23 1759, drafted by Sulivan himself, in which there were reflections on the Council in Calcutta and to which Clive and his colleagues replied defiantly. Sulivan's letter was occasioned, above all, by an excessive use of bills on the Company in London by its servants in the Indian establishments, especially in Bengal, for transferring their private money to England. Another cause for complaint was the demand for quick payment of these bills. Both caused financial difficulties to the Company at home.

But though Clive was also implicated in these transactions the directors in London, so far as possible, tried to spare his susceptibilities. They tempered the wind for a rival wolf and directed it only on those whom Sulivan, like the wolf in Aesop's fable, could put in the position of the lamb arguing in vain for his life.

The whole issue between London and Bengal was at bottom very crude: who was to get the greater share of the loot from India – those who had created the power and brought in the loot, or those who had bought East India stock at home and thereby acquired so many pounds' worth of claim on the plunder? In other words, the issue was between the tiger, which had killed the sambur, and the hyena, skulking behind to get a share of the meat which had become carrion: nobody thought of making a distinction between the killer and the carrion-eater.

Clive sensed the ill-will and was not disarmed by the attempt to disassociate him from his colleagues. So he remained watchful. The exchanges between him and Sulivan provided a very amusing spectacle until an open conflict broke out at the beginning of 1763. At one stage in the growth of this mutual distrust Clive described the game, with a sense of humour not usually attributed to him, as 'like shy cocks – at times outwardly expressing great regard and friendship for each other'.

There can be no doubt about Sulivan's motives. He was afraid for his position in the Company's direction. In the two years since he had become chairman of the Board of Directors, he had made himself a virtual autocrat, and he could easily see that if Clive sought to have a voice in the affairs of the Company, officially or unofficially, he could throw nothing in the scale against Clive's achievement, prestige, money and connections.

Perhaps the best policy for him would have been to co-operate with Clive, oblige him about his jaghir and, up to a reasonable point, about patronage, thus bringing into existence a coalition between Clive of India and Sulivan of the City. But he did not, and could not, take that course, though he had not the slightest reason to anticipate a gratuitous attack on him by Clive. This can be explained by the following assumptions, shown to be plausible by the entire subsequent behaviour of Sulivan: first, that the lesser man from Bombay was jealous of the greater man from Bengal; and that Sulivan was so fond of power that he would not share even a part of it with anybody else. No one who would objectively appraise the relative standing of the two men could have put them on the same footing. Firstly, Sulivan had done nothing to create the position for the Company which was now making the seizure of its control a great prize: Clive had done everything.

But men with only narrow abilities of a technical order can never perceive any ability of a higher order, or if they do they resent it. Secondly, those who have created a vested interest for themselves are the last men to relax their grip. Finally, a man of faction and a jack-in-office always overestimates his strength. It would also seem that the Irishman's pugnacity in Sulivan got the better of the tradesman's discretion. In any case, he tried to play the game of carrot and stick with Clive, and was throughout too cunning by half.

Relations between Clive and Sulivan
To Clive upon his return Sulivan showed outward cordiality. Besides, for many months Clive was seriously ill. So he was left alone, and no action was taken even on the strong letter from Calcutta, to which Clive was a signatory. But Sulivan was not the man to overlook an affront from anybody whom he could safely punish. Thus, on January 21 1761 the directors wrote to Calcutta to communicate their decision to dismiss the four members of the Council who were still there and had signed the letter. They observed that the letter from Calcutta 'contain

gross insults upon, and indignities offered to, the Court of Directors, tending to subversion of our authority over our servants, and a dissolution of all order and good government in the Company's affairs'. The dismissed members – Holwell, Playdell, Sumner and M'Guire, were all to be sent back to England by the first ship available. At that time Sulivan believed that Clive had repented of signing the letter.

But it was hardly possible that he would approve of the punishment of his one-time colleagues, whose indignation he had shared. He was bound to look upon it as a vicarious punishment of himself. Clive received a copy of an outspoken letter which Sulivan wrote to Eyre Coote at Madras on March 16 1761, in which he said: 'Our people at Madras we find are hotheaded, but they are able, generous and open – I can smother their rebukes, but the ungrateful wretches, late of Bengal, have hurt my temper.' He expected 'that lawless settlement of Calcutta will be reformed to decency and order'. Clive could hardly overlook the implications for himself of such opinions.

Furthermore, about this time, Sulivan seems to have conveyed to Clive a hint that his right to the jaghir might be disputed. The directors had come to know about it in June 1760, but even by March 1761 they had not expressed any opinion on it officially, for on March 13 they wrote to Calcutta that Clive's illness had prevented any conversation on the subject with him and 'we must therefore defer giving you our sentiments thereon to another opportunity'.

If any warning was given to Clive at this date, it must therefore have been done informally. But we have no information about the exact time. All that is known is derived from a letter written by Clive to Amyatt in Bengal on February 27 1762. In it Clive said that, when he was very ill and even his life was despaired of, 'I had hints given to me that either some attempts would be made upon my jaghire or some proposal made for giving it up to the Company after a certain time,' and also that he was 'given to understand by Sulivan, that the Gentlemen of the Secret Committee would wait upon me on this subject'. He added: 'But health returning, this proposal was dropt, and I have heard nothing more of it since.' So, till the end of February 1762, no definite threat about the jaghir seems to have been openly held out.

During the rest of 1761 the exchanges between the two were about patronage. Clive recommended one person in September and another in November. In both cases Sulivan pleaded inability to oblige Clive. But he did so very politely, almost obsequiously. In the first case he wrote: 'Need I say that it mortifies me when I cannot oblige you: especially as it's so rare that you call upon me.' However, he had had to refuse applications from very high places, and even Pitt received a refusal. Perhaps to work on Clive's sympathy, he complained about Vansittart's importunity, which he said was causing great embarrassment to him. He added that Calcutta had inserted a most impertinent paragraph bordering upon insolence, taxing him with injustice about certain appointments.

In the second case Sulivan assured Clive: 'Could I be influenced by any other motive than my regard for Colonel Clive?' But he pleaded prior engagements. In this letter Sulivan also requested Clive's assistance in replying to a Dutch memorandum about the treatment they had received in Bengal, which had been sent by the Government to India House for their explanation. Clive sent a long note on it. In the same letter (dated November 18) Sulivan said that a mutual friend would 'impart to you the falsity of those assertions that have been thrown out against me'. What these were is not known. At the time of the elections for 1761 certain aspersions were cast on Sulivan about taking bribes for giving jobs. But it is hardly possible that Sulivan would refer to them in November, when there had been correspondence between them in the intervening period. The assertions must have been more recent, and it would seem that they were about Sulivan's attitude to Clive.

But something seems to have happened by February 1762, which caused great alarm to Clive over his jaghir. At this period, he wrote a number of letters to his friends in India, including Vansittart, who was the Governor of Bengal, disclosing his anxiety to put the grant on a firm legal footing on the Indian side and admitting that it was very vulnerable in England. What put him in this state of mind is very difficult to guess, for on February 27 he informed Amyatt that since the vague hint was given him the previous year he had heard nothing on the matter. Yet in the same letter he requested Amyatt to see that the grant of the jaghir was regularized in the most formal manner.

All this can be explained only on one supposition – it can be nothing more – that some threat was held out that the jaghir would be challenged if he made common cause with the opponents of Sulivan in the elections to the Court of Directors next

April, when Sulivan would not be able to stand because he would have been a director for four years. Or Clive's friends may have brought this possibility to his notice, finding that the opponents of Sulivan were trying to get support from him. It is to be noted that at this time Clive was not in close touch with India House, for he wrote to Lushington on February 28 1762: 'The situation I am in at present and the part of the town where I now reside [Berkeley Square], seldom gives me an opportunity of seeing any of the Directors, to whom I have been very sparing of applications, since I do not like refusals.'

Whatever the reason, in February 1762 Clive was in a state of panic about his jaghir. There are three letters from him on this subject – one to Vansittart written on February 3; one to Amyatt dated February 27; and one to Pybus written on the same day. The letter to Vansittart is the same in which he dwelt on the importance of money. In it he also gave an account of the situation in India House. He wrote:

> Sulivan still continues at the head of the Direction and in all probability will remain so long as the War lasts. I before represented to you that the present set of Directors are without abilities, fortune, or influence, and that it was Sulivan's policy to have such that he might have the greater sway. There are not wanting opponents but in the present distracted times, no man chooses to be concerned in any direction whatever.

Then he told Vansittart that he could depend on Parliament for justice over his jaghir. Nevertheless, he requested him to take every step in his power to make his right to the jaghir as clear and unequivocal as possible by means of a confirmation from Delhi.

In the letter to Amyatt he gave an account of the threat held out in the previous year, and then wrote:

> Although I have such an interest in Court and in Parliament that I should not be afraid of an attack from the whole Court of Directors united, yet all my friends advise me I should do nothing to exasperate them, if they are silent as to my jaggeer. Indeed it is an object of such importance that I should be inexcusable if I did not make every other consideration give way to it; and this is one of the reasons why I cannot join openly with the Bengal gentlemen in their resentments. It depends upon you, my friend, to make me a free man by getting the grant confirmed from Delhi, and getting such acknowledgements from under the hands of the present Nabob as may enable me put all our enemies at defiance.

To Pybus he wrote on the same lines, showing, equally, dislike and fear of Sulivan:

> The Court of Directors seem to be much in the same situation as when you left England. Sulivan is the reigning director, and he follows the same plan of keeping every one out of the direction who is endowed with more knowledge, or would likely to have more weight and influence than himself.

This, he went on to say, was exasperating most of the Company's servants who had lately come from India, and they were surprised that he, Clive, was not joining them. But he could not, because he had such an immense stake in India. As he put it:

> My future power, my future grandeur, all depend upon the receipt of the jaghire money. I should be a madman to set at defiance those who at present show no inclination to hurt me.

This would indicate that no new threat was held out to him. He also said in this letter that he was so strongly supported by the Government and by Parliament, that 'I should not be afraid of an attack from the whole body united,' but 'there is no necessity of wantonly exciting them to attempts against my interest'. He was even trying to keep Sulivan on tenterhooks. He told Pybus that he had presided at a general meeting of a club of East Indians, and that 'this has all the effect I could wish of keeping Sulivan in awe, and of convincing him that, though I do not mean to hurt him, I can do such a thing if he attempts to hurt me'.

This leaves Clive's anxiety about his jaghir all the more unexplained. Was he thinking of attacking Sulivan himself, and taking precautions against a possible retaliatory move against the jaghir? This does not seem probable. In any case, there was no further display of rivalry between Clive and Sulivan for many months.

However, in a letter written by Clive to Vansittart on November 22 1762, there is an account of the situation in the Company and Clive's views respecting it. He wrote:

> There is a terrible storm brewing against the next general election. Sulivan, who is out of the direction this year, is strongly opposed by Rous and his party, and by part, if not all, of the East Indians (particularly the Bengalees), and matters are carried to such lengths, that either Sulivan or Rous must give way.

He was frank about his own attitude:

I must acknowledge that in my heart I am a well-wisher for the cause of Rous, although, considering the great stake I have in India, it is possible I shall remain neuter. Sulivan might have attached me to his interest if he had pleased, but he could never forgive the Bengal letter, and never has reposed that confidence in me which my services to the East India Company entitled me to.

At this time the affairs of the Company were in confusion in Bengal, and they were heading towards a military conflict with the new nawab the Company had installed – a conflict that actually broke out the following year. But as news of it did not reach London till early in 1764 it did not make any difference to the squalid rivalries in India House, which showed no party to any advantage. Nor did the negotiations for a treaty of peace with France, which raised important public issues for the Company, put an end to the quarrels. Instead, the consultations between the company and the Government about the terms of the treaty relating to India gave rise to more ill-feeling between Sulivan and Clive, though there was no difference of principle between them and neither had any official position to exercise a voice in the framing of the treaty. The aggravation was due to personal pique.

The Government did not consult the Company about the terms concerning India, and it was very brusque with the directors, and drafted the treaty in the light of their own judgement. Both Clive and the directors found the clause in the preliminary treaty unsatisfactory. Clive himself voted against it in Parliament, and annoyed the Government. However, as a result of representations the clause was amended, and the amendment was considered to be satisfactory by all, including Clive. Later he publicly approved of the amended article (XIth of the definitive treaty).

The misunderstanding was entirely over who could claim more credit for the amendment. Clive thought Sulivan, though without any official standing, was exercising his influence through Dorrien, one of the directors, who took an active part in the discussions with Wood, the under-secretary. On March 15 1763 he wrote to the General Court of Proprietors: 'All the world knows the connection between Sulivan and Mr Dorrien and that the latter took no step without the advice of Sulivan and of consequence that Mr Sulivan knew from Dorrien everything that passed with the Committee when he was not present and consulted.'

Of his own role in securing the improvement he wrote later in his letter to the proprietors of East India stock issued early in 1764:

> As my opposition arose from the defects in the Preliminary Articles (in which the interest of the East India Company appeared to me to be much exposed) it affords me a very particular pleasure to think that I have been any ways instrumental to the amendment of that article relative to the Company. Of the part I acted in it, Mr Wood himself bore testimony in the General Court.

The jealousy for relative credit was childish. But when a general antipathy has been created between two persons the occasions for arousing it can be very trivial. It might be mentioned that among other serious causes of the misunderstanding that grew up between the Mogul Emperor Shah Jahan and his son Aurangzib, which afterwards led to the dethronement and imprisonment of the father, was a suspicion on his part that his son was keeping the best of the famous mangoes which grew on the western coast of India for himself instead of sending them to Agra. By the beginning of 1763 Clive had definitely decided to oppose Sulivan's return in an official capacity to the management of the Company's affairs.

Clive's Defeat in 1763
Strong opposition to Sulivan had already been in existence for some time, as has been seen from Clive's letters, but from the end of 1762 it became active, and at the beginning of 1763 this faction began to organize its electoral campaign to keep out his party. There were two distinct groups in this opposition: first, the directors who were dissatisfied with Sulivan's control of the Company, and secondly some former servants of the Company, specially those from Bengal. The latter had personal grievances against Sulivan, and plenty of newly gained money. Clive put himself at the head of the entire opposition, with the weight of his wealth behind it.

This money was thrown lavishly into the struggle for power between the factions and used for the creation of votes. It should be remembered that the twenty-four directors of the Company were elected by the general body of those proprietors who were qualified to vote. The qualification was ownership of £500 of stock, but whatever the amount of stock held by a particular person, he had only one vote. To get round this, any additional stocks held above £500 by a person were split into units of £500 and collusively transferred to nominal owners to create new and fraudulent votes. This corrupt practice was introduced by the opponents of Sulivan in 1762–63 for factional advantage, and had to be adopted by his faction as well. It grew into a regular organized evil in the affairs of the Company until suppressed by legislation.

By this means, and by laying out money for it, Sulivan's opponents created roughly 220 votes by March 1763, when the books were closed. It is said that Clive himself contributed £100,000 for this purpose. In the same way Sulivan and his supporters created 160 votes. But about half the money for these votes came from governmental sources, because Bute's ministry decided to back Sulivan with both influence and money. Thus it happened that Henry Fox, the paymaster-general, diverted £19,000 (or enough to create 38 votes) from the department's funds to help Sulivan. More money came from other departments, and in addition prominent members of the Government like Fox and Shelburne took voting qualifications personally.*

The principle behind the Government's policy was quite palpable, and can be summed up in the words of Pope:

But Ministers like Gladiators live;
Tis half their business, Blows to ward, or give,
The Good their Virtue effect [affect], or sense,
Die between Exigents, and Self defence.

Both the exigency and the motive of self-defence decided the attitude of the Government. It needed the support of the City for its finances, and Bute's ministry was unpopular there. On the other hand, the East India Company was always a strong sup-

---

*When the power or the gains of any individual or party is made dependent on votes, dishonest creation of voters is inevitable. After the Indian National Congress had accepted office in the provinces in 1937 there was a sudden leap in the membership of the Congress, because the professional politicians who wanted to be nominated as candidates to the legislatures on behalf of the party created supporters by paying the subscription of membership themselves (which was only four annas), and making fictitious members. For years Mahatma Gandhi denounced bogus membership as the great evil of the Congress organization, without being able to remove it.

In the municipal operations congressmen and other party candidates introduced fictitious names in the official electoral lists, and sent their own men to vote under these names. Naturally, there was also condemnation of this. One day, in my presence, a reformer was holding forth on the false electoral lists for the Calcutta Corporation. One congressman contemptuously brushed aside all this as a crotchet, and said: 'All of us do that and without it we should not be returned.'

porter of the Government. So it was necessary to retain its support. To this was linked the fact that Clive and his group had opposed the terms of the preliminary treaty and were therefore considered hostile to the Government. Sulivan, on the contrary, was believed to have thrown in his influence on the side of the Government. In fact, his opponents were claiming in their campaign that he had not looked after the interests of the Company. Thus a common cause was established between Sulivan and the Bute ministry, all the more opportunistically because the Government expected an attack on the final treaty.

This in its turn prompted the opposition, led by Newcastle, to join hands with Clive and his party. Great Whig noblemen like the Duke of Portland, Marquess of Rockingham, Lord Middleton, Lord John Cavendish and others took up their voting qualifications as East India proprietors. Newcastle even wrote for support to the bishops he had created. One of them had conscientious objections and wrote: 'The contrivance of splitting the votes, seems not very consistent with his station and character,' and begged to be excused. The whole campaign was an unscrupulous faction fight for everybody concerned. Macaulay described the proceedings of the General Court of Proprietors in the following words:

> The meetings were large, stormy, even riotous, the debates indecently virulent. All the turbulence of a Westminster election, all the trickery and corruption of a Grampound election, disgraced the proceedings of this assembly on the questions of the most solemn importance.

Not even the interests of the Company, not to speak of the growing English power in India, carried any weight with these factionalists.

The struggle for power between the two factions was divided into two phases. The first, in March 1763, was a preliminary trial of strength on a secondary issue. This General Court of Proprietors was called to exonerate Rous, the chairman for the year, from the charge of mismanaging the negotiations for the treaty with France. At this meeting, held on March 16, Clive's party won by 359 to 298 votes. This made him over-confident. He wrote jubilantly: 'This is really a great victory, considering we had the united strength of the whole ministry against us.'

In ripost, the Sulivan faction and the Government mobilized all their strength for the election of the directors, which took place on April 13–14 1763. In it Clive's party was badly defeated. The majority on the Court of Directors was gained by Sulivan. However, he made Dorrien the chairman, and took the office of deputy himself – choosing to play the role of *l'eminence grise*.

The faction, led by Sulivan, took their revenge at once. Within two weeks they wrote to Calcutta ordering the stoppage of all money to Clive from his jaghir.

> With respect to the Jagueer given by the late Nabob Jaffier Ali Kawn to Lord Clive arising out of the lands granted by the said Nabob to the Company, we direct that you do not pay any further sums to the attorneys of Lord Clive on that account, and we further direct that whatever shall arise in future from the said Jagueer to be credited to our credit....

And so on. Sulivan wrote privately to Vansittart:

> That all cordiality being at an end with Lord Clive, the Court of Directors had stopped payment of his Jaghire; a measure which would have taken place years ago, had it not been for him; and that on this head the said President was to obey every order, which he might receive from the Court of Directors; and that more was not, nor must be, expected of him.

Clive came to know of it at once, and he also wrote to Vansittart:

> Upon the whole, act like an honest man, and a man of honour: do justice to your friend without injuring the Company; for I am satisfied, the more this affair is inquired into, the more it will be to my honour.

He gave a formal warning to the president in Council in Calcutta, '... forbidding them to comply with the orders sent them at their peril'. He also wrote to Carnac making him his attorney, and gave him the following instruction:

> In case the Governor and Council should retain my money, or refuse giving bills of exchange, you (or whoever acts as my attorney), are immediately to commence a suit of law against the Company, and to transmit a very exact account of all your proceedings, that it may be taken up in England.

The circumstances of the granting of the jaghir and Clive's justification of it have already been set down in the previous chapter. Still, it is necessary to go into the matter again because a good deal of misunderstanding exists even now.

The very first thing that has to be said about the stoppage is that it was wholly arbitrary, high-handed and inspired by malice. It was an exhibition of personal and factional vindictiveness. Sulivan had learnt about the jaghir before the arrival of Clive in England in July 1760, and had done nothing about it for three years. Therefore, if the grant was illegal and had harmed any interest of the Company, he had been guilty of failing in his duty. In fact, he unambiguously disclosed the motive of the stoppage in the letter in which he referred to the end of all cordiality between the Company represented by him and Clive.

So far as any legal question was raised by the grant of the jaghir, the opinion of the best legal authorities in England was on Clive's side. Its substance was given in a contemporary document in these words: 'The East India Company could not raise an objection against the grant to Lord Clive, founded on the want of right and power in the Nabob, which would not impeach their own.' Macaulay cited this opinion and as one-time Member for Law in the Governor-General's Council he knew what he was talking about. He described the withholding as unjust.

The grounds given by Sulivan and his party were the following: first, that the rents granted to Clive were the ancient imperial rents reserved to the Emperor of Delhi and could not be alienated by Mir Jafar, his deputy; second, even supposing he had had the right, with his death the grant had lapsed; third, that Clive's acceptance of the dignity of *omrah* or mansabdar of the Mogul Empire was contrary to his duty to the Company, since he might be obliged by his acceptance of the position even to help the Emperor or the Nawab in a war with the Company; fourth, that he had no legal remedy in England but must appeal to the Mayor of Calcutta, or the Nawab, or the Emperor.

All these grounds were specious to the point of low chicanery. The surprising part of it is not that Sulivan put them forward as pretexts for his exercise of power to harm Clive, but that recent historians should have been disposed to accept them and doubt Clive's right to the jaghir. These writers forget that Wellington was Prince of Waterloo in the Netherlands and had 20,000 florins as annuity to support the position; that he was the Duke of Ciudad Rodrigo in Spain and received £50,000 as his share of Spanish prize money; that he was the Duke of Vittoria in Portugal and Duke of Brunoy in France; that he was a Marshal of the armies of Spain, Portugal, Netherlands, Russia and Prussia; that he received other large sums of money from foreign governments; and, finally, that in England he received cash gifts from the Government amounting to £600,000 in addition to his pay as field-marshal.

The discrimination made between him and Clive springs from a historic difference of attitude – that European peoples have always thought more of the soldiers and statesmen who have put their *European* rivals in their place, or defeated and killed other *Europeans*, than of those who have founded empires for them. This discrimination was even seen in the treatment of Wellington. After returning from India, where he had played a brilliant part in building the Empire, he was put in charge of nothing bigger than a brigade, and he served only because, as he said, he was a *nimak-wallah*, an eater of salt. The real and adequate recognition for him came only when he had killed a sufficient number of Europeans. This tendency to form judgements in the light of the European family feuds survives even today.

In point of fact, to question Clive's right to his jaghir in law was to raise a legal point where none was applicable because the gain rested solely on one man's wish and power to give and another man's power and determination to keep. Those who had the power could also create legal justification for it.

However, an extremely important point has been overlooked in considering this dispute: that it would not have risen if the jaghir had been given elsewhere than around Calcutta. The Company's power to control the payment came from the fact that Clive's rent was to be paid by the Company itself from the total revenue of the grants made to it by Mir Jafar in and around Calcutta. A grant elsewhere would have taken Clive's income beyond the control of the Company, and he could have transferred it to England by indirect means. But, as he wrote, he thought it would be an advantage to him as well as for the Company to have the jaghir in the Company's lands.

Sulivan acted as he did simply because he had the power to harm Clive, which he wanted to do, and because he felt confident that Clive would have no immediate means of redress, and would feel the deprivation and humiliation all the more. This gave him so much satisfaction that he did not consider the possibility that his own power might come to an end through two variables in the situation: namely, developments in India and the attitude of the Government to him. But men of action are intoxicated by temporary victories and blinded by hatred, and they cannot be prudent.

Certainly, he gloated over Clive's exasperation, and the latter was quite incapable of hiding his sense of injury and always behaved like a wild bird in a cage in such situations. Clive's vain appeals to all and sundry must have delighted Sulivan. Clive wrote or spoke to Lord Hardwicke, Newcastle and others, but they could not help him. Even Pitt told him that on account of violence of the party spirit it would be futile to raise the matter in Parliament. As a last resort, Clive decided to side with the Government, and established contacts with George Grenville, who had become prime minister in April 1763, towards the end of that year.

In the meanwhile, he showed his state of mind by picking a quarrel with Vansittart over an elephant. He wanted to present some rare and large animals from India to George III, and wrote to Vansittart to send him two elephants. One of these was too large to be shipped, but the other was sent, and Vansittart wrote that, in addition, he had also sent a rhinoceros and a Persian mare and hoped Clive, accompanied by Vansittart's brother, would present them to the King. When the animals arrived, this brother asked Clive to go with him to the palace for the presentation. Clive thought that Vansittart was stealing a march on him by presenting the animals on his own behalf, and wrote angrily to the brother:

> I can plainly perceive that Mr Vansittart, declining to comply with the request I made of him, of purchasing and sending home, on my account, an elephant to be presented to his Majesty by me, has taken that hint to send one home on his own. This unkind treatment I neither deserved nor expected from Mr Vansittart.

He added that, lest the King should think him wanting in respect towards him for not being present at the ceremony, he would inform him why he could not. There was an explanation; and it was found that the captain of the ship that brought the animals had given Vansittart's brother a wrong account of Vansittart's intentions. Clive at once concluded that it was Sulivan who had incited the captain to make mischief. Later, he made it up with Vansittart but he could not forgive Sulivan. He wrote:

> I am sorry there should be any mistake about the elephant; and although I was somewhat affected at first at the commission you gave me to present the elephant to his Majesty in your name, instead of my own, yet the thing in itself appears to me of too trifling a nature for either of us to think any more about it. Your brother will inform you in what manner [the captain] has acted, owing I believe to the instigation of Sulivan.

However, by November 1763 Clive, who had drawn closer to Grenville, sought his intervention with the Company in respect of the jaghir. On November 7, in reply to Grenville's request, Clive sent him the terms upon which he was willing to make an absolute cession of the jaghir in favour of the Company. Horace Walpole, who had begun to take renewed interest in Clive, wrote to the Earl of Hertford on December 2: 'The ministry have bought off Lord Clive with a bribe that would frighten the King of France himself: they have given him back his £25,000 a year.'

Clive felt very anxious about the outcome of the offer of compromise and wrote to Grenville on December 13 1763 that a settlement of the jaghir question was 'more essentially necessary towards establishing my peace of mind than improvement of my fortune'. He even went so far as to say: 'I must confess to you, Sir, that I have so much sensibility inherent in my nature, that my mind will be too much affected to recover so severe a shock for some time.' He was thinking of the possibility that the directors would not come to a compromise. They did not: they rejected the offer. As Horace Walpole wrote on December 29 1763: 'The East India Company have come to an unanimous resolution of not paying Lord Clive the three hundred thousand pounds, which the ministry promised him in lieu Nabobical annuity.'

Clive's Victory: 1764

However, relief was soon to come to Clive from the only source on which he could always depend, namely India. In February 1764, news arrived in London of the outbreak of the war with Mir Qasim. There was at once consternation among the stockholders. The price of the stock had already begun to fall from the previous November on account of disturbing reports from Bengal. Before the news of the war arrived, Clive issued an address to the proprietors of East India stock, certainly as a preliminary to the election campaign. In this pamphlet he referred to the attacks on his character and fortune made during the previous election, and laid before the proprietors his version of the events in India since the war with the French began, and also described how he had acquired his fortune. He hoped that the proprietors would not attribute this self-defence to vanity, and would excuse the necessity under which he lay of giving his version of the facts, which he submitted to their consideration, justice and candour.

When the news of the war arrived the causes of the troubles in Bengal were widely discussed, and different interpretations were given. In March 1764 the *London Magazine* published a long letter, which was virtually an article, from an anonymous contributor who said that he had drawn up a short account of state of the late unhappy affair in Bengal after a perusal of almost everything that had been published upon the subject, and was sending it to the magazine to save it the trouble of giving an account of its own. He added that whenever the facts were contested he gave an abstract of the statements of both sides.

The writer attributed the troubles to the weakness of the Company's agents:

> Upon the whole it is evident that the present disturbance, and all misfortunes we have lately met with, in Bengal, have been owing entirely to the weakness of our own conduct, ever since the Lord Clive left that place; and ultimately to the treaty, as it is called, which our governor made with the Subah of the province of his own creating, without any authority from the Council.

He declared at the end that he would conclude his long and impartial account 'with the sincere prayer, that no British subject, either at home or abroad, may ever allow himself to be actuated by that pernicious sort of emulation which destroyed the great Roman people, *ne quis fit ditior alter*.'* Whoever he was, he was very well informed about the affairs of Bengal.

In the state of general anxiety the proprietors responded to the public mood only by asking for meetings of the General Court to consider the situation, and two were held on February 27 and March 2, at which the conditions in Bengal were generally discussed. It was at a special meeting held on March 12, 1764, that Clive was requested to take upon himself the governorship of Bengal again. At a large meeting, Sir Francis Gosling, a close associate of Clive, explained the critical situation in Bengal and moved that 'considering the great alteration of our affairs in Bengal by the late commotion in the settlement and the restoration of Meir Jaffier Ali Kawn to the subahship, the present appointment of the successor to the presidency and the appointment of the commander of our forces, are therefore improper.'

---

*'Nothing of that which makes another man rich'. This was at the bottom of the hostility to Clive.

The appointment was that of Spencer to the governorship in Bengal, about which more will be said later. The negative motion gave rise to a long debate, and a majority of the proprietors appeared to be of the view that the situation called for the appointment of some men of superior abilities and influence to restore the affairs of the Company from that anarchy and confusion in which they were involved. The account continued:

> All eyes seemed to be fixed upon one, which produced a motion, as if by inspiration, and from a candid and sensible member, who had set out with arguments against the first motion; but who had the honour of proposing this:
>
> 'That Lord Clive should be requested by this Court to take upon him the presidency of Bengal, and the command of the military forces there, upon his arrival in the province.'
>
> This met with an universal shout of approbation, which obliged his lordship to deliver his sentiments in a very manly and modest speech:
>
> 'Confessing, that though his affluence of fortune and other schemes of life were totally different; yet, if he was called on by the general sense of the proprietors, and matters could be settled, so that he could proceed with any degree of prudence, supported by a friendly and united direction, he would once more stand forth in their service.
>
> The question was carried without a division.

The idea of sending Clive to India in order to restore the Company's position seems to have been widely discussed, for even before the offer just mentioned was made on March 12, Horace Walpole had written to the Earl of Hertford on the eleventh: 'The East India Company yesterday elected Lord Clive . . . Great Mogul; that is, they have made him Governor General of Bengal, and restored his Jaghire. I daresay he will put it out of their power even to take it away again.'

But the next day he corrected himself and wrote:

> I went a little too fast in my history* of Lord Clive, and yet I had it from Mr Grenville himself. The jaghire is to be decided by law, that is, in the year 1900. Nor is it certain that his Omarship (Mansab) goes; that will depend on his obtaining a board of Directors to his mind, at the approaching election.

The Court of Directors had to act on the resolution of the General Court, and on March 16, after sending Clive a copy of it

---

*Horace Walpole was given to gallicisms – he meant *histoire*.

formally, they informed him that 'they were *unanimous* in assuring him, that they would most cheerfully concur in taking the steps necessary to carry the resolution of the General Court into effect, and in preparing every convenience for his passage'. Clive formally thanked the directors for it only the following day, and did not commit himself to acceptance of the offer. Clearly, he thought Sulivan and his party were trying to get him out of the way before the election of the directors in April. He would not oblige.

Curiously enough, Horace Walpole again anticipated events. On March 18 he wrote to Sir Horace Mann: 'Lord Clive has been suddenly nominated, by the East India Company, to the Empire in Bengal.' He seemed to have taken the resolution of the twelfth as an appointment.

A general Court of Proprietors, held on March 21 1764, took up the question formally. The two letters were read out, and as his letter did not mention his acceptance, Clive, who was present, was asked whether he was inclined to accept the post and to give his answer at once. He replied that 'he would give his answer as soon as the next election of directors should be determined'. Some considered this as a refusal and moved 'that Lord Clive declining to accept immediately the service proposed to him by the General Court, the Court of Directors be desired to make proper arrangements in the present critical situation of the Company's affairs'. It was suggested that the directors should fill up the several vacancies. There was a long debate, but the motion was rejected with much clamour.

Sulivan as deputy chairman delivered a eulogy on Clive and expressed great cordiality towards him. Clive in a reply doubted all this profession of friendship and declared unambiguously that 'it was indifferent to him who were in the Direction, provided one gentleman was not in it', and asked the Court to consider whether it was more in their interest that 'Mr Deputy Chairman should continue to assume lead in the Court of Directors or that he [Lord Clive] should proceed to India'.

Sulivan then replied, and 'endeavoured to clear himself from the charge of ever having done his Lordship any ill office, and expressing the most cordial desire of being honoured with his Lordship's friendship'. Anything more coolly impudent could hardly be conceived. Clive stuck to his disbelief in Sulivan's friendliness, though some members tried to bring about a reconciliation. I shall present the end of the discussion in the words of a report published in the *London Magazine* for March 1764. It ran:

> The altercation was put a stop to by a respectable member of the Court, who stood up, and requested Lord Clive, that, as the proprietors entertained the highest idea of his lordship's merit, and his abilities to serve them at this very critical time, his lordship would be pleased to name his terms, which, he durst undertake, would be accepted, if in any degree reasonable. After a short pause, his lordship desired a few days to give his answer:

Clive replied on March 28 1764. He wrote:

> Gentlemen, – It was agreed at the last General Court of Proprietors, that I should have a few days to consider and determine concerning the terms upon which I would accept the request of the preceding Court of Proprietors, to take upon myself the direction of their affairs in Bengal.
>
> Although I thought I had sufficiently explained myself on that head at the time the proposal was made, yet, as there seemed to be a disposition in many gentlemen of the Court for whom I have the highest respect, that a reconciliation should take place between Mr Sulivan and me, so that this gentleman might still conduct the affairs at home, and that I might nevertheless venture, without fear of my reputation, abroad. I thought the respect which was due to those Proprietors, the duty I owe to myself, and the regard I shall ever feel for the interest of the Company, all called upon me, in the strongest manner, once more to revolve in my mind the possibility of such an union, consistent with the services I would endeavour to render the Company, and consistent with that attention which is due to my own honour.
>
> This I have endeavoured to do in the coolest and most dispassionate manner, after laying aside every prejudice, and judging only from the constant experience of things.
>
> Upon the whole, I still continue to be of opinion, that, in case the Proprietors think it for their advantage that Mr Sulivan should remain at the head of the Direction (or, as he was pleased to term it himself, should continue Mr Sulivan in such authority), I cannot accept their service: but in case the Proprietors should not think it necessary to continue Mr Sulivan in such authority, I am willing and ready to accept their service, even supposing the next advices should pronounce their affairs in Bengal to be in as desperate a condition as ever they were in the time of *Suraja Dowla*.
>
> Should a Direction be settled with whom I can *possibly* co-operate, everything will be easily adjusted, since I have no interested views in going abroad.
>
> At the same time, I never desired, or even wished, to name a

Direction, as some industriously spread abroad; I only object to one man having the lead in the Company's affairs, in whom I have so often and publicly declared, I never can place any confidence, and who, in my opinion, has acted, and does continue to act, upon principles diametrically opposite to the true interest of the East India Company.

Nothing could have been more straightforward and above board. Clive had every justification for distrusting Sulivan on private as well as public grounds, and in politics the two can never be separated. Sulivan, when confident of his power, had behaved with undisguised malevolence towards Clive, and his interested profession of friendship towards Clive put his character in the worst of lights. In a Bengali collocation this sort of conduct, very frequent in the East, is described as 'being rampant when free, and quealing when cornered'. (The image concerns the toad free and under the harrow.)

If Clive had to do anything effective, he had to be sure that he would be supported at home in his actions in Bengal, which were bound to be drastic, and also that in his absence he would not be stabbed in the back in England. Sulivan in India House would have kept him exposed to danger on both the counts.

After that no further action was taken on the appointment in spite of the urgency of the question, until the election of the directors took place on April 12. Everybody wanted to see how the factional fight would go.

At the election the Court of Directors was evenly divided into two blocks of twelve, for and against Sulivan. In this election the Government's weight was thrown on the side of Clive, though the intervention was not massive – it created about eighteen votes for him. The party of Newcastle did not take any part in this contest. Of course, votes were created by splitting on both sides. What is significant is the fact that, in spite of all this and the conviction of Clive's indispensability, the result was still indecisive. This showed the strength that Sulivan had created for himself from his entrenched position. The next year he was thoroughly routed.

So, after the election of the directors, the position of the parties depended on the choice of the chairman. Sulivan was naturally the candidate from his side, and Rouse was put up by Clive's party. At the election of the chairman, Sulivan, it is generally stated, sensing the general mood, did not press his candidature. Horace Walpole, however, gave a more spicy account in a letter to Lord Hertford written on April 10 1764.

The East Indian affairs have taken a new turn. Sulivan had twelve votes to ten: Lord Clive bribed off one. When they came to the election of chairman Sulivan desired to be placed in the chair without the disgrace of a ballot; but it was denied. On the scrutiny, the votes appeared eleven and eleven. Sulivan understood the blow, and with three others left the room.*

With the election of the chairman on April 13 1764, the decks had been cleared for the final settlement of all the questions connected with Clive's new mission to Bengal, the nature of which he knew less than he did about the situation in Bengal when he set out from Madras in October 1756. Nobody in England knew as yet that in fact no military problem existed, because Mir Qasim had been defeated, or that atrocities worse than those of the Black Hole had been perpetrated on the English. So Clive could only formulate very general ideas. Apart from that, he was a pragmatist, not at all prone to act on *a priori* ideas, even when he had them. In fact, even in respect to a situation actually confronting him, he *acted* in a manner that was inconsistent with his *appraisal* of it.

But there were also practical issues to be settled, and he discussed them in two meetings with the new directors, on April 19 and 27. He confirmed verbally what he had said in a letter written on the twenty-seventh. On April 30 he was sworn in as the governor of Bengal and commander-in-chief of the Company's forces there. On May 2 and 5 there were two sessions of the General Court of Proprietors at which the various issues were discussed, and his jaghir was restored. On May 25 the Court of Directors defined his powers. On June 3 he set out from London for Portsmouth, and on the fourth sailed for Bengal on the *Kent*.

*I shall describe what happened in Calcutta in a similar situation during the election of the mayor in the early thirties, so far as I remember it. Two prominent politicians had competed, and there was some doubt about who was properly elected. So, at the next session of the Calcutta Corporation, one of the politicans came into the hall a little earlier than the other and occupied the mayoral chair. When the other arrived he would not give way (with the discretion of Sulivan). So the late-comer also went up and occupied a portion of the chair, which was large. There was a collision lasting for some time between the posteriors of the two, and I have forgotten who finally bulldozed whom. But one of these men became a member of the Viceroy's Executive Council later, and the other chief minister of Bengal under the new Government of India Act of 1935. The fact that in the last stages of their rule the British had to run the government of the country with such men showed that the end was not far off. The squalor that marked the beginning of the Empire stopped short of the lowest behaviour: if it became necessary, the men of that period could show some decency.

As regards general policy, he told the directors that he was opposed to any extension of territory for the Company, because 'if ideas of conquest were to be the rule of our conduct, I foresee that we should by necessity be led from acquisition to acquisition until we had the whole Empire against us'. He added that the Nawab of Bengal must not be allowed to be independent, for the only alternatives were that the princes of the country must be in great measure dependent on the English or the English would become totally dependent on them. But he said, the princes ought to be treated with respect, and with that honour that ought to be characteristic of Englishmen in Asia as well as Europe.

Regarding the private money-making of the Company's servants, he suggested that they should be forbidden to participate in the trade in salt, betel-nut and tobacco. But he offered to surrender the right of the governor to engage in private trade, so that his portion of the commercial advantages, which was considerable, might be divided amongst the lower employees. For himself he undertook 'not to enrich himself one farthing by any pay or emoluments he might receive'.

In regard to the military establishment he said that he hoped to reduce military expenditure, but that at least three thousand Europeans should be maintained in Bengal, and they should consist of three battalions of infantry, four companies of artillery and one regiment of light horse. In addition, of course, there were to be sepoys – and the whole was to be organized in three brigades.

In regard to command he said that, though he was willing to receive a military commission inferior to General Lawrence who was at Madras, he must have full powers over the troops in Bengal. He also insisted that any troops, treasures or other consignments sent from England to Bengal must not be stopped and employed by Bombay or Madras if the ships stopped there. At that time there was a tendency to regard Madras as the centre of the Company's power in India, though Bengal had become its most important acquisition. So Clive made a far-reaching suggestion, which was given effect only some ten years later, that if ever a governor-general was to be appointed for all the settlements in India his station should be in Bengal, 'as the greatest weight of your civil, commercial, political and military affairs will always be in that province'.

There were also two personal questions – always productive

of unpleasant sequels – about which more will be said later. But for the directors, the proprietors and Clive, the most important practical issue was the restoration of his jaghir. At the meeting with the directors on April 19 Clive said that it would be most improper for him to go to Bengal as governor whilst the lawsuit about his jaghir was still pending. His objection was very correct, for if the stoppage of the money from the jaghir remained, he as governor would be compelled to stop payments to himself. Nonetheless, he had already suggested a compromise – that he would hold the jaghir only for ten years or till his death if this was earlier. At the second meeting with the directors, he agreed to go to Bengal even if his offer over the jaghir was not accepted. The Board of Directors, however, agreed to accept the terms generally at a formal meeting, and to send their recommendations to the General Court summoned for May 2. Sulivan and his supporters opposed this, and ten directors, including Sulivan, either opposed the recommendation or abstained from voting. But the recommendations were carried by a majority.

The two meetings of the proprietors on May 2 and 5 were very stormy and violent. The first was adjourned when a proprietor rose to say that he did not think as highly of Clive as he used to. This adjournment was challenged as illegal. But even at the second meeting Clive's supporters won, although not without a tumultuous session. An account of the meetings was published in the *London Magazine,* which indicated the interest aroused by them. This discussion and Clive's victory showed how artificial and *malice prepense* the whole campaign against the jaghir had been. Horace Walpole did not comment on it. But imitating his style, one might say the entire rampage over the jaghir was *un tas d'histoires.*

There remained only the question of the powers to be given to Clive. He wanted to have the ultimate discretion for decisions in Bengal. To give such powers was wholly against the traditions of the Company, and the new directors were not ready to give him unlimited autocratic powers. But they adopted a compromise, which gave him all he wanted in an indirect form. He was to nominate a Select Committee of four to act with him as president. The position was defined by the Court of Directors on May 25 1764 in a formal resolution which ran:

> In order to restore peace and tranquillity in Bengal, full powers be given to our president and governor Lord Clive, Mr Sumner, General Carnac, Messrs Verelst and Sykes, to pursue whatever means

they judge most proper to attain the same; but that, when it can be done conveniently, they are to consult the Council at large. However, when those desirable objects are obtained the said extraordinary powers are immediately to cease.

But when he sailed Clive was not wholly at ease about the situation he was leaving behind in London. Sulivan's faction was still on the Board, and he could not expect them to be anything but unfriendly. He had expressed his misgivings on this score already in his letter to the directors written on April 27:

> I cannot avoid acknowledging that I quit my native country with some degree of regret and diffidence, on leaving behind me (as I certainly do) a very divided and distracted Direction, at a time, too, when unanimity is more than ever requisite for the carrying into execution such plans as are absolutely necessary to the well-being of the Company.

However, he was leaving trusty friends behind to see that Sulivan would do no harm to him. All this vagueness in dealing with India must be set down to the fact that in England there was as yet no crystallization of opinion about the new political responsibilities that were being created in India. There was no perception of the responsibilities at all. The proprietors thought only of their dividends and patronage. The Government did not apply its mind to India at all. When it did not want to extort money from the Company, it thought of the stakes in that country only as a secondary element in the Anglo-French rivalry.

It was in this unedifying manner that Clive was sent out to save the Company's possessions in Bengal, and he was leaving strife behind him only to face more of it in accomplishing his task. However, there was a difference. In England it was mean; in India, despite the greed and personal animosities that marked the establishment of British power, there was a counterbalancing grandeur. It was robbery like the acquisition of the china from the looting of the Summer Palace in Peking and the appropriation of the sculptures of the Parthenon, but on a more magnificent scale.

This way of looking at the beginning of the Empire is not inconsistent with the admiration one might feel for it as a fully developed historical phenomenon. It is absolutely basic for a proper historical attitude to recognize that the phenomena of history do not remain the same in the course of their total evolution. On the contrary, in every aspect they undergo startling metamorphoses like insects.

In that age English political thinking was not able to deal with the embryonic Empire at all. So far as the politically conscious upper classes thought about its gestation, they thought in terms of the only imperialism with which they were theoretically familiar – i.e. the Roman Empire. This comes out incidentally from Horace Walpole's comments on the quarrels between Clive and Sulivan. He wrote on March 11 1764:

> We have had a deluge of disputes and pamphlets on the late events in the distant provinces of our empire, the Indies. The novelty of the manners diverts me; our governors there, I think, have learned more of their treachery and injustice, than they have taught them of our discipline.

Again a week later:

> Dupleix has taught all our merchants to affect to be King-making Earls of Warwick; and the chief things they have made are blunders and confusion. It is amazing that our usurpations have not taught the Indians union, discipline, and courage. We are governing nations to which it takes a year to send our orders.

Men of Walpole's class had no other image of the Roman Empire than the literary, and so moralizing with the help of that precedent was easy. It might indeed be said that the attitude of cultured Englishmen of that age towards the rising Empire was, like the republican stance of the leaders of the French Revolution, the product of an indigestion of Roman history.

Seas between us Braid hae Roar'd

For a few months, however, there was a spell of mental peace for Clive. Those were days of sail, and, as it happened, Clive's last voyage to India like his first was lengthened by a diversion to Brazil. This gave him a respite from political worries, and he employed the forced leisure in writing letters to his wife which showed not only the intimate, but also the most human side of his personality.

It is not easy to illustrate this. Nothing substantial can be written on Clive's private life. What Masson did for Napoleon has never been done for Clive, and the reason is simple – insufficiency of material. However, the small number of letters that exist show him as a man with a very great capacity for affection and loyalty in his personal relations. It is curious that his enemies have been called as witnesses for prosecution, but not his friends in defence. Yet his family life not only soothed him, but can soothe those who write about him. Sir John Malcolm found the narration of his public life harrowing, and sought relief in describing his private life – his love for his family and friends and the uniform kindliness in his dealings with those who served him.

This self-revelation began on the very day he sailed from Portsmouth. Even then he was looking forward only to a reunion. 'My dearest wife,' he wrote on June 4 1764, 'God only knows how much I have suffer'd in my separation from the best of women, however the necessity of the thing.' The immediate cause was that at this time Lady Clive was expecting a child, and could not safely undertake so long a voyage. He observed that her good sense would make her bear the separation as he was bearing it: 'Let us look forward towards the happy day of our meeting, which I think cannot be farther distant than two years.' In the meanwhile, he told her, 'the education of our children will be a pleasing amusement'. As for himself, 'the busy scene in which I shall be employ'd . . . will greatly shorten our time of absence'.

Lady Clive, on her part, gave her instructions to Strachey, who was going with him as private secretary: 'Mr Strachey will remember to write to Lady Clive, and let her know how my Lord does while at Portsmouth, and ever after when opportunity offers.'

Clive's next letter was from Rio de Janeiro, written on October 14. He found to his surprise that two ships which had left England one month after the *Kent* had arrived at Rio a month before it. They brought a letter from Lady Clive, in reply to which he wrote: 'Nothing could afford me greater pleasure than to find you reconciled to my departure in a manner consistent with that good sense which I know you to be mistress of, and consistent with the superior duty which you owe to our children.' He told her: 'Never entertain the least doubt of our meeting again.' He added that nothing would induce him to stay in Bengal beyond the year 1765.

He was glad that she had not accompanied him in a most tedious and disagreeable passage, in which he had to suffer so many inconveniences that he would have been very anxious on her account, especially in her condition. Besides, there was on board the ship 'a woman of a most diabolic disposition, ignorant, ill-tempered, and selfish to the highest degree ... possessed of every disagreeable quality which ever belonged to the female sex without being mistress of one virtue (charity excepted) to throw into the scale'. It was with difficulty that they all behaved with common civility to her, and he added: 'I would not upon any consideration whatever you had been the companion and passenger of such a woman.'

This lady felt so hot that she kept all the doors and windows of the cabins open, and as a result Clive and all others caught cold. At last he had 'to make use of some authority' to have them closed.

As to the lady's accomplishments, Clive wrote: 'She gave us to understand that she understood music and could play upon the harpsichord, and to convince us of this she has been playing two humdrum tunes for four hours every day since she has been on board (Sunday excepted) without the least variation or improvement.'

He hoped that by this time Lady Clive 'was safely delivered and of a boy, for we have girls in abundance'. His son Edward (the future second Baron) was not very good at English. But he was not particularly uneasy on that account. He thought Edward had too many irons in the fire. Nonetheless, he observed: 'A master of the dead languages may become master of the living whenever he pleases.'

However, he was sorry about his heir's 'want of ear and awkwardness in dancing'. This, he said, 'gives me pain. There he seems to be constitutionally deficient, and I would have nothing spared to make him a tolerable proficient in that art.'

He had a fancy for rare animals and birds, and at Rio bought two for Lady Clive – a lion monkey (the marmoset *Leontideus rosalia*), and a 'pretty Pol' (Amazon parrot, second only to the grey African parrot as talker). However, he allowed his brother-in-law, Edmund Maskelyne, to present them to his sister from himself. Maskelyne congratulated her on the escape from a very tedious voyage and 'a still more tedious and teizing companion'. 'His Lordship,' he added, 'has drawn the Sultana's character so completely that one need only say she is the reverse of everything that is amiable and engaging in the fair sex.'

Clive's next letter to his wife was written from the Cape on January 2. There he heard that Mir Qasim had been defeated and that there was a prospect of peace and quietness. He also informed her that in Brazil he had bought some topazes and amethysts worth about between two and three hundred pounds, and was sending them by the captain of the *Weymouth,* so that she might get a necklace, earrings and buckles made from the best of them, and distribute the rest to his sisters and some friends. But, he wrote in the postscript: 'Upon reflection I think it will be better to bring home the topazes and amethysts myself lest the division should occasion the pulling off caps, etc., etc.'

He changed his mind again and sent the stones by the hand of the captain of a warship, with two casks of Constantia wine and one cask of Tent (a Spanish red wine) – about 120 gallons in all, which he said must be drawn off, and from which he wished two dozen bottles of red Constantia, three dozen white Constantia and one dozen Tent to be given to Lord Powis (whose daughter his son was to marry).

On March 10 the *Kent* met an English ship bound for England from Bengal at sea,* and by it Strachey sent the news to Lady Clive that 'my Lord is in perfect health [and] has begun to use the cold bath, which answers the desired purpose of preventing colds'. Clive also wrote, expressing his fear that he might not be able to leave India as soon as he had intended with any propriety.

---

*At Long. 75 E; Lat. 20.33 S.

Chapter Eleven
Saving the Conquest

Clive's Achievement and its Basis

Clive's work in India during his second governorship of Bengal has been praised by every historian. Of all this appreciation the most weighty is that of Macaulay, who judged it not only as a historian but also as a practical administrator. He wrote his famous essay, published in January 1840, with the knowledge of India gained first as secretary to the Board of Control in London, and then as a member of the Governor-General's Council in India. As he put it:

> From Clive's third visit to India dates the purity of our Eastern Empire ... if in India the yoke of foreign masters, elsewhere the heaviest of all yokes, has been found lighter than that of any native dynasty, if to that gang of public robbers, which formerly spread terror through the whole plain of Bengal, has succeeded a body of functionaries not more highly distinguished by ability and diligence than by integrity, disinterestedness, and public spirit ... the praise is in no small measure due to Clive.

Continuing, Macaulay said:

> His name stands high on the roll of conquerors. But it is found in a better list, of those who have done and suffered much for the happiness of mankind. To the warrior, history will assign a place in the same rank with Lucullus and Trajan. Nor will she deny to the reformer a share of that veneration with which France cherishes the memory of Turgot, and with which the latest generations of Hindoos will contemplate the statue of Lord William Bentinck.

History has recognized the value of Clive's reforms in India, but no comparison with those carried out by Bentinck has been made. It is curious to note that the British government in India did not erect a statue to Clive in Calcutta until that of Bentinck was green with patina; nor was the monument, when erected, as big or elaborate as that of Bentinck. Nor did Warren Hastings and Wellesley have any statue in a public place there. These are tell-tale omissions.

Macaulay's tribute has set the tone of all subsequent writing about Clive's second administration. Nonetheless, I would repeat what I have already said, that there would have been no need to save his conquest of Bengal if Clive had remained in India for five instead of two and a half years after Plassey.

Praising Clive for the work which he did in 1765–6 is like praising Churchill for saving Britain in 1940. The need would not have arisen if Churchill had not been excluded from office by mediocrities like Baldwin and Neville Chamberlain from 1934 to 1939. Churchill called the Second World War the unnecessary war. Clive's reforms would also have been unnecessary if he had remained in India after 1760. But his absence in India was due, not to exclusion by others, but to his own constitution and temperament.

However, when he was called upon to save what he had acquired, Clive accomplished this with extraordinary insight and energy. His capacity for going to the root of every military and political problem, and for separating the essential from the ancillary, was extraordinary. This is the mark of a great man of action anywhere, and in India no one can do anything at all without the capacity to brush aside the lush tropical ramifications of all problems. They become hydra-headed if allowed to arise and no one can ever solve a problem by merely cutting off the heads. One might as well try to destroy weeds by pruning. That Alexander began his conquests in the East by cutting the Gordian knot was symbolic.

So, on the very day of his arrival in Calcutta he called for the minutes of the Council and read them through, so that, as he himself wrote, 'by seeing what had been done he might be able to form a clearer opinion of the plan of operations on which it would be necessary to act'. Within a few days he had worked out his plans.

The second, and most important, element in Clive's success was the absolute authority to act, which was given to him. Formally, of course, he did not have it, but it was his for all practical purposes, because the Select Committee was composed of men nominated by him and who were also his friends. It also had the authority to act independently of the Calcutta Council. Clive was given a freedom of action which was not granted to Warren Hastings under Lord North's Regulating Act of 1773, and most of the troubles of Hastings, and the intrigues to which he had to resort in order to act according to his judgement, were due to that limitation of authority. More will be said later about the need to give absolute power to the governor-general of India. Fortunately, Clive did not lack it. Even so he was given trouble.

Beyond all this, there was an imponderable element which made Clive irresistible in India. He had an aura of personal power which made others obey him – either from trust or from fear. It is impossible to analyse all the factors that intermingle to make an individual a sort of political medicine man. His previous successes may have contributed to create the status, but his successes are also effects of the status. His character, behaviour and luck, all in their turn, played a part in building him up. The point at which this kind of leadership passes from the rational to the supra-rational can only be approximately determined. Clive seems to have approached that point when he was selected for command in Bengal in 1756, but his authority became undisputed only after Plassey – which, rationally, should not have meant much. What, however, is certain is the fact that without this intangible moral aura about him he could not have carried out the reforms he put through. In comparison, what Warren Hastings did was only rational. The quality of leadership in the one and the other are incommensurable. Just as Joan of Arc has been called the *Sainte Mascotte*, Clive, too, can be regarded as a mascot, besides being a very capable man of action.

The Task

Between 1760 and 1765 two political revolutions had taken place in Bengal. In October 1760, Mir Jafar was deposed and his son-in-law, Mir Qasim, installed in his place. Again, in June 1763, upon the outbreak of a war with Qasim, Mir Jafar was reinstated. The actions and motives of the Company's agents in Bengal who brought all this about immediately became a subject of acute controversy, and historians are generally agreed that this was a very discreditable beginning for British rule in India. The whole subject is, however, so complicated that it is impossible to deal with it briefly, nor is it necessary to go into all its details in a biography of Clive, who was concerned only with liquidating the affair. He did that, not by taking up the thread, but by breaking it. So all that is necessary is to summarize the main events.

Initially, Holwell, who acted as governor in Bengal for about six months after Clive's departure, was hostile to Mir Jafar, and urged Vansittart, who took over in August 1760, to remove him. Vansittart was also ill disposed to Mir Jafar and to the Muslim princes generally. It has to be noted that both these men were involved in the Black Hole, and also that Mir Jafar commanded the forces of Siraj in 1756 and boasted of his military success in capturing Calcutta.

Vansittart arrived at an understanding with Mir Qasim, by which Mir Jafar was to be deprived of all effective power, and Mir Qasim was to exercise it. However, when the proposal was put before the Nawab he flatly refused to fall in with it. So English troops surrounded his palace, and forced him to yield. In fear of his life, Mir Jafar chose to go to Calcutta and live under English protection, and Mir Qasim formally became nawab.

There was no doubt that Mir Jafar had proved to be a very incompetent ruler, and also he, or at all events his subordinates, were guilty of excesses. On the other hand, Mir Jafar, who had the greatest respect for Clive, regarded both Holwell and Vansittart, especially Holwell, as persons of no importance. Moreover, after the death of Miran, Mir Qasim had become the obvious successor to Mir Jafar, and being a man of ambition and capacity he was not likely to be patient.

Mir Qasim showed himself to be a strong and relatively efficient ruler, but though the English in Calcutta had grown tired of a King Log, they could not be happy with a King Stork. In any case, they were not the meek frogs that petitioned God. They defied the energetic new Nawab, and at once trouble started over the trading rights of the Company, which had never been defined with absolute clarity. The rights were certainly abused in the most scandalous manner by the servants of the Company and their agents. On this subject there was a prolonged argument between the Company and Mir Qasim, who prepared to assert his independence and resist the Company. He removed his seat of government from Murshidabad to Monghyr.

Then, in the middle of 1763 an open conflict broke out. Mir Jafar was reinstated on the throne, and an English force advanced against Mir Qasim under Major Adams. There was no question of successful military resistance by Mir Qasim, and he fled to Patna. There he held captive Ellis and the other Englishmen who were in the company's establishment, and threatened to massacre them if Adams advanced towards the city.

What then happened was quite different from what would have happened if, instead of 1763, it had been 1973. Mir Qasim found that he was born two hundred years too early. Adams paid no attention to his threat, and wrote back:

> If a hair of their heads is hurt, you can have no title to mercy from the English, and you may depend upon the utmost fury of their resentment, and that they will pursue you to the utmost extremity of the earth; and should we unfortunately not lay hold of you, the vengeance of the Almighty cannot fail overtaking you, if you perpetrate so horrid an act, as the murder of the gentlemen in your custody.

Ellis and Hay, on their part, wrote to Adams that 'they ought not to be attentive to them, for they must submit to their fate; and desired that no consideration of their situation should prevent the army from proceeding in their operation'. They, and with them all the other Englishmen, numbering forty-nine, were cruelly killed on October 4. Other English prisoners were also murdered. I am sure that Englishmen in these days would condemn not Mir Qasim, but Adams, for not saving, despite their own wishes, the lives of Ellis and others by agreeing to restore Mir Qasim and clear out of Bengal.

On October 28 1763, Adams entered Patna, and drove out Mir Qasim from Bihar. The latter took refuge with Shuja-ud-daula, the Nawab of Oudh, and persuaded him to take the field against the English. Early in 1764, he advanced into Bihar, and laid siege to Patna, where the English defended themselves successfully. So Shuja fell back on Buxar – seventy-five miles to the west – to wait for the end of the monsoons. With him was the refugee Emperor of Delhi, Shah Alam, as well as Mir Qasim.

In October 1764 the English forces under Hector Munro advanced to Buxar, and after a fierce battle, fought on the twenty-third, totally routed Shuja. This was a real battle, and the only encounter so far with any Indian prince that could be called a battle. But a British victory was never in question, and it finally placed British power in Bengal on a footing of complete military security. One important result of the victory was that the Emperor Shah Alam came over to the English side.

After the battle the English forces advanced into Shuja's territory, overran the greater part of Oudh, and forced its nawab to go further west into the Rohilla country for safety. He was summoned to surrender Mir Qasim, but refused to do so. Nevertheless, Mir Qasim was plundered of everything he had, and died in Delhi many years later.* The English forces took

*See Appendix 7 on Mir Qasim's later life.

their station at Allahabad, where the Emperor remained with them.

This was the situation in Bengal when Clive arrived in Calcutta on May 3 1765. Even before, in Madras, he had learnt enough about the general position of Bengal as to be able to give his appraisal of it, and some indication of his ideas for dealing with it – in a letter to Rous, Chairman of the Board of Directors in London on April 17 1765, i.e. only ten days after his landing.

First, he noted that the military situation was satisfactory, and, as a result, the affairs of the Company were flourishing, which he assumed must already be known in London. As he said, 'it is scarcely a hyperbole to say that the whole of the Mogul Empire is in our hands'. The troops of the Company were then half-way to Delhi.

The position facing the English was defined by him tersely: 'We have at last arrived at that critical conjuncture which renders it necessary for us to determine, whether we can, or shall take the whole to ourselves.'

He was convinced that there should be no addition to the Company's conquests and possessions. He highly disapproved of the march continuing even as far up-country as Allahabad, but added that this was forced on the Company's commanders by the action of others, meaning principally Shuja-ud-daula. He thought that after 'the lengths we have run, the Princes of Indostan must conclude our views to be boundless. . . . They have indeed seen such instances of our ambition that they cannot suppose us capable of moderation.'

For himself he said: 'I mean absolutely to bound our possessions, assistance and conquests to Bengal, never shall the going to Delhi be a plan adopted if possible to be avoided by me, and you may depend upon my putting a stop to it.' He wished that the Company's operations had been carried on 'upon a plan of moderation and we had not been obliged to maintain any other military force, than what might be sufficient to preserve and pursue our commercial advantages'.

But he realized this was no longer possible, and wrote: 'Since our views are extended and since commerce alone is not now the whole of the Company's support, we must go forward, to retract is impossible.'

Go forward to what? As he saw it, it was only to put the Company's power and position in Bengal on an absolutely secure and stable footing. From the people of the country he envisaged no resistance: 'The inhabitants of the country we know by experience, have no attachment to any Nabob whatever, their troops are neither disciplined, nor commanded, nor paid as ours.'

But he saw the possibility of continuous ill will on the part of the Muslim princes. He said that 'the very nabobs, whom we might support, would be either convetous of our possessions or jealous of our power. Ambition, fear, avarice would be hourly lying wait for an opportunity to destroy us.'

Therefore he recommended an adequate military establishment. As he put it: 'Can it then be doubted that a large army of Europeans would effectually preserve to us the sovereignty, as I may call it, not only by keeping in awe the ambition of any country prince, but by rendering us so truly formidable, that no French, Dutch or any other enemy could ever dare molest us?'

But the large army he demanded was not large in any European sense. He stuck to the original estimate he had presented in London: 3 European regiments of 1,000 each; 500 light horse; 3 or 4 companies of artillery; and he said this force 'will absolutely render us invincible. . . . In short, if riches and stability are the objects of the Company, this is the method, the only method we now have for attaining and securing them.'

But he did not think that military strength and its employment were likely to provide the final answer to the question raised by the Company's presence in India. What was basically needed was a policy. He explained himself: 'A victory would be to us but a temporary relief, for the dethroning of one nabob would be followed by the setting up of another, who actuated by the same principles, would, when his treasury could afford him an army, pursue the very path of his predecessor.' He could see only one way of escaping this vicious spiral: 'We must indeed become the nabobs ourselves in fact, if not in name, perhaps totally so without disguise.' But, he added, 'On this subject I cannot be positive until my arrival at Bengal.'

He also knew that, whatever the end in view might be, any management of the Company's affairs in the situation which had developed called for the organization of a proper administration with a suitable cadre of personnel. He had already heard of the lust for gain on the rampage in Bengal and felt that it must be checked. So he observed:

> See what an Augean stable is there to be cleansed. The confusions we behold, what does it arise from? Rapacity and luxury; the

unreasonable desire of many to acquire in an instant, what only a few can, or ought to possess. Everybody would be rich without the merits of long service and from incessant competition undoubtedly springs that disorder to which we must apply a remedy, or be undone, for it is not only malignant but contagious.

He thought the new covenants introduced for the Company's servants would make a beginning for the reforms, though he did not approve of them in their present shape. He anticipated that on account of them many of the servants of the Company would resign. So the task was to supply Bengal with a new set of recruits. He wrote:

> The Court of Directors must supply the settlement with young men more moderate, or less eager in their pursuit of wealth, and we may perhaps be reduced to the necessity of drawing some senior servants from the other settlements. It must be your care and I trust you will do all in your Power to send out proper gentlemen. Affairs seem to be coming to such a pass, that in a little time, there will hardly be anybody at the Council Board above the rank or age of a Writer.

He declared finally:

> In short, the evils, civil and military, are enormous, but they *shall* be rooted out. Whatever odium may be thrown upon me by the malice or disappointment of individuals I am resolved to act for the advantages of the Company in every respect.... I have not here time to inform you of my whole plan of reformation, but the motives upon which I have found it, being no other than the public good, you may safely exert yourself in its support if it should stand in need of your assistance, which I hardly think it can, tho' faction should be still ranging.

He gave an assurance for himself: 'I propose no advantage to myself – I am determined to return to England, without having acquired one farthing addition to my fortune. Surely then I cannot possibly design anything but public good.' All this was written before his arrival in Calcutta.

On arriving there he was even more dismayed, and wrote to his friend Carnac on the very day he arrived. i.e. May 3 1765: 'I arrived here this morning to take possession of a government, which I find in a more distracted state, if possible, than I had reason to expect.' He was deeply moved by the loss of reputation for his nation which had resulted from the corruption of the Company's servants, and wrote two days later:

> Alas! how is the English name sunk! I could not avoid paying the tribute of a few tears to the departed and lost fame of the British

nation (irrecoverably so, I fear). However, I do declare, by that Great Being who is the searcher of all hearts, and to whom we must be accountable, if there must be an hereafter, that I am come out with a mind superior to all corruption, and that I am determined to destroy those great and growing evils or perish in the attempt.

That Clive was able to put an end to the disgraceful scramble for money quickly should not obscure the real nature of the achievement. Misuse of public power and position for the sake of private gain is the greatest evil that accompanies government, and in some countries it is never suppressed. Eradication of corruption cannot be brought about without personal power and standing of an exceptional order. But even that sort of power cannot do anything unless there is something in the social outlook of a people which counteracts corruption. It is very rarely that such a combination is present in history. So it is the absence of corruption that has to be looked upon as an exceptional condition in government, and not its presence. Somehow, both at home and abroad, the British people realized this to a certain, and even a remarkable, extent. Thus they gave the impression that it was an easy thing to stamp out, which it was not. Nevertheless, as Clive feared, the corruption of those five years left a permanent stain on the British Empire in India in the eye of future generations everywhere.

Obstruction by Colleagues

Upon his arrival Clive was heartily welcomed by the inhabitants of Calcutta, both European and native. The welcome from Murshidabad was even more effusive. The two older Jagat Seths had been put to death by Mir Qasim, but their sons wrote to welcome Clive, and he assured them that 'as I loved your fathers, so I will always exert myself in supporting the dignity and welfare of their children'. Raja Durlabhram Rai wrote that the news of the arrival of Clive had brought relief to his mind, which was like the parched earth refreshed by rain or the budding flower by the spring breeze. Clive answered all these letters of welcome punctiliously. One thing that distinguished him was that he never failed in the outward forms of politeness to the native personages, whatever might be his real opinion of their character and motives. But in respect of him, the feelings of these men must have been sincere, because they could now expect firm and purposeful action from Calcutta.

The spirit of faction had been rife in Calcutta, and it tried to raise its head with Clive as well. When he met the Council for the first time on May 5 1765, he desired that the paragraphs in the instructions from the Court of Directors relating to the powers given to the Select Committee (i.e. Clive and his four associates) might be transmitted to all concerned, so that everybody might know what were the powers of the Committee.

Upon this, one member, Leycester, seemed disposed to raise a discussion about the meaning and extent of the powers. Clive at once replied that he would not suffer anyone to discuss these, and of their powers the Committee were the sole judges. Nonetheless another member, Johnstone, drew attention to certain other letters which seemed to invalidate the instructions, and he wanted these letters to be sent with the new instructions. Instead of considering this suggestion, Clive pointedly asked Johnstone whether he dared dispute the authority of the Committee. Johnstone replied that he never had the least intention of doing such a thing. As Clive informed Carnac on the same day: 'Upon which there was an appearance of very long and pale countenances, and not one of the Council uttered another syllable.'

It will be recalled that Clive's colleagues on the Select Committee were Sykes, Sumner, Verelst and Carnac. Of these, the first two had accompanied Clive from England, but the other two were away from Calcutta – Carnac with the troops up-country and Verelst at Chittagong. But Clive assembled the Committee on May 6, and opened the proceedings with a formal letter from himself. In it he pointed out the need for assuming the powers given to them at once, in order to conduct the civil and military affairs of the settlement.

He explained that even within the very few days since their arrival such things had come to their knowledge as made this absolutely necessary. He said: 'What do we hear of, what do we see, but anarchy, confusion, and, what is worse, an almost general corruption?' But he also observed that he was sure his colleagues would have been as happy as he himself if the conduct of the Governor and Council had been so irreproachable as to permit the affairs to be left in their hands. The Committee replied by promising unanimous support.

This was a formal assurance. But Clive had already given thought to the reliability of his colleagues, and since General Carnac, though a member of the Committee, was also a close friend he wrote frankly to him:'Verelst appears, as far as I can hitherto judge, to be a man of honour and integrity. Sykes may be thoroughly relied on, and Sumner must, for his own sake, be a friend to the Company.' As for Carnac, he wrote: 'Your resolution, my dear friend, and principles, almost unparalleled in these climes, will, I am sure, co-operate with me in every regulation for the public good.'

Clive regarded many things done by the Governor and the Council shortly before his arrival to have been wrong or mistaken, and he wished they had not been so precipitate. But he said: 'I am determined not to be embarrassed by the errors of others, if in my power to remedy them.' The immediate question that faced him was the nawabship of Bengal. Mir Jafar had died on February 6 1765, and the Council had agreed to the accession of his son, Najm-ud-daula, who was only eighteen and was also said to be illegitimate. But a formal recognition had been put off until the successor had signed a treaty prepared by the Council and presented to him by a deputation at Murshidabad. The signature to the treaty was secured at once. By it the young Nawab was deprived of all power and the government of the province was vested in Muhammad Riza Khan, a Muslim grandee. The Nawab was further required to have the approval of the president of the Council in Calcutta for making all appointments in the administration of revenue. Over and above this, the Calcutta Council confirmed by this treaty the British privilege of trading free of duty, except two and a half per cent on salt.

When this treaty was concluded the Nawab promised to pay about £140,000 to the Governor and the members of the Council, and the greater part of the money was paid. Clive suspected that the hurry in setting Najm-ud-daula on the throne was due to the eagerness to secure the presents of money. In any case, a month before the treaty was signed the Council in Calcutta had received specific orders from London that:

> ... all persons in the Company's service should execute covenants, restraining them from accepting directly or indirectly, from the Indian princes, any grant of lands, rents or territorial dominion, or any present whatever, exceeding the value of four thousand rupees, without the consent of the Court of Directors.

This order was received on January 24, even before the death of Mir Jafar. Yet when Clive arrived the covenants had not been signed. Moreover, the Court of Directors had sent orders directing the complete abandonment of inland trade. So what the Calcutta Council had done since Mir Jafar's death was done in deliberate disregard of instructions from London.

Clive was naturally angry both at the commissions and the omissions, and he expressed himself freely in his letters. On May 5, he wrote to Carnac:

> They have all received immense sums for this new appointment, and are so shameless, as to own it publicly. Hence we can account for the motive of paying so little respect to me and the Committee; and, in short, everything of benefit to themselves they have in this hasty manner concluded....

He wrote even more severely to Palk, the Governor of Madras, on May 11. First of all he informed Palk that only the acknowledgement of the authority given to the Select Committee by the directors prevented Clive from using force against the recalcitrant councillors. Next, at a meeting held on May 9, he got a resolution passed that the covenants required by the directors should be executed at once. In his letter, Clive reported what happened: 'After many idle and evasive arguments, and being given to understand they must either sign or be suspended by the service, they executed the covenants on the spot.'

As to the new Nawab, Clive wanted to see him before deciding on the next step concerning those who had committed the irregularities. He wrote to this affect to Palk in the same letter:

> We are awaiting the arrival of the Nabob and his ministry to determine whether we shall suspend them the service, or represent matters in a general light leaving to the Directors to determine their state; though I am persuaded they will never wait such a decision, having all received large fortunes which they barefacedly confess, for absolutely and precipitately concluding the late treaty with the young Nabob; not waiting for our approbation, or leaving it in our power to rectify the least tittle, without being guilty of a breach of faith.

Clive hoped, however, that 'a committee of gentlemen, whose emulation is not excited by the distribution of loaves and fishes, may acquire at this juncture immortal honour to themselves, and lasting advantages to the Company'.

When the young Nawab, who resented the surrender of his powers to Riza, came down to Calcutta some days later he complained to Clive that Riza had distributed twenty lakhs of rupees to the members of the Council so that he might be continued in his position.

The tale of 'presents' (a euphemism for bribes) was long and lamentable. On June 7, Clive raised the whole question in the Council, and Johnstone proposed that the question as to whether the acceptance of any present was improper should be put to each member of the Board. Three members of the Select Committee – Sykes, Verelst and Sumner – and Clive himself were opposed to their acceptance. Four members of the Council gave either a complete or a qualified approval. Johnstone said: 'Where they are not the price of unworthy services, and no trust is betrayed for them, the acceptance of them is in no way improper; and in the present case, as being previous to the execution of the deed of covenant, as warrantable as in time past by anyone who had received them.'

As John Johnstone was to become one of the instigators of the later attacks on Clive, and one of his most unscrupulous slanderers, it is necessary to say something about him here. He and John Spencer were the two men whose position in India had been raised as personal issues, before Clive came to India, at two meetings of the proprietors. Spencer had been transferred from Bombay to take up the post of president or governor in Calcutta, and his return to Bombay was demanded by Clive as a condition of his acceptance of the office. It was agreed to. The case of Johnstone was different. He, with three others, was dismissed in 1764 as members of the Council in Calcutta for resisting the authority of Vansittart over the question of private trade. He was known to be notoriously corrupt and unscrupulous. But he was reinstated by the Court of Proprietors at the time Clive's jaghir was restored. Clive's party had at first shown no readiness to do this, but later voted for the reinstatement because they did not want to lose the votes of the supporters of Johnstone in respect of the jaghir. Johnstone came from a very influential family and had three brothers in Parliament. He was only thirty-one at the time, but his assertiveness and obstreperousness were based on his consciousness of the support behind him at home.

Though overruled by Clive, he was allowed to record his dissent, and he did so in a long minute which he submitted on June 17 1765. In it he boldly attacked both Clive and the Select Committee. In regard to the money he had received he simply cited the precedent of Clive. 'With regard to presents in general, we have the approved example of the President, Lord Clive himself, for our guide.' He dwelt specifically on the jaghir.

Not satisfied with this, he questioned the bona fides of the Select Committee. He observed in the same note that the aim of the Select Committee was to render the actions of the previous governor and Council obnoxious, and he found the motive for it:

> To what cause must we attribute this temper of the Committee? One would almost think they were piqued to find the interest of the Company so well secured before their arrival; only they must know that their coming at all was doubtful, and the gentlemen who had felt the defects of the former treaty were full as qualified to remedy them in the new one, and have no doubt their masters will approve of their services.

He criticized Clive for showing disregard for Spencer, who, as he put it, was 'the darling of that party which in England opposed Lord Clive and the gentlemen of the Committee'. He also wrote that he had 'heard that the Governor [Lord Clive] had expressed much chagrin that the affair of his jaghire has been settled without his interposition'.

Clive was not the man to be intimidated by such behaviour. He recorded his observations against Johnstone's minute in a long note. In regard to his own gains he made these points: he had received his presents in a military capacity, only as a reward for real services rendered to the Nawab in a very dangerous crisis; the reward was not stipulated, required or expected by him; what he received in consequence of the battle of Plassey was the only present he had ever taken, though he remained in Bengal for the space of nearly three years at the head of the victorious army. He concluded by saying:

> Let the impartial world determine, whether those who have succeeded me with inferior pretensions, and even in inferior stations, have conducted themselves with equal propriety or moderation.... If Mr Johnstone's transactions will bear the test as well as mine, he will no doubt receive as honourable testimonials of public approbation as I did.

Clive naturally regarded Johnstone as the leader of the opposition to him. He thought Johnstone and Leycester, who had been most vocal in resisting his authority and measures, had led astray Spencer, whom he described as being deeper in the mire than the others. He had been so dominated by the Council that the dignity of the governor was 'sunk beyond contempt itself'. Clive added that only the name of the Council was heard in Bengal, and not that of the governor.

This clique carried on its ineffectual but irritating obstruction. Before Clive left Calcutta on June 25 1765 to settle the affairs of the Company at Murshidabad and up-country, he left a plan to reconstitute the Council, to be executed by one of the members, Sumner. It proposed two changes: that the number of its members should be reduced from sixteen to twelve, and that the councillors should no longer be appointed as heads of the subordinate factories like Patna or Dacca. When he was at Murshidabad he received a letter from Sumner in which he was informed that some of the councillors had produced previous letters from the directors which had fixed the number as not fewer than sixteen, and made the headship at Patna tenable only by a councillor.

Clive was extremely angry at this. In his reply on July 8 he reproached Sumner for having changed his opinion so quickly owing to opposition from members who were self-interested and had exposed themselves to severe censure. He imagined that few of them would escape being suspended from their posts. He told Sumner that he had lowered the importance of the Committee by his diffident conduct.

> A conduct that tends to abolish the power of the Committee, tends, consequently, to frustrate the intentions of the General Court of Proprietors, who thought me a proper person to curb that licentious spirit of disobedience in the servants, and at the same time to put a stop to that torrent of universal corruption and luxury which had overwhelmed the settlement.

He said that he was determined to carry out the plan. On the question of the powers of the Select Committee he repeated his previous opinion: first, that the Committee was empowered to adopt any means it thought proper and to set aside any order which it thought detrimental to the Company; secondly, that it was the Committee that was to decide what matters to lay before the Council.

The opposition was cowed and eliminated. Some of the recalcitrants were suspended, others resigned. Johnstone went home in October, with a fortune of £300,000. The Company wished to prosecute him for corruption, but at a General Court of Proprietors held in May 1767, Sulivan and his party secured the withdrawal of the prosecution despite the directors and the ministry, who were for it. Johnstone became Member of Parliament in 1774 and retained his seat till 1780. In politics, he who fights and runs away always lives to fight another day. No victory, no defeat, no reputation, no discredit is final.

However, when the directors learned about the steps taken by Clive they fully approved of them. They did not consider the presents to Johnstone and others as free gifts, and they were sorry, as they put it, 'to see some of the gentlemen have thought fit to justify their breach of trust by a breach of order in pleading the covenants were not executed, and therefore not obligatory'.

The Powers of the Country and the Company

Upon settling the affairs in Calcutta on some sort of regular footing, Clive turned his attention to the relationship of the Company with the native princes, of whom three concerned him immediately: the young Nawab at Murshidabad, the Emperor Shah Alam at Allahabad, and Shuja-ud-daula, the Nawab – Vizir of Oudh. Leaving Calcutta on June 25, he stopped at Murshidabad and finally defined the status of the Nawab *vis-à-vis* the Company and their mutual relations.

He had already formed his ideas on the general aspect of the relationship. On the day he arrived in Calcutta he wrote to Carnac:

> Since we have experienced such a series of troubles from the mismanagement of the Subahship, it is our duty to guard against future evils, by doing ourselves what no nabob will ever do for us; and never trust to the ambition of any Mussulman whatever, after what had happened. Peace upon a firm and lasting foundation must be established if possible.

After meeting the young Nawab in May 1765, he had come to the conclusion that he was quite unfit to rule, and therefore, immediately on arriving at Mushidabad, he got him to agree to transfer the administration to a sort of council of ministers composed of Muhammad Riza Khan, Durlabhram Rai and the two Jagat Seths. They were to conduct the government according to a set of regulations which were drawn up, and would be supervised by the Company's agents.

The collection of the revenues, or the *diwani* side of the government, was transferred to the Company, and the Nawab was to receive a fixed allowance of Rs5,000,000 a year for all his expenses. Clive explained to the Council that the sum might be considered large, but considering the Nawab's expenses and the demands upon him, he thought he had to be given this amount. The young Nawab on his part was perfectly satisfied. As Clive wrote to Verelst on July 11 1765: 'He received the proposal of having a sum of money for himself and household at his will with infinite pleasure; and the only reflection he made, upon leaving me, was "Thank God! I shall now have as many dancing girls as I please."'

Thus a dual system of government was established in Bengal. Clive was not wholly satisfied with the position or the person. As to the former he wrote to the Select Committee in the same letter in which he reported the new arrangement for Bengal:

> We have often lamented that the gentlemen of the Council, by precipitating the late treaty, had lost the most glorious opportunity that could ever happen of settling matters upon that solid and advantageous footing for the Company which no temporary invasion could endanger. The true and only security for our commerce and territorial possessions in this country is, in a manner, always to have it in our power to overawe the very Nabob we are bound by treaty to support. A maxim contrary to this has of late been much adopted; and from that fundamental error, as I may call it, have sprung the innumerable evils, or at least deficiencies, in our government which, I have now the pleasure to inform you, are in a fair way of being perfectly removed.

On the Nawab, he wrote:

> Although it is certain that neither his education nor his abilities will enable him to appear to any advantage at the head of these great and rich provinces, yet, I think we are bound in honour to support the dignity of his station, so far as it is consistent with the true interests of the Company.

As soon as he had come to this agreement, Clive set out for Allahabad, leaving Sykes to look to the details of execution. But even when he was engaged in other affairs, he did not forget the situation in Bengal. For instance, though he maintained friendliness with Rai Durlabh, he knew the man too well to leave him unsupervised. So he wrote to Sykes: 'Rai Durlabh must be watched and not suffered to pilfer, steal, extort or oppress.'

He also gave advice to Sykes about filling the posts in the revenue system. His recommendation was to prefer Hindus to Muslims. He wrote:

> These fat, expensive Moormen who spend the government's revenues in luxury and assuagements must pay rents regularly in future or immediately be turned out. Indeed, in my opinion, none but Gentoos [Hindus] ought to be renters of counters, who always spend less than their income and can, when called upon, make good any deficiency in the revenues.

The war with Shuja-ud-daula now had to be formally ended, and an understanding with Shah Alam, the fugitive Emperor of Delhi, arrived at. Clive gave his attention to the problem, and as he proceeded up the Ganges wrote to Carnac on July 13 that they had to be particularly careful in dealing with Shuja, so that the Company might not be exposed to future wars with him on account of Shah Alam. Before Clive's arrival the Council had decided to deprive Shuja of his kingdom and to give it to the wild Ruhela Afghans who were settled in the western part of the Gangetic plain and were in power in Delhi. To do so would have been dangerous for the Company, and Clive decided to restore to Shuja the greater portion of his kingdom. At the same time he did not want to leave Shah Alam unprovided for, and thought Bengal would furnish him with a handsome income. He also proposed to endow him with the revenues of a portion of Shuja's territories. With all this, Clive hoped, the Emperor would reside in some place of security and enjoy ease and plenty without importuning the Company to take him to Delhi. On his own behalf, Clive was ready to give every attention to Shah Alam's interest which did not hurt the Company.

On August 1 he reached Benares and had a conference with Shuja-ud-daula, to whom he made the offer of restoring Oudh. At this, Clive wrote to the Select Committee, 'his expressions of joy and gratitude were many and warm. Such an instance of generosity in a victorious army exceeded his most sanguine expectations.' Shuja agreed to pay an indemnity of Rs5,000,000. Clive thought that these moderate and equitable terms would be the best foundation for the union and amity they all earnestly wished to secure.

All this could not be incorporated in a formal treaty until an agreement had been arrived at with Shah Alam, who as titular emperor had the sole right to legalize all political arrangements in India. So Clive went to Allahabad. But he foresaw no difficulty. Even before leaving Benares, he wrote, on August 3 1765, to Sykes in Murshidabad: 'I am much mistaken if ten days does not bring to a conclusion the most glorious, honourable and advantageous event that ever happened to this Company.' And in nine days everything had gone through.

Clive arrived in Allahabad on August 9, and had many interviews with Shah Alam. At first the Emperor, though destitute and dependent, showed an inclination to fix his price too high. But he readily accepted the alternative terms offered. Of course, the English proposals had to be presented to him in the form of petitions. Then at an audience on August 11, Clive presented two petitions – the first for the formal grant of the subadarship of Bengal, Bihar and Orissa to Najm-ud-daula; and the second for the grant of *diwani* of these provinces to the Company. Shah Alam agreed, and the form of the agreement was properly established.

On the next day, the twelfth, the Emperor took his seat on a throne in Clive's tent and conferred the *diwani*. Its form was as follows:

> At this happy time our royal Firmaun, indispensably requiring obedience, is issued. That whereas in consideration of the attachment and services of the high and mighty, the noblest of exalted nobles, the Chief of illustrious warriors, our faithful servants and sincere well-wishers, worthy of all royal favours, the English Company, we have granted them the Dewannee of the provinces of Bengal, Bahar, and Orissa from the beginning of the Fussul Rubby of the Bengal year 1172 [1765], as a free gift, and Ultumgau, without association of any other person, and with an exemption from the payment of the Customs of the Dewannee, which used to be paid to the court....

Its tenure was unlimited in time. It laid down that the Emperor's heirs and all officials and subordinates should leave 'the said office in possession of the said Company from generation to generation, forever and ever; looking upon them to be insured from dismission or renewal....' (the official English translation of the firman).

This was the legal foundation for British rule in Bengal. As Burke put it:

> This is the great act of the constitutional entrance of the Company into the body politic of India. It gave to the settlement of Bengal a fixed constitutional form, with a legal title, acknowledged and recognized now for the first time by all the natural powers of the country, because it arose from the charter of the undoubted sovereign.

But of all such constitutional sanctions, it might also be said: *Populus vult decipi, ergo decipiatur*: People want to be deceived, so let them be deceived.

In addition, Shah Alam recognized the status of Najm-ud-daula, and also the territorial and other rights of the Company in the Carnatic and Northern Sircars. For the first time they were put on a legal basis. In return, the Company guaranteed to him an annual revenue of twenty-six lakhs of rupees from Bengal to Shah Alam. The two districts of Corah and Allahabad, secured from Shuja-ud-daula, were to assure an additional twenty-eight lakhs per annum.

On August 16, a formal treaty was signed with Shuja-ud-daula. He agreed to pay the compensation previously fixed, and not to allow Mir Qasim and Sumroo, who had massacred the English at Patna, or any European deserters to remain within his territories. In return, all English troops were to be withdrawn from Shuja's territory, with the exception of the garrison in the fort of Chunar and such troops as Shah Alam might require for his protection at Allahabad. Clive acknowledged that the amount of indemnity was inadequate, but Shuja's circumstances would not 'afford more without oppressing the country, and thereby laying the foundation of future contention and troubles'. Clearly, he remembered the consequences of the very large demands on Mir Jafar.

Administrative and Military Measures

In just three months since his arrival Clive had brought about a political settlement which was to remain the framework of British power in India. He returned to Calcutta on September 6, 1765, and gave his attention to the reorganization of the Company's civil and military establishments.

In his speech in the House of Commons, delivered seven years later, Clive described the choices that had been open to him when he arrived in Bengal, of which there were three.

The first

> ... was strewn with abundance of fair advantages. I might have put myself at the head of the government as I found it. I might have encouraged the resolution which the Gentlemen had taken, not to execute the new Covenants, which prohibited the receipt of presents: and although I had executed the Covenants myself, I might have contrived to return to England with an immense fortune, infamously added to the one before honourably obtained. Such an increase of wealth might have added to my weight in this country.

Secondly, 'finding my powers thus disputed, I might in despair have given up the Commonwealth, and have left Bengal without making an effort to save it'.

Last of all, he could have adopted a third course. He said:

> The third path was intricate. Dangers and difficulties were on every side. But I resolved to pursue it. In short, I was determined to do my

> duty to the public, although I should incur the odium of the whole settlement. The welfare of the Company needed required a vigorous exertion, and I took the resolution of cleaning the Augean Stable.

He had to pay the price, but in the task he undertook he was successful.

The first task was to put an end to the exactions and corrupt practices that had marked the Company's exercise of power in Bengal, and which were likely to be increased by the assumption of the *diwani*.

Clive began with the native administration at the top. The Company had taken over the collection of the revenue; military defence of the country was also its responsibility, but the executive and judicial powers of the nawab were left to him, and these were exercised by three native dignitaries, Muhammed Riza Khan, Durlabhram Rai and Shitab Rai. Clive found that the Company was incapable of collecting the revenues directly. Therefore, Riza Khan became the agent who managed the dealings with the *zamindars* in Bengal. In Bihar, too, the local governor was the intermediary. According to practice, these dignitaries were entitled for their services to various perquisites, which were undefined and left room for oppressive and corrupt practices. So Clive assigned a sum of twelve lakhs of rupees annually for the support of the three highest officials. He admitted that the sum was enormous, but he thought that in consideration of their power and responsibility, their integrity had to be safeguarded by an adequate remuneration.

Then he turned to the servants of the Company. They had two sources for making money – presents and private trade, both sources of oppression and corruption. In fact the abuse of private trade was the cause of the conflict with the Qasim. Clive could, however, go to the root of the matter, and laid the blame not so much on the British servants of the Company as on the native agents or the banians, who, he said, 'never desist till, according to the ministerial phrase, they have dragged their masters into the kennel'.

He said that the passion for gain was as strong as the passion of love, and drew a vivid parallel in his speech in 1772.

> I will suppose that two intimate friends have lived long together; that one of them has married a beautiful woman; that the friend still continues to live in the house, and that this beautiful woman, forgetting her duty to her husband, attempts to seduce the friend; who, though in the vigour of youth, may, from a high principle of

honour, at first, resist the temptation, and even rebuke the lady. But if he continues to live under the same roof and she still continues to throw out her allurements, he must be seduced at last or fly.

He went on to conclude the simile:

> Now, the Banyan is the fair lady to the Company's servant. He lays his bags of silver before him today; gold tomorrow; jewels the next day; and if they fail, he then tempts him in the way of his possession, which is trade. He assures him that goods may be had cheap, and sold to great advantage up the country. In this manner is the attack carried on; and the Company's servant has no resource, for he cannot fly. In short, flesh and blood cannot bear it.

The very upbringing and education with which the young man comes from his country, Clive felt, makes him a victim. He comes over at the age of sixteen, and his relatives have told him my Lord such a one has made so much in such a time. So they are corrupted at their very setting out, and as they go 'a good many together, they inflame one another's expectations in the course of their voyage'. Then Clive described what happened when the young man arrived in Bengal:

> A Banyan, worth perhaps one hundred thousand pounds, desires he may have the honour of serving this young gentleman at four shillings and six pence per month. The Company has provided chambers for him, but they are not good enough; – the Banyan finds better. The young man takes a walk about the town, he observes other writers, arrived only a year before him, live in splendid apartments or have houses of their own, ride upon fine prancing Arabian horses, and in palanqueens and chaises; that they keep seraglios, make entertainments, and treat with champaigne and claret. When he returns he tells the Banyan what he has observed. The Banyan assures him he may soon arrive at the same good fortune; he furnishes him with money; he is then at his mercy.

It is the banian, Clive said, who commits the acts of violence and oppression, and hence, he declared, arises the clamour against the English gentlemen in India. 'May we not conclude,' he asked, 'that if they have erred it has been because they were men, placed in situations subject to little or no control?'

The directors had already forbidden presents and had abolished private trade, and Clive had got the covenants signed by them so that they could no longer take presents. But as to private trade, Clive thought that some extra income must be provided for them before that source was taken away. The salaries of the Company's servants were miserably low. A councillor got only £300 a year – he could not live in Bengal for less than £3,000. So he thought that it was not expedient to draw the reins too tight and thus reduce the Company's servants from affluence to beggary. It was necessary, he declared, that some emoluments should accrue to the servants in general. He devised a means of doing so and put it into operation. That was done by means of the income from inland trade in salt, betel-nut and tobacco. Actually, the extra income was provided from the salt trade, which was a state monopoly under the Muslim rulers; the trade in betel-nut was not remunerative, and tobacco was afterwards excluded from the scheme.

Though the directors had totally prohibited participation by their servants in inland trade, later they reconsidered the prohibition and left it to the Select Committee to regulate trade in the three articles. So, when the matter came up for consideration, Clive left it to Sumner to prepare a plan while he himself was up-country. When Clive came back to Calcutta it was discussed and adopted on September 18 1768.

The plan was that the trade in the three articles was to be carried on by a society in which all the Company's servants, except the writers, among those in the civil employ, but including the field officers among those in the military employ, were to hold shares according to their rank, and were also to share the profit in the same proportion. The retail price of salt was fixed at twelve to fifteen per cent below the average price for the previous twenty years. A duty of thirty-five per cent was established for the Company, and it was calculated that this duty would yield £120,000 a year. The share of profit for those at the top was fairly high, e.g. £7,000 for a member of the Council or a colonel. But the amount was lower than that gained by private trade.

The plan was sanctioned for a year in the first place to see how it worked, and it was discovered that it was open to abuse. So in the second year a new system was introduced. The society was no longer to employ its agents to sell salt in the interior, but to sell all of it in Calcutta to the native merchants, and the strictest orders were issued that no Englishman or their agents could participate in the trade outside Calcutta. The duty for the Company was raised to fifty per cent, which yielded £160,000 a year.

On account of the immediate abolition of the right of private trade, the servants of the Company would have been left without proper means of living. So the schemes were put into operation at once without waiting for sanction from London. But they were not approved, and after Clive had left Bengal a different method of remunerating the Company's servants was adopted. In the meantime, however, the scheme provided adequate remuneration for them.

The next problem that Clive had to deal with was the recruitment of qualified men for carrying on the complex work of administration which had fallen on the Company. The most urgent was to fill up the vacancies in the Council created by the suspension, resignation and death of a number of members. When Clive was absent in July 1765, the Council had called two covenanted servants next in seniority to join it. This was disapproved by Clive because these men, in his opinion, were too involved in the irregularities of the past to be fit for the posts. He decided to requisition four members of the Madras service whose conduct there was exemplary. They arrived in Calcutta in February 1766.

The decision became known in January, and at once there was protest from the Bengal service. These servants sent a memorandum to the directors, which Clive described as modest though puerile and, though plaintive, not clamorous. But to Clive and members of the Select Committee who had requisitioned the men from Madras they exhibited an aggressive hostility which was insolent. They formed themselves into an association and bound themselves not to have any social relations with Clive and the members of the Select Committee except Sumner, who had dissented; similarly with the members from Madras. Those who disregarded the ban were to be stigmatized and avoided.

Clive described their conduct in a despatch to the Court of Directors dated January 31 'as destructive of that subordination without which no government can stand', and exposed their claims.

> The young gentlemen of the settlement had set themselves up of the propriety of our conduct, and the degree of their own merit: each would think himself qualified to transact your weighty affairs in Council at an age when the laws of his country adjudge him unfit to manage his own concerns to the extent of forty shillings.

He went on to say that, in short, the members of the service in Bengal were separating themselves totally from the head of the government. So, he said, 'it becomes a fair struggle whether we or the young gentlemen shall in future guide the helm of the government'. Finally, he summed up their standing:

> Look at their names, examine their standing, inquire into their services, and reflect upon the age of the four-fifths of the subscribers to this bill of grievances, who now support this association, and you will be equally surprised with us at the presumptuous intemperance of youth.

He took drastic disciplinary action against them. The Secretary to the Council, who was the ringleader, was dismissed from his post and suspended from the service, the leaders were deprived of their right to trade, and other stoppages were also made. As one servant wrote at the time, 'Every servant that had ventured to express detestation of the administration was marked and immediately stripped of all to their bare pay.' This broke the resistance, and the same correspondent wrote: 'The spirited Bengallers appeared in a body one morning at the table of their lord and master.'

In filling the higher appointments Clive thought it necessary to depart from the practice of promoting on the strength of local rank. This, he said, would 'commit into the hands of rash inexperienced young men the conduct of a system of government which demands the discretion, judgement, and steadiness of more advanced years and longer services'. In the despatch to the directors (March 24 1766) he also drew attention to the inexperience of the men in the service.

> The business of the Secretary's department was committed to a youth of three years of standing in your service; the employment of Accomptant [Accountant] is now discharged by a Writer still lower in the list of your servants; the important trusts of Military Storekeeper, Naval Storekeeper, and Storekeeper of the Works, were bestowed, when vacant, upon Writers; and a Writer held the post of Paymaster to the Army, at a period when near 20 lacks of rupees had been deposited for months together in his hands.

These young men had of necessity to depend upon their native subordinates. So Clive wrote: 'Banians became principals in the several departments; the affairs of the Company flowed through a new and unnatural channel; and your most secret concerns were publicly known in the bazaar.'

Clive observed that:

> ... circumstances are now widely different from that they were a few years since, when you confined your whole attention to commerce.... You are now become the sovereign of a rich and potent kingdom ... your interests are so extended, so complicated, and so connected with those of several surrounding powers, as to form a nice and difficult system of politics.

He was particularly anxious that in regard to appointment to the Council 'no consideration of favour or prejudice be suffered to bias you in the important business of composing your Council; and that no other distinction be admitted, except what is due to ability, to integrity, and to faithful essential services'. The Council had become so important, he explained, that everything depended on a judicious and impartial selection of its members.

Before he began to give his attention to all this he had carried out, in an altered and improved form, the plan of reorganization of the army in Bengal – a plan he had previously put forward in London. It was made up of three brigades, and as actually organized the brigade consisted of one company of artillery, one troop of European cavalry and one regiment of native cavalry, one regiment of European infantry and seven battalions of sepoys. Clive particularly wanted the officers to be familiar with the language of the different sepoy corps, without which, as he put it, 'it is impossible to bring the sepoys to that pitch of discipline which will make them truly formidable'. It is significant that the brigades were all stationed outside Bengal: the first brigade was stationed at Monghyr in eastern Bihar; the third brigade at Patna, the capital of Bihar and in the extreme west of the province; and the second at Allahabad, which was altogether beyond the limits of the territories under the Company but where it was stationed as protection to Shah Alam. In Bengal, i.e. Murshidabad and Calcutta, there were only small detachments from the first brigade.

Mutiny of the Officers

The last and the most serious trouble that faced Clive during his second governorship was also one which could have been least expected. He, a successful and glamorous commander, had to cope with a passive mutiny of the British officers of all three brigades of the army in Bengal. The threat was held out when there was a likelihood of a Maratha invasion of Bengal, and the revolt was over a question of money. Exceptional military circumstances had created a vested interest for the officers, and they were not ready to abandon it.

Remuneration for the officers and soldiers of the army varied according to conditions of service. There was first a basic pay. To this was added, from the beginning of the wars in India, a *per capita* field allowance called *batta* (literally, rice-allowance), which was paid in full when the troops were in the field and in half when they were stationed outside the territories of the Company. In Bengal, after Plassey, Mir Jafar granted a further allowance equal to the full *batta* for all, and it was called the 'double *batta*'. It was, however, to be paid by the Nawab and not the Company. All these taken together made the earnings of the officers in Bengal double that of the officers in Madras.

The Company had no objection to the double *batta* so long as it was paid by the Nawab. But as soon as, in accordance with a new arrangement with Mir Qasim, it was transferred to the Company, the directors ordered its discontinuation. However, on account of the continuance of the military operations and remonstrances from the officers, supported by the Council in Calcutta, it was not withheld. But on June 1 1764 the directors sent a definite order that the double *batta* was to be stopped. This order reached Calcutta in January 1765. However, its execution was put off until Clive arrived.

As soon as a treaty with the Nawab of Oudh was concluded Clive gave notice to the officers that the allowance would be discontinued as from January 1 1766. He had in the meanwhile introduced the system by which the field officers were to have a share in the profits of the salt trade, and he was also creating a fund for helping the soldiers and their families. In principle he was not opposed to the acquisition of wealth by the officers. As he observed: 'Honour alone is scarcely a sufficient reward for toilsome service of the field.' But he thought that 'the acquisition of wealth ought to be so gradual as to admit not a prospect of completing it, till succession by merit to the rank of a field officer should have laid a good foundation for the claim'. He had no reason to think that the stoppage of the allowance would cause great hardship.

The Select Committee as a whole did not feel happy over it. They informed the Court of Directors on March 24 1766 that the expenses of the officers in the climate of India were so heavy that the allowances of a subaltern would 'scarcely maintain him in the station of a gentleman'. They also said that the measure had produced some grumbling and complaints, and a memorandum had even been received from the first brigade at Monghyr. But being aware that the Company's military expenses had to be reduced, the directors were determined to see the order strictly enforced.

The first intimation of trouble came in the third week of April, when on the nineteenth the Select Committee forwarded to Clive at Murshidabad a remonstrance from the officers of the third brigade at Patna commanded by Sir Robert Barker, which was signed by nine captains, twelve lieutenants and twenty ensigns. Clive on the twenty-second directed that the remonstrance should come through proper channels and should be sent back to Sir Robert.

On April 28 Clive received a letter from Sir Robert Fletcher, who was in command of the first brigade at Monghyr, that the officers not only of his brigade but of the whole army proposed to resign. He also forwarded a letter from Barker at Patna in which he informed Clive that there was a secret league of officers also not confined only to his brigade. It was soon found that there was a general conspiracy, first hatched at Monghyr and then extended to the other two brigades. The officers were determined to resign on June 1, and had bound themselves to defend any officer who would be condemned to death by a court-martial. A fund was even created to indemnify those who might be dismissed from the service. On finding that the plot was discovered the officers resigned a month earlier to escape the jurisdiction of martial law. However, they offered to continue in service till May 15, by which time they expected the Marathas to take the field, and induce Clive to comply with their demands.

Clive, however, was not the man to yield. He desired the Calcutta Council to write at once to Madras and ask the Council there to keep all the officers and cadets who could be spared ready to sail for Bengal. He also wrote to the commanders of all the three brigades ordering them to keep under arrest any officer whose conduct could be regarded as mutinous until a general court-martial could be assembled. 'The ringleaders,' he wrote, 'must suffer the severest punishment that martial law can inflict, else there is an end of discipline in the army and of the authority in the East India Company over all their servants.'

On May 4 Clive received a letter from Sir Robert Fletcher at Monghyr that forty officers of his brigade were offering their resignation, and on the next day another letter from Barker arrived to say that his officers were also resigning from May 1. Clive at once sent four officers, in whom he had complete confidence, to deal with the situation at Monghyr.

The situation was hazardous in view of the possible advance

of the Marathas. Even so he wrote to Barker on May 8 that 'I must see the soldiers' bayonets levelled at my own throat before I can be induced to give way.' But in view of the Maratha threat he said he might yield temporarily to the demands of the officers. It could only be temporary, he explained, 'for I shall think Bengal in the utmost danger, when we are reduced to the necessity of submitting the civil power to the mercy of men who have gone to lengths that will frighten and astonish all England'.

He left Murshidabad for Monghyr on the same day (May 8). On the way, he found from a letter written by Colonel Smith commanding the second brigade at Allahabad that the Marathas had begun their advance. He at once instructed this commander that if the Marathas seemed still disposed to invade Bengal, or if he feared a mutiny among the whole body of troops – but in no other situation – he was to come to terms with the officers. No such yielding however, was needed.

The four officers sent to Monghyr – Majors Champion and Polier and Captains Smith and Pearson – arrived there on the eleventh, and tried to reason with the officers, but without making any impression on them. There was a possibility of the European troops joining the mutiny. So these officers marched two sepoy battalions to the fort. The next day Fletcher informed them that the European troops had mutinied. Upon this Captain Smith, with only the Indian officers, marched the sepoys, occupied a mound and threatened to fire on the Europeans. The Europeans were frightened, and at this moment Fletcher came and appeased them. Fletcher's whole conduct was equivocal.

On May 15 Clive himself arrived. He was then told that the officers wanted to lay their case before him, and they accused Sir Robert Fletcher of being the instigator and planner of the whole conspiracy. Clive harangued the soldiers and the officers, explained why the *batta* had been stopped and rewarded the native commandants. The disturbance at Monghyr was quelled. Clive ordered the recalcitrant officers to leave at once for Calcutta – which they did – and himself proceeded to Patna.

On his arrival there he found that Sir Robert Baker had sent the officers who had insisted on immediate resignation to Calcutta. When Clive arrived the others withdrew their resignation.

The situation at Allahabad was more risky, because the troops were divided. On account of the Maratha danger, a large body of them was at a place just over one hundred miles to the west.

Colonel Richard Smith, commander of the second brigade, who was at the advanced post, denounced the officers and when they protested he ordered those who had resigned to proceed to Calcutta at once. He also sent a reproof to the officers at Allahabad, who sent back a defiant reply. Then Major Smith, who commanded at Allahabad, sent for a battalion of sepoys from the advanced post, and when they arrived put all the officers except four under arrest. Then they all submitted. Major Smith released all except the leaders whom he sent down to Patna as prisoners.

The whole resistance collapsed. The majority of officers admitted that they had been indiscreet, and prayed to be restored to service. The chief participants in the mutiny were tried by court-martial and cashiered. Among them was the commander of the first brigade, Sir Robert Fletcher, whose guilt was fully established. He was an officer with a very bad record, and was notorious as an intriguer. He owed his promotion and retention in service in India to Sulivan. As a protégé of Clive's enemies, he would be disposed to harm him if he could. But it was he who suffered.

Personal Matters

Clive had given an assurance to the directors that he would not add to his wealth by virtue of his governorship, and he repeated this resolve, while in office in Bengal, to his father, his wife and his friends in his letters. What he wrote to his wife will be quoted later. In September 1765 he wrote to his father: 'I have not benefitted nor added to my fortune one farthing, nor shall I; though I might, by this time, have received 500,000 £ sterling.' At the same time he also wrote to a friend on the subject. What he said then was published in the press in London later and read out by him in the House of Commons when charges were made that he was aggrandizing himself abroad. The passage has to be quoted:

> That you may assert with confidence the justice of my cause, I do declare by the God who made me, it is my absolute determination to refuse every present of consequence and that I will not return to England with one rupee more than what arises from my jaghire. My profits arising from salt shall be divided among those friends who have endangered their lives and constitutions in attending me. The congratulatory Nuzirs [Nazars], etc., shall be set opposite to my extraordinary expences; and if aught remains, it shall go to Poplar or some other hospital.

Reading all those declarations – and they were many – it is natural to exclaim: 'The lady doth protest too much.' There is no doubt that Clive was sensitive about his monetary gains to the point of being obsessed with what he had got, and over-conscious of what he was not accepting. His gains after the battle of Plassey were exceptional, and afterwards he gave the impression of being under a continuous necessity to justify them, not only to the public, but even to himself. On the other hand, the age in which he lived was so mercenary at all levels of society, and particularly in the middle class, that he felt that he needed a moral justification for neglecting opportunities to gain more money, which was a duty. The vehement denunciation of illicit or even abnormal acquisitions in the age in which he lived was only the reverse side of its worship of money. Clive never became hard-boiled enough to keep his money-making and his ethical notions apart.

But he could certainly claim that, during his second governorship, he gained no additional wealth with the exception of the income from his jaghir; that is to say, his fortune remained what it was before he went to India in 1764. Clive kept his accounts meticulously, and proved his claim by producing figures before Parliament in 1772.

To take his receipts first. During his governorship he received money from three sources: from his regular allowances as governor, which amounted to only £841 in round figures; from the amount received from his share in the salt trade, which he capitalized by selling the profits to five of his colleagues for £30,857; from the commission, at $1\frac{1}{8}$ per cent, on the revenues of the *diwani*, which was officially sanctioned, amounting to £30,866. The total was £62,564 over a period of one year and ten months.

But he spent or gave away more. First, as soon as the commission from the *diwani* was sanctioned he gave up the income from the salt trade, and repaid with interest proportionate sums to the friends to whom he had sold his interest: this amounted to £19,986 – leaving his total gain from the salt trade at £10,870. He gave away £43,750 to Strachey, Maskelyne, Ingham and five others. His expenses in India and England were £4,641. Thus he disbursed a total sum of £68,377. This left him out of pocket to the sum of approximately £5,800 so far as the receipts during the period of governorship were concerned.

No one could dispute these figures, but he was attacked for

giving the money to Strachey and others on two grounds: first, that he was enriching his relatives; and secondly, that the money from the salt trade was itself illegitimate.

Clive never made any secret of his intention to provide for those who were on his personal staff with a competence, and informed his friends and wife about it at the time. Later, in Parliament, he justified it vigorously. He said that he was perfectly aware how this might appear to the eyes of observers. He said that what he did for his staff was closely observed, and that it was impossible for him to take any steps in respect of them without being condemned. They had executed no covenants, not being in the Company's service, and could take presents. But if Clive had allowed that, people would have said he himself intended to gain them at one remove; if they were given permission to trade, by which, on account of his influence behind them, they would have made a good deal of money, the same thing would have been said. So he decided that 'they would not benefit themselves a farthing, but by what they should receive from my hands'.

Furthermore, they were all entitled to what they received on account of the valuable service they had rendered. Strachey had been recommended as private secretary to him by George Grenville, and Clive declared that without his abilities and indefatigable industry, he could never have gone through his great and arduous undertaking.* Ingham was his personal physician and had quitted a lucrative practice to accompany Clive to Bengal. Only Maskelyne was a relative, but he had been a companion since his early Madras days and had never been able to do well in the world. So Clive thought he would give his old companion and brother-in-law a share of his own affluence, but only as a recompense for services rendered. The others had also done valuable work for him. In all that he did for them there was nothing clandestine.

As to the legitimacy of the income from the salt trade, it was never a question of morality, but of political wisdom. On this point, the directors were in complete disagreement with Clive and his colleagues on the Select Committee. As Clive told Parliament:

> The Directors disapproved of the trade in salt, betel-nut, and tobacco as carried on by their servants from the first moment that

*The Strachey family gave distinguished administrators to India; they certainly were fit subjects for the wit of their descendant, Lytton Strachey.

they became acquainted with it. They positively and repeatedly ordered that they should have no concern with it; they regarded and declared that it was an infringement of the rights of the natives.

There was a long correspondence between the two sides on this subject. Even when the directors were expressing their obligation to Clive for what he had done and requested him to remain another year, they observed in their despatch of May 17 1766 (which reached Calcutta in December) that they could not approve of the trade in salt.

> It is neither consistent with their honour nor their dignity to promote such an extensive trade, as it is now more immediately our interest and duty to protect and cherish the inhabitants, and to give no occasion to look on every Englishman as their national enemy, a sentiment we think such a monopoly would suggest.

The Committee at once decided to abolish the trade from September 1 1767, but even then they maintained that the trade was not a monopoly, nor was it oppressive. Clive reiterated this argument in Parliament in 1772. Salt was thus a political issue, and it remained so almost to the end of British rule. It has to be recalled that Mahatma Gandhi launched his civil disobedience movement in 1930 with a defiance of the state monopoly in salt.

Another opportunity for gain came to Clive from a legacy left him by the dying Mir Jafar. He told Parliament in 1772:

> The old Nabob Meer Jaffeir, if ever Mussulman had a friendship for a Christian, had a friendship for me. When the news of my appointment to the Government reached Bengal, he immediately quitted Muxudavad, came down to Calcutta; impatiently waited my arrival for six weeks; fell ill; returned to his capital and died. Two or three days before his death, in the presence of his wife, and in the presence of his minister, he said to his son and successor, whatever you may think proper to give Lord Clive on your own account the means are in your power. But as a testimony of my affection for him, I desire you will pay to him as a legacy from me of five lakhs of rupees.

Clive was informed of this when the young Nawab came to see him in Calcutta in 1765. At first Clive thought of refusing the legacy, but when the *batta* was abolished, he decided to employ it for the benefit of the soldiers of the Company. The legacy was handed to him, and he wrote to the Council in Calcutta on April 8 1766:

> I shall immediately pay the amount into the Company's treasury in Calcutta. The interest arising therefrom I propose shall be annually distributed in such proportions as I establish, among a certain

number of officers, non-commissioned officers, and private men, who are disqualified from further service, by wounds, length of service, or diseases contracted in the service of the Company.

He also intended that the widows of the soldiers would be entitled to relief from this fund. The governor and Council of Fort William were to be the perpetual trustees of this fund in India and the Board of Directors in England.

The Council gratefully accepted Clive's offer and thanked him, observing that they were unanimously of opinion that the receipt of the legacy was in no way prohibited by the new covenants. 'So noble an example of beneficence', they added, 'cannot fail to ensure the applause and approbation of every one.'

In regard to money, Clive proposed a last measure which would enable the future governors of Bengal to dispense with all perquisites, and exercise their authority without being suspected of using their public position for private gain. In a minute, laid before the Select Committee on September 23 1766, he said: 'The welfare of this great Company should be the sole study of a Governor; attached to that point alone his measures could never be thwarted by the malice of opposition, because they would all be proposed for the public good, and actions will always be justified, or condemned from the principles on which they were founded.'

So he proposed that the governor should receive as his total remuneration $1\frac{1}{8}$ per cent of the total revenues, and bind himself by a public oath not to receive anything in addition and to pay a fine of £150,000 if he broke the undertaking. He recognized that by these means a governor would not be able to amass a fortune of a million or half a million in two or three years, but he would acquire a very handsome independency and be in a position which a man of scrupulous honour and public zeal would wish to have. His political position would be strong; he would be able to disregard opposition in Council; he would have nothing to ask for, nothing to propose except what he thought was advantageous to his employers; he would be able to defy the obloquy of the world because there would be nothing censurable in his conduct. And finally he declared:

> If stability can be insured to such a government as this where riches have been acquired in abundance in a small space of time by all ways and means, and by men with or without capacities, it must be effected by a Governor thus restricted, and I shall think it an hon-

our, if my proposal be approved of to set the first example.

On October 1 he took an oath publicly to abide by the above proposal in the Town Hall, Calcutta, in the presence of the Mayor, the aldermen, and the members of the Council. All the Company's servants and inhabitants of the city were also present. This was the last public act of Clive of India.

Immediately after, Clive's health completely failed, and the worst part of his illness was a severe nervous breakdown. He had to be taken away from Calcutta to a country residence at Barasat, about fifteen miles to the north-east. He was kept there in complete seclusion during the whole month of November. On December 4 1766, General Carnac reported his condition to Lady Clive:

> His Lordship has had his mind so continually upon the strain in studying the Company's interest, and his stomach being from the malignancy of the climate overcharged with bile, from both these causes his nerves have been affected in the most violent manner: it grieved me beyond measure to see a person endowed with such extraordinary firmness so oppressed in his spirits as to exceed any degree of hysterics I was ever witness to.

He said that he was all the more shocked because he had never before seen him like this. But he was told by Ingham, his physician, who knew his condition and medical history well, that he had had such an attack, or an even worse one, in England.

He was being 'kept clear of business', and Carnac told Lady Clive that even he himself did not go near him for some days lest his presence might recall Clive's attention to public affairs and agitate him. However, with rest and the administration of a bark, he was improving, and Carnac said that he had gone to see Clive on December 3 at his own desire, and saw with inexpressible joy that his dejection of mind had 'considerably abated'.

From the Cape, on his return voyage, Clive gave a description of his illness to his wife. He said that his disorder was of a very different nature from the one he had had in England and could have had worse consequences. Ingham told him afterwards that for two days he was out of his senses and his lower jaw was immobile. On one day he had to be given fifteen grains of opium. This, however, was only a palliative. He was cured by a bark, which had a surprisingly curative effect on his nervous disorder. However, he was left so weak that he decided to leave India immediately.

Valedictory Message

When Clive left Bengal on January 29 1767, he thought that he had established the power and government of the Company on a firm basis, and it only remained for his successors to pursue his lines of policy and follow his methods of action. But he assumed too much, for what he left behind was wholly inchoate and depended too much on the accident of personality.

It has to be noted that, if he was the founder of the British Empire in India, he was this only in a limited sense – that is to say, he was the founder of British power, which could no longer be successfully challenged: the process had gone so far that it could only go forward and never be reversed. But he was not the founder of any imperial system of government, and did not even envisage one. He fully realized that 'since the acquisition of the Dewanney the power formerly belonging to the Soubah of these provinces is totally in fact vested in the East India Company. Nothing remains to him but the name and shadow of authority.'

Yet he did not adopt or approve of any system which would make the Company exercise its power to govern the country directly. Even the work of the *diwani*, which was the direct responsibility of the Company, was to be carried on indirectly through the native dignitaries.

Furthermore, he wished the moral prestige of the Nawab to be maintained fully. As he wrote: 'This name, however, this shadow, it is indispensably necessary we should seem to venerate. Every mark of distinction and respect must be shown him, and he himself encouraged to shew his resentment upon the least want of respect from other nations.'

But who was to exercise the real authority and govern at first hand? Clive neither sought nor exercised this power on behalf of the Company, nor did he think that such a function properly belonged to the Company. The practical task of government in every branch was left in the hands of the native officials.

This system was called Dual Government, but it could be called dual only in the sense that the collection of revenue was the direct responsibility of the Company, while executive government was not.

Thus what Clive left in Bengal was an administration under the titular authority of the Nawab in the executive sphere, and under the supervision of the governor in Calcutta in regard to revenue. The military responsibility for maintaining this system belonged wholly to the Company.

It was as amorphous a system of government as could be conceived, and it could provide no coherent policy or action unless this came from the governor in Calcutta. The whole system was the product of Clive's use of his own power and judgement in controlling government from the position of an adviser. It was something like Lord Cromer's position in Egypt at the end of the nineteenth century, and of the residents in the Indian states in the latter days of British rule.

Everything thus depended on the personality and position of the governor in Calcutta. As it happened, Clive fully realized the importance of the position, but not of the personality – he seems to have assumed that they would all be Clives and be capable of exercising power like him. In fact not even Warren Hastings possessed his authority and prestige, not to speak of Clive's immediate successors.

The directors at home understood this, and therefore requested him to prolong his stay in Bengal. In a letter to Clive written in May 1766, and received in Calcutta, they wrote:

> We have the most perfect sense of your Lordship's disinterestedness in every part of your conduct, and we shall not fail to represent this to the proprietors, and shall at the same time inform them of the many advantages your Lordship has obtained for the Company.

Then they added with a full perception of the basic factor in the situation:

> But we fear, my Lord, past experience will teach them as it does us, that the permanency of those advantages will depend much on your Lordship's continuing in India, till you have seen the regulations firmly established for the concluding of these important affairs: another year's experience and peaceable enjoyment of our acquisitions, might fix them on a basis that would give hopes they may be as lasting as they are great; and there is no doubt, my Lord, but the general voice of the proprietors, indeed we may say, of every man who wishes well to his country, will be to join in our request, that your Lordship will continue another year in India.

They were sensible that they were asking him for a sacrifice, but their request was made from a conviction that it was Clive's example which had been 'the principal means of restraining the general rapaciousness and corruption, which had brought our affairs so near the brink'. The directors were prescient.

But Clive's physician had advised that his life was in danger and he must leave Bengal. He himself was also convinced of this. So he pleaded the state of his health as the reason for not being able to comply with their request, and gave them an optimistic appraisal of the situation in Bengal. He told them that internally the spirit of opposition and extravagance had been subdued; the mutiny quelled; and there were now reasonable conditions created both for the civil and the military branch. On the external side, the conflicts with the native powers had been settled, and the invariable successes of the Company's arms had all combined to place the interests and power of the Company on a firm and advantageous basis, and at the same time to convince the native states that 'our ambition extends not beyond maintenance of our present position'.

'Such being the true state of affairs,' he asked, 'to what purpose should I continue longer in a climate which would certainly prove fatal to me at the end of another year?'

What he thought essential was that the position of the governor should be strong, and to secure this he had introduced the new method of remunerating him which would make him immune to any charge that he was pursuing his personal interest in deciding upon policies. Next, he urged the Council to be strict in enforcing obedience from all, and warned them particularly against delegating too much power to the military. He dwelt on obedience with an emphasis which reminds one of Rudyard Kipling's singling out obedience as the foundation of British rule in India. The heathen, his Tommy said, bows down to wood and stone, but he obeys no orders unless they are his own. This made the regiment come in and chuck the heathen out. That was realized by Clive from the beginning. He left as his parting message:

> No regulation can be carried into execution, no order obeyed, if you do not make rigorous example of the disobedient. Upon this point I rest the welfare of the Company in Bengal. The servants are now brought to a proper sense of their duty; if you slacken the reins of government, affairs will soon revert to their former channels; anarchy and corruption will again prevail, and elate with a new victory, be too headstrong for any future efforts of government.

He told the Council:

> I leave the military and civil departments under discipline and subordination. It is incumbent upon you to keep them so. You have power, you have abilities, you have integrity; let it not be said that you are deficient in resolution.

In a last letter to the Committee written five days before he sailed he said:

> The people of this Country have little or no idea of divided power; they imagine all authority is vested in one man. The Governor of Bengal should always be looked upon by them in this light, so far as is consistent with the honour of the Committee and the Council.

On the same day the members of the Council replied, setting down their appreciation of his work and their resolution to abide by his advice:

> The rules your Lordship has been pleased to recommend to our observance shall be strictly followed, as they immediately point out the only path which can lead to our own honour, to the interests of our constituents, and to the happiness of this Country.
>
> Already we have seen the unhappy effects of discord, and dissensions at this Board; we have lately experienced of union and unanimity. Your Lordship may therefore rest assured that we shall with one hand and voice, join in preserving the reputation of your government, which we shall be ambitious to transmit undiminished to our successors.

With this assurance from his colleagues Clive left India for ever.

More Letters to his Wife

Clive furnished a prologue to his work in India in his letters to his wife written during his voyage out. He could not give up the source of consolation. So he tried to bear his separation from her by writing letters whenever he could find time, which was not often. These letters were on public as well as personal matters, and they are like points of light on the stage of his work in India, which was more or less sombre.

He wrote a very long letter to her on August 24 1765, while on the Ganges near Benares, travelling down river after meeting the Emperor Shah Alam at Allahabad. He acknowledged receipt of many letters 'from the dearest of wives and best of parents, who is seldom out of my thought one day together, not withstanding the great and important concern of the Company'. He informed her that he was in better health than in England and that 'action, as formerly, agrees better with me than indolence and laziness'. He went on to say that he had settled very great matters and hoped there would be a lasting peace, 'so that tranquility is once more restored to these much ravaged and desolated provinces'.

He also told her that he himself could not receive any presents because he had signed the covenant, and therefore those who wanted to gratify him had offered Lady Clive such quantities of diamonds, rubies and gold mohurs as she could not think of. But he refused all and had maintained his dignity and integrity in the midst of ten thousand temptations. However, he added: 'this will not prevent my sending my wife some valuable presents'. But he also said that he had not been able to refuse some because they had been presented in a public manner and also that it would rest with the directors to decide whether he should pay for them, for he 'was determined to receive nothing, not even of the most trifling nature without giving them the particulars'.

He reverted to the topic of his separation from his wife. 'I am as happy', he wrote, 'as a man at such distance from his wife and family can well be.' He suffered no anxiety of mind 'but what arises on my wife's account and from the reflection of what she must suffer from so long and cruel a separation'. 'However,' he continued, 'I am persuaded your good sense will suggest to you our separation was unavoidable, and that the duty you owed to a growing and increasing family was much superior to that of attending your husband.' He told her: 'Rest satisfied in the reflection of whatever *is, is right*.' He assured her again that they would meet soon, though not as soon as he had expected. However, he again assured her that 'no consideration on earth shall induce me to stay beyond that year 1766', and that he was likely to arrive in England some time in April 1767.

He asked her to get the house at Berkeley Square refurnished:

> The chairs, couches, etc., were all worn out when I left it, I would have the grand flight of rooms furnished in the richest and most elegant manner. A man of great taste and judgement should be consulted and if any additional rooms can be built without spoiling or darkening the others you have my consent for erecting them. I do empower you to make the house at Berkeley Square as fine and convenient as you please.

More remarkable in this letter was the account he gave of his work in India and of his satisfaction with it. He wrote:

> I have the testimony of a good conscience to support me in the most arduous task that ever was undertaken, no less than a total reformation of every branch of the civil and military departments. Never was such a scene of anarchy and confusion, bribery, corruption and extortion seen or heard of as has been exhibited in the

Bengal dominions for this year past especially. However, I have made a great progress towards demolishing these great and growing evils in which I have been admirably supported by an unanimous and public-spirited Committee.

At this time, he could not be sure about his position at home, because the Sulivan faction was still influential and active in London. So, anticipating the possibility that the Court of Directors might not support him, he wrote:

> If what I have already done and propose to do doth not convince the proprietors of the disinterestedness as well as integrity of my principles and of my resolution to exert my abilities to the utmost in defence of their property which has been very much sported with of late by men of as bad hearts as heads, I shall disdain in future throwing away one thought more on so ungrateful a society.

However, as has been seen, this never happened. But he still had to remain more than a year in India, and many difficulties and troubles still lay in store for him.

In his next letter, written on September 29 1765, he expressed his satisfaction at the defeat of Sulivan in the election of the directors in April. 'The *Fox* Capt. Hume', he wrote, 'has brought us the agreeable news of Mr Sulivan's total defeat. I feel no other satisfaction on that account than for the Company. Had that man been strong enough to continue the opposition he would have destroyed one of the grandest prospects that ever fell to the lot of a trading Company.' In politics, it must be remembered, the public motive can never be separated from the personal, because success in any public cause also means tangible or intangible profit for an individual. 'Causes, not persons,' is, truly, cant in politics.

With the same letter, however, he sent a box bound with tape and affixed with his seal, which contained jewellery worth 42,000 Arcot rupees. Among these were one big diamond ring, 2 fine ruby rings (these three valued at Rs 26,000), 22 loose diamonds and 103 loose pearls. In addition, he sent 11 bundles of fine muslins and shawls and 2 boxes of otto of rose (*itr*), from which he asked his wife to give a bottle of otto to Walsh.

In addition, he sent a very small horse and a smaller mare. The horse danced and capered very prettily, and Clive wondered whether it would be worthy to be accepted by the Prince of Wales. However he thought they themselves might raise a Lilliputian breed –'you yourself being of that breed yourself'.

The next letter was written four months later – on January 31

1766. In it he complained that he could not write a long letter because 'the public business has become a burthen to me'. He told her:

> If anything endangers my constitution it will be my close application to the desk. I am no longer walking about the room talking politics and dictating Persian letters to Nabobs, Rajah etc. I am no longer making preparations for campaigns and fighting. My whole time is taken up in introducing oeconomy and subordination among the civil servants, in reforming most notorious abuses, and sometimes when I am dar'd, challenged and compelled to do it, in detecting frauds and bringing to shame individuals.

His judgement on his fellow countrymen in Calcutta was severe.

> In short, I will pronounce Calcutta to be one of the most wicked places in the universe. Corruption, licentiousness and a want of principle seem to have possessed the minds of all the civil servants. By frequent bad examples they are grown callous, rapacious and luxurious beyond conception.

He went on to say that the incapacity and iniquity of some and the immaturity of others had obliged him to send for four civil servants from Madras. This had made the Calcutta men (as he put it) mutiny, but he declared: 'They shall be brought to reason and ruled with a rod of iron until I see a reformation in their principle and manners.'

He said he had undertaken a most disagreeable task, which his honour obliged him to go through with. He knew the price he was paying: 'I am become the slave of the Company and the detestation of individuals, and my constitution cannot bear it long. . . .'

However, he gave her the pleasant news of the marriage of General Carnac, and as the General was going home with his bride, Clive sent some presents for his wife: 'An abundance of curiosities, viz, a Hookkoo [gibbon], a gold bird [a golden pheasant?], a deer no bigger than a cat [mouse deer], etc, etc, with a chestfull of shawls, pictures, swords, and many other curiosities; also one pipe of Madeira and 15 tons of Brazil wood to make furniture for the Berkeley Square house.'

He was very happy at the account his wife had given him of their son and daughters, and enclosed a letter for his son (aged twelve and at Eton), in which he praised the style and grammar of the boy's letter and observed: 'You have laid the foundation of that knowledge which alone can make you the gentleman, and distinguish you from the herd of your fellow-creatures.' He advised him to follow the advice of his tutor and above all the instructions of his mother. He hoped 'her excellent example' would be his guide, and thus he would render himself 'truly worthy of that great fortune, which providence seems to have designed for you'.

In the next letter to his wife, which he wrote on March 20 1766, he told her that the 'brute of a captain' had refused absolutely to take the animals, except the 'hookoo', though he had paid him twelve hundred guineas for the passage and found all the liquor for the ship. He added that he was putting the finishing touches to the work he had undertaken, and at the same time thought it necessary to discourage expectations about any increase in his fortune. He wrote:

> My friends will be much mistaken if they expect I shall enlarge my fortune by this my last voyage to India. I would not have given up my family relations and connections for all the riches upon the face of the earth. Nothing but the public good and my own honour (which was at stake) could have induced me to undertake so odious and disagreeable a task as restoring tranquillity to these provinces and reforming the morals and principles of this abandoned settlement.

However, he was careful to add, 'although I shall not enlarge my own fortune, which indeed wants no addition, I have it in my power of serving others by giving to them the public and allowed advantages of my government'. He meant Strachey and the other members of his personal staff.

On April 24 1767, he wrote to his wife from the Cape of Good Hope, giving her the news of his serious illness in Calcutta (already quoted), and telling her that he would see her, his dearest wife, soon. But he was afraid as to whether his handwriting would be legible, because he had not 'set pen to paper for these five months past'.

On July 13 1767, Clive wrote from the *Britannia,* which was then near Portsmouth:

> I have just time to inform my dearest wife of my safe arrival in the Channel. . . . I propose dining with you tomorrow at Berkeley Square, and lest the good news should surprise you too much, have sent forward Messrs Strachey and Ingham who will arrive a few hours before Mun and Self.

Auld Lang Syne was regained with the happiness of personal

life. But it was also to bring public persecution. Clive was not Byron, and could not shake the dust of England off his feet. This was his basic mistake.

Note: I think I can give the name of the medicine given to Clive for his stomach trouble – and which brought him relief. It must have been this paste made from the wood and bark of an Indian tree called *Daru-haridra*: it is yellow in colour and is prescribed by the practitioners of Ayurvedic medicine. I can say from personal knowledge that it is very effective against dyspepsia and all kinds of hepatic troubles.

Chapter Twelve

The Lone Wolf

After the Return

The key of Clive's life in England, which had been established during his two previous stays, was restored as soon as he landed again in his country. He came to London on July 14 1767. On the twentieth Horace Walpole wrote to his friend Mann:

> Lord Clive is arrived, has brought a million for himself, two diamond drops worth twelve thousand pounds for the Queen, a scimitar, dagger, and other matters covered with brilliants for the King, and worth twenty-four thousand more. These *baubles* are presents from the deposed and imprisoned Mogul, whose poverty can still afford to give such bribes. Lord Clive refused some overplus [surplus], and gave it some widows of officers: it amounted to ninety thousand pounds.

After this followed a Horatian comment on Clive's political work in India:

> He has reduced the appointments of the Governor of Bengal to thirty-two thousand pounds a year; and what is better has left such a chain of forts and distribution of troops as will entirely secure possession of the country – till we lose it. Thus having composed the Eastern and Western worlds, we are at leisure to kick and cuff for our little island, which is great satisfaction.

He had commented even earlier, when the news of the *diwani* reached England, in a letter to Mann: 'Lord Clive has just sent us the whole kingdom of Bengal, which the Great Mogul has yielded to this little Great Mogul without a blow. . . . East India stock has risen 10 p.c.'

George Grenville, with whom Clive was in close touch during his previous stay in England, wrote at once with the object of re-establishing the old tie. Writing on July 19 from Wotton near Thame, he informed Clive that if he came to town he himself would be extremely glad to wait on him, but if Clive was going to the country he would feel it a great honour if Clive would take in Wotton on his way.

Grenville, the creator of the troubles with the American colonies, had not changed his opinion on this issue. He told Clive: 'I think that the sovereignty of Great Britain over its colonies which is now manifestly destroyed, must be asserted and established, and for that purpose an administration should be formed which should include as much ability, credit, and authority as is possible to make it permanent.' He further assured Clive that his object was only the public good and no personal pretension of his was to stand in the way. In doing so he paid a very handsome compliment to Clive. 'I hope,' the one-time prime minister wrote to Clive, the retired servant of the East India Company, 'my conduct and sentiments will meet with your approbation, at least I can truly say that I have not consulted any interest of my own in them and so far I wish to follow your example.'

On July 20, Clive was informed by the Duke of Grafton that he had sent directions to the customs authorities that the presents that Clive wished to give to the King should be sent directly from the ship to his house in Berkeley Square, where a customs official was to examine them.

Three days later Clive had a private audience with George III and the Queen, and gave to the latter the presents from Muhammad Ali, Nawab of the Carnatic. He informed Verelst that he was in the Queen's closet nearly an hour, and she had promised to write to the Nawab in the most gracious manner. Already, within two days of his arrival in England, Clive had formally met the Court of Directors, and the chairman in their name had congratulated him on his return to his native country and thanked him for his services.

But his relations with the directors were not happy or smooth. During the six months following his return he remained in touch with them. The most urgent question discussed was concerned with the reorganization of the Company's forces and the remuneration of the officers, and the Salt Company. There was some delay in adopting the military proposals, but the use of the profits of the salt trade for giving additional income to the servants of the Company was wholly disapproved of. Clive felt strongly on both questions, and especially about the salt trade. The legacy from Mir Jafar to Clive and the creation of the fund for helping soldiers' families were also approved of, and his jaghir was extended for a period of ten more years after the expiry of the current term. Clive was informed of the decision about the jaghir on November 4 1767.

But Clive felt dissatisfied with the manner in which both the decisions were taken. In regard to the legacy, the difference between him and the Court of Directors was on a point of form. The directors thought that the acceptance of the legacy required their consent, whereas Clive maintained that it did not, because at the time the legacy was given (February 1765) he was at sea and had neither received any salary from the Company nor signed the covenant. This dispute, trivial as it was, was referred to the legal authorities, and it was only in 1770, after the Attorney-General had given the decision that Clive was entitled to the legacy without the consent of the directors, that the fund was formally constituted by a deed of agreement between him and the Company.

The extension of the jaghir was recommended by the Court of Proprietors in March 1767, but Clive felt dissatisfied that the majority for the decision was only twenty-five. Even when on September 23 the General Court approved of it unanimously he quarrelled with the directors because they had not recommended it. There were reasons for this – the directors and the proprietors were not on good terms with one another for other reasons, and the former knew that it would not be desirable that they should show themselves too decided to oblige Clive. But Clive set it down to the illwill or jealousy of the directors.

When Scrafton tried to mollify him by telling him how the directors had supported him in his work in Bengal, he replied angrily (October 6), accusing them of 'rank infernal jealousy and envy, to conceal and lessen my services'. He told Scrafton that the directors could not have done otherwise without suffering in their reputation or even quitting the directorship – for, he asked: 'Whose interest contributed to make them Directors, and keep them so?' Then he broke out in defiance and denunciation:

> My conduct wanted no support, it supported itself, because it was disinterested, and tended to nothing but the public good. From the beginning it put all mankind at defiance, as it does at this hour: and had the Court of Directors thought fit to make my conduct more public than they have done, all impartial and disinterested men must have done me justice. However, that remains for myself to make known, when convenient and proper.

Even when the jaghir had been formally extended, he complained to Verelst in Bengal against the directors in a letter written on November 7:

Indeed, their whole conduct towards me and my associates in Committee has shown weakness, or something worse; for they have upon all occasions endeavoured to lessen the acquisitions we have obtained for them, and kept everything that might contribute to our reputation as secret as possible; and if Parliament had not brought our transactions to light, mankind would have been ignorant of what has been done. In short, they appear very envious and jealous of my influence, and give ear to every idle story of my being hostile towards them.

He quarrelled with them even when they asked his advice on questions of policy, and wrote in the same letter: 'They have even asked my opinion upon their affairs in such a mean, sneaking manner, that I have informed one of them, unless I am applied to in form, and unless more attention be paid to my advice, I shall decline giving any whatsoever.'

Behind all this petulance, there was involved not only his innate but abnormally sensitive *amour propre*, but also the irritability produced by continuing illness. He had renewed attacks from August 1767 onwards, and had to go to Bath. In October he was so ill that Horace Walpole wrote to a friend: 'Lord Clive is going before his money, and not likely to live three months.'

His condition grew worse, so that he had to give up the plans for parliamentary activity suggested to him by George Grenville in December and to inform him that he was asked to go abroad for the sake of his health. He wrote on December 28 1767:

> The relapses of my disorder are so frequent and dangerous, that Dr Moysey insists upon my making all possible haste to a more temperate climate, and I have accordingly determined to set out in a week or two for the south of France and Italy. This journey I am frankly told is the only chance I have for a perfect recovery.

So early in January Clive left England for France accompanied by his wife, brother-in-law, Strachey and Ingham. The change brought about an immediate improvement, and he wrote to Verelst on February 9 1768: 'By the time I have spent a few months in the south of France, and drank the waters of Spa, I doubt not of enjoying a better state of health than I have done for some years.' He did not return to England till September 1768.

From the time of his return from France to the end of 1771 Clive was not particularly active in public life, though as a Member of Parliament he spoke on Indian questions and also took an interest in the affairs of the Company. But it was during this period that a situation was developing both within the Company and in its relations with the British Government which made possible the attacks on him in 1772–73. The incubation of the troubles will be described presently. Here it is necessary to note that in regard to India he was getting into a mood of despair, which made him think of giving up public life altogether.

For instance, on February 10 1769, Clive wrote to Claud Russell, a friend, then in Bengal: 'Our wide and extended possessions are become too great for the mother country, or for our abilities, to manage. America is making great strides towards independency; so is Ireland. The East Indies also, I think, cannot remain long to us, if our present constitution is not altered.'

He thought a director elected for only a year could not have the authority required to manage and govern such great possessions. As to the Government, he was very forthright:

> So far are our Ministers from thinking of some plan for securing this great and national object, that they think of nothing but the present moment, and of squeezing from the Company every shilling they have to spare, and even more than they can well spare, consistent with their present circumstances.

About a month later, he wrote to Sir Robert Barker:

> To tell you the truth, after the next general election, I find myself very disposed to withdraw myself from all public concerns whatever. My own happiness and that of my family is the only object I have in view, and that can only be obtained by retirement from the bustle and noise of a busy, debauched, and half-ruined nation.

A year later, in a letter written (February 15 1770) to Kelsall, another friend, he expressed even greater disillusion about the political outlook for Britain. 'I will not trouble you', he wrote, 'with the situation of affairs in England. Anarchy and confusion seem to have pervaded in every part of the British Empire. In vain can we expect our affairs to flourish abroad, when all is going to ruin at home.' In regard to himself, he wrote:

> Having struggled long enough against the tide to very little purpose, I am determined the approaching election shall put an end to my activity, in support of any set of men whatever. It is beyond my power to do the Company any farther service; and the disposition to ease and retirement gains ground upon me daily.

The death of George Grenville, with whom he was closely connected politically, on November 13 1770, made him still more indifferent to home politics. But he thought often of the future of the British possessions in India. His idea of maintaining them was set down in a letter to Warren Hastings written to him on August 1 1771, upon his appointment as governor of Bengal, in which he sent his congratulations as well as advice.

> The situation of affairs requires that you should be very circumspect and active. You are appointed Governor at a very critical time, when things are suspected to be almost at the worst, and when a general apprehension prevails of the mismanagement of the Company's affairs.
>
> The parliamentary inquiry has thrown the whole state of India before the public, and every man sees clearly, that as matters are now conducted abroad, the Company will not long be able to pay the £400,000 to Government. The late dreadful famine, or a war, either with Shuja-ud-Daulah, or the Marathas, will plunge us into still deeper distress. A discontented nation and a disappointed Minister will then call to account a weak and pusillanimous Court of Directors, who will turn the blow from themselves to their agents abroad; and the consequences must be ruinous both to the Company and the servants.

It was neither to legislation at home nor to any handling of Indian affairs from India House in London that he would look for salvation. He was emphatically of the opinion that what was required to save the British possessions in India was the character of the person in charge of them, together with the authority given to him. As to authority, he wrote:

> In the situation you see the necessity of exerting yourself in time, provided the Directors give you proper powers, without which, I confess, you can do nothing; for self-interest and ignorance will obstruct every plan you can form for the public good.

He was more emphatic on the need for certain personal qualities. He advised Hastings to be impartial and just to the public, regardless of the interest of individuals, to be resolute in executing all that he felt was necessary, not to be dependent on the opinion of others.

He warned Hastings that dangers would arise, and he must meet them with cheerfulness and confidence, never entertaining a thought of events miscarrying till the misfortune actually happened, and even then not to despair but to carry into execution schemes for retrieving affairs, always believing that time and perseverance would get the better of everything.

He was confident about the capacities and integrity of Hastings, but rather distrustful of his resolution. As he put it: 'I thought I discovered in you a diffidence in your own judgement and too great an easiness of disposition, which may subject you insensibly to be *led* where you ought to *guide*.'

He warned Hastings more especially against paying too great an attention to the reports of the natives, by which he might be inclined to look upon things in the worst instead of the best light. Finally, he said that, with confidence in himself, he hoped Hastings would make himself one of England's most distinguished characters.

Subsequent history was to prove that Hastings needed all this advice, but also that he was not himself lacking in resolution and tenacity. It was this which was to save the British Empire in India, and not the measures which were taken in 1773. But percipient as Clive was about the Indian question, he never suspected that, in the course of the debate that followed on Indian affairs, he would be personally indicted.

Government, Company and Clive

The first intimation that formal moves against him were afoot came to him in a letter dated January 7 1772, from the secretary to the Court of Directors. In it he was informed that the Company had lately received several papers containing charges against the management of the Company's affairs in Bengal in which Clive was implicated. Copies of these were sent to him and he was invited to offer his comments on them as expeditiously as was convenient to him.

Clive at once replied in his characteristic manner. First of all he said that he was not informed from whom these papers were received, nor what resolution the directors had taken on them, nor for what purpose he was asked to give his observations. As to the substance of the charges and their timing he said:

> I shall, however, observe to you, that upon the public records of the Company, where the whole of my conduct is stated, you may find a sufficient confutation of the charges which you have transmitted to me. And I cannot but suppose, that if any part of my conduct had been injurious to the service, contradictory to my engagements with the Company, or even mysterious to you, four years and a half, since my arrival in England, would not have elapsed, before your Duty would have impelled you to call me to account.

Clive here made a very cogent point, for the delay was in itself sufficient to establish as reasonable the assumption that the charges were put forward in bad faith and were meant to harm him. They were brought up because a situation had developed in respect of the Company's position both at home and in India which created an opportunity for Clive's personal enemies to attack him.

In the first place, after years of employing all the usual means, including split votes, to try and gain a majority in the General Court of Proprietors, Sulivan and his party at last came to power in the direction of the Company in 1769. They were joined by the civil and military employees of the Company who had been removed or punished by Clive during his second governorship and wanted to take their revenge on him. At their head was John Johnstone, the most corrupt and unscrupulous among them. They could not, however, do any actual harm to Clive because both he and his jaghir were now beyond the reach of the power of the directors. But they carried on an active campaign of slander and abuse in the press. To describe it in his own words: 'The public papers teemed with scurrility and abuse about me.' Much of it was believed.

For two years his enemies lay low in regard to active persecution. However, the opportunity came to them towards the end of 1771 when it became apparent that the Government was going to act in respect of the Company's affairs. Actually, by that time the Company's possessions in India had become a matter of public interest and concern second only to the trouble with the American colonies. Indeed, to the press in England, India and the misdeeds of the Company's agents there furnished more spicy material, on account of the stories of horror and scandal circulating widely.

The Company had, however, provided good reason for the Government's intervention. After Clive's departure from Bengal in 1767, there was a relapse into the conditions seen after 1760, though there were no new conflicts with the country's powers. The reason for the confusion and inefficiency was the same as before: weakness in the management in Calcutta. Clive attributed the deterioration to four causes: a relaxation of government under his successors; great neglect on the part of the administration; notorious misconduct on the part of the directors; and the violent and outrageous proceedings of the General Courts, of which contested elections were the main cause.

Clive had the greatest consideration for his successor Verelst, whom he believed to be a man of worth and honour. But he said, Verelst had too much humanity, and that was his ruin. In his diagnosis of the causes Clive was certainly right. Certainly, his own measures during 1765–66 had nothing to do with what followed.

Besides this general deterioration, there were two particular reasons for concern. There was a near collapse of the Company's financial position, in the course of which East India stocks declined so sharply in value that even Sulivan was almost ruined. Next, by the beginning of 1771 the news of the terrible famine in Bengal in the year 1769 began to reach England. Interested persons spread reports that the deaths from starvation and the suffering of the people were largely caused by the monopolies held by the Company's agents in the necessaries of life, including rice, and their determination to make money for themselves out of the shortage. Apart from these, books written by certain writers such as Bolts gave exaggerated accounts of the misuse of power and oppression by the Company's servants.

All this made the Government of Lord North ready to take measures to put the management of the Company's affairs both at home and in India on a sound footing by bringing them under the control of the Government. Already, under the ministry of Chatham in 1766 some form of intervention had begun after many decades of what might be described as untrammelled *laissez faire* for the Company. But the motive of that intervention was to get a share of the Company's increased profits from the grant of the *diwani*. By an agreement the Government then secured a tribute of £400,000 a year. There were also restrictions in minor matters like the rate of dividends. But by 1772 the Company found itself unable to give money, and even had to ask the Government for a large loan in order to escape bankruptcy.

This made the Company vulnerable and gave an opportunity for introducing measures for more thorough control. To avoid this Sulivan took the initiative in bringing in a bill for reordering the status of the Company at the beginning of 1772. But it was not found to be adequate. So a government measure was proposed, and after being discussed for months it became law as Lord North's Regulating Act in June 1773. It made the Company in effect a department of the State in the constitutional form of a controlled corporation.

Clive did not take an active part in the passing of this measure. In principle he had always been in favour of transferring the possessions of the Company in India to the State, and in so far as he spoke in Parliament on the question of government of the possessions he criticized both the Company and the directors.

There was, however, a strong body of opinion both in and outside Parliament which disapproved of the Government's interference with the rights of the Company. Of these, Burke was the most distinguished. He argued that the Government's claim infringed the rights of the Company as part of the fundamental right to property. Moreover, it was not only the Company but also the City of London and a dissenting group of peers in the Lords who took this view. In their first protest, signed on June 14 1773, these peers – thirteen in number, including the Dukes of Devonshire and Portland and the Marquis of Rockingham – concluded their protest with these words:

> If the provisions and precedent of this Bill should render the public faith of Great Britain of no estimation; the franchise, rights, and properties of Englishmen precarious . . .; if the boundless fund of corruption furnished by this Bill to servants of the Crown, should efface every idea of honour, public spirit, and independence from every rank of people, after struggling vainly against these evils, we have nothing left but the satisfaction of recording our names to posterity, as those who resisted the whole of this iniquitous system, and as men who had no share in betraying to blind prejudice or sordid interest every thing that has hitherto been held sacred in this country.

This would serve to show that even on the highest plane of principle it was possible for men who had no axe to grind to take different views of the right of the Government to take over the control of the East India Company. Neither politically nor morally was it as straightforward a question as is often assumed. It should not be overlooked that when the Crown finally took over the government of India in 1858 no less eminent a political thinker than John Stuart Mill was opposed to it.

Politics would have become a very much simpler and cleaner business if differences in it were confined to such opposition of principles, however sharp. But this is never the case. In politics all sorts of extraneous interests are involved and the rivalries and animosities they create form undercurrents almost as strong as the main current. The entire process of the British Government's relations with the Company from 1766 to 1784, when at last they became stabilized, was bedevilled by adventitious considerations which made everybody concerned with them incapable of taking any measure on its merits alone.

In consequence, the whole history of these events, and even the first legislation in 1773, had many strands. They were intermingled in so complex a pattern, and were so shot through and through with personal motivations and antagonisms, that it is quite impossible to summarize what happened in a short space. However, Clive was not involved inextricably in the complicated manoeuvres to get the Regulating Bill accepted. Those who are interested in this question as well as the detailed history of the relations between the Company and the Government from 1766 to 1784 should read Dr Lucy Sutherland's *East India Company in Eighteenth Century Politics*, published in 1952, which is a work of fundamental research. But a study of the book is likely to produce a shattering affect, on account of the bleakness of the subject, and to leave the reader with an impression that the beginnings of British rule in India were even more sordid than what the histories had shown it to be before the Namier school extracted all the pettiness from the documents.

But the main question of ensuring good administration for the Company's possessions had a side issue, and this is far more important for a biography of Clive than the Regulating Act. Through the legislative process of which a parliamentary inquiry was to form a part, Clive's enemies made an attempt to discredit him and even to deprive him of his wealth. There was no need to go into past history and open up all the things that had happened in Bengal since 1756 in order to remedy the evils that were facing the Company and the Government in 1772. Even if Clive's measures during his second governorship were relevant to the discussion, the facts of the overthrow of Siraj-ud-daula were not. But to deal simply with the present would have left the enemies of Clive without the means of attacking and harming him. In fact, so far as the group in power in the Company, as well as their parliamentary champions were concerned, no interest of theirs would have been served by extending the control of the Government over the Company. But they were out to persecute Clive, and for this it was necessary to throw open the past to an inquiry.

Colonel Burgoyne, who on April 13 1772 introduced the motion for the appointment of a Select Committee of the House of Commons to consider the affairs of the East India Company, was of course very conscious that his motives might be misunderstood; he therefore said upon rising: 'As a first step, and to remove at least any unfavourable impression that may be conceived of me, I shall beg leave to state to the House the motives and principles upon which I act.'

He disavowed personal motives, all hostility to the Company, or vindictiveness towards its servants, and put forward lofty principles. He argued that to push through a bill only on the 'present narrow and rotten system of Indian government must be a mere temporary expedient: a poor, paltry, wretched palliative'. Quoting *Hamlet* he declared:

It will but skin and film the ulcerous part,
While foul corruption mining all beneath
Infects unseen.

He also said: 'I never conceived it possible that parliament could be called upon by any man whatever, to apply a remedy without any information of the disease: to pass an act upon divination.' So he added that when he heard the notice given to bring in this bill and nothing else proposed, 'I considered the proceedings with astonishment'. He assured the House that he acted in this matter unconnected with any man whatever, unconcerned in every interest, unintentional in every purpose that might arise from it, other than a fair, a free, a direct, an impartial, a temperate but an effectual inquiry.

Others opposed the inquiry and among them Burke. When discretionary power, he said, is lodged in the hands of any man, or class of men, experience proves that it will always be abused. The directors had neither the time nor the capacity to make general regulations for the good government of so great an empire, and, even if they had, they could not enforce them from such a distance. Therefore they were obliged to leave discretionary power in the hands of the governors; and the governor who knew he did not derive any authority from law was forced occasionally to act the despot, and to terrify the refractory by the arm of power or violence. This, Burke declared, was the genuine source of that arbitrary conduct charged upon the late governors in Bengal. Where no laws exist, men must be arbitrary; and very necessary acts of government will often be, in such cases, represented by the interested and malevolent as instances of wanton oppression.

He blamed the Government for the failure in India.

> The East India Company is not punishable for not performing what no body of men in their circumstances ever did or will perform. It is the men who are at the helm of affairs, and who neglected, or wanted capacity and inclination to make the proper arrangements, that ought to be the objects of public and parliamentary vengeance.

He feared that those who had thus neglected their duty would now seek to make the Company and its servants their scapegoats. But he hoped that the House 'would have more sagacity than to suffer them to sacrifice a Byng or two to their own security'. His own recommendation was different:

> The evil has spread too widely to be probed to the bottom. A general amnesty or act of oblivion for what is past will be the most rational method of proceeding; as in a civil war, where a whole nation is engaged on either side, I would have mutual forgiveness to take place. Exact retribution for every irregularity would be the height of folly; it would only make the public wounds fester and rankle to an extreme.

Finally, he said that it was enough to provide good government for the future, and not discredit the Company which had added an empire to the possessions of Britain:

> Let the people of Bengal be not taught to despise them, by finding their authority limited and circumscribed . . . let us not check their growth by sinking them in the estimation of foreigners. . . . Hindostan should not know, that their legislature and the Company differ in opinion; but rather, that such harmony subsists between them as to render them in effect the same.

But the motion for a Select Committee was carried without a division. The moral issues raised were a convenient cover for the persecution of Clive, and there existed a state of opinion, both general and particular, which promised success for the campaign.

The Moral Situation
To describe the general aspect first. Just as the first decades of the reign of George III were a period of political disquiet and excitement, they also witnessed an almost panic-stricken moral anxiety. Its causes were many and varied, and cannot be gone into here. But the anxiety covered both public and private life. In the public sphere it made an unscrupulous adventurer like Wilkes popular, and created the appeal of an anonymous writer

like Junius who exhibited nothing but a negative rancour. In the private sphere it made people eagerly read and more than half believe the moral denunciation which the journalists and editors found it profitable to print. Some illustrations have to be given.

The *London Magazine* for 1772, for instance, published as its frontispiece an allegorical illustration of its own genius unmasking the Times – a hideous demon-like man in tightly fitted black clothes, bearing these legends all over the body: popularity, corruption, *bon ton,* bankruptcies, nabobships, continental history, state sharping, free will, bigotry, dearness of provisions, £200,000, prerogative, pension, patriotism, the drama, fraud, folly, crim. con.* From the crown of the figure's head flew a pennon, bearing the words, 'The fashions'. The list of vices, which included patriotism (perhaps on the strength of Dr Johnson's definition of it), was comprehensive, and beneath the illustration was an invocation:

Blest Genius! still be thine the arduous task;
From motley times to draw the iron mask.
On Errors eye to pour thy splendid ray –
And give the glories of eternal Day.

In the preface this moral mission was proclaimed in plain prose. 'A spirit is gone forth into the world which teems with evil affections,' the editor wrote. 'Its destructive influence is every where spread, and every where received. When we look around us, we seem to see only a scene of universal debauch. The doors of profligacy are unhinged, and morality seems overwhelmed in its own ruins.'

In this 'almost universal bankruptcy of good morals and good manners', the *London Magazine* felicitated itself 'on having continually stemmed the torrent of iniquity'. It declared: 'And yet we have painted the Times, and shall continue to paint them with a warm pencil.' This would cover not only political life, but, even more ruthlessly, private life and its vices. 'In our description of the foibles of Life, particularly those of the passions, we shall not suffer anything to escape us: if we attack too closely, let them blame themselves and mend their manners. We wound only to cure.'

The scalpel was to be used most resolutely on the festering

---

*It is significant that the cryptic 'crim. con.' was printed in a banner placed across the groin of the allegorical figure.

sore of sexual vice. 'The torch of unlawful Love,' the editor wrote, 'which now burns so fiercely, burns mostly in secret, and in darkness: it will be our business to snatch it forth into daylight, where it will expire itself.'

Not even the *Washington Post* in its exposure of the Watergate affair could be more determined than this magazine, and the editor was as good as his word. He published an article in which the writer said that his age was worse than the epoch of the Restoration.

> Nell Gwynn, though she was the loosest harlot in the king's bedchamber, was yet the modest lady in the drawing-room, and wore the chastest look in the circle. But *our* women, so distant are they from being ashamed of their follies, are sometimes the first to publish it; they glory in their infamy, and come forth in the fair face of day, with all those wanton and lascivious airs which they carried from the adulterer's arms.

The writer noticed with horror the tendency of the skirt to go up. Youthful rakes of the metropolis, he said, have already conceived the greatest hopes from this. The petticoat, which formerly 'dangled down to earth – so modest that it kissed the humble dust', was now two inches higher, almost past the ankle. He feared that it would rise as high as the mid-leg before the end of the next year. He even anticipated what sort of news would be published in the reign of George IV and gave an example:

> Yesterday noon at high-water, a young lady of fashion and fortune, for a bett of 500 guineas, leapt off Westminster Bridge into the river, naked, amidst a concourse of spectators.

The principal agents of all the adulteries, another writer said, were the men gynaecologists and obstetricians, 'men-midwives', as he called them. It was through ignorance, he said, that the husbands were asking their wives to go to them. 'They know not that they are removing the cornerstone on which the virtue of their wives is founded!' He went on to say that pregnant women would admit a man *to the most unbounded liberties* to find out how the child lay, and he asked; 'How did the dear man, sweet Dr —, find out how the child lay? – By means *sufficient to taint the purity*, and *fully the chastity* of any woman breathing!'

He did not think that women were safe even during labour, because, as he put it,

. . . even in actual labour, *a woman has many intervals of ease*, for many minutes together quite free from pain – *in those intervals*, her mind *cannot* maintain *its spotless whiteness* – *in those intervals*, her mind cannot but *be conscious*, that the DOCTOR *is infringing on* the HUSBAND.

Those who could swallow such stuff could not be expected to be critical about the slanders spread about Clive. In the very foreground was the stark fact that what he did in India set him at odds with his English environment. Just as Walpole's England could not have formed him, Lord North's could not accept him. The society of eighteenth-century England took its stand on its own concept of the *mos majorum* – ways of the ancestors – and no society that is conservative and traditional can tolerate the *novus homo*. Napoleon did not have to face that kind of hostility, at least not in an active and open form, only because in his age the ancient regime of France had been pushed out and France was all upstart. Augustus and his heirs had to feel the implacable hatred of the old patrician and senatorial order. They foiled that enemy by means of their political power. But Clive's achievements in India did not make him the emperor of the British Isles. So he had to end somewhat in the manner of Julius Caesar, instead of being able to send his freedman with a polite note to ask a senator to open his veins.

India made Clive a conquistador, and thus it also made him share the fate of other modern conquistadors, such as Cortes and Pizarro, or like Dupleix, who tried to become one but failed. These men alienated the established order at home by their exotic achievements and personalities, and so the full weight of the moral standards and outlooks of the order were brought to bear on them. They offended even by the unorthodoxy of their corrupt practices. English politics in the eighteenth century was corrupt and unprincipled enough, but it had established certain norms and conventions of corruption. Acts that went beyond them or were different shocked the conscience at home.

This natural and unavoidable antagonism was fed and exploited by another set of men. These were the less successful adventurers of the conquering people in the conquered countries, and lower in the hierarchy. They were envious of the more successful adventurers, but as they were often checked or even punished by the latter, they also returned to their countries with a sense of real injury, excited the prejudices of the home authorities, and furnished them with evidence of the misdeeds of the adventurers at the top. Pizarro was killed in Peru by the followers of a rival, but Cortes, Dupleix, Clive and Warren Hastings were persecuted by an alliance of the established order and the less successful adventurers.

The moral disapproval covered not only Clive and Hastings, but all adventurers from India, and along with them all the doings of the Company. It became all the more vocal because by this time Indian affairs had become a topic of great popular interest, and offered scope for both indignation and humour. The *London Magazine* wrote:

> [It might] not be amiss to relieve a little of the intenseness of thinking, by throwing together any pleasant stories, entertaining remarks, or witty conceits . . . with regard to that wonderful oriental empire, which this little island called Great Britain has by means of its skill and navigation, and other arts not so innocent, been able to appropriate to itself.

One line of witticism was to ridicule the pretensions of the merchants of Leadenhall Street, newly turned into rulers. One day Sir George Colebrooke, Chairman of the Court of Directors and a man with a diminutive priggish figure, made a very tedious speech in the House of Commons. After he had finished, Charles Townshend, noted for his brilliance, got up and said: 'Mr Speaker, we have heard a great deal from this lineal successor of Alexander the Great.' The physical contrast suggested by this set the whole House roaring with laughter.

But the indignation was not a less strong note. Barré said that more cruelties had been practised in India than even in Mexico. In giving an abstract of a new comedy called *The Nabob*, which was staged at the Haymarket theatre on June 29 1772, the *London Magazine* said that it was:

> . . . a pointed and judicious satire on the ill-regulated laws and conduct of a certain great trading Company, who depute servants and officers in their foreign settlements, armed with such unlimited powers, that they sacrifice their inferiors abroad to their tyranny and rapine, and on their return home treat those masters, who raised them to power and wealth, with the most extravagant insolence and pride.

When the news of the great famine of 1769 reached England, the public horror expressed, though perfectly creditable to the British people's moral sensibility, lost all sense of proportion. It is an extraordinary coincidence that both the beginning and end of British rule in India should have been marked by a terrible famine in Bengal. There is reason to believe that the famine of 1943 was largely man-made, but that of 1769 was a natural calamity. Yet even Horace Walpole with all his sophistication could write about it in the following manner. He wrote to Mann on March 2 1772:

> We have another scene coming to light of a black dye indeed. The groans of India have mounted to heaven, where the heaven-born General Lord Clive will certainly be disavowed. Oh my dear Sir, we have outdone the Spaniards in Peru! They were at least butchers on a religious principle, however diabolical their zeal. We have murdered, deposed, plundered, usurped – nay, what think you of the famine in Bengal, in which three millions perished, being caused by a monopoly of provisions, by the servants of the East India? All this is come out, is coming out – unless the gold that inspired these horrors can quash them. Voltaire says, learning, arts and philosophy have softened the manners of mankind; when tigers can read they may possibly grow tame – but man!

In this surprisingly emotional outburst from Horace Walpole is to be seen the influence of the libels that were being spread about Clive in the journals and magazines. The following letter by an anonymous writer, describing himself as an officer who had lately served in Bengal, was published in the February 1772 issue of the *Gentleman's Magazine*:

> In the year 1765, when the *Prince* and *Father* of *Nabobs*, whose nod, like that which shakes Olympus, could destroy the inhabitants of the earth, shook his awful brow, and said, 'let there be a monopoly of the necessaries of life, for the benefit of my family and friends,' he signed the death warrant for two millions of his fellow-creatures. And when he said, 'Let the coin be adulterated,' he issued an order for depopulating three thousand villages!

The officer added that he knew Bengal well; it was once a paradise on earth, but was now a forest where tigers roared and jackals howled. Such charges were believed, for the readiness to do so existed.

The general inclination to believe the worst about British rule in India and about those who carried it on was strengthened by the life and conduct of the nabobs, that is, the servants of the Company who were returning to their country with immense wealth gained within a few years. Nobody likes the neighbour who becomes a millionaire before there has been time to notice that he is getting rich, and if his behaviour is vulgarly ostentatious the dislike becomes active. The nabobs certainly did their best to become hated.

There is no more vivid description of the attitude of all classes of people in England towards these upstarts than in the essay of Macaulay on Clive. Anyone interested in the last act of Clive's life must read those pages. Macaulay had his heightened way of telling things, but about the nabobs his rhetoric in no way distorted the truth. On the contrary, it may be said that, rather, it laid a coat of undeserved literary varnish on the vulgarity and garishness of their lives.

'Wherever they settled,' says Macaulay, 'there was a kind of feud between them and the old nobility and gentry.' They made themselves obnoxious not only to these classes, but also to their own, (i.e. the commercial classes) – in England. To quote Macaulay's very words:

> The humane man was horror-struck at the way in which they had got their money, the thrifty man at the way in which they spent it. The Dilettante sneered at their want of taste. The Maccaroni blackballed them as vulgar fellows. Writers, the most unlike in sentiment and style, Methodists and libertines, philosophers and buffoons, were for once on the same side. It is hardly too much to say that, during a space of thirty years, the whole lighter literature of England was coloured by the feelings we [Macaulay] have described.

He gave an instance of two writers, Foote and Mackenzie. The chief character of Foote's comedy called *The Nabob* is an East Indian, Sir Matthew Mite, who proposes a marriage between his son and the daughter of a country gentleman named Sir John Oldham, offering a settlement of five lakhs of rupees and a jaghir. Lady Oldham is furious, but becomes pacified when she is told that the Nabob would also give her £10,000. The Nabob is shown in his house in his silk nightgown, gambling, surrounded by bad characters including a bawd, Mrs Match'em. Finally, the marriage does not come off, and the Nabob retires in disappointment and rage. Anything more insipid could hardly be written, but its topicality made it not only popular but admired. Foote proudly declared that he did not write to stand the test of serious criticism 'to be squared by the formal rules of Aristotle, or the stiffer refinements of his commentators and scholiasts, but only to give the public what they wanted from him – laughter'. He added that he was more ambitious for present than future fame, unawed by critics and unshackled by art. The reviewer of the play in the *London Magazine* suggested that the character of the Nabob, Sir Matthew Mite, was 'formed of a complex idea, and that two important personages are included in it'. One was a certain lord and the other a certain general. The lord was, of course, Clive.

This, though grotesquely inapplicable to Clive as he was, could be accepted as plausible by the general public. Even the most well-informed and educated circles in England were ignorant about what was really happening in India and of Clive's real achievements. They saw only the general run of nabobs, and in Clive saw the nabob *par excellence*.

Thus all the slanders spread about him stuck, and people of all ranks were ready to believe the worst of him. Even his creation of the fund for the soldiers and their families out of the legacy of Mir Jafar was the subject of dark hints. In the Royal Academy exhibition of 1772 an allegorical picture of this charity was shown, and it evoked both attention and appreciation. But a Member of Parliament well known for his wit and lively sallies, being, as the contemporary report put it, 'in company not a mile from Arlington Street [Horace Walpole's street], where great encomiums were passing on the subject of the picture, observed with a significant turn: "I am afraid that affair will not bear to be *canvassed*"'. The comment on this witticism was: 'This gentleman perhaps viewed the matter with too much *shade*, because at the last [1768] general election, it is believed he was opposed in *his canvass* by Lord Clive.' This MP must have been Barré. Clive's acquisitions were, of course, seen as sinister. For instance, Lady Mary Coke, who (as will be seen later) recorded the death of Clive with great sympathy and natural awe, set down, when she first heard the rumour, that Clive may have committed suicide out of horror, 'which reasonably one should have supposed would have made him dread death instead of seeking it'.

In 1779, in the course of a conversation, Dr Johnson told the story of Capability Brown's visit to Clive's house. Brown was shown a large chest at the door of his bedroom by Clive himself, who said that he had once had it full of gold. Upon this Brown observed: 'I am glad you can bear it so near your bed-chamber.'

Macaulay wrote in his essay that he himself had heard old men, who knew nothing of Clive's history, talk of him as a fiend incarnate. He also wrote that the peasants of Surrey looked with mysterious horror on the stately house which Clive was building at Claremont and whispered that the great wicked Lord had ordered the walls to be made thick in order to keep out the devil, who would one day carry him bodily away.

It is easy to establish the affiliation of these ideas with the old European stories of compacts with the devil for some worldly prize and position, which in their turn were complementary to the temptation of Jesus in the Bible. It would seem that popular imagination raised Clive to the dubious status of a man who had sold his soul to the devil for money.

Clive, people believed, had entered into such a compact. When a man acquires this stature in the popular imagination, an attack on him in Parliament by his enemies can only be a prosaic item in the legend. There are, however, two surprising things in the affair – that the House of Commons absolved Clive in spite of this, and that historians have, on the contrary, been taken in.

Dieu et mon Droit: Honi Soit qui Mal y Pense

Clive did not wait to be formally attacked to begin his defence of himself. When Sulivan's Bill was introduced on March 30 1772, Clive rose to speak on it after Sulivan, Cornwall and Rumbold. He did not, in fact, speak on the Bill at all, but defended himself against the accusation brought forward in the papers. First of all he explained the necessity for an apologia.

> With what confidence can I venture to give my sentiments upon a subject of such national importance, who myself stand charged with having been the cause of the present melancholy situation of the Company's affairs in Bengal? This House can have no reliance on my opinion, whilst such an impression remains unresolved.

So he asked the House to give him leave to remove the impression, and he hoped that he would be able to restore himself to the favourable opinion which the House entertained of him before these charges were made against him. But in so doing he intended to address himself not only to the House, but to a wider audience. 'I speak likewise', he declared, 'to my Country in general, upon whom I put myself, not only without reluctance, but with alacrity.' His speech was considered to be very honourable, and when, on account of the speech's length, he wanted to put off what more he had to say for a future occasion, there were cries of 'Go on. Go on.'

Throughout these troubles Clive maintained an unapologetic and defiant attitude, without caring whether he was carrying his listeners with him or not. To give one example, in his very last speech in the House of Commons in self-defence he said: 'I have a conscious innocence within me that tells me my conduct is irreproachable. *Frangas non flectes*.' (You will break but not bend.)

Those who were attacking Clive maintained that restitution to the public was the great object they had in view. And in fact, in adopting the two general principles applicable to the British possessions in India, namely, that all acquisitions made by means of military force or by treaties with foreign princes did of right belong to the State, and that to appropriate any part of those gains was illegal, the House of Commons did give some weight to the charges made against individuals.

But when it came to the question of punishing Clive, the general opinion was that after the great services rendered by him to the State and his quiet enjoyment of his great fortune for such a long time, it would be unjust to try to deprive him of honour and wealth by a strict and severe retrospective inquiry into the past.

Against this the accusers said that in criminal matters there was no limitation of time; and that the idea of a *set-off* of services against offence was trivial and illegal. It was further argued that it would be a gross mockery of the resolutions of the committee that had investigated embezzlement of money and other offences if those who were guilty were suffered to escape. Furthermore, it was said that Lord Clive was the oldest if not the principal delinquent and had set an evil example; so to punish those who had only followed and not those who had set the example would be gross injustice and an indemnity to the whole corps of delinquents.

All this emphasized the personal motivation of the attack. No less significant was the fact that, in considering the question of personal guilt, the House of Commons would not admit the reports of the parliamentary committee which was set up originally on the grounds of public interest. At enormous expense in time and labour the committee had gone into all the details of the establishment of British power in India since 1756, and set down the facts and its conclusions in nine reports covering in all 763 large folio pages and presented over seven months. All this was rejected on the grounds that the witnesses were personal and principal actors in the affairs and were under no guard in respect of their testimonies, so that these could not be relied on for judicial proceedings in Parliament. Moreover, the discussion of the conduct of individuals did not influence the drafting of Lord North's Regulating Bill. In fact, in the course of the debate on the Third Report of the Secret Committee on the Company's affairs on March 30 1773, Lord North 'disclaimed the thought of accusing, even in idea, any particular person'. He said:

> The reports now before the House contained matter which might serve for a ground of enquiry; and though accusations might be inferred from them, he would yet not permit himself to accuse a single individual, how mean or exalted soever.

This should be enough to establish the purely personal motivation of the attack on Clive. When dealing with such affairs in history it is necessary to keep in mind that moral issues are hardly ever raised in politics without the instigation of personal enemies. It was so with Aristides, Themistocles and Pericles; it was so with Scipio Africanus; it was so with President Nixon; and Clive's case was no exception. Politics in itself is an amoral struggle for power between individuals, parties, social classes or nations. But men in general do not like to kill or burn fellow-men except for conscience's sake. They are too afraid of naked power to be able to see a struggle for power or self-interest for what it is. So such conflicts have to be given a moral colouring. This gives politicians their chance, and among them, as a rule, morality like patriotism becomes the last refuge of the scoundrel.

There is, however, a broader historical aspect of the personal attack on Clive, which makes it part of the political life of the times, and one particular feature of a whole political scene. What has escaped historians in considering the domestic and the foreign side of English politics from the middle of the eighteenth century to the outbreak of the French Revolution is a paradoxical correlation between the two sides. There is, on the one side, an unedifying political situation in which no great political idea and no far-seeing statesmanship are seen to be at work, but in which personal rivalries are carried on to the accompaniment of clamour about corruption; there are claims from everybody that they stand for the public good, when really pursuing self-interest and seeking personal power. Against this is seen an impersonal and relentless pressure towards external expansion, natural and irresistible in the stage of evolution reached by the nation, and yet hampered and obstructed either by the vagaries of domestic politics or by public opinion shaped by traditions which have become obsolescent. Such an opposition between the internal political life and the external self-assertion of a nation seems to be the historical swaddling clothes of young empires. This was seen in Roman history from the end of the second Carthaginian war to the establishment of the Principate. It is again being seen in contemporary American history. In fact, the similarity between the situation of the American people today and the British people in the days of the acquisition of India and their loss of the American colonies is extraordinary. It is analogous even to the point of providing the press with the same sort of zeal in promoting the public good and its own circulation at the same time. Not to take into account the wider aspects of the career of Clive is to confine oneself to a narrow view and surrender naïvely to unconsciously held preconceptions.

To come back to Clive. When he went half-way towards meeting the intended attack on the measures of his second governorship, and refuted them with facts and strong arguments before they were put forward in Parliament, his enemies shifted their ground and concentrated on the period of the conflict with Siraj-ud-daula, on which different views could be held by non-party men. There can be no doubt that the leading spirits behind the campaign were John Johnstone and Sulivan, helped by the former servants of the Company with a grievance against Clive. But though they were closely in touch with Governor Johnstone, John's brother, who spoke against Clive on every possible occasion and most vehemently, they were not so unintelligent as to entrust the major role in the campaign to a member who was bound to be regarded as a mere partisan. So the leading role was given to Burgoyne, who was supported by men like Sir William Meredith and Colonel Barré. All of them could be considered independent.

Colonel Burgoyne, who was later to acquire fame for his surrender to Gates at Saratoga in the course of the American War of Independence, was the son-in-law of the Earl of Derby, but he was impecunious. He wished to be regarded as a man of fashion and of wit, and a writer. But he was not considered a good speaker. Horace Walpole called him a pompous man, whose speeches were studied but not striking, and who had more reading than parts. The second colonel, Isaac Barré, was almost the *ex officio* wit of the House of Commons. He was a dark, robust, hard-favoured man with a military figure, but he commanded a classic and eloquent diction, and was so aggressive that he was called a bravo. Sir William Meredith was a steady man, with an inflexibly serious temperament and a weighty manner of speaking. But Walpole said that he had no clear head. Being an honest man with views of his own he was disposed to be scornful of those who did not agree with him and whom he supposed to be less honest. Thus all three speakers against Clive could be regarded as parliamentary gladiators, rather than as moral crusaders.

Their style of speaking was also consistent with their role. In those days parliamentary speaking was much more literary, and while Burgoyne quoted *Hamlet,* Sir William Meredith cited *Paradise Lost.* Speaking of the horrors seen in Bengal, Sir William said:

> The reports on your table, voluminous as they are, if I may use the words of our great poet, give
>
> No light – but rather darkness visible
> Serves only to discover sights of woe.
>
> How we came by this territory may God forgive! But believing there is a God above us, I believe also, that acquisitions made by shedding the blood of innocent princes [Siraj?], and by wringing from an innocent people their substance, can never prosper.

In dealing with the misdeeds of the governors of foreign territories it was impossible that any parliamentary orator in England of those days would not quote from the Verrine orations of Cicero. Sir William quoted him twice and described what Verres would have done had he lived in his time. He had been contented with only a quarter of his ill-gotten gains, but he needed three-quarters more: one to bribe the leading senators, one to engage the greatest lawyers and the most famous orators, and another to be distributed among the common senators – such, Sir William explained, as 'we should call nowadays the dumb votes of the House'. But had he lived in England he would have employed his money better: 'He might have added parliamentary influence to the influence of money. He might have bought boroughs, and got an interest within these walls, that might have controuled this very House of Commons, and perhaps the legislature itself.'*

The preliminary attacks on Clive were made in the sessions of the committee presided over by Colonel Burgoyne. Clive was summoned before the committee, questioned and cross-examined in the manner described by him later in his speech

*Embroidered on *In Verrem,* I–14:40.

before the House on May 3 1773, in connection with the resolutions moved by Lord North for the regulation of the Company's affairs. He said:

> Not a stone has been left unturned, where the least probability could arise of discovering something of a criminal nature against me. The two Committees [Select and Secret], Sir, seem to have bent the whole of their enquiries to the conduct of their humble servant the Baron of Plassey; and I have been examined by the Select Committee more like a sheep-stealer than a member of this House. I am sure, Sir, if I had any sore places about me, they would have been found; they have probed to the bottom; no lenient plaisters have been applied to heal: no, Sir, they were all of the blister kind, prepared with Spanish flies, and other provocatives.

He closed his statement with a sally which made the House burst into applause and remain in a paroxysm of laughter for nearly ten minutes.

> The public records have been ransacked for proofs against me; and the late deputy chairman of the India Company, a worthy member of this House [Sulivan], has been very assiduous indeed, so assiduous in my affairs, that really, Sir, it appears he has entirely neglected his own. As the heads upon Temple Bar have tumbled down, and as there appears no probability of their being replaced, for Jacobitism seems at an end, at least there has been great alteration in men's sentiments within these ten years; I would propose, Sir, that my head, by way of pre-eminence, should be put upon the middle pole; and his Majesty having given me these honours, it is proper they should be supported: What think you then of my having the late chairman and deputy chairman on each side?

It was to this committee that Clive made the defiant statement about Omichand and also his famous assertion of moderation, which was as follows:

> Am I not rather deserving of praise for the moderation which marked my proceedings? Consider the situation in which the victory at Plassey had placed me. A great prince was dependent on my pleasure; an opulent city lay at my mercy; its richest bankers bid against each other for my smiles; I walked through vaults which were thrown open to me alone, piled on either hand with gold and jewels! Mr Chairman, at this moment I stand astonished at my own moderation!

Anyone who knows anything about the opportunities offered in India during imperial interregnums for amassing wealth merely by being in a position of power will accept Clive's claim to moderation. In these days, especially, it would be sheer hypocrisy or ignorance to sneer at Clive's astonishment at his own moderation, or to say that he had less right to be so astonished than has an English politician or businessman if he restricts himself only to a few professional call-girls and does not 'cultivate' every woman he meets in every conceivable situation.

The formal parliamentary attack on Clive was made on May 10 1773, in a motion from Colonel Burgoyne on Clive's conduct in India; the long debate ended on May 21. Burgoyne opened the debate by saying that the reports of the committees contained accounts of crimes which would have shocked human nature even to conceive. He said that he looked upon the deposing of Siraj and the installation of Mir Jafar as the origin of all the subsequent evils. He became expansive over the perfidy towards Omichand, and closed his speech by declaring that perfidy to be of the blackest dye.

The vote of the House on this motion was free. So the ministers voted differently according to their personal convictions. Lord North even objected when Colonel Barré called him a minister. He said that the Colonel had no right to do so, because he knew of no right of any gentleman to call him minister, but that he sat in that House as a Member of Parliament, in which light alone he desired to be considered in the course of the East India business.

Even on the first day it became apparent that the motion of censure was not likely to go through. Gibbon, engaged on his history but not yet a member of the House, wrote to his friend Holroyd (the future Lord Sheffield) on the eleventh: 'The hounds go out again next Friday. They are in high spirits; but the more sagacious ones have no idea they shall kill.'

When the debate was resumed on the nineteenth Clive spoke and justified himself, and ended his speech with the following remarks on the real aim of those who wanted to censure him.

> I cannot say that I either sit or rest easy when I find by the extensive Resolution proposed, that all I have in the world is to be confiscated, and that no one will henceforward take my security for a shilling. These, Sir, are dreadful apprehensions to remain under, and I cannot look upon myself but as a bankrupt.... I have not anything left which I can call my own, except my paternal fortune, of £500 per annum, and which has been in the family for ages past. But upon

this I am content to live, and perhaps I shall find more real content of mind and happiness therein than in trembling affluence of unsettled fortune.

He then threw out a challenge:

They may take from me what I have, they may as they think, make me poor, but I will be happy. I mean not this as my defence, though I have done for the present. My defence will be made at that bar, and before I sit down, I have one request to make to the House. That when they come to decide upon my honour, they will not forget their own.

If those who were attacking him thought that the sick lion could be kicked with impunity by the ass, they were mistaken. On that day and throughout that year of attack Clive again showed the spirit he had displayed at the siege of Arcot.

On May 21 1773, the first part of Burgoyne's motion, that Clive had received a large sum of money, was accepted, but omitting the words 'through the influence of the powers with which he was entrusted as a member of the Select Committee and commander-in-chief of the British forces'.

But as to the second part, which censured him in these words: 'That Robert lord Clive, did, in so doing abuse the power with which he was entrusted, to the evil example of the servants of the public', it was rejected, and an amendment, proposed by the Solicitor-General, carried without a division. It was this: 'That Robert lord Clive did, at the same time, render great and meritorious services to this country'. The time was four o'clock in the morning. But for Clive the rest of his life was a gloaming.

The Aftermath

Comments of two contemporaries on the outcome of the debate on the conduct of Clive have to be quoted as illustrating the basic difference in the attitudes even of men who had no motive for taking sides.

The opinion of those seriously interested in the political aspect of the matter was expressed by Burke. On May 22 1773, writing to Charles O'Hara, he said:

Lord Clive has thus come out of the fiery Trial, much brighter than he went into it. His gains are now recorded; and not only not condemned, but actually approved by parliament. His reputation for ability stands higher than ever.

In contrast, Horace Walpole spoke for the cynics, who also

stood in the line of the moral tradition bearing on politics. A week after the end of the debate Walpole wrote to Madame du Deffand:

> On a voulu faire le procès à Milord Clive. Il s'est glorifié de ses forfaits et on l'a renvoyé absous. C'est permettre tous les abus et on veut ôter le domaine à la Compagnie à cause des abus. Voilà comme nous somme consequents.

The next day – May 29 1773 – he wrote again, this time to his friend Mann:

> I told you the attack on Lord Clive has begun: oh, he is as white as snow. He has owned all, and Machiavel would be the first to acquit him – for he pleaded supreme policy as his motive. The House of Commons have been of Machiavel's opinion. The censure was rejected, and even a vote of applause passed. Cortez and his captains were not more spotless heroes.

All this was as typical of the English conscience of the age, with its seasoning of irony, as it was unrealistic, uninformed and irrelevant as political judgement. The House of Commons of the day showed no inconsistency in absolving Clive and at the same time proceeding with the measure for greater control over the East India Company. To Walpole one might say: *On ne badine pas avec l'amour ni avec l'empire non plus.*

Macaulay regarded the result of the inquiry on Clive as being on the whole honourable to the justice, moderation and discernment of the Commons. In this matter, he added, they had no great temptation to do wrong, for the question respecting Clive was not a party question. Accordingly, he said, the House acted with the good sense and good feeling which may always be expected from an assembly of English gentlemen not blinded by faction.

Macaulay contrasted the equitable and temperate proceedings of the British parliament with the mean and cruel treatment by the government of Louis XV of the Frenchmen who had served their country with distinction in the East. He added that the government had murdered them, directly or indirectly. 'The Commons of England, on the other hand, treated their living captain with that discriminating justice which is seldom shown except to the dead.' That treatment was summed up by Macaulay in the following words: 'They laid down sound general principles; they delicately pointed out where he had deviated from those principles; and they tempered the gentle censure with liberal eulogy.'

This was true so far as it went, but it did not go to the root of the matter. The majority in the House of Commons was virtuous only because it was necessary to be so. Perhaps they felt, rather than consciously realized, the seriousness of the challenge which Clive had thrown out to them by asking them not to forget their own honour when deciding upon his – a challenge which to them had a broader meaning than Clive's.

The plain issue was whether they could condemn Clive without condemning the very establishment of British power in India, which by the same moral standards that were at that moment being applied to Clive's conduct was naked aggression and usurpation, if not robbery. The East India Company had no more right to go to war with Siraj, instal Mir Jafar in his place, dethrone Mir Jafar, give the throne to Mir Qasim, go to war with Mir Qasim and restore Mir Jafar to the throne than Clive had to receive money from Mir Jafar. His misdeeds, if there were any in reality, were inconsequential and minor, compared with those of the Company. England could not retain the stolen goods if they called Clive a thief. But it must be said for the attitude of the disinterested British moralists that they did regard the acquisition of an empire in India as usurpation. This current of thought never died, and helped in the abandonment of the Empire in 1947.

Clive himself felt that he had been vindicated by the House of Commons, and wrote to Warren Hastings on October 14 1773.

> A few envious and resentful individuals turned the whole attack upon me, and aimed the ruin of my fortune and reputation. But the justice of the House of Commons defeated their intentions, and by a great majority passed a vote that I rendered great and essential services to this Country.

At this point it is necessary to put the Act of 1773 as well as the inquiry on Clive in their historical perspective, for both of these have a bearing on any interpretation that may be offered of the actions and achievements of Clive in India. On the one hand, it has been maintained that Lord North's Regulating Act inaugurated an efficient and well-regulated government for the British possessions in India; and on the other it has been said that the searching inquiry into Clive's personal conduct, followed by the trial of Warren Hastings, ensured the purity of administration there. Both ideas are unfounded.

Certainly, Lord North's Act transferred the ultimate sovereignty over the British possessions in India to the State, and the Company became, so to speak, the executor of the 'will'. This is correct, and owing to this and the system of control introduced by the Act, the government of the possessions was freed from the internal rivalries of the proprietors and the pressures of their private monetary interests. In other words, the Act regularized the existence of the Empire in India, and brought it within the constitutional structure of the British polity.

But it did not secure a more efficient and sound government in India. On the contrary, it put into operation a system so unworkable that, in order to carry on his administration and the wars, Warren Hastings was compelled to resort to means to which Clive never descended. Clive did not practise the tortuous intrigues of Hastings, nor did he present the undignified spectacle of the head of the British government in India fighting a duel with a colleague. Besides, there was such high-handedness, accompanied by irregularities, that Hastings was tried in a formal manner. In short, it might be said that Lord North's Act transferred the squalor in the higher levels of the direction of the political affairs of the Company from London to Calcutta.

This called for a new measure, and Pitt supplied this in his Act of 1784. Even that was not satisfactory, and had to be amended in 1786 in order to make British administration in India truly effective. The basic condition of this was absolute authority for the governor-general, which Clive exercised *de facto*, but not *de jure*.

Lord Cornwallis refused to accept the office until he was given that authority by legislation, and in addition he insisted that in emergencies the governor-general should also be empowered to assume the office of the commander-in-chief of the military forces in India. From the purely British point of view all this was contrary to the principles of government which were considered sacred and inviolable. Burke felt this and denounced the system created in 1786 as an arbitrary and despotic government, and the preamble to the Act of 1786 as 'a libel on the British Constitution'.

For India, however, this was fundamental, and it is interesting to note that Dr Johnson saw this, though Burke did not. One day he and Boswell were talking about the accusations against Warren Hastings. Johnson said: 'They will not get at him. When bad actions are committed at so great a distance, a delinquent can obscure evidence till the scent becomes cold; there is a cloud between, which cannot be penetrated, therefore all distant power is bad.' Johnson in a sense was right, though he underestimated the power of personal enmity.

But regarding a proper system of government in India he was certainly right. He said:

> I am clear that the best plan for the government of India is a despotick governor; for if he be a good man it is evidently the best government; and supposing him to be a bad man, it is better to have one plunderer than many. A governor whose power is checked, lets others plunder that he himself may be allowed to plunder. But if despotick, he sees that the more he lets others plunder the less there will be for himself, so he restrains them; and though he himself plunders, the country is a gainer, compared with being plundered by numbers.

As to the idea that the inquiry into Clive's conduct, in spite of being inspired by personal rancour, produced some public good by warning the administrators in India about the consequences of high-handed or corrupt conduct, it is as unfounded as the other. The persecution of Clive did not make Warren Hastings's tenure of office free from misdeeds considered punishable by the political standards accepted at home.

The purity of administration that became the general rule after Warren Hastings also owed nothing to the impeachment of Hastings. Behind this last was a personal factor which has never been noticed. By a tacit assumption, which became a constitutional convention, from that time some social status was required in the governor-general. If the tenure of Sir John Shore is left out – and he reduced the prestige of the British government of India – no servant of the Company and no commoner from England was to hold the post of governor-general; it was always reserved for a distinguished member of the British aristocracy, who not only belonged to the ruling class but also had close personal relations with the ministerial 'set' of the day at home. Neither Clive nor Hastings had that status by birth. They did only what ability and genius could do. Thus they benefited the British people, but harmed themselves.

But the cant about Clive's wrongdoings has to be disposed of. First, the only action of his that can be regarded as immoral by the customary definition is his deception of Omichand by means of a false treaty and a forged signature. Clive made no bones about it, and it has to be judged as an act of deception in war is judged. It will always be judged variously, but to think that the treatment of Omichand lowered the reputation of the Company in the eyes of the people of India is to show complete ignorance of their way of thinking. Apart from the deception of Omichand, no dishonesty in anything can be charged to Clive. Moreover, no accusation of any kind of high-handedness or cruelty to any Indian prince or notable can be brought against him. He treated all of them with respect even when he privately knew them to be villains or idiots.

In his political actions, too, Clive never showed the high-handedness of Warren Hastings, Wellesley or Dalhousie. In his political behaviour he never exhibited the lack of dignity of Hastings, and never descended to the squalor of Hastings's tortuous intrigues and mean quarrels. No one could conceive of Clive fighting a duel with any member of his Council. His personal position made all such things unnecessary, while Hastings was forced into them by the urgent necessity of self-preservation.

In respect of money-making, Clive never did anything that was not done openly and avowed openly. He never acquired money by dishonesty, by the disregard of any existing moral obligation or by oppression. Both in his public and private transactions he never resorted to extortion.

I have already dealt with the jaghir, and in regard to the presents of money he received from Mir Jafar I would say that they cannot be seen in the light in which such presents had to be judged after the British established their political power. When acting against Siraj, the Company was in the position of a mercenary auxiliary, and Clive was a commander of mercenaries. Neither the Company nor he had any political status *vis-à-vis* Mir Jafar. The argument that territorial gains made with the forces of the state belonged to the state was inapplicable then because the state itself did not exist in India. Even the presence of the regular troops of the King with the troops of the Company did not make the Company a state, because these troops were loaned to them, so that in fighting for the Company they also became mercenaries. The wars in India at that time were private wars.

If on the seas English sailors had the right to prize money when serving in the King's ships, the soldiers of the Company had an equal right. In fact, by the letters patent issued to the Company in 1758, it had the right to all booty and plunder taken in all wars carried on by the Company's forces, with some reserved for the sovereign in the case of the King's troops. This continued. Later, the whole of the prize money gained in the Mysore campaign of 1792 and from the capture of Seringapatam in 1799 was given to the captors. Even as late as 1817–18 the booty gained in the course of the Maratha and Pindari wars was claimed for himself, and for the troops under him, by the governor-general, the Marquis of Hastings, as commander-in-chief. At that time the East India Company had become the State.

Last of all, it has to be emphasized that, with the exception of totally false charges like participation in the killing of Siraj, there was not one accusation against Clive in regard to anything he had done which was not avowed by him before any charge was brought forward. The malice of the charges when made, and their vapidity and irrelevance in history afterwards, should have been recognized. Instead, the controversy about Clive's conduct still lingers on in serious histories and biographies.

Eighteen months passed between the vote of the House of Commons and Clive's death. During this period he lived uneventfully. But in this period two proposals were made to him which, if they had been accepted, would have produced interesting results. One of these is not clearly substantiated, except as a statement in the *Biographia Britannica*'s article on him, based on information derived from the family. But the other is supported by documentary evidence.

The *Biographica Britannica* says that, in view of a likelihood of war between the American colonies and Britain, a proposal was made to Clive to assume the chief command of the British forces there, but that he declined the offer on account of the state of his health, and from a consciousness that his vigour of mind was no longer what it had been. Naturally, there could not be any official document on such an approach. But inherently it is not improbable.

The other proposal came from no less a person than Voltaire. He wanted to write a book on the rise of British power in India (as Tocqueville wanted to do later) and mentioned this to Dr Moore, who paid a visit to him at Ferney. The request came to Wedderburn, the Solicitor-General, who was a friend of Clive and was interested in it. He wrote to Clive on July 9 1773, asking if material could be supplied to Voltaire. But he seems to have anticipated religious objections, for he wrote:

Lady Clive, I am afraid, will scruple at a correspondence with so free a writer; but whatever mischief his works may do for a better state [in the other world], in this world they are very entertaining: and that justice, which is everywhere due to fame, will have a very good effect in England, coming from the pen of a Frenchman, writing at the foot of the Alps.

Nothing came of the suggestion; whether for religious or any other reasons is not on record. But it gave an English solicitor-general the opportunity to refer to Voltaire as a 'Frenchman writing at the foot of the Alps'. Byron, on the contrary, wrote about Lausanne and Ferney as if they were places of pilgrimage – the first for Gibbon's and the second for Voltaire's presence.

During these months Clive was both tired and ailing. His recurring stomach ailment was accompanied by gout and kidney trouble, but it was the stomach trouble that was the most serious cause of his suffering. In his biographies the effect of his physical state from 1753, when it became chronic, has never been properly emphasized. Owing to this state, his generally assertive temperament also recoiled on himself.

His real complaint was never diagnosed. Information in the Strachey family, handed down from Henry Strachey, his secretary, was that he had a very painful form of dyspepsia accompanied by vertigo, and when an attack came he felt extremely depressed. This information, taken with the symptoms described by Carnac in his letter quoted in the last chapter, suggests a disease which is now believed to have been behind George III's recurring insanity. It is a disease affecting the metabolism called porphyria, and has two forms. It is not impossible that Clive may have developed it in its hepatic form, which gives rise to a wide variety of clinical symptoms like abdominal pain and nausea, with mental disturbances manifested in hysterical and psychotic behaviour.

Clive again went abroad for the sake of his health, this time to Italy. Lady Mary Coke met him at Florence on January 2 1774, on his way from Milan to Naples. It is not known when he came back, but towards the end of 1774 he was still suffering. Shortly before his death he wrote to Henry Strachey: 'How miserable is my condition. I have a disease which makes life insupportable, but which my doctors tell me won't shorten it an hour.'

Yet when an attack was on he must have forgotten his doctor's assurance, and become desperate. He was by nature melancholic and given to brooding, especially when without active employment. It is interesting to note that the *Encyclopaedia*

Britannica, in its first edition published in 1768 (the year in which Chatham also went mad temporarily) connected melancholia and madness. These two, it wrote,

> may be properly considered as diseases nearly allied; for we find they have both the same origin; that is, an excessive congestion of blood in the brain: they only differ in degree, and with regard to the time of invasion. Melancholy may be looked upon as the primary disease, of which madness is only the augmentation. When persons begin to be melancholy, they are sad, dejected, and dull, without apparent cause.

Certainly, this kind of depression often came upon Clive. In his last year there was no external reason for it except absence of occupation. The persecution had failed, and he himself felt that he had been not only acquitted, but also vindicated. So one would think that his depressed condition was more physiological than psychological, though in the last stage the two may have combined. That is as far as it is permissible to speculate on the cause of his death.

Death of Clive
Clive died on November 22 1774. No account of his death can be given which is not hearsay. The family disclosed nothing, and the family papers contain no information about it. He died in his house in Berkeley Square, but his body was removed to Styche, the ancestral home, and he was buried in the parish church of Moreton Say. The spot where he was buried is not known, nor is there any monument to him. Only a brass plate inside the door of the church says: 'Buried within the walls* of this church'.

Though the generally accepted view is that he committed suicide, this has been contested and it has been maintained that he died of an overdose of opium. The contemporary notices of his death in the papers are silent about the manner of his death. But there are reports and speculations in the letters and diaries written contemporaneously. I have accepted the view that he took his own life, and among other biographers – to mention the most notable – Macaulay, Gleig and Forrest have done so also. However, I shall give the most dependable contemporary statements, which show that various guesses and reports began to circulate from the very day of his death.

*'Walls' is ambiguous; the word could mean within the boundary walls of the church, or the walls of the building itself.

On the day that he died there was heavy snowfall in London. It continued till about midday, and the city looked as if it was covered with white paper. In the afternoon Lady Mary Coke went with the Duchess of Beaufort to play Lu in the house of her friend Lady Hertford, wife of Lord Hertford, the Lord Chamberlain, in Grosvenor Street. As she was coming away she was told of the death of Lord Clive. What she heard was that he was given medicine twice for great pains in the bowels, and the second administering deprived him of life.

Lady Mary set down in her journal written later in the night: 'This appears to me so extraordinary that I cannot help thinking there was some unhappy mistake in the making up of the physick.' Then she commented: 'He was certainly a Great Man, and had done considerable service to his country.'

On November 23, Horace Walpole wrote to the Countess of Upper Ossory: 'The nation had another great loss last night. Lord Clive went off suddenly.'

In the same letter he also wrote: 'Lord H [ertford] has just been here, and he told me *the manner* of Lord Clive's death. Whatever had happened, it had flung him into convulsions, to which he was subject. Dr Fothergill gave him one dose of laudanum, but he wanted another, upon which the doctor said that a second dose would result in death. Even so he took it, and with fatal effects.'

Apparently, all sorts of rumours were current in London, for Walpole wrote to his friend Mann on the twenty-fourth: 'Lord Clive has died every death in the parish register, at present it is most fashionable to believe he cut his throat. That he is dead is certain.'

On Monday November 28 the Duchess of Montagu told Lady Mary Coke: 'It is strongly reported that Lord Clive had not died a natural death, and there is one circumstance that looks very suspicious; he was put into his coffin a few hours after his death.' On November 29 Lady Mary set down: "Tis said now that 'tis certain Lord Clive kill'd himself, and the reason given for this unhappy action is the horrour of his mind.'

On December 11 Lady Mary wrote:

> The method he took to deprive himself of life was, I believe, what nobody ever thought of before; he cut his throat with a little instrument that is bought at the Stationers to scratch out anything upon paper; I don't know what it is call'd, but 'tis so small he must have been some time before he could affect his purpose, and must have

been very determined to proceed when he was giving himself such terrible pain: reason there can be none for such action, but I wish to know what it was that could give him so dreadful a thought.

Lady Mary Coke's report of the discovery of his dead body is awful in its tragic poignancy, and there is no reason to doubt its truth, for the incident is so singular that nobody could have invented it if it did not have some basis in fact. Lady Mary wrote on December 18:

> 'Tis reported that Lady Clive was the first person who found her Lord weltering in his blood; 'tis no wonder the horrour of the scene should have such an effect upon her spirits as to deprive her of her senses, and throw her with a fit, but 'tis fortunate She remained in it so long, that when She came out of it, her ideas were so confused with regard to that terrible scene, that She believed to have been a dream what was but too real, and spoke of the shocking dream She had had of her Lord: She was incouraged in this notion, and was told he was dead of an apoplectick fit.*

A later report is quite circumstantial in its account of the incident. According to this, Clive had great pain on the twenty-first, and was driven to take strong doses of opium for relief. This continued on the next day. At about noon or a little later a lady who was on a visit at his house came into his room and said: 'Lord Clive, I cannot find a good pen; will you be so good as make me one?' 'To be sure,' replied he, and, taking a penknife from his waistcoat pocket, he moved towards one of the windows, and mended the pen. The lady took it back with thanks and left the room. Some time shortly afterwards a servant entered the room and found Clive dead. The weapon with which he killed himself was seen to be the same penknife.†

Macaulay wrote severely about the general attitude to Clive's death and commented on it:

> In the awful close of so much prosperity and glory, the vulgar saw only a confirmation of all their prejudices; and some men of real piety and genius so far forgot the maxims both of religion and of philosophy as confidently to ascribe the mournful event to the just vengeance of God, and to the horrors of an evil conscience.

Clearly, in the second half of his comment Macaulay had in mind, above all, Dr Johnson, whose remarks on the death of

---

*That she went in first, and fainted away was also the version handed down in the Strachey family. See Appendix 8.

†Gleig – 2nd edition, pp. 360–1. The book was first published in 1848.

Clive showed how wrong a man could be when under the influence of a preconceived idea, even though he might otherwise be humane and generous. Johnson replied to Robertson's praise of Clive by saying: 'Yet this man cut his own throat. . . . The true strong and sound mind', he explained, 'is the mind that can embrace equally great things and small.' And he referred to Frederick the Great as an example. Johnson had heard that Frederick could say to a servant: 'Bring me a bottle of such a wine, which came in such a year; it lies in such a corner of the cellars.'

Later, he told Boswell that since Robertson had talked about someone he did not know, 'I *downed* him with the King of Prussia.' 'Yes, Sir,' was Boswell's reply, 'you threw a *bottle* at his head.' This shows that Johnson really knew nothing about the personal characteristics of Clive, whose interest in small things was no less than that in great things. Boswell, too, knew nothing. Otherwise, he might have thrown shiyagoshes, hookoos and lion monkeys, not to speak of *itr*, muslin, and a bewildering variety of other out-of-the-way things, at Johnson's head.

About two weeks later, Johnson referred again to Clive in order to support his argument that, so far as the world went, vice did not hurt a man's character and interests, about which he was having a dispute with Boswell. The conversation was as follows:

Johnson: —Will you not allow, Sir, that vice does not hurt a man's character so as to obstruct his prosperity in life, when you know that _____ _____ [Lord Clive] was loaded with wealth and honours; a man who had acquired his fortune by such crimes, that his consciousness of them impelled him to cut his own throat.

Boswell: — You will recollect, Sir, that Dr Robertson said, he cut his throat because he was weary of still life; little things not being sufficient to move his great mind.

Johnson: — (Very angry) — Nay, Sir, what stuff is this? You had no more this opinion after Robertson said it, than before. I know nothing more offensive than repeating what one knows to be foolish things, by way of continuing a dispute, to see what a man will answer, to make him your butt! (Angrier still.)

Boswell: — My dear Sir, I had no such intention as you seem to suspect; I had not indeed. Might not this nobleman have felt every thing 'weary, stale, flat, and unprofitable', as Hamlet says?

Johnson: – Nay, if you are to bring in gabble, I'll talk no more. I will not upon my honour.

On this Boswell commented: 'My readers will decide upon this dispute.' Unfortunately, as yet even history has not decided upon it.

Robertson and Boswell were more right about Clive's death, though perhaps not wholly right, than was Johnson. But Johnson's apparently heartless attitude is not to be dismissed as that of a factious and opinionated individual. Enough has been said in this book to show that in this matter Johnson duplicated a general attitude, only in his very forthright manner. This attitude was shaped by the accepted moral notions of the age.

In their entire history the English people have not passed through any epoch before or after the eighteenth century in which the human urges denounced by Christianity as lust of the flesh, lust of the eyes and pride of life were transformed more effectually into an idealized aspiration after magnificence, and, after being sublimated in this manner, had the practical effect of bringing a greater elegance and amenity into the external manifestations of human life than ever seen before. But in its most cherished and most widely preached moral notions no age was more opposed to that very ideal of magnificence. In respect of human life, its highest moral concept was embodied in the first beatitude: 'Blessed are the poor in spirit: for theirs is the kingdom of heaven.'

It was not solely the professed moralists of the century, among whom Johnson was one of the greatest, who preached this message; the poets also did it. And among the poets, too, it was not Gray alone, who, as Tennyson said, uttered 'divine truisms which make us weep'. Pope, whom nobody could suppose to be poor in spirit, did this equally. Again, it was not exclusively Gray's poetry which, as Johnson pronounced, 'abounds with images which find a mirrour in every mind, and with sentiments to which every bosom returns an echo'. Pope, too, supplied them. And Pope was no unworldly recluse.

He enunciated his ideal of life at the age of twelve in the following words:

Thus let me live, unseen, unknown;
Thus unlamented let me dye;
Steal from the world, and not a stone tell where I lye.

He repeated this throughout his life; and also almost at the end of his life, in a translation from Horace:

In unambitious silence be my lot,
Yet ne'er a friend forgetting, till forgot.

His verdict on the greatness of man as the world regarded it was:

A Wit's a feather, and a Chief a rod;
An honest Man's the noblest work of God.

As Pope saw it, of all men it was the so-called heroes who had the least of greatness:

Heroes are much the same, the point's agreed,
From Macedonia's madman to the Swede;*
The whole strange purpose of their lives, to find
Or make, an enemy of all mankind!

Even planting trees to make a beautiful park, so that visitors could say: 'They have some of the finest woods in the country,'† was a vanity. The only morally justifiable planter of trees was he

Whose rising Forests, not for pride or show,
But future Buildings, future Navies grow.

The great house at Stowe was also to be admired above the creations of Inigo Jones and Le Nôtre, because it had most of sense 'of every Art the Soul'.

Unless all this is to be set down to a repulsive hypocrisy it must be attributed to a typical moral outlook. Pope never shrank from applying his moral code to others, though in doing so he showed himself to be no practitioner of Christian charity.

Compared with Pope, Gray showed the most charitable side of the century's moralizing in seeing his villager as some mute inglorious Milton or Cromwell guiltless of his country's blood. Nevertheless, Gray's moral consciousness also had a tragic side, which is to be found in his *Ode on the Distant Prospect of Eton College*. Victorian England justified its worship of organized games by imputing to Wellington the saying: 'The battle of Waterloo was won on the playfields of Eton'. This, the Victorians said, was as typically English as Cambronne's even more famous '*La Garde meurt, ne se rend pas*', uttered at Waterloo, was typically French. Both attributions were spurious.

As to Eton, Gray, contemplating the view before him and

---

*Charles XII.
†Mrs Gardiner to her niece Elizabeth Bennet about Pemberley.

seeing the boys swimming in the river or playing football on the grass, could only think of these young Englishmen as future victims of black misfortune – as prey to anger, fear, shame, despair, infamy, falsehood and even madness.

Both attitudes, Pope's and Gray's, had a common origin in the distrust, preached in Christian morality, of worldly greatness or even mere worldliness. All of it had to be rejected and condemned because 'if any man love the world, the love of the Father is not in him'.

In his death as in his life Clive provoked the antagonism which the moral and religious ideals of his age preached towards worldly greatness. Otherwise, the misunderstanding of his exotic greatness by the general body of his countrymen would have been wholly hypocritical, as it certainly was in his active persecutors.

But the apology of the late nineteenth century did not show a truer grasp of historical truth, though Englishmen in that age were pursuing another activity which could have furnished them with a clue. They had begun to hunt big game, and they should have seen in Clive's death the end of a great beast of prey.

A fine poet has described the death of a wolf. Riddled by bullets, and with the daggers of the hunters plunged to their hilts in his ribs, the beast gets up, licks his blood, glares at the gun-barrels, still pointed at him, lies down again and closes his eyes without uttering a cry.

But at least the hunters understood the wolf's death, whereas the contemporaries of Clive did not understand his. One of the killers rested his forehead on the muzzle of his gun and read the mind of the wolf:

> Gémir, pleurer, prier est également lâche
> Fais énergiquement ta longue et lourde tâche.
> Dans la voie où le Sort a voulu t'appeler,
> Puis, après, comme moi, souffre et meurs sans parler.

Appendix 1

The Expedition to Tanjore

The existing accounts of this expedition are inaccurate on certain essential points, and the evidence on them must be considered.

1. The motive
Sir George Forrest says (*Life*, Vol. I, p. 85) that one reason was that Pratap Singh had proved himself to be an active ally of the French before and during the siege of Pondichery; and Forrest has been followed by others. There is no contemporary evidence for this. The reasons for sending the expedition in support of Shahaji were given by Governor Floyer to the Council of St David on April 10 1749, and are to be found in the Consultations for the day. The text of the proceedings is set forth below:

At a Consultation

Present

CHARLES FLOYER ESQ^F.	PRESIDENT & GOVERN^R.
EDWARD CROKE.	FOSS WESTCOTT.
RICHARD PRINCE.	WILLIAM HOLT.
ALEX^R. WYNCH.	STRINGER LAWRENCE.

   The President acquaints the Board that about two Months past he was Solicited by Messages from Sahajee MahaRajah the Right and Lawfull King of Tanjour, who had been deprived of such his Right about Seven years ago by an Illegitimate Brother, he likewise made Application to General Boscawen in the same manner, acquainting him He had Affairs of great Consequence to Impart to Us, Whereupon it was Agreed between Genl. Boscawen, himself, and M^r. Prince to Admit him into our Bounds, and further to hear what he had to propose to us. His Request being granted he came to the Garden House in Company with his Uncle, when after speaking much on the Occasion by way of setting forth the Injustice that had been done him by his Illegitimate Brother taking Possession of the

Kingdom of Tanjour, of which he as true & Lawfull Heir had an indisputable Right to, and then requested we would assist him in regaining his Kingdom, which he assur'd Us was then to be effected with little Difficulty, he having received such assurances both by Letters and Messages from the Principle Men & Officers at Tanjour, that in case he could by any means raise a Body of Forces, and March that way they would certainly Join with him, and put him in Possession of his just Right, without the Effusion of Blood. These Circumstances being duely Considered by General Boscawen the President and M^r. Richard Prince, it appeared to them that great Advantages might be made in behalf of the Hoñble Company, by granting to him the Assistance he desired, which the easier might be done at this time, having so large a Body of His Majesty's Forces now in Garrison, and the risque but small in Comparison to the Benefits that might be gain'd on the Occasion. But to come to particulars with him relating thereto, it was ask'd of the dethron'd King what Retaliation he would make to the Hoñble Company if such Assistance was given him, as might enable him to regain his Right, upon which he made the offer of giving up, and making sure to them the Fort of Deva Cota about Eleven Leagues from this Place Southward, and Thirty from Tanjour, with as much Land round it as would at least bring in yearly to the Honble Company, Ten or Twelve thousand Pagodas; Having thus talkd on the Subject for some time, he was told this Affair would be taken into further Consideration, upon which y^e. Conference broke up: But before the King withdrew he further requested the Loan of a Sum of Money from the Hoñble Company, to enable him to raise Forces in the Country, to which it was likewise Answer'd it should be Consider'd on.

The President also acquaints the Board that he with M^r. Prince frequently held Conferences with General Boscawen on this Affair, and it appearing to them that the [sic] being put in Possession of the Fort of Deva Cota with the Lands adjoining thereto annually producing to the Hoñ Company, the amount of Ten or Twelve thousand Pagodas the Greatest part of the Country thereabouts being very fruitfull in Grain, and some with Wood in abundance, an Article much wanted here, and therefore very Advantageous to the Hoñble Company, beside which there is a River from the Sea running round the Fort, at present Capable of receiveing only small Vessells, but might be made fit to receive larger; this alone would be of great Service to the Company, there being much want of such a Conveniency on this Coast. The Affair being taken into Consideration, and due Weight given to the beforemention'd Circumstances, It was Agreed on by General Boscawen, the President and M^r. Prince to grant the Dethrond King the Assistance he desired, provided he entered into an Obligation to deliver up as before mention'd to the Hoñ. Company for ever the Fort of Deva Cota, and the Lands adjoining thereto as abovemention'd, in Case he was put in Posession of the Kingdom of Tanjour, and further to pay the whole Charge of the Expedition if he Succeeded therein.

Major Lawrence being made acquainted with what had pass'd in this Affair, approved thereof, he was likewise desired by the President to meet in a private Conference with General Boscawen and M^r. Prince, in Order to a final Determination on the Subject in hand, When it was Agreed upon to assist the Dethroned King (it appearing so much to the Hoñble Companys Advantage), and to send by Land two Companys of Foot. Fifty European Horse, all the Black Horse, and about Six hundred Seapoys, & General Boscawen to send Assistance by Sea. The Hoñble Company's Forces were Ordered to be got ready with the utmost despatch. The Agreement or Obligation to the Hoñble Company being Sign'd by the Dethron'd King and approved of. It was thereupon Agreed to advance him on the Honourable Compys Account, Five thousand, five hundred (5500) Pagodas in Order to enable him to raise Forces in the Country.

As the greater the Secrecy the more to Advantage is the design of Expeditions of this nature brought to perfection, of which the President does not in the least doubt but the rest of the Gentlemen of the Board will join with him in the same Opinion, and approve of the methods taken therein, and now acquaints them that the Forces abovemention'd began their March yesterday morning early, & that the King's Forces will prepare to Embark on board such Ships as General Boscawen may please to appoint tomorrow or the next day at farthest.

Upon reading the above, the President Observeing that the Gentlemen of Council, that had not been till this time acquainted of the above Expedition disapprovd of the Proceedings, He put the Question to them, & further Ask'd their Opinion about carrying it on, as our Troops were Ten Miles on their way, and our Credit somewhat at Stake, as well as the certain Loss of the Money already Advanc'd in Case the Troops were recall'd. Messrs. Coke & Westcott dissented from the whole Proceedings, but Messrs. Holt and Wynch agreed as the Expedition had been already sett on foot, it was better to proceed on it; and the President promis'd the Board, the same should be conducted with as small an Expence to the Company as possible, and that he would from time to time acquaint them with every thing material that happened.

I dissent from this Enterprize as I fear it may prove of bad consequence.

CHARLES FLOYER.
EDW: CROKE.
STRINGER LAWRENCE.
RICH^D PRINCE.

As the Expedition is already gone on so far, I consent for the abovementioned Reasons to its being Carried on.	A^R. WYNCH.
I Dissent from the above Expedition Because I am of Opinion it is repugnant to my Honble Master's Interest.	FOSS WESTCOTT.

In his despatches to the Company also Floyer mentions no other reason. All doubt on this point is set at rest by a later statement of Dupleix himself. In a letter to Saunders (February 18 1752) he said that 'it was known to all India that the Prince on the throne [Pratap Singh of Tanjore] had, during the war between our two nations, done very material service to yours, and according to an agreement between you was to come down and lay siege to Karaikal while your troops were employed in that of Pondichery...'

2. What happened to Shahaji

Orme (Vol. I, p. 122), apparently basing himself on an account supplied to him by Clive (quoted in Forrest, Vol. I, pp. 86–91; the statement on this point is on p. 91), says that Pratap Singh accepted, along with the other terms, that of giving an allowance to Shahaji. *Proceedings* of the Council of St David for June 30 1749 expressly mentions that this made the Tanjore representatives angry and was rejected. I have not found any other mention of Shahaji in the documents of this period. However, it is not impossible, though hardly probable, that the English themselves gave Shahaji a pension.

3. Why Pratab Singh made Peace

Orme (Vol. I, p. 122), writes that the King of Tanjore agreed to the terms of the English 'without hesitation, ... but his compliance did not proceed so much from his dread of the Englishmans, as from his sense of the danger with which his kingdom was threatened, in consequence of events which happened a few days before in the Carnatic; and which had struck the whole coast of Coromandel with consternation'.

This is clearly an allusion to the defeat and death of Nawab Anwar-ud-din Khan at the battle of Ambur on August 1 1749.* But Orme's opinion cannot be correct. The Tanjore general wanted to know the English terms in May, and the discussion after which the peace was concluded took place on June 25 (July

2, n.s.), and was approved by the Council on June 30 (July 11, n.s.). The agreement under which Dupleix was to help Chanda Sahib was not disclosed till July 13 (n.s.), and though both Chanda Sahib and Muzafar Jang were on the border of the Carnatic before that date it could not be anticipated that with the forces they had they would be able to overthrow Anwar-ud-din Khan, whose army was stronger. It should be added that even after the successes of the French and Chanda Sahib, the King of Tanjore refused to join them, and risked a siege of his capital by them.

---

*The date of this battle is given as July 23 (n.s. August 3) by Orme (Vol. I, p. 132), and has been accepted by modern authors. Fort St David Consultations, July 27 1749, give it as July 21 o.s. (= August 1 n.s.) This has been adopted here.

Appendix 2

Genesis of the Arcot Expedition

It is curious that the genesis of the Arcot expedition, the sensational overture to Clive's career, should have been left as an unexamined legend. It was possible to go beyond that when at the beginning of this century the records of Madras began to be published, but even now the accounts remain imprecise and vague.

Of the contemporary authorities, Lawrence only says that 'a scheme was laid to reduce that part of the country to the Nawab's obedience. Captain Clive commanded the party'. (Cambridge, 1761, p. 14.) Lawrence at the time was not in India.

Orme (Vol. I, 1763, p. 187) wrote:

> Captain Clive, on his return from Trichinopoly in the beginning of August, represented this situation of affairs to the presidency, and proposed, as the only resource, to attack possessions of Chunda Sahib in the territory of Arcot; offering to lead the expedition himself, which he doubted not would cause a diversion of part of the enemy's force from Trichinopoly.

If he got his information from Clive, it must have been verbal, for no document on the point has been cited by those who have examined the Orme manuscripts.

Subsequent writers – the author of the article in the *Biographia Britannica*, Malcolm, Macaulay, Gleig and Malleson – have all followed Orme, some of them embroidering his account. Even Forrest, writing after the publication of the Madras records (1910), attributes it to Clive (Forrest, Vol. I, 1918, p. 137). Dodwell (*Dupleix and Clive*, 1920, p. 56 of the 1967 reprint) first mentions Muhammad Ali as the proposer of the diversion, but adds that this prince might have suggested it to Clive. Davies (1939, p. 78) only says briefly that Muhammad Ali was the proposer and Saunders the sponsor of the expedition. Neither Dodwell nor Davies gives any authority for departing from the traditional account, but the latter quotes an anonymous account of the war in the Carnatic published in 1761,

417

which says that at St David Clive heard about the resolve to send an expedition towards Arcot and offered to lead it.

So it is necessary to set forth what contemporary documentary evidence exists on the point. It leaves no doubt that Muhammad Ali, hard-pressed at Trichinopoly, suggested the diversion to Saunders again and again. His letters and replies to them, in Persian in the original but preserved only in the English translations, are all printed in the *Records of Fort St George: Country Correspondence* (1751, published by the Madras Government in 1910 and edited by A. G. Cardew). The first suggestion was received at St David on May 29 1751 (o.s.), and in his letter Muhammad Ali wrote:

> If the English troops at Madras should set out at this juncture in company with Walley Mahomed Cawn, Amuldar of Conjeverum and take possession of the countries that way, which may be easily done, it will be the same in reality as if we were Masters of three-quarters of the Carnatick. The enemy will be entirely deprived of the revenues and unable to fight which will certainly ruin their affairs. It is therefore highly necessary to be mindful of it.

On June 17 the Governor was reminded of the suggestion about 'raising disturbances in the several Parganas that way' for the purpose of depriving the enemy of his revenues, but in this letter Muhammad Ali also spoke of the possibility that troops preparing to attack Trichinopoly 'will be ordered to march there [towards Conjeverum]', and then he added: 'I therefore think it advisable to pursue this scheme, but you may act as you think proper. Let me know your resolution.'

Only a few days later (on June 27) another letter on the subject was received from Muhammad Ali. In it he said that had a diversion been attempted the enemy troops now marching on Trichinopoly would probably have discontinued the advance. He concluded the letter by saying: 'However, depending upon your true friendship I take the liberty again to desire you to lend your assistance to this business.'

Apparently Saunders informed Muhammad Ali that he had instructed the Deputy Governor at Madras to help his Amuldars, and so Muhammad Ali wrote in a letter received at St David on July 9:

> I am glad to hear you have ordered the Deputy Governor of Madras to assist my Amuldars. I must acquaint you that the countries towards Arcot are clear of the enemy's forces; if your troops went out from Madras jointly with Mahomed Cawn etc., Amuldars, and take possession of the districts it will throw the enemy into confusion.

Another letter on the subject was received on July 22.

Yet another letter, received on July 29, repeated the argument: if a disturbance could be raised in the Arcot country towards Madras it would in all likelihood confound the enemy and break his heart. 'I hope therefore that you will enter into that resolution.'

At last Saunders replied on August 3 that he had devised a scheme for the diversion. He wrote:

> I have considered we have a thousand men in the field and have wrote to Captain Gingen if he thinks himself strong enough to engage enemy, if not that he consult with you how many men may be sufficient to defend Trichinopoly and that with the rest joined to your horse he make a diversion in the Arcot country and raise contributions for you, the manner how and where to be settled with you if you approve of it.

After that there is no further communication from St David to Muhammad Ali on this subject, until on September 3 the Governor informs the latter that English troops are in possession of Arcot.

But there is additional evidence in the English records. On August 6 the Governor informed the Company that 'we purpose, agreeable to the *Nabob's desire* making a diversion in the Arcot country, and raising contributions for him which he is much in need of, and we hope it will have the desired effect.' This obviously communicates the decision of which Saunders apprised Muhammad Ali on August 3. However, a consultation of August 15 at St David records:

> The board being of opinion that a diversion in the Arcot country will oblige the enemy to withdraw part of their forces from Trichinopoly and put it in our power to attempt something that way, now agree that Captain Clive be sent with a party of all the Europeans we can possibly spare and some sepoys for this purpose.

The proceedings also recorded that Clive was to go with the troops by sea on board the *Wager* to Madras, where he was to be reinforced by all the men they can any ways furnish, and march immediately towards Arcot.

It is clear that there was a change of plan between the sixth and the fifteenth, by which the scope of the expedition was changed; the military objective became Arcot; and Clive was put in charge of the expedition. The question arises – what brought about this change? Is it possible that it was Clive who gave the expedition this new character by discussing the project with the Governor and the Council at St David? Unless it is assumed that Orme's attribution of the expedition to Clive was a fabrication, this is the only way to reconcile it with the now known fact that in a less precise form Muhammad Ali had all along been urging the diversion.

But there is no means of establishing this. All that we know is that Clive was at St David after his return from Verdachellum during the first week of August or till the middle of the month; that after that he was sent with reinforcements to Trichinopoly, recalled to command the expedition to Arcot, and set out on the expedition from Madras on the twenty-sixth. The distance between St David and Trichinopoly is about a hundred miles, and that between St David and Madras the same. On the other hand, there were only eleven days between the decision to make Clive the commander of the expedition to Arcot and its setting out on the twenty-sixth, and thus, if he was at Trichinopoly around the fifteenth, it must have been very quick work for him. However that may be, his presence at St David during the first days of August makes it probable that he had something to do with the final shape of the expedition, though not with the idea of making a diversion. That is all we can say at present about Clive's part in the genesis of the expedition.

Appendix 3

Sources used for chapter seven

In giving an account of the conquest of Bengal I have drawn mainly on the letters and other documents written at the time of the events and only in exceptional cases depended on statements made after them even by the participants. For instance, I have not used the evidence given before the Parliamentary Committee of 1772, or the accounts written years after the happenings, unless I was sure from internal evidence or other indications that there was neither interested motive nor failure of memory. I have not used the history of Orme at all, who had a habit of adding embellishments for heightening the effect of his narrative.

Others besides Clive who were present at the events have been inaccurate not only from failure of memory, but also from a desire to be picturesque. Of this the account given by Scrafton in his *Reflections* of the meeting of Mir Jafar with Clive in the morning following the battle of Plassey is a good example. He says that when the guard turned out 'to receive him as he passed, he started as if he thought it was all over with him; nor did his countenance brighten up until the Colonel embraced him, and saluted him subah of the three provinces'.

Yet it was Scrafton who had carried to Mir Jafar the congratulatory letter written to him by Clive in the morning of June 24, in which Clive informed him that he would make him nawab of Bengal. Scrafton was also asked to congratulate him on his chief's behalf. Clive in his evidence before the Parliamentary Committee only said that Mir Jafar made many apologies for the non-performance of his agreement to join him, upon which he assured Mir Jafar that the English would most religiously perform their treaty.

For the battle of Plassey I have relied on the following documents, which are placed in their chronological order:

1. Mir Jafar's letter to Clive written before 3 p.m. on June 23;

2. another letter from him written after the battle on the same day;
3. Clive's letter to Calcutta written the same evening;
4. Clive's letter to Calcutta written on June 24;
5. a description of the battle, whose date is given as June 29, which was obviously by Clive, and had a sketch map supposed to be by him;
6. Clive's letter to Madras dated July 2 1757;
7. his letter to London of July 26 1757, which is almost identical in its details with the previous letter;
8. Eyre Coote's journal (date not known);
9. Clive's journal (date not known);

but both of which journals must have been written soon after the events, if not as they were happening.

Appendix 4

Some disputed points relating to chapter seven

1. Did Admiral Watson disapprove of the deception of Omichand, and did he know of or express his anger at the insertion of his name in the false treaty?
The Admiral died on August 16 1757, and what he thought about the whole matter was described later by witnesses before the Parliamentary Committee. One witness, Captain Brereton, who was hostile to Clive, said, basing himself on the assertion of a man who was then dead, that Watson was angry at both. But certainly the Admiral did not disapprove of the treatment of Omichand. This is evident from documents written after the meeting of the Council on May 17. That he did not agree to sign the false treaty is also stated clearly. So long as he was not involved personally with the false treaty, he was probably indifferent.

There is an interesting document among the Strachey papers which contains a refutation of Captain Brereton's evidence. It is probably by Clive himself, and it showed that Brereton's evidence on another point was incorrect, so that this statement should not be taken as necessarily true. Also, in this document, the very cogent point is made that 'if the action be itself justifiable it is immaterial whether Admiral Watson did or did not consent to have his name affixed'. It further stated: 'The truth is that he did not sign it, because the whole negotiation had been left to the Secret Committee, Admiral Watson declaring that they best understood what the Company's interest required, but permitted the Committee to use his name.'

2. When did the troops cross the river at Katwa?
Coote wrote in his journal, and also said in his evidence, that they did so in the morning on June 22. Clive, dealing with this point before the Parliamentary Committee, said that this happened in the afternoon of that day. Clive's contemporary statements are not consistent. In the description written on June 29,

it is definitely stated: 'The 22nd in the morning we crossed the river.' The other documents mention the time as afternoon. However, Coote's statement is not a vague recollection of a certain time, but a clear visual impression. He wrote: 'At 6 o'clock in the morning, the army crossed the river and marched to a large *tope* [hillock] about two miles distant.' Such a concrete image cannot be mistaken. Besides, if the troops crossed in the afternoon they would not have marched only to a *tope* two miles distant, for the march to Plassey began at 4 p.m. I have assumed that a part of the force – possibly the 39th Foot, *Primus in Indis* – crossed in the morning and waited on the other side for further orders, and the main body with Clive crossed in the afternoon.

3. What Clive did before and during the battle.
a) Orme in the first draft of his history wrote the following:

> At sunrise he went with another person upon the terrace of his hunting house, from whence having contemplated the enemy's array, he was surprised at their numerous, splendid and martial appearance. His companion asked him what he thought would be the event, to which he replied: 'We must make the best fight during the day and at nights sling our muskets over our shoulders and march back to Calcutta.'

Scrafton also gives a similar picturesque account of the appearance of Siraj's army, but without the remark. The words in Orme bear all the mark of his style of devising dramatic situations and remarks. (What Clive actually decided was to attack in the night.) All this was omitted by Orme from the printed version of the battle published in 1778. There is nothing improbable in such a remark. As has already been stated, other commanders have shown such hesitations, and when facing a dangerous situation any man will think of the alternatives open to him. Clive did feel doubtful, as was shown in his letter to Mir Jafar. But that he said 'Calcutta', if he at all made the remark, is quite impossible. He may have mentioned Katwa, where he had intended to remain during the rains, and in the recollection of men who were unfamiliar with Indian place-names the two places could be confused.

b) I have not accepted Orme's statement that Clive may have gone to take a nap before the advance of Killpatrick. The testimony of Walsh who was with him is conclusive, and he sent it to Orme. The report was given currency by Clive's enemies. In his history, Orme gave the story of sleeping as hearsay and described what happened afterwards in almost the same language as is to be found in Walsh's letter. Walsh wrote (1763): 'Surprised that such a motion should be made without his orders, he instantly hastened to the party, at the head of which he found Major Killpatrick whom he reprimanded for his unsoldierlike conduct and ordered him back to the grove....' Orme wrote (1778): 'Standing up, he ran immediately to the detachment, reprimanded Killpatrick sharply for making such a motion without his orders, commanded him to return to the grove....' But this is an utterly trivial point raised by malice. Clive did not want to attack till night, and he had given instructions for his subordinate officers to remain on the defensive. If therefore he had gone to have some rest, that would have been nothing wrong.

Appendix 5
Mir Jafar and Siraj

Mir Jafar has been represented as a traitor to Siraj-ud-daula – assumed to be his master – by Indian writers (including historians), and so far as Indian opinion goes this image is fixed. But that need not be his image in history. The English, too, were disposed to think of him, when the events were unfolding, as a man who had not kept his promise to them. This notion has also to be examined historically. Later, even some British historians, curiously enough, regarded him as a traitor to Siraj. We Bengalis have a proverb: 'The man for whom I steal, calls me a thief.'

First of all, if any attempt, successful or unsuccessful, at supplanting a reigning monarch by any of his relatives, generals or ministers is regarded as treachery to him (because, being his subjects, they are *ipso facto* bound to remain loyal to him) then scores and scores of rulers and some of them great rulers have to be regarded as traitors. This notion of treachery was quite unknown in the East, and the Indians who have fastened the name of traitor to Mir Jafar would not have come into existence to do so if the British had not delivered their forbears from Siraj.

In the sense given above, Siraj himself was a traitor because he revolted against his doting grandfather. Alivardi Khan was a worse traitor because he killed his sovereign and took his throne almost gratuitously. Skipping such traitors as there are in between, the Sayyid brothers put to an ignominious death their master the Emperor Farrukh-siyar. Aurangzeb was the greatest traitor of all, for he killed his three brothers and imprisoned his father, Shah Jahan. And Shah Jahan too had revolted against his father. It is unnecessary to go outside India to find out what happened in the Islamic world generally, especially what the Abbasid Caliphs did.

To secure a crown by assassinating the previous ruler, including a father, was also a well-known practice in ancient Hindu India.

Kalidasa, the greatest of Sanskrit poets, wrote in his *Raghuvamsa* (Canto VIII, 2.) that Aja, son of Raghu, accepted the crown in obedience to the command of his father, not for his own enjoyment, nor by employing the foul means by which sons of kings try to obtain the throne (*Duritairapi Kartum-atmasat prayatante nripa-sunavo*). The commentator gives the meaning of 'by foul means' (*duritaih*) as 'by the administration of poison and such forbidden means' (*Vishaprayogadi-mishiddhena-upayaih*).

The last *Maurya* (last of the line of Asoka) was killed by his commander-in-chief Pushyamitra on the pretext of being shown a parade of soldiers. The famous Sanskrit play *Mudra-Rakshasa* shows Chanakya, who is regarded by the Hindus as the supreme exponent of statecraft, as a crude practitioner of the lowest cunning and crude intrigues, including, of course, assassination.

To give one other proof, the *Kama Sutra* (the erotic treatise which gives elaborate instructions regarding liaisons with other peoples' wives) gives this warning: *Na rajñam mahamatranam va para-bhavana-praveso vidyate* (Neither for kings, nor for the great officials, is there entry into other men's houses) – (*Kama Sutra*, 5th book, ch. 5). One reason given is that, being VIPs, their movements would be observed and would be regarded as an example. But its risk was also pointed out: 'King Abhira of Kotta was assassinated by a washerman engaged by his brother when he was in another man's house.' (Commentator added that he was having a liaison with the wife of the merchant Vasumitra.) Another example was that of a king of Kashi who was assassinated by his commander of horse.

So one might say that treachery of a kind far worse than that attributed to Mir Jafar was regarded very lightly in India, indeed as lightly as adultery by a husband or wife is regarded in the West today, though there was certainly a theoretical moral condemnation of it, which did not make any difference.

But Mir Jafar did not conform even to this tradition. The name of traitor has been fastened on him simply because he was raised to the throne by the English, by men who have never denounced any real treachery in their country, ancient or modern.

In considering Mir Jafar's relations with Siraj the nature of the relationship between a Muslim king and his commanders must be realized. It was quite different from the relationship between the feudal lord and his vassal in Europe. There was no oath of fealty (*sacramentum fidei*) in it. The whole body of the commanders (known as the *umarrah*) were the ruler's associates and supporters by voluntary choice, either on account of family or personal relationship or from interest. Whenever they found opportunity, these commanders repudiated their so-called allegiance and became independent. From Ibn Tulun under the Abbasids down to Murshid Quli Khan in the days of the later Moguls, this was the universal practice.

Mir Jafar did not try to do anything of the kind. Under Alivardi he was a competent and loyal commander. Siraj after his accession insulted and tried to harm him in every way, and before and after the conspiracy there was no pretence whatever of friendship between the two. The conspiracy was widely talked about, and even Siraj was told who were in it. He would have had Mir Jafar killed if he dared. When Watts fled, at first he tried to molest Mir Jafar, and then in a panic tried to make it up with him. As has been related in the text, Mir Jafar agreed to remain with Siraj expressly on condition he would bear no military responsibility whatever and he also got the other commanders to guarantee that he would be allowed to go wherever he liked in peace if Siraj defeated the English (see page 225).

But he also took the risk of being regarded as a traitor to the English by not joining them, because he had given a promise to Siraj to remain by his side and because when the battle had taken a bad turn Siraj threw his turban at his feet and implored his help. Remaining aloof in this manner, he was likely to forfeit the trust and help of the English, and if he did not it was only because Clive understood his position. It must also be noted that from the day he signed the treaty to the day of Plassey he had never agreed to join the English in a battle against Siraj and fight against him. Watts always warned Clive that at best he would remain 'neuter'. In the letter which he wrote at midday on June 23 he told Clive why he had not joined him, and he explained that again the next day. As a matter of fact, he went very near falling between two stools.

The only thing that can be held against him is this: while Siraj was reigning he agreed to supplant him. But with the exception of some close associates of Siraj, who would have suffered by his removal, nobody was loyal to him, because he had driven all of them to disloyalty by threatening their life and interests, and outraging their honour; and it cannot be said that they had any moral obligation to be loyal to him.

    Mir Jafar did not show himself as a capable or straightforward ruler after his accession. But that phase of his career is quite independent of what he did up to Plassey. Power and position are almost universally fatal to character in India even now.

Appendix 6
Grant of the Jaghir to Clive by Mir Jafar 1758

(Translation published with 'A Letter to the Proprietors of the East India Stock', from Lord Clive. London: Printed for J. Nourse, opposite Catherine Street, in the Strand, Bookseller in Ordinary to His Majesty. M.DCC.LXIV. With explanations of the terms by Clive himself.)

Translation of a Perwannah (or Order) from the Nabob Shujah Ulmulk Hossum o' Dowla Meer Mahmud Jaffier Cawn Bahdr Mohabut Jung, *to the Honourable President and Council.*

BE it known to the noblest of merchants, the English Company, That whereas the Glory of the Nobility, Zubdut Ulmulk Nusseera Dowla Colonel Clive Subat Jung Behadr, has been honoured with a Munsub (or title) of the rank of 6000 and 5000 horse from the Imperial Court, and has exerted himself, in conjunction with me, with the most steady attachment, and in the most strenuous manner, in the protection of the imperial territories; in recompence thereof, the Pergana (or county) of Calcutta, &c. belonging to the Chucta* (or jurisdiction of Hughley, &c. of the Sircar Sauntgaum, &c. (or treasury) dependant on the Calfa Shereefa and Jagueer, amounting to two hundred and twenty-two thousand nine hundred and fifty-eight S^a. R^s. and something more, conferred by the Dewannee Sunnud (or King's Lord Treasurer of the province) on the English Company, as their Zemindarrie, commencing from the month Poos, (or December) in the eleven hundred and sixty-fourth year of the Bengal style, from the half of the season Rabbee Sooscanneel, in the eleven hundred and sixty-fifth year of the Bengal style, is appointed the Jagueer of the glory of the nobility aforesaid. It behoves you to look upon the above-written person as the lawful Jagueerdar (or Lord) of that place; and in the same manner as you formerly delivered in the due rents of the government, according to the Kissbundee, (or written agreement) into the treasury of the court, and the Jagueer taking a receipt under the seal of the Drogha (or Receiver-General) and Mushreef, and Treasurer; now in like manner you are regularly to deliver to the above-mentioned Jagueerdar the rents, according to the stated payments, and receive a receipt from the afore said person. Be punctual in the strict execution of this writing. Written the first of Zeckaida 6^d sun (or year) of the reign.

It is passed. (The Nabob's mark.)
N. B. Endorsements.
(The Royran's signing.)
    D   H
Copied in the books of entered in the books of the Huzzoor, the Dewannee, the 1st of the 1st of the Mohurrum, the 6th sun (or year) of the reign, the Mohurrum, the 6th of the reign.
N. B.
Signed by the Dewannee Peshker, or Accomptant Secretary.   N. B.
    Signed by the Nabob Nloon.

Explanation of the Terms used in Colonel Clive's Perwannah for his Jagueer.
Perwannah, A warrant, or a letter from any person in a superior station to a dependant.
Munsul, A dignity.
Calsa Shereef, The office in which all the King's accounts are passed.
Jagueer, Lands assigned by the King for the maintenance of a Munsubdar, or contradistinction to the Calix. It signifies the revenues appropriated to the use of the Subahdre and his family.
Dewannee, The Dewan is the King's agent for the collection of his revenues.
Rebbee. The year in all public registers is divided into two seasons, the one called Kherief, which comprehends the months of Affin, Cartic, Aghnun, Poos, Maug, Phagun; the other Cheif, Bysaac, Int, Assar, Sawun, Bhadun. The latter half of the season Relba commences 1st of the month Assar, on the 12th of June, from which time the Jagueer takes place.
Kissbundee, A contract from the acquittance of a debt by stated payments.
Huzzoor, Literally the presence, applied by way of eminence to the Nabob's court.
Hoskaneel, I have not had time to inform myself of the exact meaning of this word, but believe it to be the name of the present year, the registers of this empire accounting a perpetual revolution of twelve years, each of which is differently named.

*Chucta is a misprint: chucla (old spelling) or chakta (modern spelling) is the correct word.

Appendix 7
End of Mir Qasim

What happened to Mir Qasim after his defeat was not exactly known, and even the latest histories could only say that he died after many years of wandering as a refugee and in extreme poverty. However, my late friend Brajendranath Banerji found some documents about him among the records of the Secret Department preserved in the old Imperial Records Office of the Government of India. He sent a paper on the subject to the tenth meeting of the Indian Historical Records Commission held at Rangoon in December 1927. This was published in Vol. 34, Pt. I (pp. 88–96) of *Bengal, Past and Present* (1927). This is the only account, so far as I know, of the true end of Mir Qasim.

It showed that the Company's government in Calcutta was throughout kept informed about the movements and activities of the late Nawab, and that it tried to have him surrendered to the Company. He never was. But the surprising part of the story is that Mir Qasim, after all his attempts to make the Nawab of Oude, the Emperor of Delhi (and even Ahmad Shah Abdali) intervene on his behalf had failed, himself approached the English most abjectly, asking to be restored to their favour and permitted to come back to Bengal.

As a last resort he wrote a letter to Warren Hastings on August 29 1776, trying to convince him that he was not responsible for the massacre at Patna. Only the English version of the letter is preserved. In it the following information is found: that he was extremely anxious to meet the Governor-General – ('May his heart soften towards myself so that he may not deprive me of the pleasure of an interview'); that he was a refugee for twelve years and totally destitute; also that his conduct had been misrepresented. Mir Qasim said that it was strange that the English should have allowed themselves to be misled by interested persons and ignore the dictates of justice and shut the door of friendship against him. According to him, Samru the German, who was appointed to the command of his army after

Gurgin Khan had been slain in battle, contrived with Mir Jafar to bring about the assassination of the English prisoners, the object being to create an insuperable barrier between him and the English. A more naïve exhibition of opportunism can hardly be imagined.

No attention was paid to this letter. At that time Mir Qasim was living at Paliwal near Delhi in a tent, so as to appear even more destitute than he really was. He died in June 1777; his belongings were looted by the villagers, and his last shawl had to be sold in order to provide for his winding-sheet.

I have thought it necessary to include this account of Mir Qasim's death because Banerji's paper seems to have been wholly ignored. The story also illustrates the established pattern of conduct among the Indian rulers of those times. They were as cowardly in adversity as they were cruel and arrogant when in power. A very fair estimate of Mir Qasim's character will be found in *Mir Qasim: Nawab of Bengal, 1760–63* by Nandalal Chatterji (Allahabad, India), 1935.

Appendix 8

Death of Clive

Though it was generally accepted that Clive had died by his own hand, this was emphatically denied by R. J. Minney in his life of Clive published in 1931, and he reiterated his view in reply to a remark made by a reviewer of the book in the *Morning Post*. Then followed a controversy between him and Sir Evan Cotton in the same paper. The letters were reproduced in *Bengal, Past and Present* (Vol. 47, for Jan.–Jun., 1934, pp. 36–43) with the editor's commentary. This article should be seen by all who wish to find out on what evidence the supposition of suicide by Clive can be accepted. The only additional testimonies are those which I have cited from Lady Mary Coke's journals.

Sir Evan Cotton referred to and quoted from an article on Clive's death by Sir Edward Strachey, first published in the *Spectator* for November 4 1893, and then reproduced in the same paper on November 3 1918. Sir Edward was the grandson of Henry Strachey, Clive's secretary, and nephew of the second Sir Henry Strachey. This Sir Henry got the account of Clive's death from his mother, i.e. the wife of Clive's secretary and a cousin of Lady Clive. He dictated the account to his nephew and corrected it himself. This memorandum was the basis of Sir Edward Strachey's article. It should be added that both Henry Strachey and his wife were present at Berkeley Square when Clive died.

Gleig's account seems to be derived from someone connected with the young lady who asked Clive to mend her pen. He set down in his book: 'I therefore tell the tale as it has been told to me'. The young lady was a Miss Patty Ducarel, niece of General Gustavus Ducarel, who was in both civil and military employment in Bengal. After the controversy in the *Morning Post* one Mrs Lyon wrote to Sir Evan Cotton to say that her maternal grandfather, General G. Halliday (1822–1917) left a paper on Clive's death on the basis of information given to him by Patty Ducarel, who was his aunt. The account was similar to that current in the Strachey family.

All this should be decisive in establishing Clive's suicide. But in accepting this view I have also depended on the very important entries in Lady Mary Coke's journals, which do not appear to have been seen by anybody else. I have accepted the reports placed on record by Lady Mary as very dependable contemporary testimony, more reliable than those by Horace Walpole. Lady Mary heard them from people who could not be misinformed.*

Besides, I have considered two other facts. First, Clive's burial place would never have been left unmarked if he had not been buried in unconsecrated ground, as he had to be if he had committed suicide. Chatterton's case was wholly different. His tomb in St Mary Redcliff, Bristol, was meant to evoke compassion. Clive could not be made the object of such pity.

Secondly, there is negative evidence of considerable weight in Lady Mary's journals. In the evening of November 23 1774, i.e. a day after Clive's death, Lady Mary went to Gunnersbury Park to visit Princess Amelia, and there, among others, was Lady Powis. All of them played at cards for three hours, and only this information is set down in the journal. There is no mention of any talk about Clive's death. Lady Mary would certainly have recorded it if there had been any, and Lady Powis would also have spoken about it if she had not had a special reason for keeping silent. Clive's family and the Powis family were very intimate, and afterwards Clive's son married a Powis girl and took the name. The presumption then is that Lady Powis abstained from speaking deliberately because this was an unpleasant topic.

In view of all these testimonies I do not see any reason why Clive's suicide should not be accepted as fact in a biography and in histories.

The Letters and Journals of Lady Mary Coke, 4 vols., printed privately in 100 sets (1889–96). Facsimile edition limited to 100 sets (1970). The citations are from Vol. IV. Lady Mary Coke (*née* Campbell) was the youngest daughter of the 2nd Duke of Argyll. Born in 1726, widowed at the age of 27, she died in 1811. She was a formidable personage, and could quarrel even with the Empress Maria Theresa.

Chronological Table of Clive's Life

		Early Life in England (1725–43)	**Page No.**
1725	Sept. 29	born	56
1743	March 10	sails for India	58

		First Period in India (1744–52)	
1744	June 1	arrives at Madras	58
1746	Sept.	taken prisoner by the French and escapes	63
1746–47	Dec.–June	at the siege of St David	64
1747	Sept.–Oct.	at the siege of Pondichery	65
1748	Apr.–June	Tanjore expedition	82
1751	Sept.–Nov.	capture and defence of Arcot	83 ff.
1751–52	Dec.–March	first battles	85
1752	Apr.–June	Trichinopoly campaign: Volconda	86
	Sept.	campaign against the French	86
1753	Feb. 18	marriage to Margaret Maskelyne	96
	March 23	sails for England	98

		First Intermezzo in England (1753–55)	
1753	Oct. 14	arrival in London	99
1754–55		M.P.	103
1755	March 24	accepts new appointment in India	104
	April 23	sails for India	105

		Second Period in India (1755–60)	
1755	Oct.	arrival at Bombay	143
1756	Feb.	attack on Gheria	143
	May 14	arrival at St David	144
	June 1	Dy. Governor of St David	144
	Oct. 16	sails to Bengal	147
	Dec. 15	arrives at Fulta on the Hooghly river	166
1757	Jan. 2	Calcutta reoccupied	170

			Page No.
	Feb. 5	attack on Siraj's camp in Calcutta	184
	Feb. 9	treaty with Siraj	187
	March 23	capture of Chandernagore	205
	May 19	true and false treaty with Mir Jafar	223
	June 5	Mir Jafar signs treaty	224
	June 19	Clive arrives at Katwa	226
	June 22	marches to Plassey	227
	June 23	battle of Plassey	229–33
	June 29	installs Mir Jafar as Nawab	236–37
1757–58	Nov.–May	operations in Bihar	250 ff.
1758	June	becomes provisional governor	261
	Nov.	formally governor	262
1759	Jan.	grant of jaghir	254
	Jan. 7	letter to William Pitt	266 ff.
	Nov.	war with the Dutch	260
1760	Feb. 21	sails for England	264

Second Intermezzo in England (1760–64)

1760	July 9	arrives in England	274
	July 14	audience with George III	276
	Sept. 2	doctorate of Oxford	276
1761	March 21	elected M.P.	290
	end of year	gets Irish peerage	276
1763	March–Apr.	defeated in the elections for the Directorate of the East India Co.	306 ff.
1764	March–Apr.	wins in the elections for the same	312 ff.
	April 30	appointed governor of Bengal	318
	June 4	sails for India	323

Third Period in India (1765–67)

1765	April 10	arrives at Madras	331
	May 3	arrives at Calcutta	331
	May 5	meets the Council	335
	June 7	acceptance of presents discussed	338
1765	July	settlement with the Nawab of Bengal	341
	Aug. 1	conference with Shuja-ud-daula	343
	Aug. 12	grant of the Diwani of Bengal	344
	Aug. 16	treaty with Shuja	345

			Page No.
1766	Apr.–May	mutiny of the officers	353 ff.
	Dec.	serious illness	362
1767	Jan. 29	leaves Bengal	361

Last Years in England (1767–74)

1767	July 13	arrives in England	368
	Nov.	decision about jaghir	372
1768	Jan.	goes to France	373
	Sept.	returns to England	373
1772	Jan.	informed about charges over his conduct	376
	March 30	defends his actions in Parliament	390
	April 13	Burgoyne's motion on the affairs of the Company	380
1773	May 3	Clive's speech on North's bill	395
	May 10	attack on Clive in Parliament	396
	May 21	House of Commons adopts resolution on Clive, rejecting censure	397
1774	Jan.	visits Italy	404
	Nov. 23	death by suicide	405 ff.

Glossary

AMIR:
: A Muslim nobleman or chief; collectively Umarrah. But in popular speech the plural was applied to individual noblemen and pronounced Omrah.

BANIAN:
: A native personal assistant to an English employee of the East India Company, who managed his transactions with the people of the country.

BEGUM:
: A lady, but usually the wife, daughter or mother of a Muslim ruler or nobleman.

CHAPMAN:
: (Eng.) A commercial agent or middleman.

DIWAN:
: Minister in charge of the treasury and revenue collection.

DIWANI:
: The charge of collecting revenue.

FAUJDAR:
: Military governor of a region, also in charge of criminal justice and police.

FIRMAN:
: An order of appointment to an office or dignity; literally, an order.

GOMASHTA:
: Agent, something like a bailiff.

JAGHIR:
: Grant of the revenue of a certain area or a number of villages to the holder of a command, so as to enable him to defray the expenses of his duties, or maintain his position. Usually the holder made a profit out of it.

MASNAD:
: The cushioned seat on which Muslim rulers sat.

NAWAB:
: Literally, a deputy; but in extended use, the governor of a province in the Mogul Empire. Often independent de facto.

NAZAR:
: Present of money or other valuables to a superior, when granted an audience.

PAGODA:
: Besides meaning a temple, in the Carnatic it was also the name of a gold coin, whose value varied. In the middle of the eighteenth century it was about ten times the value of a rupee, whose value was about two shillings.

PADISHA:
: Emperor of Delhi. Popular form of the word was Badshah.

POLYGAR:
: A local chief in the Carnatic.

PRESIDENCY: Each of the three centres of the East India Company, Bombay, Madras and Bengal, was called a Presidency, because they were under a President and Council. The Governor was the *ex officio* President.
RYOT: A subject, usually a farmer or agriculturist.
SANAD: A grant.
SUBAH: A province of the Mogul Empire.
SUBADAR: Governor of one of these provinces. (The English often used the contraction Subah, for the governor, instead of for the province.)
WRITER: The juniormost British employee of the East India Company.
ZAMINDAR: Literally, holder of land. A landed proprietor, who in the eighteenth century was often only a revenue farmer.

Select Bibliography

It is not possible to give in a few pages a full bibliography of the books on Clive and on British and Indian history of the epoch in which he lived. This bibliography is not a complete list even of the works used to write this biography. It only includes the main sources drawn upon for the facts of Clive's life and for the citations to which the more enterprising reader might go if he wants to get a feel of the events from original documents or to compare my presentation with that of others.

I. **Printed Collections of Documents**
Selections from the Letters, Despatches and other State Papers preserved in the Madras Secretariat. Clive Series. 3 Volumes. Edited by Sir George Forrest.
Bengal and Madras Papers, published by the Government of India. Volume III for the period 1757–85.
Records of Fort St George and Fort St David preserved at Madras. Various editors. The volumes from 1746 to 1753 cover the wars on the Coromandel coast.
Bengal in 1756–57. 3 volumes, edited by S. C. Hill. Contains all the important documents on the conquest of Bengal.
Reports from the Committees of the House of Commons, reprinted by order of the House. Vol. 3, East India, 1772–73.

II. **Contemporary or Near-Contemporary Printed Books, which have the Value of Sources**
Cambridge, Richard Owen: *An Account of the War in India between the English and French on the coast of Coromandel: 1750 to 1760.*
Orme, Robert: *A History of the Military Transactions of the British Nation in Indostan from 1745*, to which is prefaced a discussion on the Establishments made by Mohamedan Conquerors in Indostan. Vol. I, 1763; Vol. II in two parts, 1778.
Orme, Robert: *Historical Fragments of the Mogul Empire*, etc. (1805.)
Scrafton, Luke: *Reflections on the Government of Indostan.* (1763.)

Watts, William: *Memoirs of the Revolution in Bengal in the year 1757*. (1760.)
Strachey, Henry: *Narrative of the Mutiny of the Officers in Bengal*. (1772.)
Carraccioli, C.: *Life of Robert, Lord Clive*. 4 volumes. (1777.)
The *Annual Register*. From 1758 onwards.
London Magazine: 1760 ff.
The *Gentleman's Magazine:* 1750 onwards.
The Parliamentary History of England from the earliest period to the year 1803. Vol. XVII, covering 1771–74.
Ghulam Husain Tabatabai: *Siyar-ul-Mutakherin* (Seir Mutaqharin) (translated by Mustafa – really a Frenchman named Raymond) 3 vols. (1789.)
Ghulam Husain Salim Zaidpuri: *Riyazu-s-Salatin* (A history of Bengal to the beginnings of English rule, in Persian), translated by Maulvi Abdus Salam (1902–04).

III. Later Works

Malcolm, Sir John: *Life of Robert, Lord Clive*. 3 volumes. (1836.) Contains extracts from letters and other documents.
Macaulay, T. B.: 'Essay on Clive'. (Published first in the *Edinburgh Review* in January 1840.)
Gleig, G. R.: *Life of Robert, First Lord Clive*. (1848.)
Malleson, G. B.: *Lord Clive*. (1907.)
Forrest, Sir George: *Life of Lord Clive*. 2 volumes. (1918.) (Contains copious extracts from original documents.)
Minney, R. J.: *Clive*. (1931.)
Davies, A. Mervyn: *Clive of Plassey*. (1939.)
Sutherland, Lucy S.: *East India Company in Eighteenth Century Politics*. (1952.)
Dodwell, Henry: *Dupleix and Clive*. (1920.)
Cultru, Prosper: *Dupleix: ses plans politiques: sa disgrace*. (1901.)
Martineau, Alfred: *Dupleix et l'Inde française*. 4 volumes. (1920–28.)

INDEX

(This book contains roundly 400 personal and place names, many of which are Indian. As no reader will remember all of them only the very important ones are included. The abbreviation E.I.C. stands for the English East India Company.)

Adams, Major T., 329
Aix-la-Chapelle, Treaty of, 48
Akbar (Mogul Emperor), 17
Alamgir II (Mogul Emperor), 240
Alivardi Khan (Nawab of Bengal),
  accession, 28
  daughters, 31 ff., 235
  Europeans, on, 158 ff.
  family, 31 ff.
  wars and troubles of, 30 ff.
American War and Clive, 403
Anglo-French rivalry and India, 15, 38, 47, 110, 141 ff., 257
Arcot, capture and defence, 83 ff.
  genesis of expedition, 417
  significance of victory, 87 ff.
Austrian Succession, war of, 47 ff.

Badarah, battle of, 260
Barré, Col. Isaac, 297, 386, 389, 393
Bengal,
  administration by E.I.C., 247, 265, 267, 341 ff., 345 ff., 361 ff.
  Alivardi's rule, 28 ff.
  Clive's reforms in, 352 ff.
  condition of people, 32 ff.
  diwani of, 375, 378
  expedition to, 148 ff.
  famine in, 375, 387
  importance of, 257
  revenue collection, 341 ff.
  situation in 1756, 145 ff., 160 ff.
  situation in 1760–64, 313 ff., 345 ff.
  story of conquest, 167
Bengali Hindus and Siraj, 142, 248
Bihar, troubles in, 252 ff.
Black Hole, significance of, 163 ff.
Bombay, 141 ff.
British Empire in India,
  – *see under* Empire in India
Budge Budge, 169
Burke, Edmund, 3, 267, 294, 344, 381, 397
Burgoyne, Col. J., 380, 393 ff.

Bussy, C. C., 141, 181, 189
  on Indians, 114 ff.
  on Indian politics, 122 ff.
  sent to Hyderabad, 75
Buxar, battle of, 330

Calcutta,
  capture by Siraj, 161
  moral atmosphere, 367
  recaptured, 167 ff.
  Siraj's camp, 184
Calcutta Corporation incident, 318
Cambridge, R. O., on historical writing, 36
Capability Brown, 389
Carnatic, the
  Anglo-French war in, 68 ff., 74 ff., 256 ff.
  dynasties of, 22 ff.
Chanda Sahib, 26, 50, 72 ff., 76, 88
Chandernagore, 205 ff.
Clive, Robert, Baron Clive of Plassey,
  (*for the events of his life see* Chronological Table *on p. 435*.
  absolute authority of, 327
  achievements in Bengal, 326 ff.
  biographies of, 1 ff., 6, 9
  burial, 405
  Calcutta Council, relations with, 148, 172, 200 ff., 236, 261, 334 ff., 361 ff.
  character and personality, 15, 54 ff., 57, 58 ff., 100, 175, 269 ff., 273, 289 ff., 293 ff., 297, 327 ff., 385, 390, 401 ff., 411
  clothes, 269
  Directors of E.I.C., relations with, 99, 100, 263, 276, 308, 315 ff., 320, 372, 376 ff.
  early life, 57
  father, 58 ff., 99, 101, 105, 150, 185, 270 ff., 290 ff., 355
  Fordyce and, 81
  founder of empire, 15
  French opinion of, 90 ff.
  Governor-General, idea of, 204
  Hastings (Warren), advice to, 375 ff.
  houses, 278, 365, 367, 389
  illnesses and malady, 96, 100, 273, 360, 373, 404

443

jaghir, 254 ff., 300 ff., 308 ff., 320, 372
married life, 96, 322 ff., 364
military capacity, 65, 89, 91 ff., 135, 230, 232, 279
monetary gains, 83, 97, 101, 243, 244 ff., 278, 339, 355, 356, 365, 389, 395, 397, 402
mother, 57, 99, 101
Nabob, as, 387, 389
Napoleon, comparison with, 15, 54, 274, 277, 279, 280, 285, 289
Omichand and, 223, 242
opinions and pronouncements of Clive on;
   absolute power in India, 101, 262, 364
   banyans, 364
   Bengal, 257
   conquest of territory, 236, 264, 331
   discipline and obedience, 362 ff.
   English politics, 374
   French in India, 258
   military forces for E.I.C., 265, 352
   money, 294
   presents, 338
parliamentary inquiry on, 381, 391, 395
parliamentary life of, 103, 105, 290 ff., 270
poem on, 275
relatives, 100, 270, 278, 291
Scipio Africanus, comparison with, 279
speeches, 237, 376, 395
stories about, 55, 277, 381, 387
suicide, 405, 433
Clive, Lady, 323 ff., 407
Clive, Sarah, 275
Coke, Lady Mary, 389, 406 ff., 434
Comneni, 209
Coote, Sir Eyre, 134, 169, 170, 184, 258, 272, 423
Cornwallis, Lord, corruption in politics, 334, 410

Deccan project, 141
Dupleix, Joseph, François, Marquis of,
   appraisal, 106 ff.
   Austrian Succession war and, 47 ff.
   Carnatic war, 68 ff.
   Chanda Sahib and, 72
   character and policy, 48 ff., 108 ff.
   claims on French company 127
   early career, 44, 46 ff.
   English, hostility to the, 49 ff.
   English opinion of, 106 ff.
   French company and, 111
   French government and, 112
   French historians and, 108
   Godeheu and, 113
   Indians, attitude to, 113 ff.
   Lawrence and, 80
   memorandum of Oct. 1753, 108
   monetary gains of, 124 ff.
   Orme on, 107 ff.
   prestige in India, 51
   recall, 108, 113
   Saunders, correspondence with, 77 ff.

Dupleix, Mme., 47, 81
Durlabhram Rai, 183, 212, 241, 249 ff., 342, 346
Dutch, the – war with, 260
dynasties according to Khaldun, 20, 152

East India Company (English),
   British government and, 283 ff., 377, 379
   early history, 38 ff.
   factions in, 296 ff., 303 ff.
   meetings, 307
   military forces, 44, 53
   organization, 39
   policy, 128 ff.
   private trade, 347 ff., 358
   purity of administration, 401
   right to India, 133
   rulers of India and, 42
   state of, 377
East India Company (French), 44 ff.
Economic interpretation of history, 151
Elephant, quarrel over, 311
Empire in India,
   Bengal as focal point, 128
   Clive's role, 15, 361, 385
   Clive's views, 237, 265, 266, 331
   Dupleix as precursor, 106, 113
   interest in England, 287, 386
   military basis, 134 ff., 238, 332
   process of growth, 3, 14 ff., 73, 128, 133, 200, 202, 237, 267, 273, 281, 321, 361, 392, 399, 400 ff.
   Roman analogies, 216, 277, 322, 394
Empires, rise of, 393
England, moral situation, 382 ff.
England, political situation, 281 ff.
England and Clive,
   attraction for, 61, 269, 273
   maladjustment with, 269, 273, 278, 280, 310, 382, 385, 389, 409 ff.

Foote, satires on Nabobs, 388
Forde's expedition, 258
French in the Carnatic, 256 ff.
Fulta, English refugees at, 165 ff.

Gheria, capture of, 143
Gibbon, Edward, 396
Gray, Thomas, 409 ff.
Gleig on Clive's death, 407
Grenville, George, 370 ff., 375

Hastings, Warren, 6, 375, 399, 400, 401
Historiography of British India, 3 ff., 36, 167

Indianization of foreign administration, 195
Indians, European attitudes, 118 ff.

Jagat Seths, 11, 155, 195, 242
Jaghir, *see under* Clive
Johnson, Dr S., 282, 389, 401, 407
Johnstone, John, 335, 338

444

Kalidasa (Sanskrit poet), 152, 427
Khaldun, Ibn, 20, 152

Lally, Count, 257
Law, Jacques (Trichinopoly), 75, 76, 78, 90
Law, Jean (Murshidabad), 155, 189, 190
  on Siraj, 178 ff., 196, 198, 211, 214, 235
Lawrence, Major Stringer, 53, 71, 86, 91, 96, 276
London Magazine's moral campaign, 383

Macaulay, T.B.,
  as historian, 7 ff.
  on Clive, 1, 7, 277, 326, 398
  on jaghir, 309
  on money in India, 287 ff.
  on Nabobs, 388
Madras, capture by the French, 48
Marathas, 25, 30, 35
Masulipatam, 258
Meredith, Sir William, 393 ff.
Military power, need of, 134 ff., 238
Mill, James, 3
Mill, John Stuart, 379
Miran, 231, 251, 261
Mir Jafar, Nawab of Bengal,
  English, relations with, 201, 240 ff., 248
  Clive relations with, 234, 253, 254, 358, 361
  death, 336
  English, relations with, 201, 240 ff., 248
  Plassey, conduct at, 232 ff., 428
  Siraj, relations with, 225, 426 ff.
  weakness of rule, 247
Mir Madan, 232
Mir Qasim (Nawab of Bengal),
  end of, 431
  war with the English, 329 ff.
Mogul dynasty, 16 ff.
Mogul empire, 19 ff.
Mohanlal, 11, 154, 194
Money in India, 122 ff.
Muhammad Ali (Nawab of the Carnatic), 87 ff.
Mutiny of officers, 351 ff.

Nabobs, 386 ff.
Najm-ud-daula (Nawab of Bengal), 341
Namier school of history, 282
Nandakumar (Nuncomar), 7, 197
Nationalism (Indian) and Clive, 11, 243, 248
Nizam-ul-Mulk, 27, 41
North's Regulating Act, 378, 399

Omichand, 219 ff., 242
Orme, Robert,
  armies in India, 24
  Bengal expedition, 146
  Marathas, 25
  Pathans, 25
  Plassey, battle of, 421, 424
  princes of India, 24
  tyranny in India, 35
  war in India, 137

Patna, massacre of, 330
Pitt, William (the Elder),
  Clive's letter to, 266 ff.
  discussion about E.I.C., 284 ff.
Pitt's India Act (1784), 400
Plassey, battle of, 226
  Bengali poem on, 248
  Clive at, 230, 424
  sources for, 421
Political persecution and morality, 392
Pondichery, 48
Pope, Alexander, 306, 409 ff.

Rhodes, Cecil, 279
Robertson, Dr W., 282, 408

Salt duty, 348
Saunders, Thomas, 77 ff., 296
  correspondence with Dupleix, 78 ff.
  letter to Mme. Dupleix, 81
Scipio Africanus, comparison with Clive, 279
Scrafton, Luke, 33, 183, 192, 197, 279, 198, 216
Shah Alam II (Emperor of Delhi), 19, 252 ff.
  grants *diwani* to E.I.C., 378
Shuja-ud-daula (Nawab of Oudh), 330
Sirajud-ud-Daula (Nawab of Bengal)
  (*see* Ch. 5, 6, 7 generally)
  accession, 32, 151
  Black Hole, 163
  Calcutta,
    capture of, 161
    march to, 179 ff.
    retreat from, 184 ff.
  captured and killed, 234 ff.
  Chandernagore and, 207
  character of, 151 ff., 198
  conspiracy against, 215
  court and ministers, 194 ff.
  English policy towards, 202 ff.
  father of, 30
  French, the,
    correspondence with, 190 ff.
    surrender of, 212 ff.
  Law on, 155 ff., 189, 235
  Mir Jafar and, 225, 232, 424 ff.
  mother and aunt, 31 ff., 235
  Muslim historians on, 153
  Plassey, at, 232
  revolt against grandfather, 31
  treaty with the English, 187
Strachey, Henry, 323, 357, 433
Sulivan, Lawrence, 289, 305 ff., 314, 321, 377
  position and character, 285, 286, 288
  relations with Clive, 264, 297, 298, 299 ff., 308 ff., 316 ff., 366, 377
Sutherland, Lucy, 380

Tanjor expedition, 69 ff., 412
Tocqueville, Alexis de,
  on the British empire in India, 3, 5
  on Clive, 281
  on Macaulay, 8
  on military power in India, 135 ff.

Townshend, Charles, 386
Travancore, Raja of, 120
Treaty of peace with France (1763), 304

Verrine orations of Cicero, 394
Vizagapatam, 258
Voltaire, 403

Walpole, Horace,
  on Bengal famine, 375
  on Clive, 274, 276, 277, 312, 314, 370, 373, 397 ff., 406
Walsh, William, 183, 425

War in India, 134 ff.
Watson, Admiral Charles, 145, 147, 172, 173, 174, 184, 210
  correspondence with Siraj, 168, 179, 186, 193, 210, 214
  dispute with Clive in Calcutta, 170 ff.
  Omichand and, 223, 423
  reduction of Chandernagore, 205, 206, 208
Watts, William, 190, 192, 207, 211, 213, 224
Wellesley, Arthur (Duke of Wellington), 97, 98, 142, 154, 309
Women, insults to, 155
Women, rights of rulers on, 154